21.99s

ArtScroll Series®

Rabbi Nosson Scherman / Rabbi Meir Zlotowitz

General Editors

A SHABBOS

Published by

Mesorah Publications, ltd

וקראת לשבת עונג

VORT

A collection of thoughts, stories and parables
on the Weekly Parashah

RABBI YISRAEL BRONSTEIN

Adapted from the Hebrew
V'Karasa L'Shabbos Oneg
by Rabbi Moshe Gelbein

Prepared for publication by
Rabbi Yehudah Bulman

FIRST EDITION
First Impression … June 2004

Published and Distributed by
MESORAH PUBLICATIONS, LTD.
4401 Second Avenue / Brooklyn, N.Y 11232

Distributed in Europe by
LEHMANNS
Unit E, Viking Business Park
Rolling Mill Road
Jarow, Tyne & Wear, NE32 3DP
England

Distributed in Australia and New Zealand by
GOLDS WORLDS OF JUDAICA
3-13 William Street
Balaclava, Melbourne 3183
Victoria, Australia

Distributed in Israel by
SIFRIATI / A. GITLER — BOOKS
6 Hayarkon Street
Bnei Brak 51127

Distributed in South Africa by
KOLLEL BOOKSHOP
Shop 8A Norwood Hypermarket
Norwood 2196, Johannesburg, South Africa

ARTSCROLL SERIES®
A SHABBOS VORT
© Copyright 2004, by MESORAH PUBLICATIONS, Ltd.
4401 Second Avenue / Brooklyn, N.Y. 11232 / (718) 921-9000 / www.artscroll.com

Typography by CompuScribe at ArtScroll Studios, Ltd.
Printed in the United States of America by Noble Book Press Corp.
Bound by Sefercraft, Quality Bookbinders, Ltd., Brooklyn N.Y. 11232

TABLE OF CONTENTS

❧ BEREISHIS

Parashas Bereishis	10
Parashas Noach	17
Parashas Lech Lecha	27
Parashas Vayeira	33
Parashas Chayei Sarah	43
Parashas Toldos	50
Parashas Vayeitzei	56
Parashas Vayishlach	63
Parashas Vayeishev	69
Parashas Mikeitz	75
Parashas Vayigash	83
Parashas Vayechi	90

❧ SHEMOS

Parashas Shemos	100
Parashas Va'eira	108
Parashas Bo	115
Parashas Beshalach	121
Parashas Yisro	128
Parashas Mishpatim	136
Parashas Terumah	143
Parashas Tetzaveh	150
Parashas Ki Sisa	157
Parashas Vayakhel	165
Parashas Pekudei	173

❧ VAYIKRA

Parashas Vayikra	180
Parashas Tzav	187

Parashas Shemini — 194
Parashas Tazria — 202
Parashas Metzora — 208
Parashas Acharei Mos — 215
Parashas Kedoshim — 223
Parashas Emor — 231
Parashas Behar — 236
Parashas Bechukosai — 245

❧ BAMIDBAR

Parashas Bamidbar — 254
Parashas Nasso — 260
Parashas Beha'aloscha — 268
Parashas Shelach — 276
Parashas Korach — 283
Parashas Chukas — 291
Parashas Balak — 299
Parashas Pinchas — 307
Parashas Matos — 315
Parashas Masei — 322
Haftarah of Parashas Masei — 330

❧ DEVARIM

Parashas Devarim — 334
Parashas Va'eschanan — 341
Parashas Eikev — 350
Parashas Re'eh — 358
Parashas Shoftim — 368
Parashas Ki Seitzei — 377
Parashas Ki Savo — 385
Parashas Nitzavim — 394
Parashas Vayeilech — 404
Parashas Haazinu — 412
Parashas Vezos HaBerachah — 422

BEREISHIS

BEREISHIS

בְּרֵאשִׁית ...

"In the beginning..." (1:1)

T HE WRITTEN TORAH BEGINS WITH THE HEBREW LETTER *BEIS,*
Bereishis ...," while the Oral Torah begins with the letter *mem,*
"*Me'eimasai korin es haShema b'arvis*? [From what time do
we read the *Shema* at night?]" (*Berachos* 1:1). These two letters form
the word **bam** ("in them"), as in the verse, "*v'dibarta bam* [And you
shall speak of them]" (*Devarim* 6:7). This alludes to a lesson
expounded by our Sages: "'And you shall speak of them (*bam*)' — Of
them [the Torah] you may speak, but not of other matters" (*Yoma*
19b). From the outset, the Torah teaches us that the main topic of our
conversations should always be in them!

T he *Gaon* of Vilna was once present at a *pidyon haben* feast that
followed the redemption of a firstborn. One of the participants
asked the *Gaon* the following question: "There is a tradition recorded in
Kabbalistic works that all the *mitzvos* of the Torah are alluded to in

Parashas Bereishis. Our teacher! If this is true, then where in *Parashas Bereishis* is the allusion to the *mitzvah* of *pidyon haben?*" Without even pausing, the *Gaon* responded: "The *mitzvah* of *pidyon haben* is alluded to in the very word *'Bereishis'* — **B**en **R**ishon **A**char **SH**eloshim **Y**om **T**ifdeh —'You shall redeem the first son after thirty days.'"

בְּרֵאשִׁית בָּרָא אֱלֹקִים אֵת הַשָּׁמַיִם וְאֵת הָאָרֶץ.

"In the beginning of God's creating the heavens and the earth (1:1)

The *Ba'al HaTurim*, R' Yaakov ben Asher, pointed out that the last letters of the words, *"bara Elokim es,"* which begin the account of Creation, can be combined to spell the word *emes* (truth). And the words, *"Asher bara Elokim la'asos* [which God created to make]" (2:3), which conclude the account, also form the word *emes*. This comes to teach us that the attribute of truth permeates all of Hashem's creation. Without truth, the world would cease to exist.

"It is well known," remarked the *tzaddik*, R' Simchah Bunim of P'shischa, "that it is the custom among authors to hint to their names in the titles of their *sefarim*. For this reason, as well, Hashem included His Name at the outset of *His sefer*. For the last letters of '*Bereishis bara Elokim es'* spell the word *emes*, and *Chazal* teach us that 'the seal of *HaKadosh Baruch Hu* is *emes* — Truth' " (*Shabbos* 55a).

וַיְבָרֶךְ אֱלֹקִים אֶת־יוֹם הַשְּׁבִיעִי
"God blessed the seventh day" (2:3)

One day the emperor of Rome decided to take a walk. He continued until he chanced upon the Jews' street. That day happened to be Shabbos, and the pleasant aroma of Shabbos foods filled his nostrils. The emperor thoroughly enjoyed this delightful fragrance but wondered how it was produced. He summoned R' Yehoshua ben Chananyah, and asked him: "Tell me, R' Yehoshua, why are the dishes cooked by the Jews so fragrant? I have never smelled such a pleasing aroma!"

"The Jews have a special spice," answered R' Yehoshua, "and 'Shabbos' is its name. That is what gives our food its special taste and aroma."

"Please," requested the emperor, "give me some of that spice."

"I'm sorry," responded R' Yehoshua. "This spice is only effective for those who keep the Shabbos; but it is of no worth for those who do not keep Shabbos."

וַיִּיצֶר ה' אֱלֹקִים אֶת־הָאָדָם
עָפָר מִן־הָאֲדָמָה וַיִּפַּח בְּאַפָּיו נִשְׁמַת חַיִּים

"Hashem, the All-powerful, then formed the man out of dust from the ground, and He breathed into his nostrils the soul of life" (2:7)

On one occasion, Antoninus approached his close friend, R' Yehudah *HaNasi*, and said, "I thought of an idea of how man can exonerate himself from all sin before the Heavenly Court. When a person departs this world, let his body declare before the Heavenly Court, 'I am innocent because it is the soul that is responsible for this man's transgressions, for the moment the soul leaves the body, the body is nothing but a silent mass, incapable of doing anything. Does this not prove that it is the soul who is the true sinner? It should be punished, not I!'

"But then the soul would counter, 'I am not the sinner, for as all can see, the moment I take leave of the body, I ascend to the Heavens, and I am never able to sin again. Why is it that I can only sin when I am in the body? Obviously, it is because the body is the true guilty one. Punish the body!'

"With this strategy, both body and soul would have claims that would absolve them of all sin. Can this not free man of all guilt and save him from punishment?"

"Allow me to draw a parable," answered R' Yehudah *HaNasi*. "To what can this be compared? To a king who owned a beautiful orchard, which grew unique and choice fruit trees. The king wished to appoint a guard over his prized orchard, but he was concerned — perhaps the guard himself will fall to temptation and eat from them.

"The king finally devised a solution: He would appoint two guards to watch over the orchard — one lame, the other blind. One would not be able to reach the fruit while the other would not be tempted by them.

"A while later, the lame guard said to the blind one, 'My friend! I have just thought of a great idea! Put me on your shoulders, and I will direct you. This way, we will be able to take the king's fruits and split them between us.' The blind man agreed to his friend's scheme, and that is what they did.

"One day, the king visited his orchard and — much to his surprise — many of his precious fruits had vanished! The king turned to the guards and asked, 'Who dared take my fruit?' 'Your Highness,' replied the blind man, 'I am a blind man; how could I have known where they are if I cannot even see them?'

"'Your highness,' then replied the lame man, 'I am a lame man; how could I have reached them if I cannot even walk?'

"The king — who was a wise man — quickly grasped what had occurred in his orchard, so he sentenced them together: he had the lame man placed on the shoulders of the blind man, and he punished them as one.

"So too," concluded Rabbi Yehudah *HaNasi*, "the body claims that it could not have sinned without the soul, and the soul claims that it could not have sinned without the body. But their arguments will help neither of them, for when the time comes to judge a person for his deeds, his soul is immediately put together with the body and they are punished as one unit."

(Based on *Sanhedrin* 91a)

❧⊰⊱❧

וַיַּפֵּל ה' אֱלֹקִים תַּרְדֵּמָה עַל־הָאָדָם
וַיִּישָׁן וַיִּקַּח אַחַת מִצַּלְעֹתָיו וַיִּסְגֹּר בָּשָׂר תַּחְתֶּנָּה.

*"Hashem, the All-powerful, then cast
a deep sleep upon the man and he slept.
He then took one of his sides and closed
up the flesh in its place" (2:21)*

A Roman emperor once challenged Rabban Gamliel: "I have a claim against your people."

"What is your claim?" asked Rabban Gamliel.

"Your God is a thief," said the emperor. "The Torah states so explicitly, as it says, 'Hashem, the All-powerful, then cast a deep sleep upon the man and he slept. He then took one of his sides!'"

Rabban Gamliel's daughter, who was present, asked her father, "May I answer?" Rabban Gamliel allowed her to respond to the emperor. She turned to the emperor and said, "Your Highness, please bring me a judge who is prepared to sit in judgment."

"Why do you need one?" asked the emperor.

"Well," she said, "last night thieves broke into our home. They stole a silver jug, and left a gold one in its place. I would like a judge to prosecute them."

"That is your problem?" asked the surprised emperor. "I wish that such criminals would visit me every night."

"You have answered your own claim," said the daughter, "For was Hashem not benevolent with Adam? He took just one rib from Adam and gave him a wife in return!"

וַיְבִאֶהָ אֶל־הָאָדָם.

"And He brought her to the man" (2:22)

Even as a child, R' Chaim Halberstam of Sanz (the *Divrei Chaim*) was known as a prodigy. Thus many great Talmudic scholars would engage the young genius in amusing Torah discussions.

"Tell me," asked one scholar, "how did Adam betroth Chavah? After all, in order for a man to betroth a woman, two witnesses are required to view the process. Since there were no other human beings at the time, it should have been impossible for Adam to betroth Chavah."

"The *halachah* that betrothal requires two witnesses," began R' Chaim, "is traced in the Gemara (*Kiddushin* 65b) to a *gezeirah shavah* comparison to monetary ownership: just as the Torah requires two witnesses to prove monetary ownership (see *Devarim* 19:15), so too, two witnesses are required for betrothal to take effect.

"The Gemara, however, goes on to ask: Since there is a principle in monetary law that, 'The admission of the litigant is the equivalent of the testimony of one hundred witnesses,' then it should follow that if a woman admits that she is betrothed to a man, she should be believed as firmly as a hundred witnesses!

"The Gemara then explains that this cannot be true, for when a defendant admits owing money to someone, he harms no one. But if a woman says that she is betrothed to a certain man, she does cause harm to others, since no other man will be allowed to betroth her.

"The Gemara's answer," concluded the *Divrei Chaim*, "is applicable to all men — except for Adam *HaRishon*. For even if Chavah would have claimed that Adam betrothed her, she would not have caused any damage to anyone, since only Adam could have betrothed her.

"In Chavah's case, then, we can apply the principle of 'The admission of the litigant is the equivalent of the testimony of one hundred witnesses,' so Adam did not need any witnesses to betroth her."

~∞∞~

וְעָפָר תּאכַל כָּל־יְמֵי חַיֶּיךָ:

"And dust shall you eat all the days of your life" (3:14)

The *Midrash* (*Bereishis Rabbah* 20:5) asks: On the surface, the snake does not seem to be cursed at all. Since dust is its food, it has plenty of food without any exertion. How is this a curse?

We can answer this with a parable: There was a certain king who provided all the needs of his cherished son. Whatever the son needed was lovingly granted.

But the son grew up and strayed from the proper way of life. The king was furious and reprimanded him, but nothing seemed to help.

Finally, the king summoned one of his ministers and said, "Give my son whatever he needs."

The minister was taken aback by this order. "Your Highness! But your son has strayed from your path; why should he get whatever he wants?"

"You have misunderstood," responded the king. "As long as my son was acting properly, I wanted to see him as often as possible. Therefore, I would give him whatever he needed so that he would come to my palace whenever he needed something. But now that he has turned from the proper path, I don't want to see him at all. I want you to provide him with all his needs so that he will never again appear before me in the palace."

The snake was cursed in the same way. After it enticed Chavah to eat from the Tree of Knowledge, bringing about a great sin, Hashem told it, "And dust shall you eat all the days of your life." It was as if Hashem was telling the snake, "Your needs will be met wherever you go; from now on, do not turn to Me in prayer. Be gone — I do not wish to deal with you ever again."

וַיֹּאמֶר ה' אֶל־קַיִן לָמָּה חָרָה לָךְ וְלָמָּה נָפְלוּ פָנֶיךָ:

"And Hashem said to Kayin,
'Why are you angry and downcast?'" (4:6)

A story is told of two merchants who appeared before R' Chaim Soloveitchik, the Rav of Brisk, in a *din Torah*. R' Chaim listened to each of their claims and then ruled in favor of one of the litigants.

The other merchant grumbled about R' Chaim's ruling and complained that the judgment was not fair. R' Chaim, however, remained firm and ordered the man to comply with his ruling.

After the men had left, R' Chaim turned to the other people who had been present when the verdict was pronounced, and said, "I have a question for you. Why is it that when a rabbi rules that an animal worth thousands of rubles is *treif* (not kosher), the inquirer accepts the ruling and, without a second thought, sells the animal to a gentile at great loss or even abandons it — he may even thank Hashem for protecting him from eating a *treif* animal — yet when the rabbi rules against someone in a *din Torah*, that same individual will refuse to accept the ruling and will become embittered with the rabbi?"

The men stood silently, waiting for R' Chaim to continue.

"I'll tell you what the answer is," said R' Chaim. "It can be distilled to one word: jealousy. The trait of jealousy has the ability to completely override a person's intellect. A man can tolerate the prospect of losing thousands of rubles — as long as he knows that he has not lost them to someone else. But if he sees that his money will go to someone else — that he cannot bear."

R' Chaim then continued with an explanation of the verse, "And Hashem said to Kayin, 'Why are you angry and downcast?'" "Hashem's question," said R' Chaim, "is perplexing, for the Torah had already related, 'But to Kayin and to his offering He showed no regard' (4:5). Kayin seems to have had a very good reason to be downcast, as Hashem refused to accept his offering. Is it any wonder, then, why Kayin was upset?

"Rather," concluded R' Chaim, "the Holy One was asking Kayin for the true reason behind his mood. 'Was it because I did not accept your offering or was it because I accepted *his*?'"

NOACH

נֹחַ אִישׁ צַדִּיק תָּמִים הָיָה בְּדֹרֹתָיו אֶת־הָאֱלֹקִים הִתְהַלֶּךְ־נֹחַ:

"Noach was a righteous man, perfect in his generations; Noach walked with God" (6:9)

LATER, THE TORAH TELLS US THAT HASHEM TOLD AVRAHAM *AVINU*, "Walk before Me and be perfect" (17:1), but here the Torah says that Noach "walked with God." What was the difference between Noach and Avraham?

The *Midrash Rabbah* answers this question with a parable: A father was once walking down the road with his two sons. The father turned to the younger son and said, "Give me your hand and we'll walk together." But to the older son, he said, "Go ahead; you can walk before me."

"Father," asked the older son, "why won't you hold my hand as well?"

"My son," answered the father, "your brother is still young and I'm afraid that he might stumble or fall. You, however, are older and I'm not worried about your walking."

The difference between Noach and Avraham was like the difference between the two sons in the parable. Though Noach was a *tzaddik,* he nonetheless needed protection to make sure he would not stumble in his beliefs. The verse therefore describes his relationship with God as, "Noach walked *with* God," since Hashem stood by him at all times, to make sure his faith would not falter.

Avraham's faith, however, was much stronger, so Hashem told him, "Walk before Me — I'm sure you will not stumble."

Rashi expressed this idea in one sentence: "Noach needed support, but Avraham drew his strength from himself and walked in his righteousness on his own."

וַתִּמָּלֵא הָאָרֶץ חָמָס:
"And the earth had become filled with robbery" (6:11)

Throughout the generations, *gedolei Yisrael* were always careful with other people's money to make sure they would not be guilty of stealing.

R' Eliyahu Dushnitzer, the renowned *mashgiach* of the Lomza Yeshivah, was particularly careful in this regard. For example, because the electrical supply to his home was drawn from the yeshivah, he was extremely careful to use the least electricity possible. When he learned Torah late into the night, he always turned off the electric lights in his home and used a kerosene lamp instead. "Who knows," said R' Dushnitzer, "perhaps I will fall asleep while learning and the electricity will continue running on the yeshivah's expense for no reason."

וַתִּמָּלֵא הָאָרֶץ חָמָס:
"And the earth had become filled with robbery" (6:11)

R' Yosef Chaim Sonnenfeld was in charge of a *tzedakah* fund to help the people of Yerushalayim pay for their children's weddings.

Anyone who couldn't afford to pay for their wedding expenses received four gold coins — a very large sum of money in those days — from the fund.

R' Yosef Chaim himself once lacked the money to pay for his own daughter's wedding, but because of his concern for money that was not his, he did not want to withdraw anything from the fund on his own. He hoped that one of the other *gabba'im* would remember to give him the customary four gold coins. But they forgot.

When R' Yosef Chaim saw that he would not receive the assistance on time for the wedding, he approached one of the wealthier Jews of Yerushalayim and asked him for a loan. The man was happy to help the esteemed rabbi and immediately loaned him the money needed.

The wedding was held a short while later, with many guests in attendance, as befitting the rabbi of Yerushalayim.

The day after the wedding, one of the *gabba'im* suddenly remembered that he had forgotten to give R' Yosef Chaim the four gold coins. He rushed to the rabbi, begged him for his forgiveness, and presented him with the coins.

"I cannot accept this money," said R' Yosef Chaim. "The purpose of this fund is to help parents marry off their children — not to help them pay off their debts…"

צֹהַר תַּעֲשֶׂה לַתֵּבָה
"A window shall you make for the Ark" (6:16)

The word *"teivah,"* "ark," said the *Sefas Emes* (R' Yehudah Leib Alter of Gur), also means, *"a word."* The verse can therefore be read as follows: *"Tzohar,* like the afternoon *("tzohar"* resembles the word *"tzaharayim"), "ta'aseh la'teivah"* — shall you make each word." Meaning, when a Jew prays before his Creator, he must make sure that each word that leaves his mouth is pronounced as perfectly and as clearly as the sunlight that shines in the afternoon.

מִכֹּל הַבְּהֵמָה הַטְּהוֹרָה תִּקַּח־לְךָ שִׁבְעָה... גַּם מֵעוֹף הַשָּׁמַיִם שִׁבְעָה
"Of every clean animal take unto you seven pairs … of the birds of the heavens also, seven pairs" (7:2,3)

Why is it, asked the *Meshech Chochmah* (R' Meir Simchah HaCohen of Dvinsk), that when the Torah mentions the animals, it refers to them as *"tahor,"* yet it does not do so when it mentions the birds?

The physical signs that show whether an animal is kosher or not, answered the *Meshech Chochmah*, such as split hooves or chewing its cud, are external and easily identifiable. But the signs of kosher birds are internal and cannot be seen from the outside.

This is why Hashem commanded Noach to take animals that were *tahor*, for he was able to discern between them and choose only those that fit the description of kosher animals. He could not, however, identify the *tahor* birds just by looking at them, so the only way he could tell the birds' status was by seeing whether they came seven at a time.

מִן־הַבְּהֵמָה הַטְּהוֹרָה וּמִן־הַבְּהֵמָה אֲשֶׁר אֵינֶנָּה טְהֹרָה

"Of the clean animal, and of the animal that is not clean" (7:8)

I n tractate *Pesachim* (3a), *Chazal* taught: "A person should never let an unrefined expression pass his lips, for the Torah expressed itself in a roundabout way… so as to avoid using an unrefined expression, as is stated, 'Of the *tahor* animal, and of the animal that is not *tahor*.'"

Chazal's lesson was derived from the fact that the Torah said, "of the animal that is not *tahor*," instead of, "of the *tamei* animal."

The Dubno *Maggid* was once asked: If saying *tamei* is improper, then why do we find so many instances where the Torah does refer to animals as *"tamei,"* or *"timei'ah"*? Should it not always use of the more proper term, "that is not *tahor*"?

The Dubno *Maggid* answered with a parable: A wealthy Jew lived in a certain town. Aside from being very rich, he was also a noted *talmid chacham*. In the same town lived a poor Jew named Yosef. Yosef was known to be a simpleton and an ignoramus. Thus his nickname: *Yossel the fool*.

One day, there was a knock on the door of the wealthy Jew. When one of the servants opened the door, the visitor asked,"I'm trying to obtain the address of a certain Reb Yosef, who is said to live on this block."

"Whose address do you want?" asked the servant as he began to laugh heartily. "You must be referring to Yossel the fool; he lives directly opposite this house in that small dilapidated hut!"

When the wealthy man heard the words of his servant, he immediately reprimanded him, "Are you not ashamed?" he asked his servant. "How can you speak in such a manner about a neighbor — all the more so, in front of a total stranger?"

Several days later, there was, once again, a knock on the wealthy man's door. Upon opening the door, the visitor began to explain to the servant that he was a *shadchan*, and he wished to speak to the wealthy man in person.

"I have come here today," said the *shadchan* to the wealthy man, "as a messenger of your neighbor, Yosef. He would like to propose a match between his eldest son and your daughter."

"Who?" shrieked the man. "Yossel the fool and *my* daughter? You expect me to agree to a match with Yossel the fool? Do not dare to come here again with ideas such as these!"

"Pardon me, sir," said the servant to his employer. "But if I could be so bold as to ask, was it not a few days ago that you reprimanded me for calling our neighbor 'Yossel the fool'? How is it that now you are referring to him in exactly the same way?"

"When somebody arrives at our door," answered the wealthy man, "and asks for our neighbor's address, it has no bearing on us whatsoever. In such an instance it is not fitting to refer to him with a derogatory nickname. But when his son is being offered to me as a potential match for my daughter, then I must explain exactly why I am opposed to the match."

So, too, with the animals, concluded the Dubno *Maggid*. When the Torah lists which animals would be allowed to board Noach's ark and which would not, it is not a matter of our personal concern. The Torah therefore goes out of its way to use expressions that will teach us the importance of speaking in a proper manner. But when the Torah discusses a Jew's requirement to avoid certain foods that will damage his soul, then the Torah wishes to impart to us the severity of the prohibition. It therefore states clearly and forcefully: "It is *tamei* to you!" (*Vayikra* 11:6).

וַיָּבֹאוּ אֶל־נֹחַ אֶל־הַתֵּבָה שְׁנַיִם שְׁנַיִם
"They came to Noach into the ark; two by two" (7:15)

The *Midrash* (*Shocher Tov, Tehillim* 7) relates that when Hashem commanded Noach to take two of each species into the ark, Falsehood came as well and asked Noach to be admitted aboard the ark. Noach told it, "You may not enter because the Holy One said that all the creatures should enter 'two by two,' but you don't have a mate."

Falsehood set out to find itself a mate, and encountered Bad-*Mazal* (the *mazal* that causes many financial loses).

Bad-*Mazal* asked Falsehood, "Where are you coming from?"

"I am returning from Noach's ark," answered Falsehood. "Noach refused to let me come aboard because I lacked a mate."

"What will you give me if I agree to marry you?" asked Bad-*Mazal*.

"I will give you all the profit that I earn through deceit," replied Falsehood.

Bad-*Mazal* agreed to the proposition, and they boarded the ark together. And so it was; after the flood had passed, Falsehood gave

Bad-Mazal all that it had earned through acts of deception, but Bad-Mazal lost it all.

Hence the expression, concludes the *Midrash,* "Profit earned through falsehood is always lost with bad *mazal.*"

⋙◌⋘

וַיִּמַח אֶת־כָּל־הַיְקוּם אֲשֶׁר עַל־פְּנֵי הָאֲדָמָה

"And He blotted out all existence
that was on the face of the ground" (7:23)

In tractate *Sanhedrin* (108a), *Chazal* ask the following: "Man sinned, but what did the animals do wrong [to deserve annihilation]?"

The Gemara answered with a parable. There once was a father who arranged a lavish wedding for his son. The wedding feast was embellished with every type of delicacy, the finest wines available, and flowers of every kind.

On the eve of the wedding, the son suddenly took ill and died. The father, no longer having a need for the delicacies, wines, and flowers, threw them all away. For as the father himself stated, "All of the arrangements had been prepared only for my son; now that my son has died, I have no need for any of them."

So said *HaKadosh Baruch Hu:* All that I have created — the trees and the flowers, the animals and birds — I created for man alone. Now that man has sinned and has been blotted out from the face of the earth, what need do I have for the rest of creation?

⋙◌⋘

וַתָּבֹא אֵלָיו הַיּוֹנָה לְעֵת עֶרֶב וְהִנֵּה עֲלֵה־זַיִת טָרָף בְּפִיהָ

"The dove came to him toward evening, and
behold it had plucked an olive leaf with its beak" (8:11)

Rashi, quoting a *Midrash,* recounts that the dove said to Noach: "Let my food be as bitter as an olive — as long as it is provided by the hand of *HaKadosh Baruch Hu* —and not as sweet as honey — if it will be provided by the hand of flesh and blood."

Why, asked the Dubno *Maggid,* would the dove make such a statement to Noach before taking leave of him and the ark? Hadn't Noach so graciously provided for it and cared for all of its needs over the course of an entire year?

Rather, answered the *Maggid*, the dove was concerned that perhaps Noach would suspect that it had returned not because the flood had ended but because it knew that it would receive all of its food on the ark. This is why the dove told Noach, "I have not returned for food. For I prefer to be sustained with food that is as bitter as olives, as long as it is provided by Hashem, rather than with food that is as sweet as honey but provided by man! If the land had dried, I would not have returned."

וְשֵׁם אָחִיו יָקְטָן:
"His brother's name was Yoktan" (10:25)

Rashi explains that his name was Yoktan "because he was humble and would make himself small (*katan*). That is why he was privileged to establish all of these families."

Humility is a very special trait; it is the one most valued by the Holy One. But regarding a haughty person the Holy One says, "He and I cannot dwell in the same world" (*Sotah* 5a).

At the advice of his physicians, R' Yisrael Salanter once rested at a convalescent home to regain his strength and health. One of R' Yisrael's students had a relative who was also staying at that facility. The student therefore sent a letter to this relative, asking him to carefully observe the actions and behavior of the *tzaddik* and to record them for him.

The relative wrote back:

"Believe me, until I received your letter I had absolutely no idea that R' Yisrael Salanter was even staying here..."

וְשֵׁם אָחִיו יָקְטָן:
"His brother's name was Yoktan" (10:25)

Rashi explains that his name was Yoktan "because he was humble and would make himself small (*katan*). That is why he was privileged to establish all of these families."

R' Simchah Bunim of P'shischa once told his *chassidim*, "Every Jew must have two pockets; one to hold the verse, 'He created him with God's form' (1:27), and the other to hold the verse, 'I am like dust and ashes' (18:27).

"When a person has an opportunity to do a *mitzvah*, to learn Torah, or to do an act of kindness, let him not think, *Who am I to merit performing such lofty deeds? I am but a simple man, undeserving of such things* .... He must not think this way! Rather, he must immediately take the verse, 'He created him with God's form,' out of his first pocket and remember that since this is so, he *is* capable and worthy of doing all holy acts.

"However, if others deride or insult him, then let him take out the verse, 'I am like dust and ashes,' from his second pocket, and he should think to himself, *How can someone like me — who is nothing but dust and ashes — feel offended by others?*

"But," concluded the *Rebbe*, "most often the opposite is how people react. When someone is asked to do a *mitzvah*, he declines, saying, 'I am nothing but dust and ashes; I am not worthy.' But when others ridicule him or insult him, he at once begins shouting, 'He created him with God's form — look at whom you're insulting!'"

∗⃝∗

וַיְחִי־תֶרַח שִׁבְעִים שָׁנָה וַיּוֹלֶד אֶת־אַבְרָם

"Terach was seventy years old
when he fathered Avram" (11:26)

Rabbeinu Bachye quotes a *Midrash* that relates a most fascinating story:

On the night that Avraham *Avinu* was born, Nimrod's astrologers saw an unusual sight. They saw a gigantic star shoot out from the east and soar to the heavens. Once there, it swallowed four stars from the four directions of the world.

Nimrod's wise men were very startled by this extraordinary occurrence, as they understood what it foretold: One day a child would be born who would grow to be great and famous. When the time would come, he would inherit the land of Canaan and kill the kings that resided there. They discussed the matter among themselves and decided to tell the king what they had seen.

Nimrod's wise men approached him and began to relate what had happened. Said the wise men, "At night we were guests in the house of Terach, who was hosting a feast in honor of the birth of his son. After the feast, we went for a stroll in Terach's courtyard, and when we looked at the sky, we saw one star consume four other stars from the four corners of the heavens. There is no doubt that this indicates that Terach's newborn son will one day conquer the entire world! If it is proper in your eyes, then have Terach's son put to death now, before he grows up and puts an end to your reign and to your religion."

Nimrod summoned Terach at once. When Terach arrived, Nimrod made him an offer: "Hand over the son that was born to you last night, and, in return, I will reward you with a house full of gold!"

Terach grew very frightened, and at first he did not know what to say. After another moment of confusion, he replied, "By all means, I am prepared to do whatever you request and accept whatever you wish to give me."

The next day, Terach returned to the king and said: "Your Highness! I do not wish to do anything without your permission; I have therefore come to seek your advice. Last night, I was approached by a man who asked me to exchange my handsome horse for a house full of barley. I told him that I couldn't do anything without first seeking the counsel of my wise king. If Your Highness so wishes, I will give the man my horse. What is your opinion?"

"Fool!" answered Nimrod. "If you own such a valuable horse, why would you exchange it for money — and all the more so for barley!"

"May my words not anger you, Your Highness," responded Terach. "You are certainly correct. But how, then, can I exchange my precious son for money?"

When Nimrod heard Terach's words, he became furious with him and wanted to execute him.

Terach fell at Nimrod's feet and pleaded for forgiveness: "Your Highness! In my foolishness, I was merely jesting with the king! I beg of you — simply grant me a few days to appease my wife, and I will bring my son to you!"

Nimrod granted Terach's request.

After three days, Terach appeared in the palace of the king carrying an infant. Unbeknownst to Nimrod, however, the child was not Terach's son; rather, it was the son of his maidservant who had recently given birth. Nimrod took the child, and his anger subsided.

Lech Lecha

לֶךְ־לְךָ מֵאַרְצְךָ
"Go for yourself from your land" (12:1)

VRAHAM *AVINU'S* MOTIVE FOR LEAVING HIS COUNTRY WAS BECAUSE Hashem had commanded him to do so. Most people, however, leave their native land in search of livelihood; especially if they think they will become wealthy elsewhere.

In *Yalkut Shimoni, Chazal* relate a fascinating story about one of the students of R' Shimon bar Yochai. The student had traveled to *chutz la'aretz,* and after living there for some time, returned to *Eretz Yisrael* a wealthy man.

His friends envied his newfound wealth.

R' Shimon sensed their envy and asked them to come with him. He took them to a valley near Meiron, and he prayed: "O Valley! Valley! Fill yourself with gold coins!"

Immediately, the valley became filled with shiny gold coins. R' Shimon bar Yochai turned to his students and said, "Anyone who wishes to take from these coins may do so — but be aware that it will come at the cost of a portion of your *Olam Haba.*"

The students understood his message, and decided not to take any of the coins.

In the same vein, the *Chofetz Chaim* was once traveling with a student to a small town where another one of his students resided. When they arrived at the town, the local student, who had heard of his eminent *rebbi's* arrival, went out to greet him. He lauded the *Chofetz Chaim* with much praise and showered him with honor, and then begged him to be a guest at his home.

The *Chofetz Chaim* — who was known to shun honor in every possible way — refused his student's invitation.

The student who had accompanied the *Chofetz Chaim* was surprised by his *rebbi's* behavior. "Why did *Rabbeinu* not give his student an opportunity to merit performing the great *mitzvah* of serving a *talmid chacham*?" he asked.

"Tell me," responded the *Chofetz Chaim,* "in your younger years, did you ever enter the kitchen on *erev Shabbos* and ask the cook for a piece of *kugel?*"

"Certainly," answered the student.

"What did the cook reply?" asked the *Chofetz Chaim.*

"The cook told me," said the young man, "that the *kugel* has been set aside just for Shabbos, and that one who eats the *kugel* on *erev Shabbos* will have none left for Shabbos."

"It is exactly the same regarding honor," responded the *Chofetz Chaim.* "*HaKadosh Baruch Hu* has set aside honor to serve as a reward in *Olam Haba,* as the verse states, 'The wise inherit honor' (*Mishlei* 3:35). One who eats in this world from what has been prepared for him takes a 'bite' out of the portion he was supposed to receive in the next world."

❧∞❧

לֶךְ־לְךָ מֵאַרְצְךָ וּמִמּוֹלַדְתְּךָ וּמִבֵּית אָבִיךָ
"Go for yourself from your land, from your relatives, and from your father's house" (12:1)

R' Nachum of Chernobyl was famous for his efforts on behalf of Jewish captives. It was his custom to travel through towns and villages to collect money for the important *mitzvah* of *pidyon shevuyim* (redeeming captives).

Once, when he was in the town of Zhitomir, the local gentiles shamelessly accused him of some crime that he had not committed. The authorities promptly arrested him and placed R' Nachum in jail.

One of the distinguished members of the Zhitomir community paid R' Nachum a visit at the prison. There he elaborated upon the verse, **"Go for yourself from your land"**: "Avraham *Avinu,*" said the man, "excelled at *hachnasas orchim*, showing hospitality to guests, and dedicated his entire life to finding new ways to honor his guests.

"*HaKadosh Baruch Hu* therefore commanded him, 'Go for *yourself* from your land, from your relatives, and from your father's house.' Once you become a wanderer and experience what it feels like to be without shelter or a place to rest, you will be even more sensitive to the needs of your guests.

"The same applies to you, R' Nachum. Since your entire life has been dedicated to the freeing of captives, Heaven has granted you the opportunity to feel the bitter taste of captivity. Now you will possess an even greater sensitivity toward the plight of a captive."

וְאֶעֶשְׂךָ לְגוֹי גָּדוֹל וַאֲבָרֶכְךָ וַאֲגַדְּלָה שְׁמֶךָ

"And I will make of you a great nation;
I will bless you and make your name great" (12:2)

Rashi comments on the above verse: "'And make your name great' — This is [a reference to that] which they say [in the *Shemoneh Esrei*], 'God of Yaakov.'"

What is the connection, asked the great *tzaddik* and kabbalist, R' Shimshon of Ostropola, between Hashem's promise to make *Avraham's* name great and the phrase "God of *Yaakov*"?

Furthermore, continued R' Shimshon, God changed Avraham's name from Avram to Avraham and Yaakov's name to Yisrael. *Chazal* tell us, "Whoever calls Avraham, 'Avram,' violates a positive commandment" (*Berachos* 13a). However, the Gemara issues no warning against referring to Yaakov as Yisrael. What is the reason for this discrepancy?

The answer, said R' Shimshon, is as follows: In Hebrew, the names of our forefathers, Avraham, Yitzchak, and Yaakov, have a total of thirteen letters. The number thirteen is also the *gematria* of the word *"Echad"* ("One"). The Hebrew spelling of our matriarchs' names — Sarah, Rivkah, Rachel, and Leah — also contains thirteen letters, the gematria of *'Echad'*!

Together, the names of our Forefathers and Matriarchs contain a total of twenty-six letters, which is the numerical value of *yud – hei – vav – hei*, Hashem's ineffable Name! Thus the names of our Forefathers and Matriarchs allude to the idea that Hashem *Echad* — "Hashem is One."

Now, once the name Avram was switched to Avraham (adding one letter to his name), if we were to refer to Yaakov as Yisrael (which has five letters in Hebrew), then there would be fourteen letters in the names of our Forefathers and they would no longer equal *"Echad"* nor would the combined total of letters in the names of our Forefathers and Matriarchs equal Hashem's Holy Name. This is why we are not required to refer to Yaakov as Yisrael, as it would alter these numerical patterns.

Our verse can therefore be understood literally: "I will make your name great"; meaning, "I will make it longer, from Avram to Avraham." To this Rashi adds: "This is a reference to what they say... 'God of *Yaakov*'" — and not 'God of *Yisrael*.'

וַיְהִי־רִיב בֵּין רֹעֵי מִקְנֵה־אַבְרָם וּבֵין רֹעֵי מִקְנֵה־לוֹט

"And there was quarreling between the herdsmen of Avram's livestock and the herdsmen of Lot's livestock" (13:7)

Rashi comments, "[They quarreled] because Lot's shepherds were wicked and would graze their cattle in the fields of others, and Avraham's shepherds would rebuke them over the theft."

The *Chofetz Chaim* took great measures to avoid any action that could be considered theft. For example, when it rained in Radin, the *Chofetz Chaim's* town, people would place wooden boards on the muddy roads so that others would not soil their clothing. The *Chofetz Chaim,* however, never walked on these boards. *Perhaps,* he thought, *these boards belong to somebody and were taken without permission. To use them would be stealing.*

❦

וְאַנְשֵׁי סְדֹם רָעִים וְחַטָּאִים לַה׳ מְאֹד:

"Now the people of Sodom were exceedingly wicked and sinful toward Hashem" (13:13)

Yalkut Shimoni (*Bereishis* #70) relates that there were four judges in Sodom: *Shakrai, Shakrurai, Zaifai* (forgers), and *Matzli Din* (those who tipped the scales of justice in their favor). These judges acted just like their names: they were liars (*shakrai* in Aramaic), forgers (*zaifai*), and people who perverted justice (*matzli din*).

Two men once appeared at the court of Sodom, with one of them claiming that the other had cut an ear off his donkey.

The judges contemplated the matter and arrived at a verdict: The owner of the donkey must deposit his donkey with the other man, in whose possession it would remain until the ear would grow back!

There was a bridge in Sodom that crossed the river that flowed through the city. The courts in Sodom passed a law that whoever crossed the bridge would be required to pay a toll of four *zuz,* but whoever crossed the river without using the bridge would be charged eight *zuz.*

A garment cleaner once visited Sodom. He was unfamiliar with the city's laws and, so, when he noticed that there was a toll for using the bridge, he waded through the water to save himself the money.

When he reached the other side of the river, the toll collectors met him. "If you have crossed the bridge, pay us four *zuz*," they said.

"I did not use your bridge!" responded the launderer. "I cut through the river, instead."

"In that case," said the toll collectors, "you must pay us eight *zuz!*"

The man refused to pay, so the toll collectors beat and injured him. The launderer then went to the court of Sodom to sue his attackers.

Said the judge, "Since these men let your blood, which is beneficial to one's health, you are required to pay them for their great service to you. This is in addition to the toll of eight *zuz* that you incurred by crossing through the river."

Eliezer, the servant of Avraham *Avinu*, was walking through the city of Sodom. The townspeople of Sodom attacked Eliezer and injured him. Eliezer went to the city's courthouse and presented his case to the judge.

"Since these men improved your health by letting your blood," said the judge, "you are required to pay them for their services."

Upon hearing the verdict, Eliezer picked up a large stone and hurled it at the judge. The judge, now bloody and wounded, screamed at Eliezer, "What have you done?"

"Please," replied Eliezer, "give the money which you now owe me for letting your blood to my attackers. Now the money in my purse can stay where it is."

❧❀

אִם־מֵחוּט וְעַד שְׂרוֹךְ־נַעַל וְאִם־אֶקַּח מִכָּל־אֲשֶׁר־לָךְ
"I will not keep even a thread or a shoestrap" (14:23)

In tractate *Chullin* (89a), *Chazal* state the following: "As reward for having said, "I will not keep even a thread or a shoestrap," Avraham *Avinu's* children received two *mitzvos*: the string of *techeles* that is placed on the *tzitzis,* and the *tefillin* strap."

Rashi explains *Chazal's* statement: The reason that Avraham did not wish to accept anything from the king of Sodom was because he did not want to derive any benefit from stolen goods. He was duly rewarded with the *mitzvos* of *tzitzis* and *tefillin.*

Perhaps this is the reason, suggests the *Meshech Chochmah* (R' Meir Simchah of Dvinsk), that we don our *tallis* and lay our *tefillin* specifically during *Shacharis,* as this was the prayer instituted by Avraham *Avinu.*

הַבֶּט־נָא הַשָּׁמַיְמָה וּסְפֹר הַכּוֹכָבִים
אִם־תּוּכַל לִסְפֹּר אֹתָם וַיֹּאמֶר לוֹ כֹּה יִהְיֶה זַרְעֶךָ:

*"Look now toward the heavens and count
the stars, if it is possible for you to count them."
He then said to him, "So will be your descendants" (15:5)*

When we look at the stars, said R' Chaim of Sanz, they appear to be rather small. Yet in reality stars are enormous, as we would see for ourselves if we could get closer to them.

This is the message that Hashem imparted to Avraham when He stated, **"Look now toward the heavens and count the stars."** In this world, Avraham, your children are going to be considered small and insignificant among the nations of the world. However, "So will be your descendants" — In Heaven they are considered far more important than any of the nations!

וְהֶאֱמִן בַּה' וַיַּחְשְׁבֶהָ לוֹ צְדָקָה:

*"He trusted in Hashem, and He considered
this for him as an act of righteousness" (15:6)*

Why, asked the *Chofetz Chaim,* was Avraham's trust in Hashem considered "righteousness" — as though it was something above and beyond what was demanded of him? After all, Avraham fulfilled every commandment in the Torah; what was so unique about his trust in Hashem?

We see from here, answered the *Chofetz Chaim,* that trust in Hashem is more than just another *mitzvah;* rather, it is the foundation of the entire Torah.

To what can this be compared? To a man drowning in the sea who suddenly sees a tree extending from the shore. Which part of the tree will he attempt to grab? Not the branches, for they can easily be broken off; rather, he grabs hold of the roots.

So too, concluded the *Chofetz Chaim,* is trust in Hashem. Trust in Hashem is comparable to the sturdy roots of a tree, which serve as a foundation and a base for the entire tree.

וַיֹּאמַר ה' אֱלֹקִים בַּמָּה אֵדַע כִּי אִירָשֶׁנָּה:

"My Lord, Eternal God! How will I know that I shall take possession of it?" (15:8)

Chazal teach us in tractate *Berachos* (7a), "Said R' Yochanan in the name of R' Shimon bar Yochai: Since the day that *HaKadosh Baruch Hu* created the world, there was no one who referred to Hashem as *'Adon'* ('Master'), until Avraham came and referred to Him as *'Adon.'* As the verse states, *'Ado-nai Elokim!* How will I know that I shall take possession of it?'"

A young *talmid chacham* once appeared before the Vilna *Gaon* with a commentary he had written on the *Siddur.* He presented it to the *Gaon* and requested his approbation.

The *Gaon* began to leaf through the *sefer,* and saw that the author had asked the following question at the outset of his work: Why is it, he asked, that our Sages placed the prayer *"Adon Olam"* at the very beginning of the *Shacharis* service that we recite each morning?

The answer, he wrote, is as follows: Since it was Avraham *Avinu* that instituted *Shacharis,* and it was he who first called Hashem *"Adon,"* it is fitting that *Shacharis* commence with the prayer *Adon Olam!*

The *Gaon* was impressed with this insight; he praised the commentary and gave the *sefer* a glowing approbation. He then commented that for this *d'var Torah* alone, it was worth publishing the *sefer.*

After relating the above story to a group of students, the Brisker *Rav* (R' Yitzchak Zev HaLevi Soloveitchik) concluded by teaching them a valuable lesson:

"Do you know why the Vilna *Gaon* was so impressed by an explanation that to us seems so simple?" asked the Brisker *Rav.*

"The Vilna Gaon," he answered, "strove his entire life to reveal the true meaning of the Torah. Therefore, whenever he learned of *any* Torah truth — albeit a simple one — he was filled with great joy."

✿❀✿

יָדֹעַ תֵּדַע כִּי־גֵר יִהְיֶה זַרְעֲךָ בְּאֶרֶץ לֹא לָהֶם

"Know with certainty that your descendants will be foreigners in a land that is not theirs " (15:13)

This verse speaks of the slavery that the Jewish nation would be forced to endure in Egypt. Yet our Sages tell us that this verse also alludes to the six fast days that have been set in the Jewish calendar:

The letter *yud* (*yud* has the numerical value of ten) in *"yado'a"* alludes to the **Tenth** of Teves.

The letter *taf* of *"teida"* alludes to *Ta'anis Esther* and *Tishah B'Av.*

The letters *kaf* and *yud* in *"ki"* allude to *Yom HaKippurim,* which falls on the **tenth** of Tishrei.

The letter *gimmel* (which has the numerical value of three) in *"ger"* alludes to *Tzom Gedalyah,* which falls on the **third** of Tishrei.

The letters *yud* and *zayin* (which together equal seventeen) in *"yihe'yeh zaracha"* allude to the **Seventeenth** of Tammuz.

PARASHAS VAYEIRA

וַיִּשָּׂא עֵינָיו וַיַּרְא וְהִנֵּה שְׁלֹשָׁה אֲנָשִׁים נִצָּבִים עָלָיו
*"[Avraham] looked up and saw: And behold!
three men were standing near him" (18:2)*

RASHI EXPLAINS THAT THE THREE "MEN" WERE ACTUALLY ANGELS THAT HAD been sent to carry out specific missions. One angel was to inform Sarah that she was going to bear a son, another angel was sent to destroy Sodom, and yet another one was sent to heal Avraham. Each angel was to perform only one task, as an angel is never sent to carry out more than one mission at a time.

Rashi goes on to inform us that the angel that healed Avraham subsequently traveled to Sodom in order to save Lot.

Soon after being appointed as rabbi of Brod, R' Shlomo Kluger was given the honor of being the *sandak* at the *bris milah* of one of the distinguished members of the town.

However, when he arrived at the *shul* where the *bris* was to be held he noticed that everyone there seemed downcast and dispirited. R'

Kluger approached one of his congregants and asked him what was the matter.

"The father of the infant is deathly ill," responded the man. "Being that his end is near, the family decided to delay the *bris* so that they could name the child after his father."

"Hurry," exclaimed R' Kluger, "bring the father here and perform the *bris* immediately!"

The father was brought to the *shul* and the *bris* was performed. Amazingly, as soon as the *bris* concluded, the father's medical condition improved! The father's life was, miraculously, no longer in danger. News of the miracle brought about by the new rabbi spread quickly throughout the town.

R' Kluger, however, dismissed the rumors about his "miraculous powers." "It wasn't a miracle at all," he insisted. "I learned to do so from the words of Rashi in *Parashas Vayeira*. Rashi there explains that the angel that cured Avraham later went on to Sodom to save Lot. But this is perplexing," continued R' Kluger. "Were there not enough angels available that one had to be sent to carry out two missions?

"Rather," he answered, "Lot's merit was not great enough to earn him an angel that could be sent specifically to save him, so the angel that was sent to cure Avraham was then sent to save Lot.

"It occurred to me," concluded R' Kluger, "that in all likelihood the father's life was being weighed at that very moment. But I was concerned that perhaps the father would not have sufficient merit to deserve a special angel to cure him. But since Eliyahu *HaNavi*, the angel of the *bris,* is present when the infant is circumcised, it was possible that he would bring about a recovery for the father as well."

וַיַּרְא וַיָּרָץ לִקְרָאתָם
"He noticed this, so he ran toward them" (18:2)

R' Isser Zalman Meltzer was once sitting in his home, discussing Torah thoughts with a group of disciples. Suddenly, one of his family members informed him that R' Yitzchak Zev Soloveitchik, the Brisker *Rav*, was about to arrive.

R' Meltzer immediately stood up and went to change from his weekday clothing that he had been wearing to his Shabbos finery. He put on his special Shabbos hat, and went out to greet his esteemed guest.

When he got to the door, however, it became clear that an error had been made. The visitor was not the great Brisker *Rav* but an ordinary Jew who looked like him.

R' Meltzer welcomed this Jew into his home with much honor. He then sat him at the head of the table, personally served him refreshments, and showed him great respect.

The students watched their *rebbi* with astonishment. When the visitor had left, they took the opportunity to ask R' Meltzer about his behavior. "Why did the *Rav* display such great respect toward an ordinary guest?" they asked.

"My students," answered R' Meltzer, "you must know that we are required to shower each and every Jew with an abundance of honor. Every Jew is a child of The One and Only King and must therefore be treated like royalty! However, it is not always feasible to do so. But since I had already prepared myself to honor the person whom I thought was the Brisker *Rav*, I was able to give this Jew the honor he rightfully deserved."

יֻקַּח־נָא מְעַט־מַיִם
"Let some water be brought" (18:4)

R' Yisrael Salanter once went to a small *shul* in Vilna to *daven Minchah*. Shortly before *Minchah* commenced, the congregants went to wash their hands. While the men spared little water when they washed, each one pouring an abundance on his hands, R' Salanter merely wet his hands with a few drops of water.

The people were surprised by what they had just seen. "Isn't the *Rav* accustomed to washing his hands before praying?" they asked.

"I certainly am," responded R' Salanter. "However, the water that we are using is brought by the *shamash*, and I do not want him to expend any extra effort on my behalf."

"This is a lesson that we were taught by Avraham *Avinu*," continued R' Salanter. "The verse states, 'Let some water be brought.' This is surprising, for Avraham had prepared lavishly for his guests: he brought them three *se'ahs* of fine flour and slaughtered three calves in order to serve each of them tongue with mustard. Considering his generosity, why did Avraham offer them only a small amount of water, as the expression, 'Let some water be brought' implies?

"The answer," concluded R' Salanter, "can be derived from the Gemara in *Bava Metzia* (86b). *Chazal* teach us that Avraham himself hastened to select the fine flour and calves, while a servant drew the water. When it came to his own efforts, he felt free to be lavish, but when it came to work that would be done by others, he made sure not to cause them any unnecessary effort. Since the water was to be brought by his servant, Avraham requested only a small amount of water, which is why he said, 'Let *some* water be brought.'"

וְאֶל־הַבָּקָר רָץ אַבְרָהָם
"Avraham then ran to the cattle" (18:7)

Chazal teach us (*Bava Metzia* 86b) that Avraham served his guests three tongues in mustard *(b'chardal)* — one for each guest.

The Vilna *Gaon* was sitting and teaching Torah to a group of students. Said the *Gaon*, "We find that there are three positive characteristics that can be found in all righteous men:

1. They feel compassion for the poor.
2. They suffice with little.
3. Their hearts quake with fear of Hashem.

These qualities are alluded to in the word *"b'chardal,"* as the Hebrew letters of this word can be rearranged in three different ways:

1. *bachar-dal* — they choose the poor and love them.
2. *chadal-rav* — they shun excessive lifestyles and make do with less.
3. *charad-lev* — their hearts quake with the fear of Heaven.

וַיִּקַּח בֶּן־בָּקָר רַךְ וָטוֹב
"He took tender, choice calves" (18:7)

In *Parashas Vayeira*, Avraham *Avinu* teaches us many lessons about the great importance of *hachnasas orchim* (hospitality).

Chazal (*Avos d'Rebbe Nasan*, Chapter 7) tell us that Iyov, as well, excelled at the *mitzvah* of *hachnasas orchim*, though he never reached the level of Avraham *Avinu*. *Chazal* explain the reason for this distinction: Iyov used to present each of his guests with the exact food that they were accustomed to eating. To one whose usual meal consisted of bread, Iyov gave bread. To one who normally ate meals of fattened fowl with aged wine, Iyov gave exactly that. Avraham *Avinu's* measure of hospitality, however, was far greater. To each one of his guests — even to the most destitute pauper — he presented a sumptuous feast of beef tongue dipped in mustard.

The *mussar* masters explain Avraham's motive: Avraham was not interested in simply providing for his guests. Rather, he also wished to instill within them a desire to praise and offer thanks to Hashem. He therefore provided for them in such a plentiful way in order that they would feel satiated and happy. This would then lead them to praise and thank Hashem with joy.

By giving his guests food of the finest quality, Avraham was also hinting to them the importance of constantly striving toward greater spiritual heights. It was as if he was telling them, "Why should you be satisfied with a simple meal of bread? Have tongue dipped in mustard instead!" Similarly, a person should never be satisfied with the spiritual level that he has attained; rather, he should constantly push himself to climb ever higher.

It is told of R' Chaim Soloveitchik, the *rav* of Brisk and *rosh yeshivah* of Volozhin, that despite his extensive involvement with communal affairs he always set aside time to perform the *mitzvah* of *hachnasas orchim*. He would personally care for each guest that entered his home, giving them to eat and drink, and providing for all of their needs.

On one occasion, however, R' Chaim was host to an individual who turned out to be a thief. Betraying R' Chaim's hospitality, this "guest" arose early one morning and stole many of the valuables in R' Chaim's house.

The members of the household were very distressed by the theft and even went so far as to accuse R' Chaim of not properly investigating the character of the people whom he allowed to reside in their home.

"Let me ask you a question," said R' Chaim to his family. "When Hashem wished to enable Avraham *Avinu* to perform the *mitzvah* of *hachnasas orchim,* he sent him angels in the form of desert nomads. Why did He not send Avraham angels in the form of fine, upstanding Jews?

"Hashem did this," he explained, "in order to teach us that the door of one's home must be open to everyone, without first investigating the personality and character of each potential guest. No one should ever be prevented from being the recipient of *hachnasas orchim*."

וַיֹּאמֶר ה' זַעֲקַת סְדֹם וַעֲמֹרָה כִּי־רָבָּה
וְחַטָּאתָם כִּי כָבְדָה מְאֹד:

"Hashem then said [to Avraham], 'The cries of Sodom and Amorah have become great, and their sin is very grave'"
(18:20)

Despite the fact that the residents of Sodom were extremely wealthy, they allowed no one to derive any benefit whatsoever from their property and they never permitted guests to enter their city.

However, it was not only people to whom the gates of Sodom were closed, but even to animals. *Chazal* relate that the wicked inhabitants of Sodom used to chop down all the trees surrounding the city so that the birds would be unable to rest on them and derive enjoyment from their property!

The *Midrash* tells a story of a starving man who once visited Sodom and asked for charity. The people gave him a coin, but in their cruelty, engraved their names on it and sent a message to all the storeowners in Sodom not to accept a coin that had their names etched upon it. The unfortunate man, coin in hand, made his way to each and every store in Sodom, but was unable to purchase any food. Finally, the man died from starvation.

One day, Avraham's servant, Eliezer, was passing through Sodom. Several townspeople invited him to their homes for a short rest, but Eliezer was not fooled by their offer. He had heard of the Sodomites' cruelty, and he knew the fate of anyone who risked being their guest: Every guest was made to lie down on a bed. If the person was short, they would stretch his body until it reached the length of the bed; if he was tall, they would cut off his legs to make him fit the bed. So Eliezer replied, "I cannot accept your offer. My mother passed away recently, and on account of my grief, I have decided not to lie in a bed for an entire year."

Eliezer continued to walk the streets of Sodom and entered the house of a person who was hosting a lavish feast. There was a well-known law in Sodom that prohibited inviting an outsider to a local feast. Anyone who violated this law was severely punished.

Eliezer took a seat at the table. It was not long before he was noticed.

"Who invited you?" asked the man sitting beside him. The man was hoping to secure a punishment for whomever it was that had committed this "crime."

"Why, *you* invited me!" replied Eliezer.

The man was terrified by the response; if anybody heard it, *he* would be incriminated for this offense. So he promptly got up and left the feast. This scene replayed itself several times until Eliezer was left sitting alone at the table. He finished his meal and left Sodom unharmed.

❦

רַק לָאֲנָשִׁים הָאֵל אַל־תַּעֲשׂוּ
דָבָר כִּי־עַל־כֵּן בָּאוּ בְּצֵל קֹרָתִי:

"Do not do anything to these men, however, because they have come under the shelter of my roof" (19:8)

The *Beis HaLevi* (R' Yosef Dov HaLevi Soloveitchik) once traveled to the city of Baranovitch. During the trip, the weather changed and it became very cold. It was so cold, in fact, that he could not continue his journey. Fortunately, he spotted a Jewish-owned inn on the side of the road. He asked the wagon driver to pull over so they could rest at the inn.

The *Beis HaLevi* knocked on the door, but there was no response. The wagon driver then approached the door and pounded on it with all his might. Suddenly, a light was seen flickering from a window on the second floor. A few moments later, the innkeeper opened the door. He was clearly annoyed by the disturbance.

"There are no vacancies!" he shouted. "Every room is reserved as I am expecting men of great importance."

"Please sir," said the *Beis HaLevi*, "traveling in this bitter cold is literally life threatening. All I ask is for some shelter for my wagon driver and myself."

The *Beis HaLevi* finally persuaded the innkeeper to allow them to remain in the inn. The innkeeper showed them to a corridor in the inn and pointed to a space on the floor next to the oven — that was to be their accommodations.

The *Beis HaLevi* at once lit a small candle and engrossed himself in Torah learning.

"Put out that candle," yelled the innkeeper. "You're disturbing our sleep!"

The *Beis HaLevi* extinguished the small flame and continued to learn by heart.

A short time later, the sound of galloping horses could be heard. A magnificent stagecoach pulled up alongside the inn. It was carrying the *Rebbe*, R' Aharon of Koidanov, and an entourage of his *chassidim*.

The innkeeper rushed downstairs and greeted his esteemed guests with a radiant face and bright smile.

The *Rebbe* entered the inn and passed through the corridor. He was surprised to see a man lying on the floor. The *Rebbe* looked closely at the man and was shocked to see that the man was none other than the *Beis HaLevi!*

"R' Yosef Dov! R' Yosef Dov!" he cried. "Why are you lying on the floor?"

The innkeeper now realized whom it was that he had treated so horribly. Now shamefaced and distraught, he begged the *Beis HaLevi* for his forgiveness.

The *Beis HaLevi* forgave the innkeeper immediately, but made one request of him. He asked him to visit Brisk and to spend some time in his home. There, the *Beis HaLevi* would teach him how to properly perform the *mitzvah* of *hachnasas orchim*.

"Now I understand something that has been troubling me," said the *Beis HaLevi*. "In *Parashas Vayeira* we find two remarkable stories of *hachnasas orchim*. The first is about Avraham *Avinu;* the second is about Lot. The Torah elaborates on and lauds Avraham's hospitality. Yet the Torah makes no mention of Lot's hospitality, even though Lot and his family had literally placed their lives in danger by taking in guests, which was a serious crime in Sodom. Why, then, does the Torah not praise his act of hospitality as well?

"The answer," said the *Beis HaLevi*, "is as follows: When the angels visited Avraham they appeared as desert wanderers. Yet despite their lowly appeerance, Avraham accorded them great honor. Lot, however, knew of the angels' true identity as soon as they entered his home. Showing honor to angels is not difficult, so according them hospitality is not a real achievement. While it is true that Lot endangered the lives of his family, yet he thought that the angels would protect him. It is for this reason that the Torah specifically praises the *hachnasas orchim* of Avraham but not of Lot."

וַיִּטַּע אֶשֶׁל בִּבְאֵר שָׁבַע
"He planted an eishel in Be'er-sheva" (21:33)

"Said R' Azaryah: What is an *eishel*? [It is an acronym for the words,] *achilah* (eating), *shesiyah* (drinking), and *levayah* (accompaniment)" (*Midrash Tehillim*).

R' Chaim of Volozhin related the following story: In a certain town there lived a wealthy man who spent an enormous sum of money in performing the *mitzvos* of *tzedakah* and *hachnasas orchim*. One day, a raging fire broke out in his town, and it consumed his home and everything he owned. The man came before the Vilna *Gaon* and asked, *"Rebbe,* is this the reward for all my efforts? My entire life was dedicated to giving *tzedakah,* and I spent vast sums of money on *hachnasas orchim*. Is this what I have to show for it?"

The *Gaon* responded: "The verse states concerning Avraham *Avinu,* 'He planted an *eishel* in Be'er-sheva.' *Chazal* have taught us that the word *'eishel'* is the acronym for '*achilah, shesiyah,* and *levayah.'*

"Now, you provided your guests with food and drink, but you did not accompany them and escort them when they left your home. So you only merited performing *achilah* and *shesiyah*. The acronym of *achilah* and *shesiyah,* without *levayah,* is **eish** — fire."

קַח־נָא אֶת־בִּנְךָ אֶת יְחִידְךָ ...וְלֶךְ־לְךָ אֶל־אֶרֶץ הַמֹּרִיָּה
"Please take your son, your only one ...
and go to the land of Moriah" (22:2)

The Torah tells us about two important mountains, said the *Divrei Chaim* (R' Chaim of Sanz). The first is *Har HaMoriah,* the mountain where *Akeidas Yitzchak* took place. The second is *Har Sinai,* the mountain on which the Torah was given to the Jewish people.

When Hashem chose a mountain upon which to build the *Beis HaMikdash,* which mountain did He select?

One would think that He would have selected *Har Sinai,* as that is where the Jews received the Torah. Surprisingly, He did not select *Har Sinai* but *Har HaMoriah*. What is the reason for this?

It is in order to teach us, answered the *Divrei Chaim*, just how beloved the quality of *mesirus nefesh* is to Hashem! *Har HaMoriah* is the site where, with extraordinary self-sacrifice, Avraham *Avinu* bound his dear son Yitzchak as an offering to Hashem. It was this *mesirus nefesh* which sanctified *Har HaMoriah* forever and rendered it the most appropriate site on which to build the *Beis HaMikdash.*

וַיָּשָׁב אַבְרָהָם אֶל־נְעָרָיו וַיָּקֻמוּ וַיֵּלְכוּ יַחְדָּו
אֶל־בְּאֵר שָׁבַע וַיֵּשֶׁב אַבְרָהָם בִּבְאֵר שָׁבַע:

"Avraham returned to his young men, and they stood up and went together to Be'er Sheva, and Avraham stayed in Be'er Sheva" (22:19)

At the very beginning of the Torah's account of the *Akeidah,* we read, "And the two of them walked together" (22:6). The Torah is telling us that both Yitzchak — who was soon to be sacrificed — and Avraham — who was about to sacrifice his beloved son — journeyed *together* to *Har HaMoriah,* united in their dedication to Hashem and in their unwavering commitment to perform His will.

But why, asked R' Menachem Mendel of Vorka, does the Torah tell us that after the *Akeidah* Avraham and his *young men* "went together"? What is this supposed to teach us?

The Torah is revealing to us, answered R' Menachem Mendel, just how humble a man Avraham *Avinu* truly was. Despite the fact that he had just triumphed in the face of his most difficult trial, Avraham felt no haughtiness whatsoever. This, then, is what the verse means when it states that Avraham and his young men "went together." In the same way that Avraham's young men were not beset by feelings of pride and arrogance, so too was Avraham free from such feelings despite his extraordinary achievement!

CHAYEI SARAH

גֵּר־וְתוֹשָׁב אָנֹכִי עִמָּכֶם
"I am an alien and a resident among you" (23:4)

WHAT IS THE MEANING, ASKED THE DUBNO *MAGGID*, OF THE expression "alien and resident"? An alien is a person who resides in a land temporarily, while a resident's status is a permanent one. An alien, therefore, is not a resident, nor is a resident an alien.

The answer, said the *Maggid*, is as follows: *Chazal* comment on the verse, "For you are aliens and residents with Me" (*Vayikra* 25:23) — "This world is like a lobby before the World to Come; prepare yourself in the lobby so that you may enter the banquet hall" (*Avos* 4:21).

Each individual is required to prepare himself for his eternal residence in the World to Come by performing *mitzvos* and good deeds in this world, his temporary dwelling. Thus Avraham *Avinu* was saying, I am both an "alien" and a "resident"; I am an alien temporarily living in this world before I will become a permanent resident of the World to Come.

The *Chofetz Chaim* illustrated this idea by way of the following parable: There was a very wealthy man who wished to build himself a luxurious house. He contracted an architect who began to draw blueprints for the future home.

"It is very important to me," said the wealthy man to the architect, "that the living room be spacious and comfortable. Yet it also important that the hallway leading to the living room be very large as well."

The architect took the necessary measurements and began to tell the man what he thought: "There is most certainly not going to be enough space for both the living room and the hallway to be large and roomy. You are going to have to make a decision — do you want a spacious living room or a spacious hallway?

"I'll give you a bit of advice," continued the architect. "Being that the prevailing custom is to make the living room as large as possible and not to invest very much in the hallway, I'd suggest that you do the same.

It would be ridiculous to do the opposite and make the hallway larger than the living room. After all, you don't want people to laugh at you."

So it is with us, said the *Chofetz Chaim*. Our duty in this world is to prepare ourselves for the eternal life, so that our portion in the World to Come will be as great as possible. How are we supposed to do this? By living our lives according to the Torah and by performing the *mitzvos*.

How foolish is the man whose sole concern is to insure himself a comfortable life in this world. He is comparable to the wealthy man who requests a large hallway but a small living room. When he arrives in the World to Come everyone will laugh at him!

עֹבֵר לַסֹּחֵר:
"In negotiable currency" (23:16)

The rabbi of Brod, R' Efraim Zalman Margolios, went to speak with a high-ranking government official about matters pertaining to the Jewish community.

The official — who routinely accepted bribes — wanted to indicate to R' Margolios that a bribe would certainly be "appropriate" but, he felt, he could not say so openly to the rabbi.

He therefore took a different approach: "Rabbi," said the official, "being that I owe money to one of the local merchants, it would be most appreciated if you would settle the payment for me."

"With this," the rabbi later reflected, "I came to understand why the verse states that Efron accepted payment *'oveir la'socheir.'* [The commentators explain that this means "the currency was acceptable to all merchants," but the literal meaning of *oveir la'socheir* is "payment that is transferred to the merchant."] As it was uncomfortable for him to demand such an exorbitant fee from Avraham *Avinu*, he had a merchant accept the money on his behalf."

וַה' בֵּרַךְ אֶת־אַבְרָהָם בַּכֹּל:
"And Hashem blessed Avraham with everything" (24:1)

One Sukkos, the Vilna *Gaon* was sitting in his *sukkah* with several guests. He turned to them and asked, "From where do we know that Avraham fulfilled the *mitzvah* of *sukkah*?"

His guests sat in silence and could not think of the answer.

Said the *Gaon:* "The *Midrash* tells us, 'And Hashem blessed Avraham *bakol* — this refers to the *mitzvah* of *Sukkah.*' Where do we find any reference to the *mitzvah* of *Sukkah* in this verse? Look at the word *bakol.*

"Its three letters allude to the three verses that describe the *mitzvah* of *sukkah:*

"*Basukkos teishvu shivas yamim*" — "You shall live in *sukkahs* for seven days" (*Vayikra* 23:42);

"*Kol ha'ezrach b'Yisrael yeishvu basukkos*" — "All natives among Israel shall live in *sukkahs*" (ibid.);

"*L'ma'an yeidu doroseichem ki vasukkos hoshavti es Bnei Yisrael*" — "So that your generations will be aware that I settled the Children of Israel in *sukkahs*" (ibid. 23:43)!

וַה׳ בֵּרַךְ אֶת־אַבְרָהָם בַּכֹּל:
"And Hashem blessed Avraham with everything" (24:1)

A true *tzaddik*, said R' Levi Yitzchak of Berdichev, does not pray and beseech Hashem for his own personal needs, but rather for the needs of *Bnei Yisrael.* Even if he is blessed with good fortune, he does not view it as being truly good, unless it will benefit the Jewish people as a whole.

Therefore, he continued, when Heaven decrees to grant a *tzaddik* an abundance of blessing, the Jewish people prosper as well.

This is what the verse means when it states, "And Hashem blessed Avraham *bakol.*" When was Avraham truly blessed? When Hashem blessed *"hakol"* — the entire Jewish nation in his merit.

וְלָקַחְתָּ אִשָּׁה לִבְנִי לְיִצְחָק:
"And take a wife for my son, for Yitzchak" (24:4)

Why is it, asked R' Yosef Dov Soloveitchik, that in this verse Avraham says, "Take a wife for my son, *for Yitzchak*," but when Eliezer later relates Avraham's instructions to Lavan he quotes only, "Take a wife for my son" (24:38)? Why did Eliezer not repeat Avraham's words exactly as he had heard them?

The answer, said R' Soloveitchik, can be explained with the following parable: There was a wealthy man who was looking for a suitable match for his only daughter. Of course, he did not want just anybody for his daughter; the prospective son-in-law would have to be of dignified character and the son of a great Torah scholar.

One day, a matchmaker approached the man:

"I have the perfect match for your daughter!" said the matchmaker. "Though the young man is not the son of a Torah scholar, he *himself* is an outstanding *talmid chacham*!"

"I am not interested in having a Torah scholar as a son-in-law," responded the father. "I don't want my daughter to be a *rebbetzin*; I only want the *son* of a scholar"

Now we can understand the discrepancies between the verses, said R' Soloveitchik. When Avraham was describing his son to Eliezer, he referred to him as "my son...Yitzchak." This young man is not only my son, but he is Yitzchak the *tzaddik*.

However, when Eliezer arrived in Lavan's home he suspected that the potential in-laws would not be very impressed with praise depicting the righteousness of Yitzchak and might even reject the match because of it. He therefore said only, "Take a wife for my son" — the young man is the son of Avraham. While praise of Yitzchak's spiritual greatness might not have impressed them, praise of his father's lofty stature certainly would!

וַיָּרָץ הָעֶבֶד לִקְרָאתָהּ
"The servant ran toward her" (24:17)

Rashi comments, "Because he saw that the waters went up toward her."

Where does the verse indicate, asks the Ramban, that the waters actually went up toward her?

Later on, answers the Ramban, the verse states, "She *drew* for all his camels" (24:20). In this verse, however, we find no mention of Rivkah "drawing" any water. This teaches us that Rivkah, in fact, had no need to draw water, for the water rose up toward her.

Yet, asked R' Levi Yitzchak of Berdichev, why did the water not rise for her when she drew water for Eliezer's camels?

Initially, Rivkah had gone to draw water for her own personal needs. In order that the *tzaddekes* should not have to burden herself with the task of drawing water, the water, instead, rose to her. However, when Rivkah went to draw water for Eliezer's camels, she had undertaken to perform a *mitzvah*. Heaven wanted Rivkah to earn as much merit as possible for her act of kindness, so, this time, the water was not allowed to rise for her. In this way, Rivkah would receive maximum merit for performing this *mitzvah*, for as *Chazal* teach us, "According to the exertion is the merit" (*Avos* 5:26). Thus the more she exerted herself, the more merit she would receive.

וַיְפַתַּח הַגְּמַלִּים
"And (the man) unmuzzled the camels" (24:32)

Rashi comments: "He untied their muzzles because [whenever they traveled] he would block their mouths to prevent them from grazing along the way in other people's fields."

Gedolei Yisrael have always exercised great caution not to be guilty of the sin of theft in any way.

On one occasion, the *Chofetz Chaim's* wife and a neighbor purchased a very large fish. They made up to meet later at the *rebbetzin's* house where they would cut up the fish and divide the pieces between them.

The neighbor remained in the marketplace longer than she had planned and was late in returning home. When morning gave way to the afternoon and her neighbor still had not arrived, the *Chofetz Chaim's* wife decided to divide the fish on her own. She set aside what appeared to be the better of the two halves for her neighbor, and cooked the other half for her family.

At lunch, she set a plate of fish before the *Chofetz Chaim*, but he did not eat it. Instead, he moved the plate aside and only ate the bread.

Witnessing his father's action and knowing that there was surely a motive behind it, the *Chofetz Chaim's* son, R' Leib, asked his mother, "Could you please tell me, Mother, exactly what transpired today when you purchased this fish?"

His mother related to him all that had happened.

"Now I understand!" remarked R' Leib. "For the *Shulchan Aruch* (*Hilchos Shutfim* 176) clearly rules that if one of two partners wishes to divide and take his portion, he must do so in the presence of three bystanders!

"There is no doubt," concluded R' Leib, "that Father sensed that this fish had not been handled according to the dictates of *halachah* and therefore it might be considered stolen. Father would never allow anything with a questionable status to enter his mouth!"

וַיּוּשַׂם לְפָנָיו לֶאֱכֹל וַיֹּאמֶר לֹא אֹכַל עַד אִם־דִּבַּרְתִּי דְּבָרָי

"(Food) was set before him to eat, but he said, 'I will not eat until I have spoken what I have to say'" (24:33)

A pair of feuding in-laws appeared before the Dubno *Maggid* at a *din Torah*. The father of the groom was the owner of an inn, and he had invited the parents of his future daughter-in-law to the inn in order to finalize the match.

When the girl's parents arrived at the inn, they were served a lavish meal "fit for a king." After the meal, the in-laws sat down, and in, good spirits, came to an agreement.

"However," stated the father of the groom before the *Maggid*, "I demand payment for the meal that I served! After all, at the time of the meal we had not yet agreed upon the match so there was no family relationship then. They were, therefore, no different than ordinary guests who are obligated to pay for the food they eat."

"Hearing your argument," remarked the *Maggid*, "has enabled me to answer a question that has been troubling me. The Torah tells us that when Eliezer arrived at Besuel's home, food was placed before him, but he refrained from eating, saying, 'I will not eat until I have spoken what I have to say' (24:33). Why did Eliezer not wish to eat before he had spoken?

"It must be," concluded the *Maggid*, "that Eliezer quickly assessed the nature of Yitzchak's father-in-law. He feared that if he ate first and only afterwards said his piece, Besuel would charge him for the cost of the food. After all, at the time of the meal, Besu'el would have not yet become Avraham's relative by marriage."

אֵלַי לֹא־תֵלֵךְ הָאִשָּׁה אַחֲרָי:
"Perhaps the woman will not follow me" (24:39)

Rashi explains that Eliezer had a daughter whom he hoped would marry Yitzchak. Therefore, while the verse is read "*ulai,*" "perhaps," it is spelled in a way that can be read as "*eilai,*" "to me." In other words, Eliezer was suggesting that Yitzchak be given "to me" for my daughter. But Avraham told him, "My son is blessed; you are cursed [because you are a descendant of Cham], and the cursed can not join with the blessed."

How did *Chazal* know, asked the Vilna *Gaon,* that this was Eliezer's intention?

The Torah, explained the *Gaon,* uses one of two words when it wishes to convey the idea of doubt: "lest (*pen*)" or "perhaps (*ulai*)."

The word "lest" is used when the Torah refers to something negative and undesirable. As the verse states, "Lest your heart be seduced" (*Devarim* 11:16); "Lest there be a lawless thought in your heart" (*Devarim* 15: 9).

The word "perhaps," on the other hand, is used when the Torah speaks of a desirable result, as in the verse, "Perhaps I will be built up through her" (16:2); "Perhaps there are fifty righteous people" (18:24).

If Eliezer had deemed the possibility of Yitzchak's potential wife refusing to return with him as a negative thing, then the Torah should have said, "*Lest* the woman will not follow me." Eliezer, however, said, "*Perhaps* the woman will not follow me," indicating that he actually desired that the woman not return with him! Why would Eliezer desire such a thing? The answer must be that he wanted *his* daughter to marry Yitzchak.

וַיֵּצֵא יִצְחָק לָשׂוּחַ בַּשָּׂדֶה
"Yitzchak went out toward evening to pray in the field" (24:63

It was at that time, *Chazal* teach us, that Yitzchak instituted the *Minchah* prayer. *Chazal* state, "The prayers were instituted by the Forefathers" (*Berachos* 26a). Avraham instituted *Shacharis;* Yitzchak, *Minchah;* and Yaakov, *Maariv.*

The second letter of each of their names alludes to the prayer that they were responsible for instituting: The second letter in the name "Avraham" is "beis." This is the first letter of the word boker, morning — alluding to the Shacharis prayer, which is recited in the morning.

The second letter in the name "Yitzchok" is "tzaddi." This is the first letter of tzaharayim, afternoon, which is the time that Minchah is recited.

The second letter in the name "Yaakov" is "ayin," which is the first letter of the word erev, evening, which is the time for reciting Maariv.

PARASHAS TOLDOS

וַיִּתְרֹצְצוּ הַבָּנִים בְּקִרְבָּה

"The children struggled inside her" (25:22)

RASHI EXPLAINS THAT WHEN RIVKAH PASSED BY THE BEIS MIDRASH OF Shem and Ever, Yaakov would attempt to leave his mother's womb. When she passed a house of idol worship, Esav would attempt to leave.

R' Yechezkel of Kuzemir posed the following question to his students: It is understandable why Yaakov was unable to leave Rivkah's womb when she passed by the beis midrash of Shem and Ever. Since Esav was the intended firstborn, he was in a position that blocked Yaakov's exit. But why was Esav unable to leave the womb when Rivkah passed by a house of idol worship? Who was blocking his exit?

From here we can see just how wicked Esav really was, answered the tzaddik. For he was willing to delay his birth and forgo his idol worship as long as it would prevent Yaakov from entering the beis midrash.

וַיִּתְרֹצְצוּ הַבָּנִים בְּקִרְבָּה

"The children struggled inside her" (25:22)

Why is it, asked the Chasam Sofer (R' Moshe Sofer), that when Rivkah passed the beis midrash, Yaakov attempted to escape from her womb? After all, *Chazal* (*Niddah* 30b) teach us that during the time a child is in its mother's womb, an angel comes and teaches it the entire Torah. Did Yaakov think that he would actually be able to learn more in the *beis midrash* than he would from the angel?

The answer, said the *Chasam Sofer*, is that though Yaakov was learning the entire Torah from the mouth of an angel, he was forced to do so in the presence of Esav. Yaakov preferred to learn Torah in a *beis midrash,* free from the company of his wicked brother, than to be taught the entire Torah directly from the mouth of a holy angel!

From the words of the *Chasam Sofer* we are able to learn, remarked the *Chofetz Chaim*, just how important it is to stay far away from people who may have a negative influence on us.

וַיִּגְדְּלוּ הַנְּעָרִים

"The boys grew up" (25:27)

Rashi comments on this verse: "All the while that they were young, they were not distinguishable in their deeds, but once they turned thirteen years old, this one set out for the houses of Torah study, and the other one set out for idolatry."

R' Yechiel Michel of Zlochov had a son named Zev. Zev was no different from the other children his age; he learned as they learned and played as they played. When Zev neared the age of thirteen, his father approached an expert *sofer* and requested that he write *parshiyos* (the Torah portions) for the *tefillin* that his son would soon be wearing.

The *sofer* set about the task with utmost holiness and purity; after all, it is not every day that one has the opportunity to write *tefillin* for the son of one of the greatest *tzaddikim* of the generation.

When the *sofer* completed the *parshiyos*, he brought them to R' Yechiel Michel, who was delighted to see the beautifully written *parshiyos*. He had one request, though: Before the *sofer* would place the *parshiyos* in the *batim* (the *tefillin* boxes), he wished to have the boxes brought to him.

A short while later, the *sofer* brought the *parshiyos* and the *batim* to R' Yechiel Michel.

When R' Yechiel Michel picked up the *tefillin*, he began to cry from the innermost depths of his heart. The *sofer* watched in astonishment as the *tzaddik's* holy tears ran down his cheeks and into the *batim* of the *tefillin*.

By the time the *tzaddik* had finished crying, the *batim* were filled with his tears. The *Rebbe* then emptied and dried the *batim* and handed them to the *sofer*. "Now," said R' Yechiel Michel, "you may place the *parshiyos* inside the *batim*."

On the day Zev began wearing his *tefillin*, an amazing transformation came over him. For on that day his heart became full of love for Torah and fear of Hashem. From then on, he was set on the path that would eventually lead him to become one of the *gedolei hador*.

וַיַּעֲקֹב אִישׁ תָּם יֹשֵׁב אֹהָלִים:

"But Yaakov was a wholesome man, dwelling in tents" (25:27)

R ashi comments: "One who is not sharp to deceive is called 'wholesome.'"

Someone who is "not sharp to deceive," said the Lubliner *Rav*, is the type of person who has no notion of how to go about deceiving another person. Such a person is called a *"tam,"* "a simple one." However, somebody who knows how to deceive others yet chooses not to act in such a manner is referred to as an *"ish tam,"* "a wholesome *man*."

Yaakov *Avinu* was familiar with the ploys of deception, as he testified about himself during his stay in the house of Lavan, "I am his brother in trickery." Nevertheless, he chose to walk along the path of truth and honesty, thereby earning himself the title, "wholesome man."

וַיַּעֲקֹב אִישׁ תָּם יֹשֵׁב אֹהָלִים:

"But Yaakov was a wholesome man, dwelling in tents" (25:27)

F rom this verse we see, said the *Sh'lah HaKadosh* (R' Yeshayah HaLevi Horowitz), that the trait of wholesomeness is the most noble of all the traits.

For there is no doubt, reasoned the *Sh'lah*, that Yaakov pos-sessed every good character trait possible. Yet the only trait that Yaakov is explicitly praised for in the Torah is his wholesome char-acter. This implies that there is no trait more exalted than whole-someness.

לֵךְ מֵעִמָּנוּ כִּי־עָצַמְתָּ מִמֶּנּוּ מְאֹד:

"Go away from us, for you have become much mightier than we" (26:16)

This verse reveals to us, said the *Chofetz Chaim*, the true reason for the hatred that the nations of the world feel toward the Jewish people. Where does the animosity stem from? From the claim, "You have become much mightier than we." Thus the Egyptian advisers told Pharaoh, "The Children of Israel are more numerous and stronger than we."

It is such jealousy that causes the nations of the world to hate us so.

וְנִכְרְתָה בְרִית עִמָּךְ: אִם־תַּעֲשֵׂה עִמָּנוּ רָעָה כַּאֲשֶׁר לֹא נְגַעֲנוּךָ וְכַאֲשֶׁר עָשִׂינוּ עִמְּךָ רַק־טוֹב וַנְּשַׁלֵּחֲךָ בְּשָׁלוֹם אַתָּה

"Let us form a treaty with you, that you do no evil with us, just like we did not harm you; and just as we only treated you well and sent you away in peace, you [shall do likewise]" (26:28-29)

The *Midrash Rabbah* uses the following parable to explain this verse: A lion was devouring its prey, when suddenly a bone got caught in its throat. The lion declared that anyone who would be able to remove the bone from its throat would receive a generous reward.

An Egyptian *kora* (a bird with a long and thin beak) approached the lion and, with its long beak, managed to reach deep into the throat of the lion and dislodge the bone.

Said the bird to the lion: "Now that I have removed the bone from your throat, kindly grant me the reward that you promised."

"For an animal to stick its head into the mouth of a lion and come out alive," replied the lion, "there is no greater reward than that."

וַתֹּאמֶר לוֹ אִמּוֹ עָלַי קִלְלָתְךָ בְּנִי

"His mother said to him, 'My son, let your curse be upon me'" (27:13)

Why, asked the Vilna *Gaon*, would Rivkah invite a curse upon herself? Why did she not simply say, "He will not curse you, my son"?

Rivkah, answered the *Gaon*, was hinting to Yaakov that he would face three main forms of hardship in his life. These hardships are alluded to in the acronym of the word *"alai"*: *Esav, Lavan,* and *Yosef.*

וַתִּקַּח רִבְקָה אֶת־בִּגְדֵי עֵשָׂו בְּנָהּ הַגָּדֹל הַחֲמֻדֹת אֲשֶׁר אִתָּהּ בַּבָּיִת וַתַּלְבֵּשׁ אֶת־יַעֲקֹב בְּנָהּ הַקָּטָן:

"Rivkah then took the cleanest clothes of Esav, her elder son, that were with her in the house, and she fitted them on Yaakov, her younger son" (27:15)

The *Midrash Rabbah* quotes R' Shimon ben Gamliel: "I served my father throughout my entire life, yet my service did not reach even one hundredth of the service Esav extended to his father.

"For when I attended to my father, I wore soiled garments. Yet when I went on the way, my clothing was immaculate.

"But when Esav attended to his father, he wore nothing less than royal garments!"

One of the *chassidim* of R' Yaakov Yitzchak of P'shischa (the "*Yid HaKadosh*") had earned himself an unfavorable reputation. Nevertheless, he one day arrived at the court of his *Rebbe* and requested an audience with the *tzaddik*.

Before entering the *Rebbe's* study, the *chassid* made extensive preparations. He immersed himself in a *mikveh* and donned his finest clothing. He now felt ready to face the *tzaddik*, and he entered the study.

As soon as the *Yid HaKadosh* noticed the *chassid's* innocent-looking countenance and his fancy attire, he asked the *chassid:* "In the *Midrash* it states that Esav displayed extraordinary respect for his father, tending to his every need. That being the case," asked the *Rebbe,* "how is it possible that after having spent so much time with Yitzchak *Avinu,* Esav could have remained such a *rasha?*

"Yaakov," answered the *Rebbe,* "always appeared before his father the way he was, without making any advance preparations. Therefore, Yitzchak was able to instruct him on how to better himself and perfect his personality.

"Esav, on the other hand, always appeared before his father in regal attire, pretending that he was a God-fearing Jew. He would act piously, asking Yitzchak about the proper method with which to tithe straw and salt. Due to Esav's deceit, Yitzchak was unable to detect any flaw in him and therefore offered him no instructions on how to improve himself. This is why Esav remained a *rasha.*"

הַקֹּל קוֹל יַעֲקֹב וְהַיָּדַיִם יְדֵי עֵשָׂו:

"The voice is the voice of Yaakov, but the hands are the hands of Esav " (27:22)

"There are certain Jews," the Dubno *Maggid* once said, "who are the very personification of the words, 'The voice is Yaakov's voice,' as the way they pray and study conforms perfectly with all the pertinent *halachos.*

"Unfortunately," continued the *Maggid,* "their 'hands are Esav's hands.' For when it comes to the *mitzvos* of *tzedakah* or *gemilus chasadim,* these same Jews keep their hands tightly shut.

"It is vital for such individuals to know that one aspect of *avodas Hashem* without the other will not last."

PARASHAS VAYEITZEI

וַיֵּצֵא יַעֲקֹב מִבְּאֵר שָׁבַע

"Yaakov left Be'er Sheva" (28:10)

R ASHI ASKS: "IT NEED ONLY HAVE WRITTEN 'AND YAAKOV *WENT* TO Charan.' Why does it mention his departure? Rather," answers Rashi, "it is teaching us that the departure of a righteous person from a place makes an impression. For at the time that a righteous person is in a city, he is its magnificence, he is its splendor, and he is its grandeur. Once he has departed from there, its magnificence (*hodah*) has gone away (*panah*), its splendor (*zeevah*) has gone away, and its grandeur (*hadarah*) has gone away."

Rashi's words are alluded to in the verse by way of *gematriya*:

If we take "Yaakov out of Be'er Sheva," that is, if we subtract the numerical value of the word Yaakov (182) from Be'er Sheva (575), we are left with the number 393 — the exact numerical value of the words: *"panah hodah zeevah v'hadarah"* — "its magnificence, splendor, and grandeur have gone away"!

וַיֵּצֵא יַעֲקֹב מִבְּאֵר שֶׁבַע וַיֵּלֶךְ חָרָנָה:

"Yaakov left Be'er Sheva and set out for Charan" (28:10)

T he *Midrash* relates that when Yaakov *Avinu* left Be'er Sheva he said, "'I raise my eyes to the mountains, from whence will come my help?' (*Tehillim* 121:1). When Eliezer set out to find a bride for Yitzchak, he took with him ten camels loaded with bounty for gifts to the bride and her family. He said: But I have neither a nose-ring nor even a bracelet. Yet should I lose trust in my Creator on account of this? 'My help is from Hashem, Maker of heaven and earth!' (*Tehillim* 121:2)."

"If you wish to learn what it means to have true *bitachon* (trust) in Hashem," said R' Yisrael Ba'al Shem Tov to his *chassidim*, "then travel to the neighboring town and visit the home of Reb Yechezkel the innkeeper. There you will see genuine *bitachon* in Hashem!"

Without a moment's hesitation, the *chassidim* set out for the house of Reb Yechezkel. Upon arriving there, they asked him if they could spend the night in his home.

Reb Yechezkel greeted them warmly, and after they had *davened Maariv* and eaten to their hearts' content, they sat down and engrossed themselves in Torah study. A sense of serenity pervaded Reb Yechezkel's home. Late at night one of the governor's officers arrived at the inn. But he did not even enter; he simply lifted his club, banged on the door three times, and went on his way.

The *chassidim* wondered momentarily about what had just transpired, but then returned to their Torah study. All the while, Reb Yechezkel sat with them, happily listening to their words of Torah.

About a half-hour later, the officer returned. Once again, he did not enter Reb Yechezkel's home but knocked on the door three times and then left.

"Who is this officer," asked the *chassidim*, "and what does he want of you?"

"The officer is coming as a messenger from the governor of the town," answered Reb Yechezkel. "He has come to remind me to pay the rent for my inn. I have been warned that should I fail to do so, the governor will have me and my family sent to prison."

"From the calm look on your face," said the *chassidim*, "it appears that you have the money in your wallet. Why not just go and pay your rent?"

"At this moment," responded Reb Yechezkel, "I have not even one *perutah* in my wallet. However, I have complete faith that Hashem will provide me with the required sum of money. There are three hours remaining before the rent is due."

When the three hours had passed, Reb Yechezkel put on his coat and hat and bid the *chassidim* farewell and told them that he was setting out for the governor's house, in order to pay his rent.

"Does that mean that you have obtained the full amount of money?" asked the *chassidim*.

"I still do not have even one *perutah*," responded Reb Yechezkel. "But I have complete faith that Hashem will have mercy on me and grant me the rent money before I arrive at the governor's house."

The *chassidim* stood by the door of the inn and watched Reb Yechezkel as he calmly walked off. Suddenly, a horse-drawn wagon pulled up alongside him. The *chassidim* saw the wagon driver conversing with Reb Yechezkel and then he handed Reb Yechezkel an envelope. He then gave his horses a light smack and went on his way.

The amazed *chassidim* ran over to Reb Yechezkel and asked him what had just happened.

"It's just as I told you," said Reb Yechezkel. "Hashem sent me an individual who wished to purchase all of the beer that I will brew next winter. What's more, he agreed to pay me the entire sum in advance."

"They saw and they were indeed astonished" (*Tehillim* 48:6).

וַיֵּצֵא יַעֲקֹב מִבְּאֵר שֶׁבַע וַיֵּלֶךְ חָרָנָה:

"Yaakov left Be'er Sheva and set out for Charan" (28:10)

R' Chaim of Volozhin was once delivering a *shiur* (lecture) to his disciples on the subject of *bitachon*. Being that the hour was late, R' Chaim turned to his students and asked, "Would anyone happen to know the time?" R' Chaim did not receive a response as none of the students had a watch. R' Chaim decided to continue with his *shiur*.

"It appears to me," said R' Chaim, "that we have not yet acquired true *bitachon* in Hashem, for if we had, we would surely have been sent a watch from Heaven. In fact, we would have even received a golden watch, no less —"

Suddenly, there was a loud knock on the door, and in walked a Russian soldier. The soldier glanced nervously in every direction, and finally turned to R' Chaim and said, *"Rebbe,* I am a Jew, the only Jew among scores of gentile soldiers. I fear that the soldiers will attempt to steal my precious watch, a watch that I received as a gift from my father.

"I am presenting this watch to you, *Rebbe,* as a gift," said the soldier, as he removed a beautiful gold watch from his pocket. "Better that I give my watch to a Jewish *rebbe* than to have it stolen by a gentile soldier."

With that, the soldier hurriedly turned and left the room.

וַיִּיקַץ יַעֲקֹב מִשְּׁנָתוֹ וַיֹּאמֶר אָכֵן יֵשׁ ה' בַּמָּקוֹם הַזֶּה

"Yaakov awoke from his sleep and said, "Surely Hashem is present in this place" (28:16)

When a person wakes up in the morning, said R' Meir of Premishlan, he is required to strengthen himself like a lion in order to serve Hashem, as it is stated in the beginning of the *Shulchan Aruch*.

Thus "Yaakov awoke from his sleep and said, 'Surely Hashem is present in this place'" — immediately upon waking, Yaakov set out to serve Hashem!

But when the Torah refers to Pharaoh, continued R' Meir, we find just the opposite. For about Pharaoh the verse states, "Pharaoh then woke up. He fell asleep and dreamt a second time" (41:4-5). As soon as Pharaoh woke up, he went right back to sleep!

❧❀❧

מַה־נּוֹרָא הַמָּקוֹם הַזֶּה אֵין זֶה כִּי אִם־בֵּית אֱלֹקִים

"How awesome is this place. This [place] is none other than the House of God" (28:17)

R' Meir of Premishlan once visited a small town in Galicia and, upon arriving there, headed directly for the town's *shul.*

When he entered the *shul,* R' Meir was taken aback at its dilapidated state. The *shul* had obviously been neglected for some time. "How awesome is this place. This [place] is none other than the House of God," exclaimed R' Meir.

The *Rebbe* then explained what he meant: "How awesome (*nora*) is this place" — how terrifying it is to enter such a run-down shul. With its shaky walls and aged ceiling, it is truly a dangerous place. "This is none other than the House of God" — it is *only* His abode, for there are no people here who are concerned for its upkeep.

וַיִּדַּר יַעֲקֹב נֶדֶר לֵאמֹר אִם־יִהְיֶה אֱלֹקִים עִמָּדִי ... וְנָתַן־לִי לֶחֶם
לֶאֱכֹל וּבֶגֶד לִלְבּשׁ ... וְהָיָה ה' לִי לֵאלֹקִים ...

"Yaakov made a vow, saying, "If God is with me ...
and gives me food to eat and clothes to wear ... and
Hashem acts for me as God ...." (28:20-21)

R' Levi Yitzchak of Berdichev and R' Shneur Zalman of Liadi sat together at the wedding of their grandchildren.

At one point during the wedding, R' Shneur Zalman turned to R' Levi Yitzchak and said, "*L'chaim*, my *mechutan*! May Hashem provide us with our physical and spiritual needs!"

"Could it be, my *mechutan*," asked R' Levi Yitzchak, "that you are giving materialism precedence over spirituality?"

"I was merely following the sequence of the verse," answered R' Shneur Zalman. "Yaakov *Avinu* first requested 'food to eat and clothes to wear,' and only afterwards said, 'and Hashem acts for me as God.'"

"But how can we compare our materialism to Yaakov *Avinu's* — by our standards, we would consider his *material* concerns *spiritual!*" asked R' Levi Yitzchak.

"And our meager level of spirituality," responded R' Shneur Zalman, "can be compared to Yaakov *Avinu's* spirituality?"

וַיֹּאמֶר הֵן עוֹד הַיּוֹם גָּדוֹל לֹא־עֵת הֵאָסֵף
הַמִּקְנֶה הַשְׁקוּ הַצֹּאן וּלְכוּ רְעוּ:

"He said, 'Look, the day is still long; it is not yet
time to gather in the livestock! Give the sheep to
drink and go, take them out to the pasture'" (29:7)

When R' Meir of Premishlan would read this verse, he would lift his eyes to Heaven and pronounce, "Master of the World! If 'it is not yet time to gather in the livestock' — if, because of our sins, we have still not merited having the dispersed of Israel gathered into our homeland, than at least 'give the sheep to drink and take them to the pasture' — provide Your flock with whatever they need to sustain themselves. This way, they will have the strength to continue yearning for the final redemption."

When R' Moshe of Kobrin would read this verse, he would tell his *chassidim*, "We must prepare! *'Hein od hayom gadol,'* very soon we will have to face 'the great day' of reckoning. On that day, each individual will have to give a detailed account of his deeds, and will be judged accordingly.

"'*Lo eis hei'aseif hamikneh*,' this is not the proper time to engage in amassing the material acquisitions (*mikneh*) of this world. Instead, we must concern ourselves with amassing as many *mitzvos* and good deeds as we can, so that we should have what to take with us to *Olam Haba*."

וַיֶּאֱסֹף לָבָן אֶת־כָּל־אַנְשֵׁי הַמָּקוֹם וַיַּעַשׂ מִשְׁתֶּה:

"So Lavan gathered all the local people and made a feast" (29:22)

The *Midrash Rabbah* states that in order to finance the wedding feast, Lavan borrowed clothing and vessels from the people who lived in his neighborhood. He then took the clothing and vessels and used them as collateral in order to secure a loan. With the money that he borrowed, he arranged a lavish feast. After the feast, Lavan went around to each of his guests and told them, "Since I hosted you and you partook of the food, please go and redeem your items."

The words of this *Midrash*, said the *Chofetz Chaim*, are hinted to in the verse: The prevailing custom in the world is to first prepare a feast and only afterwards invite the guests. Lavan, however, did just the opposite, as the verse states, "So Lavan gathered all the local people and made a feast." In other words, he first invited the guests to give him their belongings, and then he arranged a lavish feast for them.

לָקַח יַעֲקֹב אֵת כָּל־אֲשֶׁר לְאָבִינוּ וּמֵאֲשֶׁר לְאָבִינוּ
עָשָׂה אֵת כָּל־הַכָּבֹד הַזֶּה:

"Ya'akov has taken everything that belongs to our father, and from what belongs to our father he has amassed all his wealth" (31:1)

The following question was once posed to the Vilna *Gaon*: The *Midrash Rabbah* states in relation to the aforementioned verse,

"There is no honor except for [that accrued by] silver and gold." Yet in *Shemos Rabbah* (Ch. 38) it states, "There is no honor except for [that accrued by] Torah, as the verse states, 'The wise inherit honor.'" The question is: Is it the Torah or one's wealth that brings a person honor?

Wherever we find the word *kavod* spelled without a *vav*, answered the *Gaon*, we are meant to apply *Chazal's* statement, "There is no honor except for [that accrued by] silver and gold." For that type of honor is superficial and false.

However, continued the *Gaon*, when *kavod* is spelled in its complete spelling, with a *vav*, *Chazal's* statement, "There is no honor except for [that accrued by] the Torah," applies. For the honor that comes from the Torah is genuine and full.

❦

כִּי רָאִיתִי אֵת כָּל־אֲשֶׁר לָבָן עֹשֶׂה לָּךְ

"For I have seen all that Lavan is doing to you" (31:12)

The *Chofetz Chaim* expounded on this verse by giving the following parable: A father gave out portions of food to each of his sons. When they had received their portions, one of the sons quickly snatched away his brother's portion.

The son whose portion had been stolen approached his father and said, "Father, I asked my brother to return my portion, but he refuses to do so. I know that you do not want me to quarrel with him and forcibly take it back. I am therefore requesting, Father, that you give me another portion."

When the father heard these words from his son, he kissed him on the head. In addition, he gave him another portion that was bigger than the one he had received previously. Said the father, "My son, your fine character has found favor in my eyes. Your brother who has stolen from you can keep the portion that he has stolen. But at our next meal, I will not give him anything at all. To you, however, I will give twice as much!"

The same is true, said the *Chofetz Chaim*, of one's livelihood. Hashem's concern extends to each and every individual, and He graciously provides each person with sustenance. On occasion, an individual may infringe upon another's livelihood, causing him to lose business and profit. The victim will probably ask the person to stop his infringement, but the request may be ignored.

At this point, the wise individual will turn to Hashem and request that He provide him with an alternate means of earning a livelihood, so that he should not be forced to quarrel with the other fellow.

Such a request, concluded the *Chofetz Chaim*, will certainly find favor in the eyes of Hashem, and He will provide the person with a livelihood many times greater than what was originally intended for him.

PARASHAS VAYISHLACH

וַיִּשְׁלַח יַעֲקֹב מַלְאָכִים לְפָנָיו אֶל־עֵשָׂו
"And Yaakov sent angels ahead of him to Esav" (32:4)

Rashi comments: "And Yaakov sent angels — Literally (*mamash*), angels."

R' Meir of Premishlan explained Rashi's words with the Mishnah in *Pirkei Avos* (4:13): "He who fulfills one *mitzvah* gains one advocate for himself." When an individual performs a *mitzvah*, he creates an angel that speaks favorably on his behalf in Heaven.

The verse tells us that Yaakov sent angels as messengers to Esav. Which angels did Yaakov send? Those angels that had been created through the *mitzvos* that he had performed.

This is what Rashi is alluding to when he says, "*mamash*, angels." For "*mamash*" is the acronym of the words "*malachim me'mitzvos she'asah*" ("angels from the *mitzvos* he performed").

וַיִּירָא יַעֲקֹב מְאֹד וַיֵּצֶר לוֹ
"Yaakov was extremely afraid and distressed" (32:8)

Rashi explains: "'Yaakov was extremely afraid' — lest he be killed. 'And distressed' — that he may have to kill others."

The Dubno *Maggid* explained this verse with the following parable:

There was a certain town that had several ill residents, but there was no doctor in the town to treat them.

Near this town, however, there was a large city that was home to the governor of the entire district. Unlike the town, the city was fortunate to have a prominent physician to tend to its sick.

There was one person in the small town who was a relative of the governor. One day, this man woke up with a slight headache. Now, it was not a severe headache, and it did not really require any special medical care. Nevertheless, the man began to groan loudly, and sent a message to his relative, the governor, asking him to please send the doctor to him in the town.

"Your headache is so minor, so why are you groaning so much?" the man's family asked him.

"Fools," he responded. "Do you really think that I am groaning for my own sake? I want the doctor to be sent to our town and then we can get him to treat all those who are truly ill and are suffering so much. I know that the governor would not send the doctor for their sake. I am therefore pretending to be ill, and I'm hoping that the governor will send the doctor for me. Once the doctor arrives, he will be able to provide his services to those in need."

So too, continued the *Maggid*, there are "small" generations, when the Jewish people don't have enough merits to deserve Divine protection. The Holy One foresaw this and therefore placed our great forefathers in situations that would prompt them to pray for the welfare of their children and descendants in all future generations.

Yaakov *Avinu*, concluded the *Maggid*, was certainly capable of defeating Esav. Yet he beseeched Hashem, "Rescue me, please, from the hand of my brother, from the hand of Esav" (32:12). For even though *I* can overcome the wicked Esav, what will be with my descendants? Yaakov, then, was not merely praying for his own survival, but, rather, for the survival of all the ensuing generations of Jews as well. This is what Scripture states in *Tehillim* (20:2), "May Hashem answer you on the day of distress; may the Name of Yaakov's God make you impregnable."

אִם־יָבוֹא עֵשָׂו אֶל־הַמַּחֲנֶה הָאַחַת וְהִכָּהוּ
וְהָיָה הַמַּחֲנֶה הַנִּשְׁאָר לִפְלֵיטָה

"If Esav comes to one camp and strikes it down, then the remaining camp will escape" (32:9)

When the Nazi party came to power in 1933, one of the *roshei yeshivah* of Radin approached the *Chofetz Chaim* and asked him, "*Rabbeinu*, what will be in store for the Jews of Germany and Poland? The wicked one has openly declared his intentions to destroy the entire Jewish nation!"

"Do not fear," responded the *Chofetz Chaim*. "For he will certainly not succeed in destroying the entire Jewish nation. In truth, it is stated explicitly in the Torah: 'If Esav comes to one camp and strikes it down, then the remaining camp will escape.'"

From the *Chofetz Chaim*'s words, the *rosh yeshivah* ascertained that the destruction of European Jewry was imminent. He therefore asked, "If the wicked one succeeds in decimating the Jews of Europe, God forbid, then which Jews will be in the 'remaining camp'?"

"That too," answered the *Chofetz Chaim*, "is stated explicitly by the *Navi*: 'On Mount Zion there will be refuge, and it will be holy' (*Ovadiah* 1:17)."

And so it was; the *Chofetz Chaim*'s prediction came true. The wicked one did succeed in destroying European Jewry, but his army was defeated at the gates of *Eretz Yisrael*, and the Jews of *Eretz Yisrael* survived.

⸎

אִם־יָבוֹא עֵשָׂו אֶל־הַמַּחֲנֶה הָאַחַת וְהִכָּהוּ
וְהָיָה הַמַּחֲנֶה הַנִּשְׁאָר לִפְלֵיטָה

"If Esav comes to one camp and strikes it down, then the remaining camp will escape" (32:9)

Before his meeting with Esav, Yaakov prepared himself in three ways: by giving gifts, by praying, and by planning for war.

In the same manner that Yaakov prepared himself for his war with Esav, said the *Sefas Emes* (R' Yehudah Leib of Gur), so too must each Jew prepare himself for his great war against the *yetzer hara*. If one prepares in such a manner, he will undoubtedly achieve very lofty levels in his service of the Creator.

We allude to these three measures of preparation when we recite the *Shema* each day. As the verse states, "You shall love Hashem, your God, with all your heart, with all your soul, and with all your resources":

"*With all your heart*" is a reference to prayer, as *Chazal* referred to prayer as "service of the heart."

"*With all your soul*" is a reference to war, as *Chazal* have expounded on this verse, "[One should serve Hashem] even to the point of giving up his life."

"*And with all your resources*" is a reference to gifts, as a person is required to graciously give *tzedakah* and perform acts of kindness.

קָטֹנְתִּי מִכֹּל הַחֲסָדִים

"I have become unworthy through all the acts of kindness" (32:11)

The Vilna *Gaon* was once asked to explain *Chazal's* statement (*Sotah* 5a): "Said R' Chiya bar Ashi in the name of *Rav*: A *talmid chacham* must have one-eighth of an eighth [of haughtiness]." (Rashi explains that it is essential for a *talmid chacham* to possess this minute amount of pride in order to prevent those who are ignorant in Torah learning from making light of him and his words.) Why did *Chazal* choose specifically the measure of one-eighth of an eighth?

The term "one-eighth of an eighth," answered the Gaon, is not a reference to a particular measure. Rather it is hinting at the *eighth* verse of the *eighth* portion of the Torah. The eighth portion in the Torah is *Parashas Vayishlach*, and the eighth verse of the *parashah* (i.e. 32:11) begins with the word, "*katonti*" ("I am very small").

While a *talmid chacham* must possess a certain amount of arrogance, it must be a "very small" amount.

וַיִּוָּתֵר יַעֲקֹב לְבַדּוֹ
"Yaakov was left all alone" (32:25)

In *Maseches Chullin* (91a), *Chazal* state the following: "Why was Yaakov left all alone? Because he returned to retrieve small vessels which he had left behind. From here it is said, "The property of *tzaddikim* is dearer to them than their own bodies.""

Look at what we can learn from this, said R' Yisrael Salanter: The property of *tzaddikim* is dearer to them than their *own* bodies but it is not dearer to them than other people's bodies. Whenever it comes to the welfare of your fellow man, do not be stingy with your money; rather, give him all that he needs.

❧⌘❧

וַיֵּאָבֵק אִישׁ עִמּוֹ עַד עֲלוֹת הַשָּׁחַר:
"And a man wrestled with him until dawn" (32:25)

At an assembly aimed at encouraging Torah study, the *Chofetz Chaim* asked the following question: "Why is it that the ministering angel of Esav wrestled specifically with Yaakov *Avinu*? Why did he not fight against Avraham or Yitzchak?

"The answer," said the *Chofetz Chaim*, "is that Avraham *Avinu* represented the *middah* of *chesed*, kindness; Yitzchak *Avinu* represented *avodah*, Divine service; and Yaakov *Avinu* represented Torah. Esav's ministering angel could tolerate the outstanding quality of *chesed*, he could bear with *avodah*, but he could not tolerate Torah study. For Torah," concluded the *Chofetz Chaim*, "is the very foundation upon which the existence of the Jewish nation rests. This is why the *yetzer hara* constantly declares war against the Torah and those who study it. We must band together to fight this fierce war against him and defeat him!"

וְלָקַחְתָּ מִנְחָתִי מִיָּדִי כִּי עַל־כֵּן רָאִיתִי
פָנֶיךָ כִּרְאֹת פְּנֵי אֱלֹקִים וַתִּרְצֵנִי:

"Accept my gift, since I have seen you — which [is to me] like seeing the face of a divine being — and you have become reconciled with me" (33:10)

On the surface, this verse is difficult to understand: Can seeing the face of the wicked Esav be compared in any way to seeing the face of a divine being?

Chazal (*Sotah* 41b), however, have explained the matter by way of a parable: A man invited a friend to visit his home and join him for a meal. As the meal proceeded, the guest sensed that the invitation he received was part of a plot to kill him. The guest, of course, became rather frightened but quickly thought of a plan that, he hoped, would save his life.

"You know," said the guest to his host, "your food tastes very similar to the food which I ate in the king's palace!"

I must have a very distinguished individual as a guest, thought the host to himself. *After all, he is an acquaintance of the king and has even eaten in his palace! If I harm him in any way, word will get back to the king, and I will be severely punished. It is certainly not worth it for me to do him any damage.*

The guest finished his meal, and he left the host's home unharmed.

Now we are able to understand the aforementioned verse: Once Esav heard that Yaakov keeps company with a divine being, he came to the conclusion that it would be unwise to harm him.

❧◯❧

וַיָּבֹא יַעֲקֹב שָׁלֵם עִיר שְׁכֶם

"Yaakov arrived intact at the city of Shechem" (33:18)

Despite the fact, said R' Tzvi Elimelech Shapira, that Yaakov *Avinu* spent many years in the house of the wicked Lavan, he did not change his name, his language, or his mode of dress. Rather, he remained the same person that he was on the day that he left his father's home.

The acronym of the word "*shalem*" spells **shem** (name), *lashon* (language), and *malbush* (dress). Thus the verse states, "Yaakov arrived intact (*shalem*) at the city of Shechem."

A Jew is "intact" and whole, continued R' Shapira, when he does not alter these three things.

PARASHAS VAYEISHEV

וַיֵּשֶׁב יַעֲקֹב בְּאֶרֶץ מְגוּרֵי אָבִיו

"Yaakov settled in the land of his father's sojourning" (37:1)

THE *MIDRASH* EXPOUNDS ON THIS VERSE, "YAAKOV WISHED TO LIVE in tranquility, but the ordeal of Yosef suddenly came upon him. When the righteous seek to live at ease, the Holy One says, 'Is the portion set aside for the righteous in the World to Come not enough for them that they seek to dwell in tranquility in this world as well?'"

At one point, the two *roshei yeshivah* of Volozhin, R' Naftali Tzvi Yehudah Berlin (the *Netziv*) and R' Yosef Dov Soloveitchik (the *Beis HaLevi*), had a disagreement about how the yeshivah should be led.

These two *gedolei Yisrael* decided to present the issue before R' Zev, the *maggid* of Vilna, and R' Yitzchak Elchanan Spector of Kovno.

After hearing both sides of the disagreement, the rabbis immersed themselves in thought, trying to decide which one had the superior claim.

"You should know," said R' Zev, "that I am presently holding in *Parashas Vayeishev.*" They all looked at R' Zev in bewilderment. It was now the end of winter, and *Parashas Vayeishev* had been read many weeks ago.

"Let me explain what I mean," said R' Zev. "You see, I am a *maggid* in the city of Vilna, and each Shabbos I deliver a *derashah* in the main *shul.* In my *derashos,* I always attempt to contrast good and evil and the ways of the *tzaddik* versus those of the *rasha.* For example, when I speak on *Parashas Bereishis*, I show the contrast between Adam *HaRishon* and the wicked serpent, or between Kayin and Hevel.

"The following Shabbos, *Parashas Noach*, I depict Noach as the embodiment of good and the Generation of the Flood as the manifestation of all that is evil.

"For *Parashas Lech Lecha*, I contrast the ways of Avraham with those of the evil Pharaoh.

"*Parashas Vayeira* offers the stark contrast between Avraham and the kings of Sodom and Amorah.

"All in all, each Shabbos I am presented with a *tzaddik* and a *rasha* around whom I can base my remarks. But when *Parashas Vayeishev* comes around, and we learn about the strife between Yosef and his brothers, I am faced with a dilemma. After all, both Yosef and his brothers were *tzaddikim* of the highest caliber.

"I find myself in the same situation today," concluded R' Zev. "For I cannot even attempt to decide which one of you is correct, as both of you are *tzaddikim* and *geonim,* and you are both correct."

אֵלֶּה תֹלְדוֹת יַעֲקֹב יוֹסֵף
"These are Yaakov's descendants: Yosef..." (37:2)

R' Mendel of Riminov once remarked that each and every Jew is called "Yaakov." What, asked the *Rebbe*, are the "descendants" of a "Yaakov" (in other words, what should spawn from a Jew)? — "Yosef" (the name Yosef is similar to the word "*hosif*," to increase); it is incumbent upon each and every Jew to constantly strive to increase his levels of *yiras Shamayim* and *avodas Hashem.*

אֵלֶּה תֹלְדוֹת יַעֲקֹב יוֹסֵף בֶּן־שְׁבַע־עֶשְׂרֵה שָׁנָה ...וְהוּא נַעַר
"These are [the experiences of] Yaakov's descendants: Yosef was in his seventeenth year ... but he was a youth" (37:2)

The *Midrash* asks: "Yosef was seventeen years old, and yet you say that he was but 'a youth'? Rather, it is because he acted like a youth."

Why is it, asked the *Sefas Emes* (R' Yehudah Leib Alter of Gur), that the *Midrash* poses its question specifically in *Parashas Vayeishev*? The *Midrash* could have asked the same question in *Parashas Vayeira* where the Torah recounts that Avraham *Avinu* stated, "I and the lad will go yonder" (22:5), though he was referring to Yitzchak who was already thirty-six years old!

In truth, answered the *Sefas Emes*, Avraham's calling Yitzchak a "lad" is not surprising. Avraham was referring to his beloved son who, in his fatherly eyes, would always be but a lad.

But in *Parashas Vayeishev*, it is the *Torah* that refers to Yosef as a "youth." The *Midrash* therefore asks, "Yosef was seventeen years of age, and yet you say that he was but 'a youth'?"

⚜

כִּי־בֶן־זְקֻנִים הוּא לוֹ

"Since he was a son of his old age" (37:3)

The acronym of the word "zekunim," says the *Ba'al HaTurim*, alludes to the five orders of *mishnayos* that Yaakov taught Yosef: Zera'im, Kodshim, Nashim, Yeshu'os (Nezikin), and Mo'ed.

On this comment by the *Ba'al HaTurim*, the *Imrei Emes* (R' Avraham Mordechai Alter of Gur) asked the obvious question: There is one more order of *mishnayos* that the *Ba'al HaTurim* ignores — *Taharos* ("Purity"). Why did Yaakov not teach Yosef *Taharos*?

Seder Taharos, answered the *Rebbe*, cannot be taught. Purity can only be acquired after an individual strives and exerts himself to achieve it on his own.

⚜

וַיִּרְאוּ אֶחָיו כִּי־אֹתוֹ אָהַב אֲבִיהֶם מִכָּל־אֶחָיו וַיִּשְׂנְאוּ אֹתוֹ וְלֹא יָכְלוּ דַּבְּרוֹ לְשָׁלֹם:

"His brothers realized that their father loved him more than all his brothers so they hated him; and they could not speak to him peaceably" (37:4)

In *Maseches Berachos* (64b), *Chazal* teach us the following: "One who is parting from his friend should not say, 'Go *in* peace (*b'shalom*),' rather, 'Go *to* peace (*l'shalom*).' For Yisro said to Moshe, 'Go to peace,' and Moshe ascended and was successful. But David said to Avshalom, 'Go in peace,' and Avshalom went and was hanged."

In light of this Gemara, the Vilna Gaon explained the verse: "His brothers realized that their father loved him more than all his brothers … and they could not speak to him peaceably (*l'shalom*)" — because of their hatred toward Yosef, the brothers could not use the expression "*l'shalom*," for doing so would guarantee Yosef success.

לֶךְ־נָא רְאֵה אֶת־שְׁלוֹם אַחֶיךָ

"Go now, look into the welfare of your brothers (shelom achecha)" (37:14)

R' Simchah Bunim of P'shischa explained this verse in the following manner: Since the Torah relates that "Yosef would bring evil reports about them to their father" (37:2), Yaakov instructed Yosef, "Look into *shelom achecha* (*shelom* is similar to the word *shalem*, whole)." Instead of only seeing the flaws that your brothers may possess, try to see their wholesomeness and good qualities.

מַה־בֶּצַע כִּי נַהֲרֹג אֶת־אָחִינוּ

"What gain will there be if we kill our brother" (37:26)

R' Yechiel Meir Lifshitz of Gostynin once rebuked a storeowner for exploiting the poor and unfortunate people that resided in his town. Instead of showing them mercy, he cruelly charged exorbitant prices for his goods.

"What you are doing," said R' Lifshitz, "is hinted to in a verse. The Torah states, 'What gain (*betza*) will there be if we kill our brother?' The acronym of the word '*betza*' is *boker* (morning), *tzaharayim* (afternoon), and *erev* (evening) — the three periods of the day when a Jew is required to pray to Hashem.

"Now tell me," concluded R' Lifshitz, "*mah betza*" — why bother praying three times a day — "if we kill our brother" — if at the same time we are busy cruelly exploiting our poor and needy brethren.

בְּעוֹד שְׁלֹשֶׁת יָמִים יִשָּׂא פַרְעֹה אֶת־רֹאשְׁךָ מֵעָלֶיךָ

"In three days Pharaoh will remove your head" (40:19)

The dreams of the chief baker and the chief wine butler, noted the Dubno *Maggid*, were very similar. Why, then, did Yosef interpret the dream of the chief wine butler favorably — that Pharaoh would soon reinstate him to his post — but that of the chief baker unfavorably — that he was about to meet his end?

The answer, explained the *Maggid*, can be understood with a parable: An artist painted a magnificent portrait of a man balancing a basket full of bread on his head. Two men came to admire the painting. While they stood there, a bird landed atop it and began to peck away at the bread, which it thought was genuine.

"Such a marvelous artist!" said one man to the other. "This bird actually believes that the bread is real!"

"No," responded the other, "he is not much of an artist at all. For while the bread may be quite realistic, the man carrying it is not, for if it was, the bird would be afraid to approach the painting."

We are now able to understand, concluded the Dubno *Maggid*, why Yosef interpreted the dream of the chief baker unfavorably. When the chief baker related his dream to Yosef, he said, "And the birds were eating them from the basket above my head." Yosef understood that if the birds were unafraid to approach him, it was an indication that he was soon to be executed by Pharaoh and was already considered a "dead man." For had he been "alive," the birds would have refrained from eating the food on his head!

וְלֹא־זָכַר שַׂר־הַמַּשְׁקִים אֶת־יוֹסֵף וַיִּשְׁכָּחֵהוּ:

"Yet the chief wine butler did not remember Yosef, and he forgot him" (40:23)

Rashi explains that Heaven punished Yosef and made him remain in prison an additional two years because he placed his trust in the chief wine butler.

The *Alter* of Novarodok's (R' Yosef Yozel Horowitz) level of *bitachon* was legendary.

One night, the *Alter* was sitting alone in his house in the woods learning Torah by candlelight. He continued learning until his very last candle burned out.

The *Alter* was now left sitting in complete darkness and it saddened him that he would have to stop learning for lack of a candle. But then the *Alter* decided that he must strengthen his faith in Hashem and trust that He would provide him with all that he needed — including a candle.

The *Alter* quickly got up and opened the door of his home. At that very moment, a man stepped out of the forest, handed him a candle, and disappeared.

For twenty-five years, the *Alter* saved the candle as a remembrance of that miracle and to show his students that Hashem takes special care of those who sincerely trust Him.

But then a fire broke out in Novarodok. The *Alter*'s home was among the many homes that were destroyed in the fire. The fire consumed everything that was in the house, including the wondrous candle.

"You should know," said the *Alter* to his students, "that Heaven made us lose the candle in order to teach us that we must trust in Hashem even when we have no proof that He will help us."

וְלֹא־זָכַר שַׂר־הַמַּשְׁקִים אֶת־יוֹסֵף וַיִּשְׁכָּחֵהוּ:

"Yet the chief wine butler did not remember Yosef, and he forgot him" (40:23)

This verse seems redundant, noted the *Maharam* of Amshinov. Why must it state that "he forgot him," once it already informed us that "the chief wine butler did not remember Yosef"?

The *Rebbe* answered: As soon as Yosef uttered his request to the chief wine butler he realized that he had sinned, as he had trusted in a human being instead of Hashem. He therefore prayed to Hashem that the butler would forget his request entirely! And, indeed, "he forgot him."

Parashas Mikeitz

וַיְהִי בַבֹּקֶר וַתִּפָּעֶם רוּחוֹ וַיִּשְׁלַח וַיִּקְרָא אֶת־כָּל־
חַרְטֻמֵּי מִצְרַיִם וְאֶת־כָּל־חֲכָמֶיהָ וַיְסַפֵּר פַּרְעֹה
לָהֶם אֶת־חֲלֹמוֹ וְאֵין־פּוֹתֵר אוֹתָם לְפַרְעֹה:

"In the morning he felt agitated, so he sent for
and called all the sorcerers and wise men
of Egypt. Pharaoh told them his dream, but
none could interpret them for Pharaoh" (41:8)

RASHI COMMENTS THAT THE SORCERERS *DID* OFFER PHARAOH SEVER-
AL interpretations of his dream, but he rejected all of them.
For example, one sorcerer predicted: "Seven daughters shall
you father, and seven daughters shall you bury." Pharaoh, however,
was not satisfied with this interpretation just as he was not satisfied
with the others.

The Dubno *Maggid* explained this with the following parable: There
once was a king who wanted his son to gain wisdom and erudition. He
therefore sent him to a faraway land where he would receive guidance
and instruction from the greatest scholars and sages in the world.

The son spent several years under their tutelage until, one day, he
sent a letter to his father requesting permission to return home.

The king granted his permission, and some time later, his son
returned to his native country.

The king was overjoyed to see his son and, in his honor, arranged
a lavish feast to which he invited all of the kingdom's noblemen.

After becoming merry with wine, one of the king's ministers decided to test the prince to find out whether he had truly grown wise in the
faraway land.

The minister placed a round ring in the palm of his hand. He then
approached the prince and showed him his closed fist. "Tell me,"
asked the minister, "what lies in the palm of my hand?"

The son gazed at the minister's hand and responded, "There is a
round, hollow object in your hand."

"You are correct!" exclaimed the minister in amazement. "Perhaps you can tell me specifically which object it is that I am holding?"

"I'm afraid I cannot," replied the prince to the minister. "For while the wisdom that I have been taught enables one to ascertain the shape of a concealed object, it does not provide one with the ability to identify the object."

So too, concluded the Dubno *Maggid*, was the case with Pharaoh's sorcerers. While their sorcery gave them the ability to ascertain that his dream was alluding to seven events that would transpire in the future, it did not enable them to discern exactly *which* events were going to transpire. They therefore simply guessed at what those seven events would be. As the verse tells us, none of their interpretations found favor in Pharaoh's eyes.

וַיְרִיצֻהוּ מִן־הַבּוֹר

"And they rushed him out of the dungeon" (41:14)

I n the *Chofetz Chaim*'s later years, the Communist Revolution raged in Russia. One of the aims of the wicked Communists was to stamp out any trace of Judaism from the hearts of the Jewish people. They spared no effort at trying to achieve this goal. They mercilessly leveled harsh decrees against the Jews, and only thanks to the mercy of Heaven were Jews able to remain firm in their faith.

"Look at what the Torah states in *Parashas Mikeitz*," said the *Chofetz Chaim* to one of his students. "The verse says that 'Pharaoh sent [messengers] and called Yosef, and they rushed him out of the dungeon.' For twelve years Yosef languished in prison and no one paid any attention to him.

"But when the moment that Hashem had designated for Yosef's salvation finally arrived, he was immediately rushed out of the dungeon.

"We are in a similar situation. Our predicament appears to be hopeless; the Communist regime, in their cruelty, will stop at nothing to sever our ties with the holy Torah. Yet when *Mashiach* comes and our moment of redemption arrives there will be no delays and, we, too, will be rushed to our Land."

חֲלוֹם חָלַמְתִּי וּפֹתֵר אֵין אֹתוֹ וַאֲנִי שָׁמַעְתִּי
עָלֶיךָ לֵאמֹר תִּשְׁמַע חֲלוֹם לִפְתֹּר אֹתוֹ:

*"Pharaoh said to Yosef, 'I have had a dream,
but there is no one who can interpret it.
Now I have heard about you that you can
understand a dream to interpret it" (41:15)*

The Dubno *Maggid* explained this verse with a parable: There once was a wealthy factory owner who lived in a certain town. All of the merchants of the area did business with him.

Every morning he stayed in *shul* after *Shacharis* to study Torah. He would learn for about two hours and then go home to eat a modest breakfast before setting off for work.

One morning, a businessman came to the wealthy man's home to do some business. The man's wife, however, told the businessman that her husband was still in *shul* and that he was due to return in about two hours. The disappointed businessman thanked her and left.

When the wealthy man came home, his wife told him what had transpired in his absence. The man was greatly distressed. *Who knows*, he thought to himself, *perhaps this businessman wanted to purchase a large amount of merchandise; I could have made a fortune.* He therefore instructed his wife that if a businessman should ever come, she should immediately send a message to him in *shul* to come home.

Several days later, a different individual visited the house of the wealthy man. Following her husband's instructions, his wife said to the visitor, "Please wait here and I will call for him." She sent an urgent message to her husband in *shul* that he had a visitor.

The wealthy man rushed home and arrived at his house out of breath. "What do you want?" he asked the visitor.

"I would like to know if you would be kind enough to help me with some money," was the visitor's response.

"What?" yelled the wealthy man to his wife. "For *this* you interrupted my Torah study?"

"But I did exactly as you told me," said his wife defensively. "Didn't you say that if someone came looking for you, I should notify you immediately?"

"Yes, that is what I said," replied the husband. "But why did you not ask him what he wanted *before* you called me?"

So too, concluded the Dubno *Maggid*, was the scenario with Pharaoh and his interpreters. Pharaoh dreamt a most disturbing dream but feared to relate it to his wise men, lest they interpret it in an unfavorable light.

Therefore, when Pharaoh related his dream to Yosef, he preceded it with the following words: "I have had a dream, but there is no one who can interpret it" — because I do not want to hear a negative interpretation. "Now I have heard about you that you can understand a dream to interpret it" — but only interpret the dream for me if you think that it means something good.

וַיְדַבֵּר פַּרְעֹה אֶל-יוֹסֵף בַּחֲלֹמִי הִנְנִי עֹמֵד עַל-שְׂפַת הַיְאֹר

"Pharaoh then spoke to Yosef: 'In my dream, there I was, standing upon the bank of the River'" (41:17)

T he *Midrash Rabbah* states in relation to this verse, "Thus it is written, 'He appointed it as a testimony for Yosef when he went out over the land of Egypt, when I heard a language unknown to me' (*Tehillim* 81:6)."

R' Meir of Premishlan offered the following elaboration of this *Midrash*: When the Torah relates the details of Pharaoh's dream, it states, "Pharaoh was dreaming, and there he was, standing *over* the River" (41:1).

Yet when Pharaoh related his dream to Yosef, he wished to test Yosef to see whether or not he was truly wise. He therefore slightly altered his account of his dream and told Yosef, "In my dream, there I was, standing upon the *bank* of the River," to see if Yosef would know that the dream did not occur as it was retold.

Yosef did notice, and as soon as he heard Pharaoh's dream, Yosef corrected him and told him that he had not been standing on the riverbank, but over the river itself.

Thus the verse states: "He appointed it as a testimony for Yosef when he went out over the land of Egypt" — what was the testimony that convinced Pharaoh that Yosef was, indeed, a wise and capable individual, fit to be a leader over Egypt? "When I heard a language (*sefas*) unknown to me" — when Yosef corrected Pharaoh and told him that the description of the "*bank* of the River" (the word "*sefas*" also means "riverbank") was "unknown" to him because it was not part of the dream!

אַחֲרֵי הוֹדִיעַ אֱלֹקִים אוֹתְךָ אֶת־
כָּל־זֹאת אֵין־נָבוֹן וְחָכָם כָּמוֹךָ:

"Since God has made all this known to you, then there is no one as intelligent and wise as you" (41:39)

The Dubno *Maggid* explained this verse by way of the following parable: There once was a wealthy and well-respected Jewish businessman who owned a very large store. One day, he appeared before the leaders of the community to complain about the amount of tax that he had to pay to the community. "Why do you level such enormous taxes upon us? I may own a large store, but the merchandise in the warehouses is not mine! Wholesalers give me the merchandise on credit. Only once I have sold it do I pay the wholesalers for the produce they deposit with me."

"It is specifically for this reason," responded the community leaders, "that you are charged such heavy taxes. Why do wholesalers give you so much merchandise on credit? Is it not because you *are* a wealthy man? After all, if you were poor, would anyone trust you with such a large amount of merchandise without making you pay for it first?"

We are now able to understand the aforementioned verse, concluded the *maggid*. Before Yosef offered Pharaoh an interpretation of his dream, he said, "It is God Who will provide an answer [that will be for] Pharaoh's welfare" (41:16). Yosef told Pharaoh that the wisdom in me is not my own but God's, for it is He Who guides me when I interpret dreams.

To this Pharaoh responded, "Since God has made all this known to you" — If Hashem, in all His glory, has granted *you* the hidden meanings of my dreams, then that is the best proof that "there is no one as intelligent and wise as you"!

וַיִּקְרָא פַרְעֹה שֵׁם־יוֹסֵף צָפְנַת פַּעְנֵחַ

"Pharaoh called Yosef by the name Tzafnas-pane'ach" (41:45)

Rashi explains: "*Tzafnas-pane'ach* — *mepharesh hatzefunos* (decipherer of the cryptic)."

If that is the meaning of Yosef's title, asked the *Sefas Emes* (R' Yehudah Leib Alter of Gur), then would it not have been more appropriate to reverse the order of the words and refer to him as *"Pane'ach-tzefunos"*?

Yosef, answered the *Sefas Emes*, merited his unique ability to reveal that which was concealed, on account of the fact that he acted with extreme modesty, always concealing his own righteousness from the eyes of others.

It is for this reason, he concluded, that he was referred to as *Tzafnas-pane'ach*. *"Tzafnas"* — because he went to great lengths to hide his greatness (*"tzafnas"* — the hidden one), *"pane'ach"* — he merited to decipher hidden matters.

כֻּלָּנוּ בְּנֵי אִישׁ־אֶחָד נָחְנוּ
"We, all of us, are the sons of one man" (42:11)

The word *"nachnu,"* noted the Ba'al HaTurim, can be found in three verses in *Tanach*:

(1) "We (*nachnu*), all of us, are the sons of one man."

(2) "We (*nachnu*) shall cross over armed, before Hashem" (*Bamidbar* 32:32).

(3) "We (*nachnu*) have transgressed and rebelled" (*Eichah* 3:42).

What is the connection between these three seemingly unrelated verses?

These verses, explained the *Ba'al HaTurim*, are indeed related: When a man acknowledges and confesses his sin before his Creator, he says, "We have transgressed and rebelled." Then he becomes determined to return to Hashem and to be included among His people, so he declares, "We (*nachnu*), all of us, are the sons of one man." Finally, when the person reaches this level of unity with Hashem and his fellow Jews, no nation can cause him any harm, as the verse states, "We shall cross over armed, before Hashem."

וַיִּקַּח מֵאִתָּם אֶת־שִׁמְעוֹן וַיֶּאֱסֹר אֹתוֹ לְעֵינֵיהֶם:
"He took Shimon away from them and imprisoned him before their eyes" (42:24)

Rashi explains: "He imprisoned him only *before their eyes*, but once the brothers departed, [Yosef] brought [Shimon] out and gave him food and drink."

A story is told of an individual who once insulted R' Yisrael Salanter. The man was very distraught about having offended this great *tzaddik*; he therefore approached R' Salanter to beg for forgiveness.

R' Salanter received the man warmly and with a big smile, as if nothing at all had happened.

"*Rebbe*," said the man, "Please forgive me for the way I behaved. I so regret that I insulted you."

R' Salanter immediately forgave the man and then asked him, "Is there perhaps some way in which I can help you? Might you need a loan or a particular act of kindness?"

"*Rebbe*," responded the man, "Is it not enough that the *Rav* has forgiven me for slighting his honor? Must he offer to bestow kindness upon me as well?"

"Let me explain to you my intention," said R' Salanter. "*Chazal* teach us (*Kiddushin* 59a), 'An action removes the original thought.' If an individual wishes to uproot a feeling from his heart, he must perform a deed!

"The same thing applies to one who harbors ill feelings toward another person. If he wishes to eradicate those feelings, he should perform an act of kindness for that person. By doing so, he will eliminate any bad feelings he may have had.

"This was the practice," continued R' Salanter, "that Yosef employed with his brothers. For we find that it was Shimon who was the first to plot against Yosef — as *Chazal* have taught us that it was Shimon who said, 'So now, come and let us kill him, and throw him into one of the pits' (37:20).

"When Yosef desired to uproot the feelings of anger that he had felt toward Shimon, he was not content with simply telling Shimon that he forgave him. Rather, he went one step further and also did a kind act to Shimon. This is why as soon as the brothers parted with him, he released Shimon and gave him food and drink."

עַל־דְּבַר הַכֶּסֶף הַשָּׁב בְּאַמְתְּחֹתֵינוּ בַּתְּחִלָּה אֲנַחְנוּ מוּבָאִים

"It is because of the money that was put back into our sacks at first that we are being brought here" (43:18)

Once, when the Vilna *Gaon* was sitting with a group of *talmidei chachamim*, one of them turned to the *Gaon* and asked, "We are taught that an allusion to all matters can be found in the Torah. If so, where in the Torah do we find an allusion to *Chazal*'s statement (*Shabbos* 31a): At the time an individual is brought to stand before the Heavenly Tribune, the first thing he is asked is, 'Were you honest in your business dealings?'

"Indeed," answered the Gaon, "an allusion to that statement can be found in the following verse: 'It is because of the money that was put back into our sacks …' — this refers to the money that we earn through business transactions, '*at first* … we are being brought' before the Heavenly Tribune!"

જી

מַשְׂאַת בִּנְיָמִן מִמַּשְׂאֹת כֻּלָּם חָמֵשׁ יָדוֹת

"And Binyamin's portion was five times as large as any of them" (43:34)

A s is well known, said R' Naftali of Ropshitz, Chanukah always falls out during the week that we read *Parashas Mikeitz*. This is hinted to in the Torah, as the verse states, "And Binyamin's portion was five times (*chamesh yados*) as large as any of them."

"*Chamesh yados*" alludes to the five instances that we mention the word "*yad*" (literally, "hand") in the special Chanukah prayer, *Al Hanissim*: "You delivered the strong into the hands (*yad*) of the weak, the many into the hands (*yad*) of the few, the impure into the hands (*yad*) of the pure, the wicked into the hands (*yad*) of the righteous, and the wanton into the hands (*yad*) of the diligent students of Your Torah."

וַיִּגַּשׁ אֵלָיו יְהוּדָה

"Then Yehudah stepped forward" (44:18)

ASHI EXPLAINS THAT YEHUDAH SPOKE TO YOSEF HARSHLY. The *Alshich HaKadosh* (R' Moshe Alshich) asked: Why did Yehudah confront Yosef and speak to him in an aggressive manner? After all, was not Yehudah the one who said, "We are ready to be slaves to my lord — both we and the one in whose hand the goblet was found"?

The answer, said the *Alshich*, is as follows: Originally, Yehudah thought that the troubles that had befallen them were Heavenly decreed for having sold Yosef.

But when he saw that each one of them had been exonerated except for Binyamin — who was not involved in Yosef's sale in the first place — he realized that their present woes were not on account of their sin of selling Yosef.

That is why Yehudah approached Yosef and spoke to him harshly.

כִּי־לֹא נוּכַל לִרְאוֹת פְּנֵי הָאִישׁ וְאָחִינוּ הַקָּטֹן אֵינֶנּוּ אִתָּנוּ:

"For we cannot go to see the man if our youngest brother is not with us" (44:26)

A grave fear had fallen upon the inhabitants of the town, Kelin. Someone had been murdered in the center of town, and a knife had been found alongside his body. The authorities' careful investigation revealed that the knife had been taken from the home of R' Shmuel HaLevi, author of the classic work *Machtzis HaShekel*, and the Rabbi of Kelin.

The Jews of Kelin realized at once that the episode was a crude libel designed to falsely accuse the Rabbi of killing the victim. The true murderer had apparently stolen a knife from the Rabbi's home, in order to make it appear as if the Rabbi had committed the depraved act.

The distinguished members of Kelin approached the Rabbi with a plan. "When the judge inquires," they said, "as to whether or not the knife belongs to you, simply respond that it doesn't! This will be sure to clear you from these false charges!"

The Rabbi rejected their advice. Thus, on the day of the trial, when the judge asked him, "Does this knife belong to you?" he replied, "Indeed, it does. But I am not guilty of this murder! Someone has set up a disgraceful libel to ruin me!"

After further investigation, the Rabbi was cleared of all charges, and he returned to his home.

A short time later, the Rabbi told the leaders of the community, "Do you know why I did not accept your advice? I took a lesson from the words of Yehudah, who said, 'We cannot go to see the man if our youngest brother is not with us.' Why did Yehudah not simply bring a different child down to Egypt and claim that he was their younger brother? Why did he take the great risk of bringing Binyamin before Yosef?

"From here we can learn a very great lesson," concluded the Rabbi. "Yehudah was so committed to truth that he refused to lie even in the face of great danger. I, too," concluded the Rabbi, "will not utter a lie even if I will pay a very dear price for it!"

כִּי־אֵיךְ אֶעֱלֶה אֶל־אָבִי וְהַנַּעַר אֵינֶנּוּ אִתִּי

"For how can I go up to my father
if the youth is not with me" (44:34)

R' Meir of Premishlan often remarked, "Every individual who passes on — after one hundred and twenty years — is required to stand before the Heavenly Tribune and give an accounting of the years that he spent in this world. At that time, he will be questioned regarding the way he raised his children. 'Did you raise them in the ways of the Torah,' he will be asked, 'or, God forbid, in a way that is contradictory to the Torah's ideals?'

"This is alluded to in the following verse: 'For how can I go up to my Father' in Heaven and stand trial before the Heavenly Tribune 'if the youth is not with me?' — if I did not ensure that my child was with me to receive a Torah education?"

אֲנִי יוֹסֵף

"I am Yosef!" (45:3)

The *Chofetz Chaim* offered the following explanation of this verse: When the brothers had initially arrived in Egypt, they were treated harshly by Yosef, who accused them of being spies. The brothers were startled by what was happening to them, and they asked one another, "Why is this happening to us? Who among us is guilty of a sin that would have brought this upon us?"

On the brothers' second trip to Egypt, they once again asked one another, "What is this that Hashem has done to us?"

However, continued the *Chofetz Chaim*, when the brothers heard but two words, "*Ani Yosef*" ("I am Yosef"), all of their questions were answered. Suddenly, everything was clear — all of their misfortune had occurred as a result of having sold Yosef.

Today, as well, concluded the *Chofetz Chaim*, there are many people who question the way that Hashem runs His world. "Why do the righteous suffer?" they ask. "Why can the wicked prosper?"

However, at the End of Days, when the entire world hears Hashem utter but two words, "*Ani Hashem!*" ("I am Hashem!") all of the questions will vanish.

✦✦✦

אֲנִי יוֹסֵף הַעוֹד אָבִי חָי וְלֹא־יָכְלוּ
אֶחָיו לַעֲנוֹת אֹתוֹ כִּי נִבְהֲלוּ מִפָּנָיו:

"'I am Yosef! Is my father still alive?' But his brothers could not answer him because they were bewildered before him" (45:3)

The *Midrash* on this verse comments, "Woe to us from the Day of Judgment! Woe to us from the Day of Rebuke!"

The commentators explain that in the same way that the brothers were unable to offer any response to Yosef's rebuke, so too will we be unable to respond to Hashem's claims against us, when we stand trial before Him.

"Can someone enlighten me," asked the *Beis HaLevi* (R' Yosef Dov Soloveitchik) of his companions, "as to where we find any words of rebuke in this verse?

"I'll tell you," said the *Beis HaLevi*. "Yehudah claimed to Yosef that he could not allow Binyamin to remain in Egypt, for to do so would be putting Yaakov's life in jeopardy, as he stated, 'It will happen that when he sees the youth is missing he will die.'

"To this Yosef responded, 'I am Yosef' — I am your brother Yosef who you sold to the Egyptians. 'Is *my* father still alive?' — when you sold me, did you give any thought to Yaakov's welfare *then*, about the danger you would be bringing upon Father by returning from the fields without me?

"To this rebuke," concluded the *Beis HaLevi*, "the brothers had nothing to say."

וְלֹא־יָכְלוּ אֶחָיו לַעֲנוֹת אֹתוֹ כִּי נִבְהֲלוּ מִפָּנָיו:

"But his brothers could not answer him, because they were bewildered before him" (45:3)

The *Midrash* on this verse comments, "Woe to us from the Day of Judgment! Woe to us from the Day of Rebuke!"

In the *Ba'al HaTanya*'s (R' Shneur Zalman of Liadi) town lived a *maggid* who regularly offered words of reproof to the townspeople and inspired them to repent.

On one occasion, the *Ba'al HaTanya* approached the *maggid* and said, "You offer words of reproof to the entire town, but to me you never say a word! I, too, desire to hear your reproof!"

The *maggid* was taken aback by the *Ba'al HaTanya*'s request and at first did not know what to say. On the one hand, how he could he rebuke the *Rebbe*? The *Rebbe* was a greater Torah scholar than he was. On the other hand, how could he refuse the *Rebbe*'s request?

"*Rebbe*," began the *maggid*, "whatever I know, you already know, and whatever you don't know, I certainly don't know.

"What, then, is the difference between the *Rebbe* and myself? The only difference lies in that which I don't know and the *Rebbe* does know!

"But *Rebbe*," concluded the *maggid*, "the difference between what I don't know and what the *Rebbe* does know is far smaller than the difference between what the *Rebbe* does know and what he has yet to learn!"

When the *Ba'al HaTanya* heard these words, he began to weep.

וְהִגַּדְתֶּם לְאָבִי אֶת־כָּל־כְּבוֹדִי בְּמִצְרַיִם

"Therefore, tell my father of all the honor that is given me in Egypt"(45:13)

The *Ohev Yisrael* (R' Avraham Yehoshua Heschel of Apta) was traveling with his son, R' Yitzchak Meir, through the neighboring towns. Wherever he went, hundreds of Jews came out to greet him, the *gadol b'Yisrael*, and showed him great honor.

The *Ohev Yisrael* was distressed by the amount of honor that he was receiving, and, because of his great modesty, he truly believed that he did not deserve it. He therefore turned to his son and asked, "My son, why is everybody honoring me so much, being that I am not worthy of it?"

R' Yitzchak Meir saw how distraught his father was, so he consoled him: "Do not let it worry you, Father. For these people have come to honor *me*."

"And why do you deserve such honor?" asked the *Ohev Yisrael*.

"That us obvious," replied R' Yitzchak Meir. "It is because I am the son of the Apter *Rav*."

The *Rebbe* smiled, and he said, "This, my son, is what Yosef meant when he stated, 'Therefore, tell my father of all the honor that is given me in Egypt' — for all of the fame and honor that I receive in Egypt is only thanks to my father's merit!"

וַיֶּאְסֹר יוֹסֵף מֶרְכַּבְתּוֹ וַיַּעַל לִקְרַאת־יִשְׂרָאֵל אָבִיו גֹּשְׁנָה וַיֵּרָא אֵלָיו וַיִּפֹּל עַל־צַוָּארָיו

"Yosef harnessed his chariot and went up to Goshen to meet Yisrael, his father. [Yosef] appeared before him and fell on his neck ..." (46:29)

Rashi comments: "But Yaakov did not fall on Yosef's neck nor did he kiss him. Our Rabbis said [that he did not do so] because he was reciting *Shema*."

This, says the *Maharal of Prague* (R' Yehudah Lowe of Prague), is the way of the *tzaddikim*. When their hearts are suddenly overcome with feelings of love and joy, they immediately direct those feelings toward Hashem. When Yaakov was finally reunited with his beloved son after so many years, his heart surged with love toward Yosef. He therefore immediately channeled it toward Hashem and recited the *Shema*.

וַיֹּאמֶר פַּרְעֹה אֶל־יַעֲקֹב כַּמָּה יְמֵי שְׁנֵי חַיֶּיךָ:

"Pharaoh asked Yaakov, "How old are you?" (47:8)

The *Sha'agas Aryeh* (R' Aryeh Leib Ginsberg) was seventy years old when he was appointed *Rav* of Metz.

Upon arriving in Metz, the *Sha'agas Aryeh* heard that their were members of the community who were grumbling over the selection of a rabbi so advanced in age. "Why did we select such an elderly rabbi? We should have appointed a younger rabbi, one who would remain at the helm of the community for many years to come!"

The first Shabbos the *Sha'agas Aryeh* was in Metz, he delivered his first *derashah* to the townspeople. The Torah reading that week was *Parashas Vayigash*.

"In this week's *parashah*," said the *Sha'agas Aryeh*, "we find that when Yaakov arrived in Egypt, Pharaoh asked him, 'How old are you?' To this, Yaakov answered, 'The span of the years of my sojourning have been one hundred and thirty years, [but] the years of my lifetime have been short and harsh, and have not approached the years of my fathers' lifetimes.'

"There are a few questions we may ask about this exchange. First, why did Pharaoh want to know how old Yaakov was? Second, why did Yaakov feel the need to add, 'the years of my lifetime have been short and harsh'? Pharaoh did not ask for a description of his lifetime; why did Yaakov deem it necessary to provide him with one?

"The answer," said the *Sha'agas Aryeh*, "is as follows: Pharaoh saw that the land of Egypt was blessed and that the famine ended as soon as Yaakov arrived. He realized that the new prosperity was thanks to Yaakov's presence, but he was concerned that it would not last, as Yaakov was apparently already old. This is why Pharaoh asked Yaakov, 'How old are you?'

"Yaakov, however, understood why Pharaoh asked him that question, so he responded, 'The years of my lifetime have been short and harsh — it may seem that I am very old and at the end of my life, but my years have actually been "short" compared to "my fathers' lifetimes," as they lived for one hundred and *eighty* years.'

"'So why do I look so old?' asked Yaakov rhetorically to Pharaoh. 'It is due to the fact that "the years of my lifetime have been short and harsh" — The stress of a difficult life,' said Yaakov, 'has made me appear older than I actually am.'

"The same applies to me," continued the *Sha'agas Aryeh*. "The reason I may look well on in years is actually only because of the hardship and persecution that I have faced throughout my life.

"But I assure you," concluded the *Sha'agas Aryeh*, "that with Hashem's help, I will serve as your rabbi for more than twenty years."

The words of this great sage were fulfilled, as the *Sha'agas Aryeh* served as the rabbi of Metz for over twenty years!

❧○❧

וַיְכַלְכֵּל יוֹסֵף אֶת־אָבִיו וְאֶת־אֶחָיו
וְאֵת כָּל־בֵּית אָבִיו לֶחֶם לְפִי הַטָּף:

"Yosef provided enough bread for his father and his brothers, and for his father's entire household, [and even]what the children were used to eating" (47:12)

This verse inspired the *Chofetz Chaim* to draw a parable: There once was a king who, one day, decided to visit his troops. He was extremely impressed by what he saw. The soldiers he viewed showed true loyalty and allegiance to him, and this pleased the king greatly.

"Request anything that your heart desires," said the king to his soldiers, "and it will be granted to you!"

"Your Highness," said one of the soldiers, "I would like you to know that I have dedicated my body and soul to your service; I would therefore like to request that you supply me with the sustenance that I need, each and every day."

The rest of the soldiers found his request ridiculous. "You fool!" they laughed. "Why do you request food? Don't you — along with the rest of the king's men — receive rations each and every day from the king's food supply? You will be provided for, even if you don't ask for it."

The same is true, said the *Chofetz Chaim*, regarding man's livelihood. We pray to Hashem that He should provide us with a decent livelihood. However, we lose sight of the fact it is not necessary for us to make such requests, as Hashem always cares for all of His creatures and He provides them with their needs.

What we should be beseeching Hashem for is that His honor and the honor of the Torah may spread throughout the world!

PARASHAS VAYECHI

וַיְחִי יַעֲקֹב בְּאֶרֶץ מִצְרַיִם שְׁבַע עֶשְׂרֵה שָׁנָה

"Yaakov lived seventeen years in the land of Egypt" (47:28)

RASHI EXPLAINS: "[YAAKOV] WISHED TO REVEAL TO HIS SONS [WHEN] the end [of Israel's exile would finally take place (*ha'keitz*)], but [the prophetic vision] was closed off from him."

Rabbeinu Bachye elaborated on Rashi's words: Yaakov observed that the letters *ches* and *tes* do not appear in any of the brothers' names. These are the two main letters of the word *chet*, sin. Yaakov took the fact that the brothers' names did not contain this word as an indication that they were clean of sin and worthy of being told when the future redemption would occur.

But then Yaakov noticed that the letters *kuf* and *tzaddi*, which together spell the word *keitz* ("the end" of the exiles), also do not appear in their names. At that point Yaakov thought that perhaps his sons were not worthy of knowing this secret after all. Because of his hesitation, Yaakov kept the secret closed and he did not reveal the information to his sons.

וַיְחִי יַעֲקֹב בְּאֶרֶץ מִצְרַיִם שְׁבַע עֶשְׂרֵה שָׁנָה

"Yaakov lived seventeen years in the land of Egypt" (47:28)

Rabbeinu Bachye points out that the *gematriya* of the word *vayechi* ("and he *lived*") equals thirty-four (6+10+8+10). This alludes to the thirty-four "good" years of Yaakov's *life*: the seventeen years before Yosef was sold plus the seventeen after Yaakov and Yosef were reunited in Egypt. These two periods were the best years of his life.

❧◌❧

וַיֻּגַּד לְיַעֲקֹב וַיֹּאמֶר הִנֵּה בִּנְךָ יוֹסֵף בָּא
אֵלֶיךָ וַיִּתְחַזֵּק יִשְׂרָאֵל וַיֵּשֶׁב עַל־הַמִּטָּה:

"Yaakov was told, 'Behold! Your son Yosef has come to [see] you.' So Yisrael summoned his strength and sat on the bed" (48:2)

Chazal (*Nedarim* 39b) teach us that "one who visits a sick person removes one-sixtieth of his ailment."

We can therefore assume, said the Vilna *Gaon*, that when Yosef visited his ill father, he alleviated one-sixtieth of his suffering. Consequently, Yaakov was left with fifty-nine sixtieths of his ailment.

This, said the *Gaon*, is alluded to in the verse: The *gematriya* of the word *hinei* is sixty. However, when the Torah describes what happened after Yosef had arrived to visit Yaakov, the verse states: "So Yisrael summoned his strength and sat on the bed (*ha'mitah*)." Amazingly, the *gematriya* of *ha'mitah* is fifty-nine!

❧◌❧

וַיִּשְׁלַח יִשְׂרָאֵל אֶת־יְמִינוֹ וַיָּשֶׁת
עַל־רֹאשׁ אֶפְרַיִם וְהוּא הַצָּעִיר

"Yisrael put out his right hand and placed it on Efraim's head, though he was the younger" (48:14)

Why, asked the *Chofetz Chaim*, did Efraim merit being blessed before Menasheh? Because, as the Torah described him, "he was the younger" one. In other words, he was free of arrogance and always acted with humility. His special character made him worthy of receiving Yaakov's first blessing.

Throughout his entire life, the *Chofetz Chaim* shunned every form of honor that came his way. For instance, whenever he received a letter that was full of praise and adulation, he made light of it.

He once told over a story that he had heard from R' Zev, the *mag-gid* of Vilna: There once was a villager who, despite his ignorance in all areas of Torah knowledge, had managed to memorize the entire Jewish calendar by heart. Whenever anyone asked him for the date and the time of the next *molad* (before the appearance of the new moon) or when a particular holiday was to begin, he could give the answer instantly.

Eventually the people of his town began referring to him as "the Rabbi." Soon he had deluded himself into believing that he was a *talmid chacham* of note.

One day, he happened to be in Vilna and went to the "GRA" *shul* to *daven Minchah*. When *davening* concluded, he approached the table where the Talmudic scholars had gathered. The scholars quickly delved into a deep Torah discussion. The poor "rabbi" felt so out of place, for he could not follow even one word of their discussion.

This is the nature of all honor, said the *Chofetz Chaim*. It is never more than a figment of one's imagination.

זְבוּלֻן לְחוֹף יַמִּים יִשְׁכֹּן

"Zevulun will dwell by the seashore" (49:13)

The *Yalkut Shimoni* states that Yissachar and Zevulun were part-ners in this world and divided their ultimate reward in the World to Come.

How were they partners in this world? The tribe of Zevulun earned their livelihood through their shipping industry, and they regularly gave a portion of their profits to the tribe of Yissachar. This enabled the schol-ars of Yissachar to dedicate themselves entirely to learning the Torah.

How did they divide their reward in the World to Come? They shared equally in the reward generated from Yissachar's Torah study.

The *Zohar HaKadosh* (*Parashas Terumah*) relates a story:

One night, R' Chiya, R' Abba, and R' Yosi took up lodging at an inn. At midnight, when all the other guests were fast asleep, they arose to learn Torah. The innkeeper's daughter heard them studying and arose from her bed as well. She lit a candle and then stood behind them so that it would be easier for them to see and so that she could hear the sweet sounds of their Torah learning.

R' Yosi glanced over his shoulder, noticed the innkeeper's daughter, and commented: "'For a *mitzvah* is a candle (*Mishlei* 6:23)' — what is the '*mitzvah* candle' that brings a woman merit? It is the candle that she kindles in honor of Shabbos! 'And Torah is light' (ibid.) — even though women are not commanded to study the Torah, nevertheless, the light generated by their husband's Torah study will serve as illumination for them as well." When the innkeeper's daughter heard R' Yosi's comment, she began to weep. Her father heard his daughter crying, so he arose from his bed and asked her, "Why are you crying, my daughter?"

His daughter related to him all that she had heard from R' Yosi, and with that, he too began to weep.

R' Yosi turned to them and asked, "Why are you both crying?"

The father began to explain the reason behind his sadness: "When it came time for my daughter to marry," he said, "I searched for a son-in-law that was a *talmid chacham*. I was willing to support the couple — in the tradition of Yissachar and Zevulun — while my son-in-law learned.

"One day," continued the innkeeper, "I spotted a young man standing on the roof of a *shul*. When the congregation inside the *shul* began to recite *Kaddish*, I noticed that this young man wished to descend from the roof and enter the *shul* in order to answer '*amen.*' But when he realized that he didn't have enough time to descend by way of the staircase, he jumped off the roof! He rushed into the *shul* and answered '*amen.*'

"A young man such as this," I said to myself, "must be a great Torah scholar. After all, he was willing to risk his life just to answer *amen* to *Kaddish*! I immediately gave him my daughter as a wife, despite the fact that I did not know anything about him. However, I have since discovered that my son-in-law is not a *talmid chacham* but an *am ha'aretz*. He doesn't even know how to recite *bircas ha'mazon* properly! That is why we are crying."

Meanwhile, the son-in-law awoke as well. R' Yosi looked at the young man and ascertained that, in fact, he was an extraordinary *talmid chacham*. Because of his humility, he concealed his greatness from the eyes of others, and acted as if he was totally ignorant of Torah learning.

"I see that an eternal light will one day emanate from him!" said R' Yosi. And so it was.

יִשָּׂשכָר חֲמֹר גָּרֶם

"Yissachar is [like] a strong-boned donkey" (49:14)

The *Chofetz Chaim* held financial supporters of Torah learning in very high regard. He used to recount the following parable about them:

"There was a king who had a very brave soldier in his army who fearlessly fought against the king's enemies.

"In a display of supreme dedication to the king, this soldier made his own arrows.

"Amid one battle, the arrows that he had prepared for himself ran out. He therefore turned to the king and asked, 'Your Highness, may I use arrows that were prepared by another soldier?'

"'What difference does it make?' replied the king to the soldier, 'Use whatever arrows you want as long as you win the war!'

"So it is with man in this world," concluded the *Chofetz Chaim*. "A man's entire life is spent waging the fiercest of wars — the war against the *yetzer hara*.

"When someone raises his children to follow the Torah path, they are the 'arrows' that he has made. But someone who has no children should at least use his money to support others who have dedicated their lives to the service of Hashem. Though he has no 'arrows' of his own, he can use the arrows made by others.

"When the enemy has been conquered and the victory sealed, there is no doubt that he, too, will receive credit for the triumph."

וַיַּרְא מְנֻחָה כִּי טוֹב וְאֶת־הָאָרֶץ
כִּי נָעֵמָה וַיֵּט שִׁכְמוֹ לִסְבֹּל

"He saw that tranquility was good, and that [his] land was pleasant, yet he bent his shoulder to bear" (49:15)

Rashi offers the following explanation: "'He saw that tranquility was good' — He saw that his portion [in the Land of Israel] was blessed and good for producing fruit. 'Yet he bent his shoulder to bear' the yoke of Torah."

Yissachar saw that the land it had been granted was fertile and blessed, capable of yielding luscious fruit and bringing it great wealth.

Yet he chose to make do with little and to dedicate his life to the study of Torah.

The *Chofetz Chaim* compared this to the story of a high-ranking official who took a trip by sea. The ship that he was sailing upon was the epitome of beauty and luxury — even the crew aboard the ship was dressed elegantly. The official strolled along the deck, and was overcome by the ship's magnificence.

Then the official became curious of how the ship worked, so he requested to be shown exactly how it operated. The captain of the ship took the official down below the deck of the ship. The official was shocked by what he saw. He saw dusty engine chambers filled with black soot, machines producing a horrible noise, and filthy crewmen covered with grease and fuel.

"There you have it," said the captain to the officer. "This is what enables you to ride upon such a smooth-sailing ship."

This is not what I expected, thought the officer. *That such a magnificent ship is operated by workers in soiled garments who look more like beggars than anything else is an absolute disgrace!*

The official commanded the captain to clean all the engines and not sully them ever again with grease or fuel.

Obviously, an engine that does not have fuel or oil in it cannot move the ship at all.

The same idea can be applied to the world in which we live, said the *Chofetz Chaim*. The world is blessed with beautiful trees and springs — it is such a marvelous creation! But it is important for us to realize that the entire world only exists thanks to the *talmidei chachamim* who sit in the *batei midrash* and engage in Torah study, sufficing with the barest minimum. The world runs only by their merit!

✒️🌤

וַיַּרְא מְנֻחָה כִּי טוֹב וְאֶת־הָאָרֶץ
כִּי נָעֵמָה וַיֵּט שִׁכְמוֹ לִסְבֹּל

"He saw that tranquility was good, and that [his] land was pleasant, yet he bent his shoulder to bear" (49:15)

R' Yitzchak of Vorka explained this verse in the following manner: "He saw that tranquility was good" — When does a person achieve true tranquility? When he bends "his shoulder to bear" —

When he decides to be a patient person, ready to bear everything that comes his way.

וַיֵּט שִׁכְמוֹ לִסְבֹּל

"Yet he bent his shoulder to bear" (49:15)

T he *Chofetz Chaim* was once asked the meaning of the words, "yet he bent his shoulder to bear." "Is the Torah not sweeter than honey? How can it be called a burden?"

The *Chofetz Chaim* answered by way of a parable. There once was a wealthy man who made his living by selling precious gems and pearls. One day, he was informed that there were mines in Africa that were laden with precious stones. He therefore decided to journey to Africa, intending to purchase these gems at a low cost and eventually sell them at a high price.

He made all the necessary preparations for his trip. He took with him 3,000 gold coins for purchasing the stones and an additional 400 to insure himself a comfortable trip, as was fitting for him, the successful businessman.

As soon as he arrived at his destination, he immediately began working on buying the precious gems. When he located the mines where the gems were sold, he spent all the 3,000 gold coins to purchase a sizable amount of valuable gems. As he turned to leave however, one of the owners of the mine motioned for him to wait.

"Pardon me," said the dealer to the wealthy man. "I was wondering if you would be interested in some gems that I have to sell. These stones are very rare, yet I am prepared to sell them to you at an unbelievably low price!"

"Your offer does sound appealing," replied the wealthy man, "but I have no more money for them; whatever money I have is just enough for my return trip home. I'm sorry."

"Please," pressed the dealer, "just come and take a look at my merchandise. And if you still feel that you don't have enough money, then I won't press you anymore."

The wealthy man finally gave in and went along with the dealer. When he saw the gems, he realized that the man had been telling the truth. The gems were truly of outstanding quality and their beauty was unmatched by any gem that he had ever seen.

It would be a pity, thought the wealthy man, *to pass up such a fantastic opportunity. I don't know when I'll ever have a chance like this again. But if I do buy these gems, then how will I ever get back home?*

After giving the matter some thought, the man decided that it was worthwhile to purchase the gems with the money he had planned on using for his trip home. *True, my trip will not be easy; I will have to forgo good food and sleeping properly at a hotel, but for gems of this quality, it will certainly be worthwhile. After all,* thought the wealthy man, *the journey will not last forever and the discomfort will pass, but this opportunity might never return.*

The wealthy man purchased the gems and set out for home. His journey was rough; wherever he stopped to rest, he was unable to take up lodging like one of the rich; instead, he slept outdoors on straw, like a lowly pauper.

On one of his stops, he met a friend who, like him, was a successful businessman. Needless to say, his friend was shocked to see this man of prominence living so miserably. "What has happened to you, my friend?" he asked. "Have you lost all of your money?"

The wealthy man told his friend the whole story of his trip to Africa and of his last business deal there. The friend listened to the man's explanation but there was still something troubling him.

"Please tell me," said the friend to the wealthy man, "I know you quite well, and I know that you are used to the finer luxuries in life. Are you not suffering from the hardships of your journey?"

"I am indeed suffering," responded the wealthy man, "but each time I stop I open my treasure box and look at the gems that I am carrying. That fills me with joy and I console myself with the special gems I bought. After that, the conditions of the trip don't bother me at all."

So it is with man in this world, said the *Chofetz Chaim*. Man descends to the world in order to fulfill the *mitzvos* and perform good deeds for as long as he lives. However, at certain times an individual may be overcome with a desire to derive pleasure from all the illusory delights that this world has to offer. How can he overcome this urge? He need only look at the great reward awaiting him in the World to Come, and then his heart will become filled with joy!

This, concluded the *Chofetz Chaim*, is the meaning of "yet he bent his shoulder to bear" — Yissachar appreciates the value of Torah, so he is willing to bear much suffering in this world.

SHEMOS

SHEMOS

וְאֵלֶּה שְׁמוֹת בְּנֵי יִשְׂרָאֵל

**"And these are the names of
the Children of Israel" (1:1)**

T HE *SHULCHAN ARUCH* (*ORACH CHAIM* 285) RULES THAT EVERY INDI-
vidual is required to read the weekly *parashah* twice (*shnayim
Mikra*) and its Aramaic translation once (*v'echad Targum*).
This requirement is alluded to in the acronym of the word "she-
mos," which is formed by the letters *shin, mem, vav, tes*": *shnayim
Mikra, v'echad targum.*

Similarly, *Chazal* note that the word "*shemos*" alludes to three *mitzvos*:
Shabbos, milah, v'tefillin ("Shabbos, circumcision and *tefillin*"). These are
the three *mitzvos* that the Torah refers to as "a sign." That is, these *mitzvos*
signify the unbreakable bond between Hashem and the Jewish people.

In regard to the *mitzvah* of Shabbos the Torah states, "For *it is a
sign* between Me and you for your generations" (31:13).

In connection with the *mitzvah* of bris milah the Torah tells us,
"And that shall be *the sign* of the covenant between Me and you"
(*Bereishis* 17:11).

When describing the *mitzvah* of *tefillin*, the Torah says, "And it shall be for you *a sign* on your arm" (13:9).

Accordingly, by stating "And these are the *shemos* of the Children of Israel who were coming to Egypt," the Torah is hinting to the idea that when the Jews enter a foreign land, these are the three *mitzvos* that protect them from assimilating with the nations.

৵৩৫

הִנֵּה עַם בְּנֵי יִשְׂרָאֵל רַב וְעָצוּם מִמֶּנּוּ:
"Behold! the people, the Children of Israel,
are more numerous and stronger than we" (1:9)

This verse teaches us, said R' Yisrael of Rizhin, that when the Jews act as one people, free of discord and strife, then the nations of the world see them as "more numerous and stronger" than themselves and realize that they cannot dominate the Jews.

This can be compared to a father who invited all of his children to his home. When they arrived, they gathered around him.

The father held several thin twigs in his hand. He gave one to each of his children and then asked them to break them.

His children snapped the dry twigs with ease.

The father then passed around a bundle of several twigs. "Now," said the father, "please try breaking this bundle." Each one tried to break the bundle but none succeeded.

"You see," said the father, "as long as you remain united in the same way that these branches are united, nobody will ever be able to harm you! But if you act divisively and there is disharmony among you, then be aware that a lone individual is as feeble and easily broken as a thin twig."

৵৩৫

וַתִּירֶאןָ הַמְיַלְּדֹת אֶת־הָאֱלֹקִים וְלֹא עָשׂוּ כַּאֲשֶׁר
דִּבֶּר אֲלֵיהֶן מֶלֶךְ מִצְרָיִם וַתְּחַיֶּיןָ אֶת־הַיְלָדִים:
"But the midwives feared God and they did not
do as the king of Egypt spoke to them" (1:17)

One of the *Chofetz Chaim*'s students approached him for his advice. A certain Lithuanian community had invited him to be their rabbi. However, he was hesitant to accept the position lest he inadvertently rule incorrectly regarding halachic matters. But the community was being persistent, and they were pressuring upon him to accept the prestigious position.

"You should certainly accept the position," answered the *Chofetz Chaim*, "and I will bring you a proof from the Torah that you should do so. In *Parashas Shemos* it states that Pharaoh ordered the Jewish midwives to murder every male child. The Torah, however, testifies that the midwives feared Hashem, and they therefore defied Pharaoh's command.

"Yet," continued the *Chofetz Chaim*, "why did the midwives not resign from their posts as soon as they received Pharaoh's cruel command? Why did they choose to stay on as midwives?

"Rather," answered the *Chofetz Chaim*, "it is specifically because of their deeply ingrained fear of God that they chose *not* to leave their positions. For who would have taken over their jobs had they resigned? Perhaps it would be unscrupulous women who would carry out Pharaoh's wicked decree! This is why they chose to remain at their posts but to defy Pharaoh's words.

"The same idea can be applied to the rabbinate," explained the *Chofetz Chaim*. "It is precisely because you are God fearing and you worry about possibly ruling incorrectly that you should accept the offer to become their rabbi! For if someone like yourself turns down the position, who knows who will be hired instead of you?"

וַיֵּלֶךְ אִישׁ מִבֵּית לֵוִי וַיִּקַּח אֶת־בַּת־לֵוִי:

*"A man went from the house of Levi
and he took a daughter of Levi" (2:1)*

Rashi explains that the "daughter of Levi" mentioned in the verse refers to Yocheved, who at the time was 130 years old! Hashem, however, performed a miracle and Yocheved returned to a state of youthfulness, and she was able to give birth to Moshe and Aharon.

But why, asks the Ibn Ezra, does the Torah not even mention this astounding miracle? When Sarah *Imeinu* gave birth to Yitzchak when she was 90 years old, the Torah describes it as a momentous miracle. The miracle that occurred to Yocheved was seemingly even greater, yet the Torah tells us nothing about it at all!

The Dubno *Maggid*, in his style, answered this question with a wonderful parable:

There was a group of paupers sitting together, discussing their difficult predicament. In particular, they were bemoaning the fact that people seemed to be giving less and less *tzedakah.*

"Even the wealthiest Jew in the city," complained one pauper, "who once graciously gave a ruble to each hungry man, now gives nothing!"

"You're absolutely right," agreed his friend. "I've noticed the same thing myself. People just seem to be giving less *tzedakah* these days."

"I don't have any idea what you fellows are talking about," said a third pauper. "The last time I went around collecting, each family happily gave me an entire ruble!"

"When was this?" asked his friend.

"Why, it was on Purim," he responded.

"What happened to you on Purim," said the friend, "doesn't prove anything. For on Purim there is a special *mitzvah* to give charity to the needy. It is therefore no wonder that you received so much *tzedakah.* Had you told us that each family gave you a ruble on an ordinary weekday, *that* would have been amazing!"

This is also the case regarding Sarah and Yocheved, answered the *maggid.* Sarah gave birth at the age of 90, and the Torah elaborates about the miraculous nature of that event. Why? Because in Sarah's day, such an event was truly astounding.

However, for the Jews in Egypt miracles were commonplace, as *Chazal* tell us that in Egypt the Jewish women gave birth to as many as six children at one time! In such an era, there is nothing extraordinary about a woman giving birth at the age of 130.

וַתִּשְׁלַח אֶת־אֲמָתָהּ וַתִּקָּחֶהָ:

"She sent her maidservant and she took it" (2:5)

Chazal inform us that the basket carrying Moshe was too far for Pharaoh's daughter to reach from where she was standing. Still, she stretched out her hand (*amasah*) in the direction of the basket and Hashem miraculously lengthened her arm for her.

R' Meir Shapiro, the *rosh yeshivah* of Yeshivas Chachmei Lublin, called for an emergency meeting of the leaders of Lublin to discuss a certain person whose life was in danger. R' Shapiro demanded of them to do something to save his life.

"This matter that you speak of," responded one of the leaders, "is beyond our capabilities. We regrettably do not believe that we can carry it out."

"In this week's *parashah*," replied R' Shapiro, "the Torah states, 'And she sent her maidservant.' *Chazal* teach us that the arm of Pharaoh's daughter was miraculously lengthened in order for her to take hold of Moshe's basket.

"I wonder," continued R' Shapiro, "why did Pharaoh's daughter even attempt to retrieve the basket in the first place? After all, if it is obvious to an individual that something is not within his reach, does he waste his energy trying to obtain it?

"We see from here," concluded R' Shapiro, "that when a person is expected to accomplish something, he should not deliberate whether or not he is capable of succeeding — he must try! Let him first make an effort, and then Heaven will assist him."

וַיַּרְא כִּי אֵין אִישׁ וַיַּךְ אֶת־הַמִּצְרִי וַיִּטְמְנֵהוּ בַּחוֹל:

"And he saw that there was no man, so he struck down the Egyptian and hid him in the sand" (2:12)

On *Motza'ei Shabbos, Parashas Shemos*, a group of *chassidim* entered the study of their *rebbe*, R' Baruch of Mezibuzh. The *rebbe* greeted them warmly and asked why they had come.

The *chassidim* sighed. "A great trouble has befallen us, *Rebbe*," said one of the *chassidim*. "For a cruel Jew-hater has recently been appointed governor of our town. His wickedness knows no bounds, as he has raised our taxes, disrupted our day-to-day lives, and has even gone so far as to imprison several distinguished Jews."

The *rebbe* closed his eyes for a short while. When he opened them, he looked at his *chassidim* and said, "Earlier today we read, 'And he saw that there was no man, so he struck down the Egyptian and hid him in the sand.'

"These words," continued the *rebbe*, "apply to me as well: 'And he saw that there was no man' — when I closed my eyes, I envisioned the tyrant who presently controls your town, and I realized that he does not even deserve to be called a man! 'So he struck down the Egyptian' — your governor deserves to be smitten as well, and a punishment from Heaven is certainly forthcoming. 'And hid him in *chol*' — however, I do not want him to be afflicted on *Motza'ei Shabbos* but only on a *yom chol*, on a weekday (the simple meaning of '*chol*' in this verse is 'sand,' but the word '*chol*' also means 'weekday')."

The *chassidim* emotionally took leave of their *rebbe* and returned to their homes. Later that week, there was a thunderstorm in their town and a bolt of lightning struck and killed the wicked governor.

וַיְהִי בַיָּמִים הָרַבִּים הָהֵם וַיָּמָת מֶלֶךְ מִצְרַיִם וַיֵּאָנְחוּ בְנֵי־יִשְׂרָאֵל מִן־הָעֲבֹדָה וַיִּזְעָקוּ וַתַּעַל שַׁוְעָתָם אֶל־הָאֱלֹקִים מִן־הָעֲבֹדָה:

"It happened that the king of Egypt died, and the Children of Israel groaned because of the work and they cried out. Their outcry because of the work went up to God" (2:23)

Why did the Jewish people cry about their work now, specifically after the king of Egypt died?

R' Yitzchak, the son of R' Yehudah HaLevi and one of the *Ba'alei Tosafos*, answers: It is customary, said R' Yitzchak, that when a new king assumes the throne, he pardons the prisoners of the state. Some are granted complete freedom, while others have their punishment reduced.

So when the king of Egypt died and a new one was appointed, the Jews hoped that their suffering would be lessened and he would free them of their hard labor. How terribly disappointing it was for them when the new king not only refused to lighten their crushing labor — but even added to it! This is why the Jewish people groaned and cried out specifically after the death of the king of Egypt.

וַיֵּרָא מַלְאַךְ ה' אֵלָיו בְּלַבַּת־אֵשׁ מִתּוֹךְ הַסְּנֶה

"An angel of Hashem appeared to him in a blaze of fire from amid the bush" (3:2)

R' Yehoshua ben Karchah was approached by a gentile who challenged him with a question:

"Tell me, please," asked the gentile, "why did Hashem choose to speak with Moshe *Rabbeinu* specifically from within a bush? Why did He not speak to him from inside a different type of tree?"

"And if Hashem would have spoken to Moshe," answered R' Yehoshua ben Karchah, "from within a carob tree or a sycamore — then you would not have had a question?

"Nevertheless," he continued, "I will answer you. Why did Hashem speak to Moshe specifically from inside a bush? Hashem wished to teach us that His Glory fills the entire world, and that there is not a single space that is devoid of His Presence — not even a plant as lowly as a bush."

ﬡﬡﬡ

מִי אָנֹכִי כִּי אֵלֵךְ אֶל־פַּרְעֹה וְכִי אוֹצִיא אֶת־בְּנֵי יִשְׂרָאֵל מִמִּצְרָיִם:

"Who am I that I should go to Pharaoh and that I should take the Children of Israel out of Egypt?" (3:11)

Rashi explains that Moshe *Rabbeinu* was asking Hashem two questions: "Who am I" — am I really distinguished enough to speak with kings? "And that I should take the Children of Israel out of Egypt" — why is Israel worthy of having a miracle done for them?

In his later years, the *Chasam Sofer*'s (R' Moshe Sofer) eyesight had dimmed. Nevertheless, countless letters continued to arrive at his home from around the world asking for his opinion regarding halachic matters and proper conduct. Because of this, his son, R' Shimon Sofer, would sit with him and read him each letter, to which he would then relay his response.

One day, R' Shimon read the *Chasam Sofer* a letter which commenced with lavish praise, showering him with the accolades befitting the *gadol hador*.

Upon hearing the praise, the *Chasam Sofer* sighed deeply.

"Why do you sigh, Father?" asked R' Shimon. "Certainly you realize that you are the *gadol hador!*"

"It is specifically for this reason that I groan!" replied the *Chasam Sofer* with humility. "How low our generation has fallen because of its sins — that I am considered the *gadol hador!*"

"Now I understand the words of Rashi on the verse, 'Who am I that I should go to Pharaoh,'" said R' Shimon.

"In his extreme humility, Moshe *Rabbeinu* asked Hashem, 'Who am I?' To which Rashi comments, 'Who am I that I should speak to kings?' I am not fitting in the least, exclaimed Moshe to Hashem, to be the leader of the Jewish people. And if it is I who is actually more deserving than anyone else, then it is a sign that the generation must be of very low stature.

"This, in turn, led Moshe to ask a second question. As Rashi explains: 'And that I should take the Children of Israel out of Egypt' — if the Jewish Nation has descended so low a level that I am their leader, then 'why is Israel worthy of having a miracle done for them?'"

⚜

וַיַּשְׁלִכֵהוּ אַרְצָה וַיְהִי לְנָחָשׁ וַיָּנָס מֹשֶׁה מִפָּנָיו

"And he cast it to the ground and it became a snake. Moshe fled from it" (4:3)

A gentile woman once turned to R' Yosi and declared, "My god is greater than your God!"

"From where do you know about the greatness of your god?" asked R' Yosi.

"I have derived it from your Torah!" she responded. "For when your God appeared to Moshe in the bush, he hid his face. But when Moshe saw the snake — our god — it was not sufficient for him to simply cover his face; rather, he fled from before it! This is proof that our god is greater than your God!"

R' Yosi replied: "When Hashem appeared to Moshe," he answered, "where could he have fled to? To the end of the earth? To the heavens? It would have served no purpose whatsoever — for the whole world is filled with His glory! Therefore, Moshe simply hid his face. Yet when he saw your god, all he had to do was take two or three steps, and the snake would no longer be able to harm him! Is this the great might of your god?!"

PARASHAS VA'EIRA

וָאֵרָא אֶל־אַבְרָהָם אֶל־יִצְחָק וְאֶל־יַעֲקֹב

*"I appeared to Avraham, to
Yitzchak, and to Yaakov" (6:3)*

Rashi writes: "'I appeared' — to the Forefathers."

Rashi's words are puzzling, commented R' Meir of Premishlan. What has Rashi added with his explanation? Is not everyone aware that Avraham, Yitzchak, and Yaakov were our holy forefathers?

Rashi wishes to teach us, answered the *rebbe*, that each one of our forefathers merited Divine revelation not because of his lineage but because of the merit he earned for himself.

וְגַם אֲנִי שָׁמַעְתִּי אֶת־נַאֲקַת בְּנֵי יִשְׂרָאֵל אֲשֶׁר מִצְרַיִם מַעֲבִדִים אֹתָם

*"I have also heard the groaning of the Children
of Israel whom Egypt enslaves" (6:5)*

One of the most successful businessmen in Pressburg visited the *Chasam Sofer* (R' Moshe Sofer) and requested his assistance.

"As the *Rav* knows," began the businessman, "I am the proprietor of a very large business. Recently, however, my business has been failing. I have come to ask the *Rav* for his blessing so that I can once again prosper."

"I am well aware of your trying situation," replied the *Chasam Sofer.* "Yet I am also aware of the fact that your brother is absolutely penniless and needs help with his livelihood. Yet you have ignored his situation."

"Forgive me, my *Rav*," responded the businessman. "I truly wish to help my brother. It's just that right now my own financial situation does not allow me to help him. If my fortune turns for the better, I will certainly help him."

"In this week's *parashah*," said the *Chasam Sofer*, "Hashem tells Moshe *Rabbeinu*: 'I have also heard the groaning of the Children of Israel.' How are we to understand the word, '*also*,' in this verse? Who else besides Hashem heard the groaning of the Jewish people?

"The answer is as follows: When the Jews groaned and cried under the yoke of Egyptian slavery, each one of them heard the cries of his fellow Jew, and despite his horrible suffering, he would strive to lighten his friend's burden. In the merit of their hearing the groans of their brethren, Hashem *also* listened to them and rescued them from Egypt.

"Help others," exclaimed the *Chasam Sofer*, "and you can be sure that Hashem will help you as well!"

✥

וְהוֹצֵאתִי אֶתְכֶם מִתַּחַת סִבְלֹת מִצְרַיִם וְהִצַּלְתִּי אֶתְכֶם מֵעֲבֹדָתָם

"I shall take you out from under the burdens of Egypt; I shall rescue you from their service" (6:6)

The *Imrei Emes* (R' Avraham Mordechai Alter of Gur) drew a parable in light of this verse: There was a king whose son had strayed from the proper path. He had begun to act recklessly, spending large amounts of his father's money. In a short period of time, he had caused the king great financial harm.

The king, needless to say, was furious with his son and, as a punishment, banished him from the palace without giving him a penny. The king hoped that after tasting the bitter taste of poverty, his son would begin to appreciate the value of money.

For many years, the son dwelled with the paupers of the city, eventually forgetting that he was the son of a king.

One day, a feeling of mercy flickered within the king's heart for his son that he had not seen in so many years. He therefore dispatched a messenger with specific instructions to find his son and to find out what he needed.

The messenger searched thoroughly among the city's poor, and after much difficulty, located the king's son, whom he almost did not recognize.

"Do you need anything?" asked the messenger.

"There most certainly is!" answered the son happily. "I could use a new beggar's sack. My old one is in tatters."

The Jewish people, explained the *Imrei Emes*, are the son in the parable. Sadly, we have sunken to such depths in our *galus*, that when we beseech Hashem, we request no more than a beggar's sack. But when the ultimate redemption arrives, we will come to realize that there are other, more important things that we have been lacking throughout our bitter exile. Then we will know what to ask for.

הוּא אַהֲרֹן וּמֹשֶׁה

"This was the Aharon and Moshe ..." (6:26)

The *Midrash Rabbah* states that there are instances when the Torah mentions the name of Moshe before that of Aharon, and other times when Aharon's name precedes Moshe's. This is meant to teach us, says the *Midrash*, that they were of equal stature.

How is it possible, asked the *Chozeh* of Lublin (R' Yaakov Yitzchak Horowitz of Lublin), for two individuals to be on exactly the same level of spirituality? Do not all people have spiritual "ups and downs"?

Perhaps we can answer this question, said the *Chozeh*, with what *Chazal* have taught us in *Maseches Chullin* (89a). *Chazal* state, "What is said regarding Moshe and Aharon is greater than what is said regarding Avraham. For Avraham exclaimed, 'I am but dust and ash' (*Bereishis* 18:27), but Moshe and Aharon said about themselves, 'For what are we?' (16:7)."

Chazal are telling us that Moshe and Aharon achieved a greater degree of self-nullification than Avraham *Avinu*. For Avraham stated that he is "but dust and ash," yet even dust and ash are still something! However Moshe and Aharon said, "For what are we?" — *we are nothing at all!*

We can now answer our question, said the *Chozeh*. For when a person believes that he is something — even something as small and insignificant as dust and ash — he will never be able to be on the exact same level as his fellow man.

But when two individuals both claim to be nothing at all, then they certainly can be equal!

וַיֹּאמֶר מֹשֶׁה ... הֵן אֲנִי עֲרַל שְׂפָתַיִם וְאֵיךְ יִשְׁמַע אֵלַי פַּרְעֹה

"Moshe said ... 'Behold! I have sealed lips, so how shall Pharaoh heed me?'" (6:30)

The *Midrash* relates that one day when Moshe was still a small child growing up in Pharaoh's palace, he was sitting on Pharaoh's lap. Surrounding Pharaoh were his officers and sorcerers.

Suddenly, Moshe reached up, removed the crown from Pharaoh's head, and placed it on his own. The sorcerers were alarmed by what they had just witnessed, and they said to Pharaoh, "Our king! We are concerned that this child will one day seize your kingdom and rule in your stead!"

Sitting among the Egyptian officers was Yisro — who at the time was one of Pharaoh's advisers — and he belittled the sorcerers' prediction, "Listen to me," said Yisro. "We have witnessed nothing more than childish play. This boy does not yet possess understanding; he is in no way a threat to the kingdom."

"We can easily check whether this boy is intelligent or not," said the sorcerers.

The sorcerers took two bowls; they placed gold coins in one, and burning coals in the other. "If the child reaches for the gold," said the sorcerers, "then it is an indication that he does possess understanding, and we will have him executed. However, if he tries to grab the coals, then he apparently is not very intelligent, and we will leave him be."

The bowls were placed in front of Moshe. He tried reaching for the gold coins, but the angel Gavriel moved Moshe's hand over to the bowl that held the burning coals. Moshe burned his hand when he touched a coal, so he tried soothing his pain by putting his hand into his mouth. When he touched his tongue, however, he scalded it as well, and thus he developed a speech impediment.

In light of this *Midrash*, there are those who explain the aforementioned verse as follows: "Moshe said before Hashem, 'Behold! I have sealed lips' — When I speak to Pharaoh he will instantly recognize me by my speech impediment and he will remember what the sorcerers had said about me. He will then suspect that I want to overthrow him. 'So how shall Pharaoh heed me?'"

תְּנוּ לָכֶם מוֹפֵת

"Provide a wonder for yourselves" (7:9)

Why, asked R' Elimelech of Lizhensk, would Pharaoh ask Moshe to "Provide a wonder for *yourselves*"? Since Pharaoh was the one who wanted proof of Moshe's legitimacy, would it not have made more sense for him to say, "Provide a wonder for *me*"?

The difference, answered the *rebbe*, between a genuine wonder and one which is no more than an optical illusion is that the illusion amazes only those who witness it. However, the one who performs the feat is not impressed in the least, since he knows that it was no more than a delusion. A genuine wonder, on the other hand, amazes not only its spectators, but even the *tzaddik* who performs it.

This, then, was Pharaoh's intention when he said, "Provide a wonder for *yourselves*" — Provide us with a true wonder, one that will not only dazzle us but will even make an impression upon yourselves.

וַיִּצְעַק מֹשֶׁה אֶל־ה' עַל־דְּבַר הַצְפַרְדְּעִים
וַיַּעַשׂ ה' כִּדְבַר מֹשֶׁה וַיָּמֻתוּ הַצְפַרְדְּעִים...

Moshe cried out to Hashem concerning the frogs ... Hashem carried out the word of Moshe, and the frogs died (8:8-9)

Why is it, asked the *Chofetz Chaim*, that at the Plague of Frogs, Hashem accepted Moshe's prayer as soon as he uttered it and immediately stopped the devastating plague, yet when the Jews were in the wilderness and were attacked by fiery serpents, Moshe's prayers did not have an immediate affect? For, in that case, Hashem told Moshe, "Make yourself [the image of] a venomous snake, and place it on a pole" (*Bamidbar* 21:8), and only by gazing at the copper "snake" did those who were bitten survive. Why was it necessary for Moshe to perform an action in order to save the Jewish people in the wilderness, yet in Egypt, no additional action was required?

This is meant to teach us, answered the *Chofetz Chaim*, the severity of the sin of speaking *lashon hara*.

As a rule, prayer is effective for removing all misfortunes and calamities. Therefore, when Moshe beseeched Hashem to remove the frogs from Egypt, Hashem accepted his prayer and instantly stopped the plague. However, the fiery serpents were sent to attack the Jewish people as a punishment for speaking *lashon hara*. Since they had committed a sin which the Heavenly court judges with exactitude, Moshe's prayers were not immediately effective. Instead, Hashem instructed him to make an image of a venomous snake for the people to gaze at. This way, each Jew would think of his Father in Heaven and personally repent for his sin. Each Jew would then be forgiven and granted life.

וּמָלְאוּ בָּתֵּי מִצְרַיִם אֶת־הֶעָרֹב וְגַם הָאֲדָמָה אֲשֶׁר־הֵם עָלֶיהָ:

"The houses of Egypt will be filled with the swarm [of creatures] — and even the ground upon which they stand" (8:17)

Explains Rashi: "'The swarm' — A mixture of all sorts of harmful beasts, snakes, and scorpions. These [creatures] wreaked destruction [upon the Egyptians]."

This verse can be understood, said the *Rebbe* R' Heschel of Cracow, with a comment made by R' Shimon of Shantz in *Maseches Keilim* (8:5). There he states that there is an animal called the *Yidoni* that "ties" itself to the ground with a ropelike organ that extends from its body. The Yidoni, states R' Shimon of Shantz, is extremely dangerous and cannot be approached.

If this is so, asked the *rebbe*, how can Rashi say that "*all* sorts" of creatures attacked the Egyptians? After all, it would have been impossible for the Yidoni to be brought to Egypt, as it constantly clings to the ground!

This, he answered, is what the verse means when it states, "And even the ground upon which they stand": the Yidoni arrived in Egypt *together* with the ground to which it was attached!

וְהִתְיַצֵּב לִפְנֵי פַרְעֹה

"Stand before Pharaoh" (9:13)

The *Midrash* relates that the doorway to Pharaoh's palace was very low so that anyone who wished to enter the palace was forced to bow toward an Egyptian idol that was placed opposite the doorway.

But when Moshe and Aharon approached the doorway it miraculously became higher and they did not even need to bend their heads in order to enter.

This, said R' Moshe Alshich, is what Hashem meant when He said to Moshe, "*Stand* before Pharaoh" — when you come before Pharaoh you will not need to bend at all; go in *standing straight.*

Similarly, continued the Alshich, when Yaakov *Avinu* went to meet Pharaoh, Hashem made a miracle for him and the doorway to Pharaoh's palace was enlarged so that the *tzaddik* would not unwittingly commit the sin of idol worship. Thus the verse (*Bereishis* 47:7) states, "Yosef brought his father Yaakov and presented him *standing* before Pharaoh." Yaakov entered Pharaoh's palace standing erect, and he did not have to bow to the idol.

וַיְהִי בָרָד וְאֵשׁ מִתְלַקַּחַת בְּתוֹךְ הַבָּרָד

"There was hail, and fire flaming amid the hail" (9:24)

The *Midrash* states that the Plague of Hail was a miracle within a miracle: the hail did not extinguish the fire and the fire did not melt the hail. Rather, both elements joined forces in smiting the Egyptians.

R' Acha compared this to a king who had two very powerful legions of soldiers. To find greater favor in the king's eyes, each legion tried outdoing the other when they went out to war. The competition between the two legions escalated to the point that they hated one another.

This hatred continued for some time until a major war threatened to break out in the king's land. The king summoned both legions to appear before him, and he told them the following:

"I know," said the king, "that you are both very powerful and dedicated to my service. I usually send only one of you at a time to the battlefront. But now a major war looms on the horizon, and I need assistance from both of you. But what shall I do about your mutual hatred? You must make peace between yourselves and go out to war united. Then we will be victorious!"

So it was with the Plague of Hail. Hail and fire cannot coexist because the nature of fire is to melt hail and the nature of hail is to extinguish fire. But in this instance, Hashem made peace between them and together they struck at the Egyptians.

Parashas Bo

בֹּא אֶל־פַּרְעֹה

"Come to Pharaoh" (10:1)

WHY IS IT, ASKED R' MENACHEM MENDEL OF KOTZK, THAT Hashem told Moshe to "*Come* to Pharaoh"? Would it not have been more appropriate to state, "*Go* to Pharaoh"? Rather, answered the *rebbe*, one should never *leave* Hashem's presence, as He fills the entire world with His glory. This is why Hashem said, "Come to Pharaoh," but *do not go away* from Me.

❧❦❧

וַיְהִי חֹשֶׁךְ־אֲפֵלָה בְּכָל־אֶרֶץ מִצְרַיִם ... לֹא־רָאוּ
אִישׁ אֶת־אָחִיו וְלֹא־קָמוּ אִישׁ מִתַּחְתָּיו

"And there was a thick darkness throughout the land of Egypt ... No man could see his brother nor could any man rise from his place" (10:22-23)

This verse, said R' Chanoch of Alexander, teaches us a valuable lesson in Divine service:

"And there was a thick darkness throughout the land of Egypt" — when it is a period of spiritual darkness — and "No man could see his brother" — when somebody only cares about himself and ignores the plight of others — then "nor could any man rise from his place" — he will not be able to rise from his low spiritual state.

❧❦❧

וּלְכֹל בְּנֵי יִשְׂרָאֵל לֹא יֶחֱרַץ־כֶּלֶב לְשֹׁנוֹ

"But against all the Children of Israel, no dog shall whet its tongue" (11:7)

A chassid once appeared before R' Meir of Premishlan and lamented to the *rebbe* about his difficult financial situation.

"*Rebbe*," said the *chassid*, "I just don't know what to do. I work diligently from morning until night, yet I have no livelihood. What should I do?"

"I will teach you an important principle," answered the *rebbe*, "that will enable you to earn a living. In this week's *parashah* it states, 'But against all the Children of Israel, no dog shall whet its tongue.' This verse can be read in the following manner: '*U'lichol B'nei Yisrael lo yecheratz*' — it is important for every Jew to realize that it is not his "*charitzus*" (his strenuous efforts) that gives him a livelihood. Rather, "*k'lev leshono*" — he must make his heart (*leebo*) and tongue (*leshono*) match each other. In other words, a man's words should reflect his heart, and he should not act deceitfully. If he is honest and conducts his business with integrity, then he will be successful!"

וּלְכֹל בְּנֵי יִשְׂרָאֵל לֹא יֶחֱרַץ־כֶּלֶב לְשֹׁנוֹ

"But against all the Children of Israel, no dog shall whet its tongue" (11:7)

R' David Bodnick, one of the outstanding disciples of the *Alter* of Novaradok, was taking a stroll. Along the way, he passed the estate of an extraordinarily wealthy family.

There was a ferocious dog chained to a pole near the gate of the mansion to deter intruders. When the dog saw R' Bodnick, it began to bark wildly and it pulled on its chain. The chain was not strong enough and it finally snapped. The dog charged at R' Bodnick.

The master of the estate saw what was happening and realized that this was a life-threatening situation. He attempted to restrain his dog, but it was of no use; the dog overpowered its master and continued its charge towards R' Bodnick.

This dog is simply following the will of its Creator, thought R' Bodnick. *I too must now do the will of my Creator — I must now arouse myself to repent.*

R' Bodnick did just that. Amazingly, the fearsome dog calmed down and meekly returned to its pen.

וּלְכֹל בְּנֵי יִשְׂרָאֵל לֹא יֶחֱרַץ־כֶּלֶב לְשֹׁנוֹ

"But against all the Children of Israel,
no dog shall whet its tongue" (11:7)

The Dubno *Maggid* once visited to a certain town, and as was his custom, requested to deliver a *derashah* in the local *shul*.

The members of the congregation, who had drifted far away from the proper path, agreed to allow the *maggid* to speak — on one condition.

"We have heard, " said the community leaders, "that you illustrate your ideas with splendid parables. We would very much like to hear your parables. However, the members of this congregation have absolutely no interest in hearing *pesukim* from the Torah. We are therefore allowing you to speak, but with one stipulation: parables are fine, but no *pesukim*!"

"Perhaps you will allow me to first draw a parable to the words which you have just spoken," said the *maggid*. "A teacher decided to take his students on a hike through a nearby forest. As they neared the forest, the teacher turned to his students and exhorted them, 'My dear students! If on our way through the forest, dogs attack us — have no fear! Simply recite the verse, "But against all the Children of Israel, no dog shall whet its tongue." It is known that saying this verse is beneficial as a protection against dogs.'

"After several minutes of hiking, the teacher and his students were attacked by a pack of dogs. When he caught a glimpse of the dogs, the teacher wasted little time — and fled. The students, seeing their teacher run for his life, did the same.

"When they reached an area where they thought they would be safe, the students asked their teacher, 'Our teacher, why did you flee? Why did you not recite the verse "But against all the Children of Israel, no dog shall whet its tongue"'?

"'My students,' responded the teacher, 'you are correct, the verse would have indeed protected me. But what could I do, as the dogs didn't give me a chance to recite any *pesukim*.'"

וַיֹּאמֶר ה' אֶל־מֹשֶׁה וְאֶל־אַהֲרֹן ... דַּבְּרוּ אֶל־כָּל־עֲדַת יִשְׂרָאֵל

"Hashem said to Moshe and Aharon ...
Speak to the entire assembly of Israel" (12:1-3)

"**B**ut did Aharon speak?" asks Rashi. "Has it not already been said [to Moshe], '*You* shall speak'? Rather, [Moshe and Aharon] gave honor to one another ... and [Hashem's] speech would emerge from between the two of them as though they were both speaking."

R' Akiva Eiger and R' Yaakov of Lisa were traveling together to Warsaw to take part in a large rabbinical gathering.

The two *gedolei Yisrael* sat next to each other and discussed Torah topics the entire trip.

The Jews of Warsaw gathered in the hundreds to greet the two greatest Torah scholars of the generation, and led them in a magnificent horse-drawn coach.

In their desire to accord honor to the *gedolim*, the *talmidei chachamim* of Warsaw released the horses and began to pull the coach themselves instead of the horses!

When R' Akiva Eiger witnessed this staggering display of honor, he thought, "*To whom are these people paying tribute? To R' Yaakov, of course!* With that, he got off the coach, and he, too, began to pull the coach.

R' Yaakov, who had not even noticed that R' Eiger had left the coach, peered from the window and thought, *This is honor fit for a king! Can there be any doubt that it is for the great R' Akiva Eiger?* R' Yaakov immediately descended and joined the others in pulling the coach. In their excitement, the people of Warsaw continued drawing the coach until someone noticed that it was empty.

Such was the honor that *gedolei Yisrael* would accord to one another!

וַיְהִי בַּחֲצִי הַלַּיְלָה וַה' הִכָּה כָל־בְּכוֹר

"It was at midnight that Hashem
smote every firstborn" (12:29)

The *Midrash Rabbah* learns from this verse that on that night the sun shone at midnight just as brightly as it shines at midday.

From where did the *Midrash* derive, asked the *Rebbe* R' Heschel of Cracow that the sun was shining at midnight?

The Torah states, answered R' Heschel, that "God named the light 'Day,' and the darkness He named 'Night'" (*Bereishis* 1:5). The *Midrash* notes that the verse does not say, "*God* called the darkness 'Night.'" Why is Hashem's Name not mentioned in reference to the night? The answer, says the *Midrash*, is that Hashem does not associate His Name with anything bad, only with that which is good.

Here, said R' Heschel, the verse states, "It was at midnight that *Hashem* smote every firstborn." Why did the Holy One allow His Name to be mentioned in a verse dealing with the night?

This is how *Chazal* deduced, concluded R' Heschel, that the sun must have been shining at midnight in the same way that it shines at noon!

✎⃝❧

וּמוֹשַׁב בְּנֵי יִשְׂרָאֵל אֲשֶׁר יָשְׁבוּ בְּמִצְרָיִם
שְׁלֹשִׁים שָׁנָה וְאַרְבַּע מֵאוֹת שָׁנָה:

"The habitation of the Children of Israel during which they dwelled in Egypt was four hundred and thirty years" (12:40)

The Gemara (*Sanhedrin* 91a) relates the following story: A delegation of the Egyptian people once appeared before Alexander the Great and made a claim against the Jewish nation.

"The Jews," claimed the Egyptians, "owe us all the gold and silver that they took from us before they left Egypt."

An elderly Jew by the name of Geviha ben Pesisa turned to the Sages of Israel and made the following request: "Please permit me to respond to their claim," he said. "For if my argument is rebuffed, the Egyptians can be told that they defeated no more than a simple old man. However, if I succeed, we can declare that the Torah of Moshe *Rabbeinu* has triumphed."

The Sages granted Gevihah permission to offer a rebuttal.

He rose to his feet and asked the Egyptians, "How do you know that we took your silver and gold before we left Egypt?"

"Why, this is a fact that is stated explicitly in the Torah!" was their response.

"In that case," said Gevihah, "I, too, would like to bring a proof from the Torah. Scripture states, 'The habitation of the Children of

Israel during which they dwelled in Egypt was 430 years.' During those years the Egyptians forced 600,000 Jews to perform oppressive labor. If so, first reimburse us for the work we did; that is, the work that 600,000 laborers endured at your hands for 430 years!"

The Egyptians, needless to say, were taken aback by his response and quickly ran away.

שִׁבְעַת יָמִים תֹּאכַל מַצֹּת וּבַיּוֹם ... מַצּוֹת יֵאָכֵל אֵת שִׁבְעַת הַיָּמִים

"For a seven-day period shall you eat matzos ... Matzos shall be eaten throughout the seven-day period" (13:6-7)

Due to a terrible famine, the *gabbai tzedakah* of Vilna's *kimcha d'pischa* fund decided to give less money to the poor of the city than what they used to give.

When the Vilna *Gaon* heard of this decision, he immediately summoned the *gabba'im*. When they arrived, he asked them the following:

"Why is it that in *Parashas Bo* the word 'matzos' is first spelled without the letter *vav* while in the next verse it is spelled *with* the *vav*?

"The answer," said the *Gaon*, "is as follows: In the first verse (13:6), the Torah is discussing an individual's personal obligation to eat matzah on Pesach, as the verse states, 'For a seven-day period shall *you* eat matzos.' When you are dealing only with yourself, you have the right to limit how much you eat, and to abstain to whatever degree you choose. The Torah is alluding to this by spelling 'matzos' lacking a *vav*. But in the next verse (13:7) the Torah is referring to matzah that others will eat. This is as the verse states, 'Matzos shall be eaten.' When it comes to the needs of others, we have no right to be thrifty; we are required to provide them with all that they need. That is why in this verse, the Torah spells '*matzos*' in its complete form, including the '*vav*.'"

אֶרֶץ זָבַת חָלָב וּדְבָשׁ

"A land flowing with milk and honey" (13:5)

All his life, the *Chofetz Chaim* yearned to emigrate to *Eretz Yisrael*. His love for the Holy Land ran very deep, and he constantly referred to it with longing.

In the year 5640, the *Chofetz Chaim* married off his daughter to R' Aharon HaKohen. As was the custom in those times, the *Chofetz Chaim* pledged to provide his son-in-law with his daily meals for a number of years.

"But I am making a clear stipulation with you," said the *Chofetz Chaim*, "that under no circumstances will you prevent me from moving to *Eretz Yisrael* during those years."

PARASHAS BESHALACH

דַּבֵּר אֶל־בְּנֵי יִשְׂרָאֵל וְיָשֻׁבוּ וְיַחֲנוּ לִפְנֵי פִּי הַחִירֹת

"Speak to the Children of Israel and let them turn back and encamp before Pi-hachiros" (14:2)

THIS VERSE, SAID THE *OHEV YISRAEL* (R' AVRAHAM YEHOSHUA OF Apta), hints at an important lesson. It teaches us just how cautious one has to be not to violate the grave sin of *lashon hara*. "*V'yashuvu V'yachanu*" — A person is required to sit (*lasheves*) and pause for a moment (*v'yachanu*) — "*lifnei Pi-hachiros*" — before (*lifnei*) he lets his mouth (*peev*) loose (*cheirus*).

וַיִּקַּח שֵׁשׁ־מֵאוֹת רֶכֶב בָּחוּר

"He took six hundred elite chariots" (14:7)

The *Midrash* asks: Whose horses were used for the Egyptians' chariots and army? If you suggest that the horses belonged to the Egyptians themselves, that would be impossible, as the Torah has previously stated, "And all the livestock of Egypt died" (9:6). Perhaps they were Jewish-owned horses that the Jews left behind? This, too, cannot be, as Moshe *Rabbeinu* told Pharaoh earlier, "And our livestock, as well, will go with us — not a hoof will be left" (10:26).

So whose horses were they?

The Torah tells us concerning the Plague of Hail, "Whoever among Pharaoh's servants feared the word of Hashem hurried his servants and his livestock into the houses" (9:20).

We can therefore deduce that the horses used by the Egyptians to pursue the Jewish people were the ones that belonged to those who "feared the word of Hashem." Whatever fear of Heaven they possessed, however, was apparently not enough to prevent them from handing over their horses for the express purpose of chasing the Jews!

This prompted R' Shimon to say, "Even the best of snakes — crush its head."

וַיִּקַּח שֵׁשׁ־מֵאוֹת רֶכֶב בָּחוּר
"He took six hundred elite chariots" (14:7)

Several students and relatives of the Maharam Shif were puzzled by something that they had seen in his writings.

They noticed that he had jotted down the aforementioned verse, but in an unusual fashion. He had written the following: "*Vayikach shesh, me'os rechev, bachur.*" What did this cryptic inscription mean? They finally decided to approach the rav and ask him personally.

"I will explain my intentions to you," said the Maharam Shif. "'*Vayikach shesh*' — if one subtracts the number six (literally, "takes six"), '*me'os rechev*' — from the word, '*rechev*' (*me'os* literally means "hundreds," but the Maharam Shif homiletically read it, "*mei'os*," "from the word"), which has the numerical value of two hundred and twenty two, he is left with the number two hundred and sixteen — the exact numerical value of the word '*bachur*.'"

ה' יִלָּחֵם לָכֶם וְאַתֶּם תַּחֲרִשׁוּן:
"Hashem will do battle for you,
but you shall remain silent" (14:14)

R' Yaakov Yosef of Ostroh was a well-known *maggid* and one of the foremost disciples of the legendary *Maggid* of Mezirich. On one occasion, he visited a town and noticed that its inhabitants appeared depressed and worried.

R' Yaakov Yosef approached one of the them and asked him, "Why are you all so unhappy?"

"We have recently received very bad tidings," he responded. "The *poritz* (landlord) has demanded that the townspeople pay him an exorbitant amount of money; needless to say, we don't have that much money. When the *poritz* doesn't receive his money there is no telling what he might do, and we are afraid of his wrath."

When R' Yaakov Yosef ascended the podium, he began to speak with much emotion. "My dear Jews," he pleaded, "I am well aware that this is a time of great distress for you. But I assure you that if you commit yourselves to not speaking about mundane matters in *shul*, all of your worries will vanish! For this is as the verse teaches us, 'Hashem will do battle for you, but you shall remain silent.' If *you remain silent* then *Hashem will do battle for you*, and you will be saved."

⋘⊙⋙

וַיִּירְאוּ הָעָם אֶת־ה' וַיַּאֲמִינוּ בַּה' וּבְמֹשֶׁה עַבְדּוֹ:

"And the people revered Hashem, and they had faith in Hashem and Moshe, his servant" (14:31)

A t that moment, said the *mashgiach* of the Mir Yeshivah, R' Yerucham Levovitz, the Jewish people reached the highest level of faith in Hashem. They achieved the level of pure and unshakable faith. They had faith in Him and they followed His servant Moshe.

A simple Jew once had attended a fiery speech delivered by R' Yisrael Salanter on the topic of placing one's trust in Hashem. At one point during the speech, R' Salanter stated that an individual who trusts Hashem wholeheartedly is guaranteed to receive all of his needs by Hashem.

R' Salanter's words made a strong impression upon the man. He quit his job and waited in his home for his livelihood to come to him. He believed in his heart that Hashem would send him 10,000 rubles.

After some time had passed and the money had not arrived, the man went to R' Salanter and asked him, "*Rebbe*, I have done as you instructed. I even left my job and trusted that Hashem would provide me with 10,000 rubles — but the money still has not come"

"I'll tell you what," answered R' Salanter. "I am willing to give you 5,000 rubles now, for the 10,000 that Hashem is soon to send your way."

The man agreed happily and accepted R' Salanter's strange offer.

"You now see for yourself," said R' Yisrael, "that you don't truly believe that you are going to receive the money. For if you did, would you ever be willing to exchange 10,000 rubles for a mere 5,000? This is a sign that your faith is not complete!"

❧◊❧

כָּל־הַמַּחֲלָה אֲשֶׁר־שַׂמְתִּי בְמִצְרַיִם
לֹא־אָשִׂים עָלֶיךָ כִּי אֲנִי ה' רֹפְאֶךָ:

"Then any of the diseases that I placed in Egypt, I will not bring upon you, for I am Hashem, your healer" (15:26)

The Rambam was the personal physician of the king of Egypt. Under his care, the king never took ill and always remained in the best of health.

"How can I be sure," said the king to the Rambam, "that you are truly a proficient physician? After all, my health never falters. What if I would take ill — would you be adept at healing me?"

"The best type of doctor," answered the Rambam, "is one who is able to prevent the patient from getting sick in the first place — and *not* the one who proves capable of healing him once he has taken ill. This is as it states in our holy Torah, "Then any of the diseases that I placed in Egypt, I will not bring upon you, for I am Hashem, your healer" — I am Hashem your healer, who will make sure that all of the diseases that were prevalent in Egypt will not come upon you to begin with."

הִנְנִי מַמְטִיר לָכֶם לֶחֶם מִן־הַשָּׁמַיִם וְיָצָא הָעָם וְלָקְטוּ
דְּבַר־יוֹם בְּיוֹמוֹ לְמַעַן אֲנַסֶּנּוּ הֲיֵלֵךְ בְּתוֹרָתִי אִם־לֹא:

"Behold — I shall rain down for you food from heaven; let the people go out and pick each day's portion on its day, so that I can test them, whether they will follow My teaching or not" (16:4)

Commenting on this verse, the *Mechilta* states, "The Torah was not given to anyone other than those who ate the *manna*."

The Kotzker *rebbe* opened the door to his study and called for his attendant.

"Tell me," asked the Kotzker. "How do people explain the *Mechilta's* statement, 'The Torah was not given to anyone other than those who ate the *manna*'?"

"The explanation that I have heard," replied the attendant, "is that this statement refers to those individuals who are supported by others and are spared the concern of having to earn a livelihood on their own. Because they are free of the yoke of earning a living, they are able to sit and study Torah with peace of mind — these individuals are the eaters of *manna* that *Chazal* are referring to."

"I say it means the exact opposite!" countered the Kotzker. "The *Mechilta* is referring to those individuals who have to struggle day after day just to provide bread for their families! Despite their hardship, however, they do not worry; they simply place their trust in Hashem, knowing that He will provide them with their daily sustenance. Such individuals are truly similar to the generation that ate the *manna*, who gathered each day's portion, without the slightest concern over where the next day's sustenance would come from. It is to Jews such as these — Jews who trust in Hashem wholeheartedly — that the Torah was given!"

וְלָקְטוּ דְּבַר־יוֹם בְּיוֹמוֹ

The *Midrash* relates that R' Shimon bar Yochai was asked by his students why were the Jews only given one day's worth of *manna* at a time instead of giving them the *manna* once a year for the entire year.

"And pick each day's portion on its day" (16:4)

"I will answer with a parable," said R' Shimon. "To what can this idea be compared? To the son of a king, whose father provided him with an entire year's worth of sustenance and necessities at one time. How often did the king get to see his son? No more than once a year.

"The king thought, *I love my son so much yet I only get to see him once a year.* The king therefore called for his son and told him, "Until today, you have received your yearly sustenance all at once; from now on it will be given to you on a daily basis."

"The same is true," said R' Shimon, "regarding the Jewish people. Anybody who had children would say to himself, *It is true that today there was a sufficient amount of manna for my entire family — but what will be tomorrow? Perhaps tomorrow manna will not fall from*

heaven? I must pray to Hashem that He send us manna every day.
Thus the Jews turned to Hashem each and every day."

❧❦

לִקְטוּ מִמֶּנּוּ אִישׁ לְפִי אָכְלוֹ

"Collect from it, each man according to what he eats" (16:16)

The leaders of Vilna's Jewish community tried many times to convince R' Moshe Kramer to accept the position of Rabbi of Vilna, but due to his great humility, he consistently refused their offer.

After much imploring, R' Kramer finally agreed to assume the position as rabbi but with one condition. He would serve as their rabbi only if they would not give him a salary.

In order to provide for his family, R' Kramer opened a small grocery shop. He spent the entire day in the *beis midrash* engrossed in Torah study, while his wife managed the store.

The people of Vilna liked shopping at R' Kramer's store because they knew that his wife was impeccably honest and that the produce in the store was always fresh and of good quality. In addition, they knew that by purchasing from the grocery they would be supporting their great rabbi.

Eventually, R' Kramer realized that his store was reaping substantial profits and the till was always full of money. He turned to his wife and said, "I have a request to ask of you: At some point each day, check the register and see if we have earned enough for our needs that day. If you find that we have, then, please, close the store immediately."

"Why?" asked his wife. "The business is faring well, and we are earning such large profits!"

"In this week's *parashah*," responded R' Kramer, "the Torah tells us that Moshe *Rabbeinu* said to the Jewish people, 'Collect from it, each man according to what he eats. This comes to teach us that a person should not try to amass more than what he needs for that day."

❧❦

וַיְהִי בַּיּוֹם הַשְּׁבִיעִי יָצְאוּ מִן־הָעָם לִלְקֹט וְלֹא מָצָאוּ:

"It happened on the seventh day that some of the people did go out to collect [manna], but they did not find any" (16:27).

Why, asked R' Meir of Premishlan, does the verse use the expression, "but they did not find any," implying that there was *manna* but they couldn't find it. After all, the *manna* did not fall on Shabbos at all, so the verse should have read, "but there wasn't any."

The wording of the verse, answered the *rebbe*, can be explained with what is taught in the *Yalkut Shimoni*: When Moshe *Rabbeinu* informed the Jews that the *manna* would not fall on Shabbos so they should gather a double portion on *erev Shabbos*, Dasan and Aviram thought of a scheme that would make it appear to the people that Moshe does not speak the truth.

"Moshe *Rabbeinu* is mistaken!" they announced to the people. "When you wake up on Shabbos morning, you will see that the *manna* will have fallen just as it falls on every other day of the week."

What did they do? Early Shabbos morning, before anyone else had risen, Dasan and Aviram quietly left their tents, and maliciously scattered some of their *manna* around the tents of the Jewish people. This way, they reasoned, when the Jews wake up in the morning and see the *manna*, they will think that it had descended on Shabbos and that Moshe had lied to them.

Hashem, however, saw to it that their wicked scheme would not succeed. He sent birds to the Jewish encampment to eat all the *manna* that had been placed around the tents.

When the Jews awoke and saw that *manna* had not descended that day, they immediately declared, "Moshe is truth!"

This is why, concluded the *rebbe*, the verse states, "but they did not find any," as the Jewish people did not find any of the *manna* that Dasan and Aviram said they would find.

שֵׁם הָאֶחָד גֵּרְשֹׁם כִּי אָמַר גֵּר הָיִיתִי בְּאֶרֶץ נָכְרִיָּה:

"The name of one was Gershom (stranger there),
for [Moshe] had said, 'I was a stranger
in a foreign land'" (18:3)

MOSHE *RABBEINU*, SAID THE *CHOFETZ CHAIM*, CALLED HIS SON Gershom because he wished to be reminded daily that his life in this world was but a temporary one, like a stranger living in a foreign land.

The *Chofetz Chaim* explained this idea with a parable: A merchant once went to a fair in order to purchase merchandise at a low cost. The fair was being held in a distant location, so the merchant was forced to part with his family for a long time.

Before he left home, the merchant comforted his wife and children: "Do not be upset. Its true that I will be away for long time and I will certainly miss all of you, but the time will pass quickly and, with the help of Hashem, I will soon return home. You have my word that I will not tarry a moment longer than necessary." The merchant then gathered his belongings and went on his way.

After a long trip, the merchant arrived at the fair. Without wasting any time, he hurried to the marketplace and began investigating the merchandise.

At one of the booths, he met a friend whom he had not seen in many years. After exchanging warm greetings, the friend suggested to the merchant that they leave the fair and go to a quiet area for a day or two, where they could sit and share memories from the past.

"I'm sorry," replied the merchant, "but I cannot accept your offer. Do you think I left my wife and children to engage in frivolous conversations? Did I travel to such a distant land for my amusement? As soon as I finish acquiring the merchandise I need, I will immediately rush home."

So it is with man, said the *Chofetz Chaim*. Every individual is placed in the world for the express purpose of fulfilling Hashem's will by doing *mitzvos* and performing good deeds. But then the *yetzer hara* tries to lure the person into wasting his precious time on meaningless pursuits.

Therefore, concluded the *Chofetz Chaim*, a person must say to his *yetzer hara* exactly what the merchant said to his friend: Did I come to this world in order to engage in foolishness? Do not even attempt to beguile me into wasting my precious time!

✦✦✦

וַיָּבֹא יִתְרוֹ חֹתֵן מֹשֶׁה וּבָנָיו וְאִשְׁתּוֹ אֶל־מֹשֶׁה

"Yisro, Moshe's father-in-law, came to Moshe" (18:5).

R' Yehoshua of Belz asked: Why does the verse state, "Yisro … came (*vayavo*)," and not "Yisro *went* (*vayeilech*) from Midyan," as the Torah says in relation to Yaakov *Avinu*, "And he went (*vayeilech*) toward Charan?"

The word "*vayeilech*," answered the *rebbe*, connotes an individual's leaving slowly and against his will. "*Vayavo*," on the other hand, implies a going that is full of joy and eagerness.

Yaakov *Avinu* did not want to leave his home in *Eretz Yisrael*, but he was forced to do so and go to Charan on account of Esav's wicked intentions. His departure is therefore aptly described as "*vayeilech*." But Yisro was eager to become part of the Jewish people and to find his place under the protection of Hashem's Divine presence. For him, then, the appropriate wording is "*vayavo*" — he *came* eagerly and full of joy.

✦✦✦

וְאַתָּה תֶחֱזֶה מִכָּל־הָעָם אַנְשֵׁי־חַיִל
יִרְאֵי אֱלֹקִים אַנְשֵׁי אֱמֶת שֹׂנְאֵי בָצַע

"And you shall select from among the entire people, men of wealth who are God fearing, men of truth who despise monetary gain" (18:21).

Why, asked the Kotzker *Rebbe*, did Moshe *Rabbeinu* appoint "leaders of thousands, leaders of hundreds, leaders of fifty and leaders of tens"? Was he not afraid that perhaps such an appointment might offend some of them if they would be appointed to a post of lesser status than that of their fellows?

However, answered the Kotzker, remember that the Torah describes these individuals as being "men of truth." A man of truth knows that honor is a lie and an illusion. Therefore none of these individuals felt offended by seeing someone else receive a higher position than they.

✿❦✿

וַיִּחַן־שָׁם יִשְׂרָאֵל נֶגֶד הָהָר:

"And Israel camped there facing the mountain" (19:2)

Rashi points out that the word "*vayichan*" is in the singular, despite the fact that the Torah was describing the encampment of thousands of Jews. This teaches us, says Rashi, that at this particular encampment the Jewish people were united — "as one man, with one heart."

In the Pesach *Haggadah*, asked R' Yitzchak of Vorki, it states, "Had He brought us before Har Sinai, but not given us the Torah, it would have sufficed us." These words are perplexing, for why would simply arriving at Har Sinai suffice for us if it would not have resulted in our receiving the Torah?

The answer, said the *rebbe*, is as follows: When describing the Jewish nation's encampment at Har Sinai, the Torah tells us, "And Israel encamped there facing the mountain" — as one man, with one heart. Even had we not received the Torah, it would have been worthwhile for us to be brought before Har Sinai just so that we could achieve such complete unity.

✿❦✿

וּמֹשֶׁה עָלָה אֶל־הָאֱלֹקִים

"Moshe went up to God" (19:3)

The Gemara (*Shabbos* 88b) relates that when Moshe *Rabbeinu* ascended on high to receive the Torah, the angels came before Hashem and asked, "What is this mortal doing among us?"

"He has come to receive the Torah," was Hashem's response.

"This Torah, the treasure that has been concealed for nine hundred and seventy-four generations before the world was created, you wish to give to Man? But is it not written, 'Place Your majesty on the heavens' (*Tehillim* 8:2)? So give *us* the Torah!"

"Give the angels an answer to their claim," said Hashem to Moshe.

"I am afraid," replied Moshe, "lest the angels incinerate me with the breath of their mouths."

"In that case," said Hashem, "take hold of My throne of glory and then answer them!"

"Master of the World," said Moshe, "what is written in this Torah that You are giving me? — 'I am Hashem, your God, Who has taken you out of the land of Egypt, from the house of slavery' (*Shemos* 20:2)."

Moshe then turned to the angels and asked, "Did you descend to Egypt? Were you ever enslaved to Pharaoh? If not, why do you need the Torah?"

Moshe continued to press the angels: "The Torah states," said Moshe, 'You shall not recognize the gods of others' (ibid. 3). Do you dwell among nations that worship false gods? Furthermore, in the Torah it is written, 'Remember the Shabbos day to sanctify it' (ibid. 8). Do you engage in any type of labor from which you would need to refrain?

"The Torah also states 'Honor your father and your mother' (ibid. 12). Do you have a father or mother to honor?"

Immediately, the angels conceded to Hashem that the appropriate place for the Torah is earth, and they said, "Hashem, our Master, how mighty is Your Name throughout the earth!" (*Tehillim* 8:2).

וַיִּתְיַצְּבוּ בְּתַחְתִּית הָהָר:

"And they stood at the bottom of the mountain" (19:17)

Chazal (*Shabbos* 88a) expound on this verse, "This teaches us that [Hashem] suspended the mountain on them like a barrel and said, 'If you will accept the Torah then it will be good [for you], but if you will not — there you shall be buried!'"

Chazal are telling us, said the *Chofetz Chaim*, that if not for the Torah, the entire world would simply cease to exist. This is as the verse states, "If not for My covenant with the night and with the day, I would not have set up the laws of heaven and earth" (*Yirmeyahu* 33:25).

Had the Jewish people refused to accept the Torah, *every* living being — and not only those who were present at the giving of the Torah — would have been buried beneath the ruins of an overturned world. This is also implied by *Chazal*'s wording: "*there* you shall be buried," and not, "*here* you shall be buried" — not only will those who are here be buried but also those who are not here will be buried "there" — wherever they may be.

The *Chofetz Chaim* expended much effort in distributing his *sefarim*. He would travel from city to city selling his works and spreading his Torah. One of his trips took him to the city of Warsaw, where he was the guest of R' Naftali Zilberberg. R' Naftali, who did not recognize his guest, asked him for the purpose of his trip.

"*Baruch Hashem*, I have merited to author a small *sefer*," answered the *Chofetz Chaim*, "and I travel from city to city selling copies of it."

Their conversation carried on for approximately an hour. R' Naftali then rose from his chair and apologized, "Please excuse me, but I must go and deliver a *shiur* in the local *shul*. It was truly a pleasure speaking with you and making your acquaintance, but if we would carry on like this, when would we be able to occupy ourselves with Torah study?"

"I most certainly agree with the *Rav*," answered the *Chofetz Chaim*, "that there is nothing loftier than the study of Torah. However, don't think that our discussion was a mundane conversation, for neither of us said a word of *lashon hara* during the entire discussion. Such a conversation can also be considered Torah."

When R' Naftali heard these words from his guest, he began to wonder.

"What exactly is the title of the *sefer* you authored?" asked R' Naftali.

"*Chofetz Chaim*," was the response.

R' Naftali jumped from his place in awe and said, "I beg the *Rav's* forgiveness for showing disrespect to your honor with my previous comment."

From then on, R' Naftali made it a point to meet with the *Chofetz Chaim* from time to time and engage him in conversations that would last for many hours.

"Listening to the *Chofetz Chaim*," said R' Naftali, "is learning *divrei Torah* in the fullest sense of the word!"

זָכוֹר אֶת־יוֹם הַשַּׁבָּת לְקַדְּשׁוֹ:

"Remember the Shabbos day to sanctify it" (20:8)

Hashem proclaimed the commandments to "Remember the Shabbos" and "Safeguard the Shabbos" in a single utterance. This is derived from the fact that in *Parashas Yisro* the Torah lists "*Remember the Shabbos*" as one of the Ten Commandments, yet in *Parashas Va'eschanan* (*Devarim* 5:12) it is listed as "*Safeguard* the Shabbos."

We *remember* the Shabbos by honoring Shabbos with eating delicacies, wearing special clothes and doing other acts of respect. But we *safeguard* the Shabbos when we are careful not to desecrate the Shabbos and we avoid certain forbidden activities.

For the poor and unfortunate, said the Dubno *Maggid*, it is very easy to fulfill the *mitzvah* of safeguarding the Shabbos. After all, they are not involved in very many activities to begin with, and whatever work they do to earn their meager livelihood can be put off until after Shabbos. However, the *mitzvah* of remembering the Shabbos is so difficult for them to fulfill, as they can afford neither meat nor wine. All they get to eat is plain bread and water.

On the other hand, continued the *Maggid*, the wealthy encounter very little difficulty when it comes to honoring the Shabbos. They can afford the tastiest foods, the most regal garments, and the fanciest dishes. For them, "remembering the Shabbos" is easy, but safeguarding the Shabbos can be very difficult for them. It is so hard for them to refrain from thinking about their business affairs and various ways to earn more profit.

This is why, concluded the *Maggid*, Hashem stated, "Remember the Shabbos" and "Safeguard the Shabbos" in one utterance. It is meant to teach us that every single Jew — whether rich or poor — must do his utmost to fulfill *both* remembering and safeguarding the Shabbos!

לֹא־תַעֲשֶׂה כָל־מְלָאכָה
"You must not do any work" (20:10)

When R' Yaakov Yosef Herman decided to emigrate to *Eretz Yisrael*, he packed up all his belongings and, along with his wife, boarded a ship that was to sail for the Holy Land.

Then, in the middle of their trip, World War II broke out. When the captain of the ship heard that war had begun, he became afraid that their ship may be attacked. He therefore decided to take a safer, but roundabout route that would extend the trip by several days.

The ship finally reached *Eretz Yisrael* on a Friday afternoon with only one hour left before Shabbos. The port was bustling with activity. On all sides there were loudspeakers blaring an announcement to the passengers telling them to leave the ship at once and to wait for their luggage to be unloaded.

If I wait for my luggage, thought R' Herman, *it will certainly result in my desecrating the Shabbos, and that I am not about to do.*

R' Herman turned to a senior official and said, "Please stamp our passports; we would like to leave."

"But what about your luggage?" asked the surprised officer.

"All my life," responded R' Herman, "I have taken great care not to desecrate the holy Shabbos. I will certainly not do so now, when I have finally merited moving to *Eretz Yisrael!*"

"Do what you like," said the officer, "but I must warn you that all of your belongings will by stolen by the Arab porters. When they see unclaimed baggage they will not hesitate to take it all. You and your wife will be left with nothing."

"I am willing to declare all of my property ownerless," exclaimed R' Herman, "as long as I will not have to desecrate the Shabbos!"

The officer stamped their passports and permitted them to leave.

That Shabbos R' Herman was very happy. "Hashem does absolutely everything for me," said R' Herman. "Finally, I was given a chance to do a small something for Him."

After Shabbos, R' Herman's wife suggested that they return to the port. "Maybe there is something left of our luggage after all," she said.

R' Herman and his wife arrived at the desolate port and encountered no one but a lone watchman standing alongside the ship.

"Who are you?" asked the watchman.

"My name is Yaakov Herman," answered the rabbi.

"It's a good thing that you came," said the watchman. "The port manager ordered me to remain here and look after your luggage. He gave me specific instructions that I dare not leave my post until you return to claim your belongings. They're untouched and you are free to take them."

כַּבֵּד אֶת־אָבִיךָ וְאֶת־אִמֶּךָ

"Honor your father and your mother" (20:12)

One night, the holy Tanna R' Yehoshua ben Elam was told in a dream, "Be happy with your portion, for you and Nanas the butcher will sit together in *Gan Eden*. His portion and yours are equal!"

R' Yehoshua awoke in a terrible fright. He was very distraught, as he thought, *Woe is me! Since the day that I was born, I have constantly feared Hashem. All my days I have toiled in Torah study; I have eighty students, and I do not walk even four amos without tallis and tefillin. Can it be that all of my deeds are no greater than those of an ordinary butcher? Why does my portion equal his?"*

I must seek out this butcher, thought R' Yehoshua, *and discover the noteworthy deeds that he has done to earn himself a place in Gan Eden alongside me.*

R' Yehoshua and his students traveled from city to city and from town to town, trying to locate the butcher. In each place that they stopped, they asked the inhabitants, "Perhaps one of you has heard of Nanas the butcher?" But no one had.

They continued traveling for many days, until R' Yehoshua and his students arrived in a small town.

"Of course we know Nanas," answered one of the townspeople, "but why would such a holy Jew as yourself want to meet with a *butcher?*"

"I wish to speak with him," replied R' Yehoshua. "Please ask him to come to me."

The townspeople arrived at the home of Nanas the butcher. "R' Yehoshua ben Elam wishes to see you," they said to Nanas. "Come immediately!"

They must be jesting with me, thought the butcher. *What business do I have with R' Yehoshua?* "I will not come with you!" answered Nanas to the townspeople, "You are only teasing me!"

The townspeople returned to R' Yehoshua. "Nanas refuses to come," they said. "He didn't believe us when we told him that you want to see him."

So R' Yehoshua set out for the house of Nanas the butcher. When Nanas saw R' Yehoshua, he became very frightened. He immediately fell on his face and pleaded with R' Yehoshua to forgive him for troubling a *tzaddik* of his stature to walk to his home.

"Please tell me," R' Yehoshua asked the butcher, "what are your deeds?"

"I am but a simple butcher," responded Nanas, "and all my days are spent in my butcher shop. However, I have an aged father and mother who are unable to stand on their feet. Day after day, I wash them, dress them, and feed them."

R' Yehoshua stood up, kissed the butcher on his head, and said to him, "My son, You are praiseworthy and your lot is praiseworthy — how good it is and how pleasant! I am so fortunate that I have merited being your peer to sit in your section of *Gan Eden!*"

וְכָל־הָעָם רֹאִים אֶת־הַקּוֹלֹת
"The entire people saw the sounds" (20:15)

E ven as a young child, the *Chiddushei HaRim* (R' Yitzchak Meir of Gur) was hailed as a future *gadol b'Yisrael*; He was diligent and intellectually gifted. The scholars of his city very much enjoyed engaging him in Torah discussions.

"Perhaps you can tell me," said one of the scholars to the young Yitzchak Meir, "why the Torah tells us that the 'The entire people *saw* the sounds'? Would it not have been enough if they had only *heard* the sounds that came from Hashem? Why did they have to see the sounds as well?"

"Imagine for a moment," answered the child, "what would have happened had they not seen His voice. All the thieves would have claimed that when Hashem said '*lo signov,*' He meant *lo* spelled with a *vav*, which means '*his* you *should* steal,' so there is nothing wrong with stealing. Hashem therefore made a miracle that enabled everyone to see His voice. This way, it would be clear that Hashem said '*lo signov*' with the word '*lo*' spelled with a *lamed* and an *alef*, meaning, 'Do *not* steal.'"

PARASHAS MISHPATIM

וְאֵלֶּה הַמִּשְׁפָּטִים אֲשֶׁר תָּשִׂים לִפְנֵיהֶם
"These are the laws that you should present before them" (21:1)

T HE WORDS OF THIS VERSE, NOTED THE *BA'AL HATURIM*, CONTAINS an allusion to how a judge must conduct himself during a hearing:

"*V'eileh*" — **V**'chayav **a**dam **l**achkor **h**adin (An individual is required to investigate the case).

"hamishpatim" — **Ha**dayan **m**etzuveh **sh**eya'aseh **p**e'sharah **t**erem **y**a'aseh **m**ishpat (The judge is obligated to find a middle ground before he imposes a ruling),

"asher" — **i**m **sh**neihem **r**otzim (assuming that both parties are willing [to compromise]).

"tasim" — **T**ishma Shneihem **y**achad **m**edabrim (Listen to both parties as they speak).

"lifneihem" — **L**o **p**nei **n**adiv **y**ehader, **h**isnaker **m**eihem (Do not show favor to the wealthy man. Estrange yourself from them [from the litigants]).

⋰⋱

וְאֵלֶּה הַמִּשְׁפָּטִים אֲשֶׁר תָּשִׂים לִפְנֵיהֶם:

"These are the laws that you should present before them" (21:1)

The words, "*And* these," says Rashi, is used to add to the previous portion, the Ten Commandments. They imply that just as the Ten Commandments are from Sinai, so, too, these commandments that the Torah is about to state were given at Sinai.

Rashi's comment is hard to understand, noted the *Chiddushei HaRim*: The entire Torah, including all the novel interpretations that will ever be formulated, was presented to the Jewish people at Mount Sinai. Why, then, must we be told separately that the civil laws were given to us on Mount Sinai?

There are certain *mitzvos*, answered the *rebbe*, that are logical and self-explanatory. For instance, the Torah forbids stealing, but even without the Torah's prohibition, common sense would have told us that it's wrong to steal. Similarly, it seems to us that even if the Torah had not prohibited striking a fellow Jew we would nevertheless intuitively know that it's wrong to hit someone.

This is why, explained the *Chiddushei HaRim*, Rashi told us that these commandments were also given on Mount Sinai. He wanted us to realize that although these laws may be self-evident, if not for the fact that they were written in the Torah they would be absolutely meaningless. It is only due to the Torah's prohibitions that we are obligated to refrain from doing them.

הַמַּכֶּה רַק שִׁבְתּוֹ יִתֵּן וְרַפֹּא יְרַפֵּא:

"He shall, however, pay for his lost work-time and provide for his complete recovery " (21:19)

A Jew once came to R' Baruch Mordechai of Koidanov. Signs of intense suffering were etched on the man's face.

"*Rebbe*," said the man, "I have been suffering terribly for a long time. Please give me a *berachah* that I should recover from my illness."

"I will give you some advice," responded the *rebbe*. "Be extra careful to avoid Shabbos violations, and try your utmost to honor the Shabbos. Do so and Hashem will grant you a speedy recovery."

The man did as the *rebbe* had instructed. Shortly thereafter, the excruciating pain that he had been feeling began to subside. Finally, it went away altogether.

"Do not think that I performed a miracle," the *rebbe* later told his students. "It is a 'treatment' that the Torah itself recommends, as the verse states, '*Rak shivto yiten v'rapo yerapei.*' The word '*shivto*' can also be read '*shabato*,' meaning, 'his Shabbos.' The verse can therefore be read as follows: 'Let him give his Shabbos, and he will surely be healed.' That is, if a person pays attention to his Shabbos observance and honors it properly, then Hashem will provide him with a complete recovery."

וְרַפֹּא יְרַפֵּא:

"And he shall provide for his complete recovery" (21:19)

"From here we learn," state *Chazal* (*Berachos* 60a), "that a doctor has permission to heal."

In a certain city lived a wealthy businessman who used to mock the *chassidic* custom of asking *rebbes* for blessings for prosperity and salvation.

One day, the daughter of this businessman was stricken with a serious illness. The physicians did all they could to help the girl, but none of the remedies were successful. Finally, the doctors gave up hope.

The wealthy man had never been so distraught. He walked around all day with a somber face and a heavy heart. One day, a neighbor of his turned to him with a suggestion. "Listen to my advice. Go to the *tzaddik*, R' David Moshe of Chortkov, and ask him to pray for your sick daughter."

I should go to a rebbe and ask for a berachah? thought the man. *I have belittled such notions my entire life! But who knows? Maybe his berachah can help.* The wealthy man traveled to R' David Moshe and requested a *berachah* for his daughter.

"Tell me," said the *rebbe*, "What do the doctors say about your daughter's condition?"

"To my great sorrow, the doctors were unable to find a cure for her illness," responded the man sadly. "They have given up all hope, saying that she is beyond any form of treatment."

"Who gave these doctors the right to give up hope?" asked the *rebbe*. "They have been granted the right to heal — but not to give up hope!

"In our *Shacharis* prayers each morning," continued the *rebbe*, "we say that Hashem '*makes* salvations flourish,' but we do not say that He has '*made* salvations flourish' because Hashem constantly makes new salvations flourish. Return to your home, and Hashem will send salvation to your daughter!"

The wealthy man hurried home, and, to his amazement, he discovered that his daughter's condition had already improved. Within a few days her illness vanished, and she regained her former health.

עַיִן תַּחַת עַיִן
"An eye for an eye (21:24)

The term "eye for an eye," explain *Chazal* (*Bava Kamma* 84a), is not meant to be taken literally — one who causes another the loss of an eye is not punished by having to lose his own eye. Rather, it means that the responsible party must pay the monetary value of an eye.

Chazal's interpretation of this *halachah*, said the Vilna *Gaon*, is alluded to in words of the verse: Why does the verse state, "*Ayin tachas ayin*" — which literally means, "an eye *beneath* an eye" — and not "*Ayin be'ad ayin*" — which means "an eye *for* an eye"?

The Torah, explained the *Gaon,* is hinting to us that in order to discover the true meaning of the verse, we must look at what is "beneath" the *ayin,* that is the letters that follow the word "*ayin*":

The letter *ayin* is followed by the letter *Pei.*
The letter *yud* is followed by the letter *Kaf.*
The letter *nun* is followed by the letter *Samech.*
These letters form the word *keSePh,* "money"!

ഉ⊃൭

אִם־הִמָּצֵא תִמָּצֵא בְיָדוֹ הַגְּנֵבָה ... שְׁנַיִם יְשַׁלֵּם:

"If the stolen object is actually found in his possession ... he shall pay double" (22:3)

The students of R' Yochanan ben Zakkai asked him the following question: "Why is the Torah more stringent with a *ganav* (thief) than with a *gazlan* (robber), for a *ganav* is required to pay double the value of the item he stole while a *gazlan* does not have to pay double?"

"A *gazlan,*" answered R' Yochanan, "is one who fears neither Hashem nor the public. He steals openly, without the slightest feelings of embarrassment. Since he doesn't place society's opinion of him before Hashem's, he is free from paying the double payment. The *ganav,* on the other hand, does his deed furtively so that nobody will see him. Since he is more ashamed before man than before Hashem, he deserves a more severe penalty so he pays double."

R' Meir illustrated this distinction with a parable: There were once two people who each made a banquet. One invited everyone in the city to his banquet except for the king's sons. The other invited neither the city's residents nor the king's sons.

Both individuals displayed a lack of honor for the king, but which one will receive a harsher punishment? It will certainly be the one who invited all the city's residents but kept the king's sons out, as he demonstrated a greater degree of disrespect for the king.

וְנִקְרַב בַּעַל־הַבַּיִת אֶל־הָאֱלֹקִים
אִם־לֹא שָׁלַח יָדוֹ בִּמְלֶאכֶת רֵעֵהוּ:

"Then the owner of the house shall approach the judges that he did not lay his hand upon his fellow's property" (22:7)

The standard meaning of the word "*elohim*" in this verse is, "the judges"; but elsewhere it means "God" ("*Elokim*").

R' Meir of Premishlan once made the following remark to his *chassidim*: "*V'nikrav ba'al habayis el ha'Elokim*" — When does a person merit being drawn close to Hashem? "*Im lo shalach yado bi'meleches re'eihu*" — when he is free of any transgressions involving his fellow Jews and he makes sure not to harm others or their property.

כָּל־אַלְמָנָה וְיָתוֹם לֹא תְעַנּוּן:

"You shall not cause any pain to any widow or orphan" (22:21)

R' Levi Yitzchak of Berdichev lifted his pure eyes to Heaven and said, "Master of the World! You have exhorted us in Your Torah, 'You shall not cause any pain to any widow or orphan.' We, Your nation Israel, are orphans, as the *Navi* laments, 'We have become [like] orphans, and there is no father' (*Eichah* 5:3).

"I turn to You today, O Father in Heaven, and I beseech You to have mercy upon Your nation of orphans who are languishing in a bitter exile. The time has come for You to take us from darkness into light!"

אַחֲרֵי רַבִּים לְהַטֹּת

"By yielding to the majority to pervert [the law]" (23:2)

As a young child, R' Yitzchak Seckel (better known as the *Ba'al Shem* of Michelstadt) was known to be an outstanding prodigy.

Word of his genius eventually reached the ears of the Duke, who invited young R' Yitzchak to his palace for an audience.

The Duke's palace was enormous, containing scores of rooms and lavish halls. Wishing to test the child's intelligence, he ordered his entire staff of servants and housekeepers to leave his palace at once. *Let's see*, said the Duke to himself, *if this boy can locate my chamber without any assistance or direction.*

When R' Yitzchak arrived at the palace, he looked around but saw no sign of the Duke, nor did he have any idea where he might be. He began searching for clues that would enable him to discover the Duke's whereabouts. Then he noticed that there was one room in which the curtains were drawn.

This is a sure a sign, thought the young R' Yitzchak, *that the Duke is inside the room.* And so it was.

"How did you find me so quickly?" asked the Duke in amazement.

"It was not very difficult," he responded. "When I saw that the curtains were drawn in only one of your many rooms, I realized that you must have been hiding behind them."

"Now, what would you have done," asked the Duke, "if I had allowed my servants to remain in the palace but gave them instructions to mislead you and direct you to different rooms?"

"I would have listened to what each servant had to say," responded R' Yitzchak, "and then I would have looked in the room which the majority of servants said you were in."

"If you are so committed to following the majority," the Duke continued to ask, "why do you remain Jewish? After all, are not the Jews a minority?"

"Your highness, the Duke," answered R' Yitzchak, "Right now, you are sitting in this room. Even if your entire staff would try to persuade me that you are not in this room I would not believe them, for I can clearly see you sitting directly in front of me! The majority is only followed in a case of doubt, but when the matter is clear and obvious, the majority is irrelevant.

"That is why I remain a Jew," concluded young R' Yitzchak. "The Jewish people may be a minority in relation to the rest of the world, but the truth of Judaism is so clear that there is no reason to follow the majority."

מִדְּבַר־שֶׁקֶר תִּרְחָק

"Distance yourself from a false word" (23:7)

The following story illustrates the extraordinary care taken by
Gedolei Yisrael to cling to the truth and avoid any form of
falsehood:

R' Akiva Eiger received a letter containing a complex question sent
to him by the judges of the city of Blostok.

"I would like you to know," wrote R' Eiger, "that I generally do not
respond to questions that are sent to me from outside my district,
as you have your own rabbis and judges who are capable of
answering your questions. In this instance, however, I will deviate
from my custom and answer your question. Why? — because I
recently attended a *simchah* at which a member of your community was present. He approached me and requested that I respond to
your question, but I remained silent.

"Yet I fear," continued R' Eiger, "that I may have nodded my head
ever so slightly, and I may have given this man the false impression
that I agreed to respond to your question. That is why, this time, I will
answer your query ..."

PARASHAS TERUMAH

דַּבֵּר אֶל־בְּנֵי יִשְׂרָאֵל וְיִקְחוּ־לִי תְּרוּמָה

"Speak to the Children of Israel and let them take for Me a portion" (25:2)

WHY DOES THE VERSE STATE, "*TAKE* FOR ME A PORTION" AND
not "*give* Me a portion"?

The Torah is showing us the greatness vested in the *mitzvah* of giving *tzedakah*. When we fulfill the *mitzvah* of *tzedakah*, it may appear

as if we are giving, but in truth, we are actually *taking* (receiving) for ourselves a very great *mitzvah*.

The *Midrash Rabbah* elaborates on this idea: "More than what the host does for the poor man, the poor man does for the host." The host may have given the poor person a *perutah* for *tzedakah*, but the poor person has enabled the host to earn a *mitzvah* that is more valuable than "thousands in gold and silver" (*Tehillim* 119:72).

Someone who refuses to assist a poor person, said the *Chofetz Chaim*, can be compared to a farmer who piled up his wagon with wheat and then traveled to a large city in order to sell it. When the farmer arrived at the city, he was immediately met by dozens of eager customers waiting to purchase his produce. He was afraid, however, that the customers would attempt to deceive him by taking bundles of wheat without paying for them. He therefore told them, "Go ahead and fill your bags with wheat. But each time you fill up a bag, place one copper coin into my hat. When you finish filling your sacks, we will count the coins in my hat, and that way we will know how many sacks you have to pay for."

The customers agreed to the farmer's method and followed his instructions. The farmer's hat was soon full of shiny copper coins.

The farmer saw all the coins in his hat and was overcome by temptation. He quickly stole some of the coins and put them in his pocket.

How foolish is that farmer! remarked the *Chofetz Chaim*. He may have managed to swipe a few coins, but he will lose much more than he gained because when the time comes to pay for the wheat and the coins are counted, there will be less coins than sacks, and he will lose the payment for all those sacks. This foolish farmer will lose the payment of an entire sack of wheat for every coin that he took for himself!

This is also the case, said the *Chofetz Chaim*, when someone refuses to give *tzedakah*. He may hold on to a coin or two, but he will lose the immense reward from a *mitzvah* that could have been his.

וְיִקְחוּ־לִי תְּרוּמָה

"Take for Me a portion" (25:2)

S ays the *Yalkut Shimoni*: "'V'yikchu' — This is as the verse states, 'For I have given you a *lekach tov* (a good acquisition), do not forsake My Torah' (*Mishlei* 4:2)."

The Torah is the best "merchandise" that can ever be purchased.

This can be compared to two merchants who were in the same city doing business. One of the merchants purchased an array of silk and cotton materials; the other bought garments that were embroidered with gold trimmings.

That evening, the merchants met at an inn. They showed one another what they had acquired, and each one was very impressed by what he saw.

"Perhaps you would care to exchange goods?" said one merchant to the other. "Give me the materials that you bought, and I will give you the garments with the gold trimmings."

The other merchant agreed and they traded goods. When they set out for home, the one who had originally bought silk and cotton materials now had gold-trimmed garments instead, and the other businessman now had only the silk and cotton materials.

However, says the *Midrash*, this is not the case when it comes to the holy Torah. When an individual who has learned *Seder Mo'ed* meets an individual who has learned *Seder Zera'im*, he says to him, "Teach me *Seder Zera'im* and I will teach you *Seder Mo'ed*." After they have taught one another and learned from each other, they now possess not one but two *sedarim*!

Can there be a better type of acquisition?

מֵאֵת כָּל־אִישׁ אֲשֶׁר יִדְּבֶנּוּ לִבּוֹ

"From every man who feels generous" (25:2)

A pauper approached R' Shmelke of Nikolsburg and related a story of bitter misfortune and distress. "*Rebbe*," said the unfortunate Jew, "I am struggling to earn a livelihood, and I am unable to provide for my wife and children. My house is cold and bare of even the most basic necessities. I beg of you, *Rebbe*, please help me."

The *rebbe* listened to the man's words with compassion and concern. But he lacked any money to give the pauper, as he himself was quite poor, so he gave the man his wife's ring — it was the only item of value in the *rebbe*'s home.

When the *rebbetzin* discovered that her husband had given away her ring, she was shocked. "*Oy vey!*" she cried. "There is a diamond of great value set in that ring!"

When R' Shmelke heard his wife's words, he donned his coat and ran after the pauper.

A short while later, he returned home happy and in high spirits.

"Where is the ring?" asked the *rebbetzin*.

"Why, the pauper has it," responded R' Shmelke.

"So why did you run after the pauper?" asked the *rebbetzin*. "Did you not chase after the pauper in order to retrieve the ring?"

"Certainly not!" he answered. "I pursued him because I wanted to tell him that the ring contained a precious jewel and that he should make sure not to sell it at less than its true value."

מֵאֵת כָּל־אִישׁ אֲשֶׁר יִדְּבֶנּוּ לִבּוֹ

"From every man who feels generous" (25:2)

One day, a widow appeared before R' Aharon of Karlin, sobbing.

"What is the matter?" asked the *rebbe*. "Why are you crying?"

"My daughter recently got engaged," said the woman. "As is customary, I promised to provide the *chasan* with a dowry, but as I am a poor widow, I don't possess the means to keep my promise. The *chasan* has threatened to break off the match if I am unable to pay."

"How much have you promised to pay?" asked the *rebbe*.

"One hundred rubles," she answered.

The *rebbe* walked over to his bureau, removed one hundred rubles and handed it to the woman. The woman graciously thanked the *rebbe* and went on her way.

A few days later, the widow once again appeared before the *rebbe*, crying as before.

"Why are you crying now?" he asked her.

"How can I possibly marry off my daughter," she cried, "if I cannot afford to buy her a gown?"

R' Aharon inquired as to the cost of the gown. When the widow told him, he handed her the exact sum that she needed.

R' Aharon's *rebbetzin* turned to him and asked, "When the woman came to you the first time, her daughter's match was on the verge of being broken. You therefore provided her with the necessary funds, as it is a very great *mitzvah* to come to the aid of a *kallah*. The second time, however, the woman appealed to you for a gown for her daughter. Not having a gown would not have resulted in the breaking of the match. Why, then, did you give her the sum that she needed; would it not have been better for the money to be given to the poor and needy?"

"I, too," answered the *rebbe*, "had similar thoughts. *Maybe this money should be given to a poor person who is unable to meet his most basic needs*, I wondered. But then I asked myself: *Where did my thought to give money to the poor come from? Did it stem from my yetzer tov or from my yetzer hara?* If it truly came from my *yetzer tov*, then why did he not urge me to give the money to the poor yesterday? Was it only today, at exactly the moment the crying woman approached me, that the *yetzer tov* remembered the suffering of the poor?

"It must be," concluded the *rebbe*, "that it was the *yetzer hara*'s plot! Once I realized this, I refused to listen to him."

וְיִקְחוּ־לִי תְרוּמָה מֵאֵת כָּל־אִישׁ אֲשֶׁר יִדְּבֶנּוּ לִבּוֹ

"You shall take selected contributions for Me from every man who feels generous" (25:2)

A wealthy Jew approached the *Chofetz Chaim* and said, "*Rebbe*, the Holy One has blessed me with much success in my endeavors. I am a very wealthy man, and I would like to finance the building of a magnificent new yeshivah. My only condition is that the yeshivah be named after me."

"You have very good intentions," responded the *Chofetz Chaim*, "but I cannot accept your offer because I would like to give all Jews the opportunity to partake in the special *mitzvah* of building a yeshivah. For the verse states, 'You shall take selected contributions from every man who feels generous,' despite the fact that the Jews had left Egypt with an abundance of wealth and each one of them could have afforded funding the building of the entire *Mishkan*. Why was it necessary for *all* the Jews to contribute towards its erection? The answer is that Hashem wanted to give each and every member of the Jewish people the opportunity to partake of this lofty *mitzvah*. This is why He commanded that donations be taken from 'from every man.'"

זָהָב וָכֶסֶף וּנְחֹשֶׁת:

"Gold, silver, and copper" (25:3)

The Chasam Sofer found in these words an amazing allusion to all the days of the year on which we read from the Torah:

Zahav — Zayin (Shabbos, the seventh day of the week), hei (Thursday, the fifth day), and beis (Monday, the second day)

Keseph — Kippurim, Sukkos, Pesach, and Purim

Nechoshes — neiros (candles, an allusion to Chanukah), chodesh (Rosh Chodesh as well as Rosh Hashanah, which falls on Rosh Chodesh), Shavuos, Shemini Atzeres, and Ta'anis tzibbur (a public fast day).

❦

וְעָשׂוּ לִי מִקְדָּשׁ וְשָׁכַנְתִּי בְּתוֹכָם:

"They shall make a sanctuary for Me, so that I may dwell among them" (25:8)

The Midrash elaborated on this verse with a parable: There once was a king who had an only daughter. The king loved his daughter dearly, and he was very attached to her.

One day, a king from a different land came and married her.

Said the king: "She is my only daughter, and the thought of having to part with her when she journeys with you to your land is too difficult to bear; who knows when I will see her again? On the other hand, I cannot tell you to leave her here, for she is your wife. But I do have one favor to ask of you: build one small chamber in your palace, so that I may dwell together with you."

The Holy One, Blessed is He, said the same to the Jewish people: My children, I have given you the Torah. I cannot tell you to take her, for I cannot part from her. But I also cannot tell you not to take her. So, I ask of you, make for Me an abode, so that I may dwell with you. As the verse states, "They shall make a sanctuary for Me, so that I may dwell among them." The verse does not say, "That I may dwell within it," alluding to the Mishkan itself, but rather "That I may dwell among them" — within the hearts of each and every Jew.

מִבַּיִת וּמִחוּץ תְּצַפֶּנּוּ
"From inside and outside you shall cover it" (25:11)

Rava (in *Yoma* 72b) expounded on this verse, "Any *talmid chacham* whose interior does not match his exterior is not a *talmid chacham*."

The Kotzker *Rebbe* had a *chassid* who, while being quite scholarly, lacked a proper Torah perspective on many issues.

On one occasion, the *chassid* boasted before his *rebbe* that he does not walk even four *amos* without occupying his mind with Torah thoughts.

"And how many *amos*," retorted the *rebbe*, "do you walk without *yiras Shamayim*?"

מִבַּיִת וּמִחוּץ תְּצַפֶּנּוּ
"From inside and outside you shall cover it" (25:11)

The Gemara (*Berachos* 28a) relates that when Rabban Gamliel became the *Nasi* he declared that any *talmid chacham* whose interior did not match his exterior was not allowed to enter the *beis hamidrash*.

Only once R' Elazar ben Azaryah became *Nasi* was the guard at the door of the *beis hamidrash* removed from his post, and all were permitted to enter to learn Torah. In a short while, four hundred benches were added to the *beis hamidrash*!

R' Avraham Yaakov of Sadigura asked: Who was this extraordinary *beis hamidrash* guard who was perceptive enough to detect which of the *talmidei chachamim* were sincere and worthy of entering and which were not?

In truth, answered the *rebbe*, there was no guard at all. Rather, the door to the *beis hamidrash* was sealed shut, under lock and bolt, and *nobody* was allowed to enter. If a Jew truly wished to learn Torah, he would have to make use of every means at his disposal in order to get inside.

When a *talmid chacham*, said R' Avraham Yaakov, displayed that much desire to learn Torah, he demonstrated the best proof that his interior matched his exterior.

וְעָשִׂיתָ שְׁנַיִם כְּרֻבִים זָהָב

"You shall make two keruvim of gold" (25:18)

T he *Mechilta* teaches us that when gold is not available, the vessels of the *Mishkan* were permitted to be made out of other met-
als as well, such as silver or copper. The exception to this was the
Keruvim, as it was only allowed to be made of pure gold.

The reason for this difference, noted R' Meir Shapiro of Lublin, is
that the *Keruvim* — which had faces of young children — symbolized
tinokos shel beis rabban, young Jewish schoolchildren. It was placed
atop the *Aron*, which contained the Tablets of the Law, to remind us
that we must always make sure that our children are being educated
in the ways of the Torah.

This is why, concluded R' Shapiro, the *Keruvim* had to be made out
of pure gold. Our children must receive a *pure* Torah education and
not any other.

PARASHAS TETZAVEH

וְאַתָּה תְּצַוֶּה אֶת־בְּנֵי יִשְׂרָאֵל

"And you will command the Children of Israel" (27:20)

W HY, ASKED VILNA GAON, DOES THE VERSE BEGIN WITH HASHEM
instructing Moshe, "And you will command ..." without
first stating the standard opening, "Hashem spoke to
Moshe, saying ..."?

The answer, said the *Gaon*, is as follows: The day of Moshe
Rabbeinu's passing was the seventh of Adar. In most years, this day
falls out during the week in which *Parashas Tetzaveh* is read. Now, in
the entire *Parashas Tetzaveh*, Moshe's name is not mentioned even
once. This alludes to the fact that Moshe's demise took place during
this week.

However, continued the *Gaon*, even though Moshe's name is not mentioned explicitly in *Tetzaveh*, it is nevertheless there in a hint:

There are one hundred and one verses in *Parashas Tetzaveh*. If the letters that comprise the name "Moshe" are spelled out in their entirety, one would have the following:

Mem — The letters comprising the letter *mem* are *mem* and *mem*.

Shin —The letters comprising the letter *shin* are *shin*, *yud*, and *nun*.

He**i**— The letters comprising the letter *hei* are *hei* and *alef*.

If one adds up the numerical value of all of these letters and then subtracts the numerical value of the letters, *mem*, *shin*, and *hei* — the name Moshe — he will be left with the number one hundred and one — the exact number of verses in *Parashas Tetzaveh*!

וְיִקְחוּ אֵלֶיךָ שֶׁמֶן זַךְ כָּתִית לַמָּאוֹר

"They shall obtain for you clear olive oil, pressed for the light "(27:20)

R' Moshe Leib of Sasov expounded on this verse in the following manner: "*V'yikchu eilecha shemen zayis*" — If an individual desires to learn Torah, which *Chazal* compare to olive oil, then "*kasis*" (broken) — he must first break the *yetzer hara* that resides within him. Only by doing so will he reach the level of "*lama'or*" (light), the level at which he is capable of truly comprehending the Torah, which is compared to light.

וְיִקְחוּ אֵלֶיךָ שֶׁמֶן זַךְ כָּתִית לַמָּאוֹר לְהַעֲלֹת נֵר תָּמִיד:

"They shall obtain for you clear olive oil, pressed for the light, to light up the lamp continuously" (27:20)

R' Dov Ber, the *Maggid* of Mezirich, offered the following interpretation to this verse: "*Kasis*" — To the extent that a Jew wearies (*me'chateis*) his legs by traveling to a proper place in which to learn Torah (as *Chazal* teach, "Exile yourself to a place of Torah learning") will he purify himself from all of his flaws until he is as pure (*zach*) as olive oil. Eventually, he will achieve the lofty level where the Torah illuminates him at every moment (*l'ha'alos ner tamid*).

לְהַעֲלֹת נֵר תָּמִיד:
"To light up the lamp continuously" (27:20)

The *Ner Tamid* which the *Kohen Gadol* kindled in the *Beis HaMikdash* symbolized the Torah, as the verse states, "The Torah is light" (*Mishlei* 6:23).

In the same way that the *Ner Tamid* was never extinguished, and its light was a constant source of illumination, so too, the radiance of the Torah will always shine upon the world and its inhabitants.

Each and every individual is commanded to fulfill the precept of, "You should contemplate it day and night" (*Yehoshua* 1:8). By upholding this commandment we ensure that the Torah's light continuously shines and illuminates the world.

The Vilna *Gaon*'s diligence in Torah study was legendary. His days were spent in his room, delving into the depths of the Torah with every ounce of strength that he possessed.

On one occasion, the *Gaon*'s sister arrived from a distant land in order to pay him a visit. This was by no means a minor event, as the two had not seen each other for some fifty years!

The *Gaon* went out to greet his sister and, as the *halachah* dictates, recited the *berachah* that is said upon seeing an acquaintance that one has not seen for a long time — "Blessed are You, Hashem ... Who resuscitates the dead."

After concluding the *berachah*, the *Gaon* said to his sister, "My dear sister, I know that we have not seen one another for quite some time. However, when I leave this world and am called before the Heavenly Tribune, I will be asked to give an accounting for every single second of my life. Each moment of time will be scrutinized and judged on whether or not it was utilized studying Torah and performing Hashem's *mitzvos*. How, then, can I waste away the precious time that I have been allotted, by engaging in trivial conversations?

"I therefore beg your forgiveness, but I must return to my room and resume my Torah study."

לְהַעֲלֹת נֵר תָּמִיד:
"To light up the lamp continuously" (27:20)

The following story is a vivid portrait of a *tzaddik's* unyielding diligence and dedication to Torah study, even under the most dire circumstances.

As World War I raged, the Russian army declared that it was strictly forbidden for Russia's inhabitants to light candles, in order to prevent the enemy from locating the populated areas.

A brigade of Russian soldiers once set up an ambush along the border, directly adjacent to the town of Tevrig. Suddenly, a soldier noticed a small light flickering in one of the windows of the town.

Convinced that they had detected a spy whose goal was to enable the Germans to locate Tevrig, the Russian brigade surrounded the small house in which the light was kindled and, once they had received orders from their commander, broke down the door and entered the house.

Next to a small candle and bent over his *sefarim* sat the Rav of Tevrig, engrossed in Torah study.

"Get on your feet!" shouted the commander. "You are a spy, and you will be put to death. Come with us immediately!"

The rabbi's response befuddled the commander. "Since I have already been sentenced to death," he said, "I would like to make but one request. I am presently trying to resolve an apparent difficulty in the words of the Rambam. I beg of you, please allow me to solve the difficulty, and then you may do with me as you wish."

The commander was stunned by the rabbi's unexpected response and agreed to his request.

With total peace of mind, the rabbi happily returned to his studies, seemingly oblivious to the large brigade of soldiers that was standing around him.

Suddenly, the sound of gunfire and explosions filled the air — the Germans had mounted a ferocious attack against the Russian army.

"Leave the man," ordered the commander, "and retaliate against the enemy!" The soldiers quickly left the house, and the rabbi was left sitting alone with his *sefarim*. The merit of Torah study had protected him and saved his life.

וְעָשִׂיתָ בִגְדֵי־קֹדֶשׁ לְאַהֲרֹן אָחִיךָ לְכָבוֹד וּלְתִפְאָרֶת ...
וְעָשׂוּ אֶת־בִּגְדֵי אַהֲרֹן לְקַדְּשׁוֹ לְכַהֲנוֹ־לִי:

"You shall make sacred garments for your brother, Aharon, for honor and splendor ... And they shall make Aharon's garments to sanctify him as a priest for Me" (28:2-3)

What was the purpose of the *Kohen's* garments? asked R' Shimon Sofer. Were they made in order to be "for honor and splendor," or in order "to sanctify him as a priest for Me"?

Rather, answered R' Sofer, it is the nature of simple-minded people to accord honor only to those who dress elegantly. It is for such people that the verse states, "You shall make sacred garments for your brother, Aharon, for honor and splendor."

However, for the wise-hearted people of the nation who appreciate the holiness of the *Kohen's* garments, the verse states, "And they shall make Aharon's garments to sanctify him as a priest for Me."

וְאֵלֶּה הַבְּגָדִים אֲשֶׁר יַעֲשׂוּ חֹשֶׁן וְאֵפוֹד
וּמְעִיל וּכְתֹנֶת תַּשְׁבֵּץ מִצְנֶפֶת וְאַבְנֵט

"These are the garments that they shall make: a breastplate, an ephod, a robe, a shirt [woven] with indentations, a turban, and a belt" (28:4)

There once was a gentile who passed by a *shul* just as the *melamed* was reading the following verse to his young students, "These are the garments that they shall make: a breastplate, an ephod, a robe ...."

He entered the *shul* and asked the teacher, "Tell me about these magnificent garments. To whom do they belong?"

"They belong to the *Kohen Gadol* who serves in the *Beis HaMikdash*," answered the teacher.

In that case, thought the gentile, *I will become a convert so that I can be appointed as Kohen Gadol.* He went to Shammai the Elder and told him his plans: "Please convert me," he requested, "as I wish to assume the post of *Kohen Gadol.*"

Shammai was incensed by the gentile's request, and he pushed the man out of the house with a measuring rod.

The gentile then headed for the house of Hillel the Elder and requested that he be converted so that he could become the *Kohen Gadol.* Hillel consented and performed the conversion.

After he had been converted, Hillel turned to him and said, "Just as we only appoint a king who is familiar with the rules and customs of royalty, so, too, a *Kohen Gadol* can only be appointed if he is well versed in the order of the Temple service. Go and learn the laws that pertain to the *Kohanim.*"

So he began to learn. He came to the verse which read, "And the outsider who approaches [to perform this service] will be put to death" (*Bamidbar* 3:10).

"To whom does this verse refer?" he asked Hillel.

"It refers even to David, king of Israel!" answered Hillel. "One who is not a *Kohen* is forbidden to serve in the Temple."

The former gentile now realized that he would not be able to become a *Kohen Gadol* after all. He approached Hillel and said, "Hillel the humble one, may you be showered with blessings for bringing me under the wings of the Divine Presence."

❦

וְחֵשֶׁב אֲפֻדָּתוֹ אֲשֶׁר עָלָיו כְּמַעֲשֵׂהוּ מִמֶּנּוּ יִהְיֶה

"And the belt which is on [the ephod], [with which the priest is] to adorn himself shall be made by the same method" (28:8)

Chazal teach us (*Zevachim* 88b) that the ephod atoned for the sin of idol worship. The sin of idol worship, say *Chazal* (*Kiddushin* 39b), is unique in its severity. It is so severe, they say, that one is punished for simply *thinking* about performing the act of idolatry, even though he has not actually committed it!

These two statements of *Chazal*, said the Vilna *Gaon*, are alluded to in the aforementioned verse: "*V'cheishev*" — even if one has only thought (*chashav*) about transgressing the sin of idolatry, which "*afudaso asher alav*" — which the ephod atones for, "*k'ma'aseihu mimenu yihiyeh*" — it is considered as if he has actually performed it!

פִּתּוּחֵי חֹתָם קֹדֶשׁ לַה':

"Engrave on it with signet-ring [type] engraving: 'Holy to Hashem'"(28:36)

In *Maseches Ta'anis* (2a), R' Yochanan states that there are three *maftechos*, three keys, in Hashem's possession that He never entrusts to others: the key to childbirth, the key to rain, and the key to resuscitating the dead.

The Gemara derived this from three verses:

Hashem does not entrust the key to childbirth to a messenger, as the verse states, "God remembered Rachel; God hearkened to her and *He opened (vayiftach)* her womb" (*Bereishis* 30:22).

Hashem does not entrust the key of rain to a messenger, as the verse states, "*Hashem shall open* for you His storehouse of goodness, the heavens, to provide rain for your Land in its time" (*Devarim* 28:12).

And Hashem does not entrust the key of resuscitating the dead to a messenger, as the verse states, "Then you will know that I am Hashem, *when I open your graves*" (*Yechezkel* 37:13).

These three keys, remarked the Vilna *Gaon*, are alluded to in the verse, "*Pituchei chosam kodesh laHashem*":

The acronym of the word *chosam* (*ches, taf, mem*), which means "seal," hints to the following words:

Ches — ***Ch***ayah (a woman who has recently given birth)
Taf — ***T***echiyas HaMeisim (the resuscitation of the dead)
Mem — ***M***atar (rain)

The verse can therefore be read as follows: "The keys of (*pituchei*) childbirth, resuscitation of the dead, and rain ("***Ch***o***T***a***M***") are designated for Hashem's use only ("*kodesh laHashem*")!

כְּבָשִׂים בְּנֵי־שָׁנָה שְׁנַיִם לַיּוֹם תָּמִיד:

"Two sheep in their first year, each day, on a regular basis" (29:38)

The Rav of Lisa, R' Yaakov Loberbaum (the author of *Nesivos HaMishpat*), was lodging in Brisk, at the home of R' Leib Katzenelenbogen.

R' Katzenelenbogen was famous for his exceptional diligence in Torah study. He would sit day and night bent over his *sefarim*, learning Torah for hours without taking breaks. He often forgot to eat and drink, and he hardly slept.

Before taking leave of R' Katzenelenbogen, R' Loberbaum turned to him and blessed him, "R' Leib, may the verse, 'Two ... each day, on a regular basis (*tamid*)' be said of you!"

R' Katzenelenbogen was puzzled by the cryptic blessing. "What do you mean?" he asked.

"I will explain," said R' Loberbaum. "The *Shulchan Aruch* begins with the words, 'I have set Hashem before me always (*tamid*)' (*Tehillim* 16:8), and it ends with the words, 'But a good-hearted person feasts all the time (*tamid*)' (*Mishlei* 15:15). I am concerned about your health because you seem to have only the first '*tamid*.' I therefore blessed you with 'Two ... each day, on a regular basis (*tamid*)' — may you achieve both types of *tamid*'s at their proper times."

PARASHAS KI SISA

וְנָתְנוּ אִישׁ כֹּפֶר נַפְשׁוֹ לַה':

"Each man shall give (v'nasnu) his personal redemption to Hashem" (30:12)

THE BA'AL HATURIM NOTES THAT THE WORD, "V'NASNU," WHICH IS spelled with the letters *vav*, *nun*, *saf*, *nun*, and *vav*, can be read backwards and forwards. This is to teach us that whatever a person donates to *tzedakah* will ultimately be returned to him; one never loses by giving charity.

There was a rich man in Volozhin who used to give generously to the poor of his city. Misfortune struck, however, and he lost much of his wealth.

He approached R' Chaim of Volozhin with the following question: "*Rebbe*," he said, "I do not know what to do. As you know, I used to give a large sum of money each month to the poor people of Volozhin.

Due to the hard times which have befallen me, however, I don't have that much money to give. Should I simply give a smaller sum than I have in the past, or should I borrow money from others and give the same amount that I am accustomed to giving?"

R' Chaim thought for a moment and then responded, "Continue to give the exact amount that you have always given. As far as your livelihood is concerned, do not worry, for Hashem will provide you with all that you need."

A few weeks later, the man returned to R' Chaim, but now, he was happy. "*Rebbe*," he said, "your words have been fulfilled! I did exactly as you said; I borrowed money and distributed it to the poor. Shortly thereafter, I participated in a lottery and won an enormous sum of money."

וְנָתְנוּ אִישׁ כֹּפֶר נַפְשׁוֹ לַה׳ ... מַחֲצִית הַשֶּׁקֶל תְּרוּמָה לַה׳:

"Each man shall give his personal redemption to Hashem ... half a shekel as a selected contribution to Hashem" (30:12-13)

The *Ba'al HaTurim* points out that the word "*shekel*" has the same numerical value as the word, "*nefesh*" (soul). This alludes to the fact that when someone gives *tzedakah* he gains protection for his soul, as the verse states, "But charity rescues from death" (*Mishlei* 10:2).

The Gemara in *Maseches Shabbos* (156b) relates that soothsayers told R' Akiva that on the day of his daughter's wedding, a snake will bite her and she will die.

R' Akiva was very frightened by this information, but he related it to no one.

On the day of her wedding, his daughter was in her room, fixing her hair. She removed a pin from her hair, and, to make sure that it would not get lost, placed it inside a crack in the wall.

When she removed the pin from the wall, she saw that it had pierced the head of a dangerous snake — she had unknowingly killed a deadly serpent that was hiding in the wall!

"Tell me, my daughter," said R' Akiva. "What *mitzvos* did you perform today? I want to know in what merit you have been spared."

"This evening," responded his daughter, "a pauper came to our home and asked for charity, but because of the large crowd that had gathered here, nobody heard him. I, however, did hear him and took pity on him, so I gave him the portion of food that had been placed before me."

"Now I understand," said R' Akiva, "how you were saved from the bite of the dangerous serpent. It is as the verse states, 'But charity rescues from death.'"

זֶה יִתְּנוּ
"This shall they give" (30:13)

Rashi explains: "[Hashem] showed [Moshe] an image of a coin made of fire whose weight was a half a *shekel* and said to him, 'They should give [a coin] like this.'"

Why, asked R' Moshe of Kobrin, did Hashem only show Moshe how to make the half-*shekel*, but not any of the other vessels of the *Mishkan*?

Furthermore, asked the *rebbe*, can it be that Moshe *Rabbeinu* did not know what coins look like?

The answer, said the *rebbe*, is as follows: Moshe *Rabbeinu* wondered how a mere half-*shekel* coin could bring atonement for a man's soul. Hashem therefore showed him a "coin of fire," hinting to the fact that every coin that goes to *tzedakah* "burns" with the fire of the *yetzer hara*. Whenever someone considers giving a coin to *tzedakah*, the *yetzer hara* tries to prevent the person from doing the *mitzvah*. It uses all sorts of tactics and excuses in order to prevent the person from giving *tzedakah*. The coin he wishes to donate may be small in size, but it requires an extraordinary amount of will-power and perseverance to defeat the *yetzer hara* and carry out the *mitzvah*. By doing so, he earns a merit that is very great and capable of bringing atonement for his soul.

זֶה יִתְּנוּ
"This shall they give" (30:13)

Rashi explains: "[Hashem] showed [Moshe] an image of a coin made of fire whose weight was a half a *shekel* and said to him, 'They should give [a coin] like this.'"

Fire, said R' Nachman of Breslav, is one of man's most needed elements. When he is cold in the winter, it gives him warmth; and when he is hungry, it enables him to cook his food. Yet fire can also consume and destroy.

It is vital that man learns how to use fire properly.

The same applies to money. On the one hand, it can be put to very good use if it enables man to perform *mitzvos* and good deeds. But on the other hand, money can completely consume a person's character. Man must therefore learn how to use his money properly, for otherwise …

❦

מַחֲצִית הַשֶּׁקֶל תְּרוּמָה לַה':

"Half a shekel as a selected contribution to Hashem" (30:13)

The great R' Abish of Frankfurt opened his hand freely to the poor to the point that he often gave away all his earnings to charity.

One day, his congregants asked him the following question: "Why do you give away all that you own to the needy. After all, do *Chazal* (*Kesubos* 50b) not teach us that 'one should not spend more than one-fifth' of his assets to *tzedakah*?"

"You are indeed correct," responded R' Abish, "that it is forbidden for an individual to *spend* more than one-fifth of his assets. However, Shlomo *HaMelech* has taught us, 'But charity rescues from death.' Consequently giving *tzedakah* can be considered a matter of *pikuach nefesh*, of life and death. Now, if it is even permitted to desecrate the Shabbos in order to save one's life, how much more so may one give away more than one-fifth of what he owns!"

A similar question was posed to R' Chaim Eliyahu Meisel, the rabbi of Lodz, by his family. They wanted to know how it was permissible for him to give so much of his money to *tzedakah*. "Does the Gemara not teach," they asked, "that one should not donate more than one-fifth of his assets to *tzedakah*?"

"You are right," answered R' Meisel, "and I have indeed sinned. However, the verse states, 'Redeem your sin through *tzedakah*' (*Daniel* 4:24). An individual who has committed a sin must give extra *tzedakah* in order to atone for what he has done. Since I have sinned by giving too much, I must give even more charity; but that just makes my sin worse, for I am already giving more than a fifth, so I need another atonement for my new sin."

וַאֲמַלֵּא אֹתוֹ רוּחַ אֱלֹקִים בְּחָכְמָה וּבִתְבוּנָה
וּבְדַעַת וּבְכָל־מְלָאכָה: לַחְשֹׁב מַחֲשָׁבֹת
לַעֲשׂוֹת בַּזָּהָב וּבַכֶּסֶף וּבַנְּחֹשֶׁת:

I have endowed him with a Divine spirit, with knowledge, understanding, and inspiration, and with [the skill of] every craft; lachshov machashavos (to think thoughts), to work with gold, silver, and copper" (31:3-4)

The fund-raiser of the Volozhin Yeshivah approached R' Chaim of Volozhin with an issue to discuss. He related to R' Chaim how one of the yeshivah's biggest supporters, a wealthy man who, year after year, never hesitated to donate generously, suddenly refused to offer even the slightest contribution.

R' Chaim traveled to the wealthy man's home and asked to speak with him. "Why have you stopped supporting our yeshivah?" asked R' Chaim.

"I will tell you," answered the wealthy man. "You see, I have always given happily to the Volozhin Yeshivah, knowing that my money was helping poor yeshivah students study Torah. The other day, however, your fund-raiser pulled up to my home in a carriage drawn by two healthy-looking horses.

"I thought to myself," continued the wealthy man, "that this horse-drawn carriage must also have been paid for by donations to the yeshivah — maybe even from my own money. To make sizable contributions, only that the money should be spent on horses, that I am not about to do!"

"My dear sir," responded R' Chaim, "in this week's *parashah* it states, 'I have endowed him with a Divine spirit, with knowledge, understanding, and inspiration, and with [the skill of] every craft; *lachshov machashavos* (to think thoughts), to work with gold, silver, and copper.'

"What is the wisdom of *lachshov machshavos*, of 'thinking thoughts'? What exactly does it mean?

"When the donations for the *Mishkan* were being collected," answered R' Chaim, "there were some Jews who contributed graciously and with good hearts, and there were others who only gave reluctantly, after they were persuaded to do so.

"One of Betzalel's unique gifts of wisdom was that he could discern which donations were given willingly, and which were given grudgingly. From the donations that were given with enthusiasm, he made the sacred vessels of the *Mishkan*; but from those given reluctantly, he made the items of lesser importance.

"The same thing applies to a yeshivah," concluded R' Chaim. "The contributions that are given with a happy heart are used to support the young Torah scholars so they can study diligently. But the contributions that are given with a heavy heart are used towards buying horses."

❦

אַךְ אֶת־שַׁבְּתֹתַי תִּשְׁמֹרוּ

"However, keep My Sabbaths" (31:13)

This verse, remarked the *Sefas Emes* (R' Yehudah Leib Alter of Gur), teaches us how to properly prepare for Shabbos.

In the Torah portion that discusses the purging of nonkosher utensils (*kashering*), it states (*Bamidbar* 31:22), "Only (*Ach*) the gold and the silver ..." *Chazal* explain that the word "ach" is coming to exclude any extraneous matter that may be stuck to the gold and silver. In other words, if one wishes to *kasher* gold or silver vessels, he must first clean them thoroughly and remove any rust or dirt that may be attached to them.

Here, too, noted the *Sefas Emes*, the Torah uses the word "ach." This is meant to teach us that before we usher in the holy Shabbos day, we must first cleanse ourselves of all the "dirt" that has become attached to ourselves as a result of our sins. Only then will we merit to "keep My Sabbaths."

❦

וְעַתָּה אִם־תִּשָּׂא חַטָּאתָם וְאִם־אַיִן
מְחֵנִי נָא מִסִּפְרְךָ אֲשֶׁר כָּתָבְתָּ:

*"So now, if You will bear their sin, [fine,]
but if not, please erase me from Your Book
that You have written" (32:32)*

The Dubno *Maggid* explained this verse with the following parable: There once was a minister to a king whose relative frequently stole from the king's treasury. Each time the relative was caught stealing, the minister defended him before the king and each time he was released without punishment.

On one occasion, however, the relative stole an extremely large sum of money from the king's treasury. This time the minister could not think of any way to justify what his relative had done.

"Your highness," said the minister to the king, "I wish to be dismissed from my post."

"Why?" asked the king in surprise.

"Each time my relative steals from your treasury," responded the minister, "he counts on me to come to his defense, so there is nothing to dissuade him from stealing. But if I leave my position he will have no one to defend him and he will be afraid to steal."

This, explained the Dubno *Maggid*, is why Moshe said to Hashem, "Erase me from Your Book that You have written." Once I am gone, said Moshe, the Jewish people will no longer have me to rely on and they will refrain from sinning.

இ೧௦ೞ

וְעַתָּה אִם־נָא מָצָאתִי חֵן בְּעֵינֶיךָ הוֹדִעֵנִי נָא אֶת־דְּרָכֶךָ

"If indeed you regard me favorably, please let me know Your way [of rewarding]" (33:13)

In *Maseches Berachos* (7b) *Chazal* explain that Moshe *Rabbeinu's* request of Hashem to "please let me know Your way" was actually a request to be shown why the righteous suffer and the wicked prosper.

This is a question, remarked the *Chofetz Chaim*, that bothers many people: Why are there wicked people who live in luxury and comfort, while many righteous people live in poverty and suffering?

Perhaps we can gain some insight, said the *Chofetz Chaim*, from the following parable: An individual was visiting a certain *shul* on Shabbos day. He watched carefully as the *gabbai* called up various congregants to recite the blessings over the Torah reading. The *Kohen* was selected from the back row of the *shul*, the *Levi* was chosen from a different row, the *Yisrael* was chosen from a third, and so on. In the end, all the people called up to the Torah were selected from different sections of the *shul*.

After *davening*, the visitor approached the *gabbai*. "Excuse me," he asked, "why did you select people who are sitting in different sections of the *shul*? Would it not have made more sense to simply choose seven men from the same row?"

"My dear sir," responded the *gabbai*, "you have been a guest in our *shul* for only one Shabbos, so it seems to you that there was no order to how I distributed the *aliyos*. But if you would pray here on a regular basis you would see that I give out the *aliyos* according to a specific order that is based on several factors ..."

The same thing can be said about this world, said the *Chofetz Chaim*. We come to this world as guests for just a few fleeting years, so we cannot grasp the sense and the order of the way Hashem governs His world. However we must believe that there is Judgment and there is a Judge Who masterfully guides our world!

❧☙

יֵלֶךְ־נָא ה' בְּקִרְבֵּנוּ כִּי עַם־קְשֵׁה־עֹרֶף
הוּא וְסָלַחְתָּ לַעֲוֺנֵנוּ וּלְחַטָּאתֵנוּ וּנְחַלְתָּנוּ:

"May the Lord['s Presence] please go among us,
for this is a stiff-necked people, and may You
forgive our transgressions and sins, and make us
Your [special] possession" (34:9)

The Dubno *Maggid* drew a parable to explain this verse: There once was a poor peddler who owned several simple wooden spoons and forks. *I should probably stand on the rich people's street,* thought the peddler to himself. *Wealthy people have plenty of money and they spend it easily.*

The peddler spent an entire day on that street, but he did not sell even a single utensil.

"You're wasting your time," said a passerby. "Rich people don't use wooden cutlery; they use silverware. Go stand in the poor part of town where you might find a customer."

Similarly, explained the Dubno *Maggid*, Moshe *Rabbeinu* pleaded with Hashem, "May the Lord['s Presence] please go among us" — the most appropriate place for Your Thirteen Attributes of Mercy is down below, in our world, and not in Heaven with the angels. "For this is a stiff-necked people" — humans are the ones who sin from time to time. So "may You forgive our transgressions and sins" — for they are the ones who need Your forgiveness!

Parashas Vayakhel

שֵׁשֶׁת יָמִים תֵּעָשֶׂה מְלָאכָה וּבַיּוֹם הַשְּׁבִיעִי
יִהְיֶה לָכֶם קֹדֶשׁ שַׁבַּת שַׁבָּתוֹן לַה׳

"Work may be done for six days, but the seventh day shall be holy for you — a day of complete rest [designated] for Hashem" (35:2)

UPON ARRIVING IN A CERTAIN CITY, THE *CHOFETZ CHAIM* WAS informed that one of the wealthy Jews in the vicinity had hired Jewish workers to work in his factory on Shabbos. The *Chofetz Chaim* went to the man's house and asked him to close the factory for Shabbos.

"But, Rabbi," exclaimed the man, "do you have any idea how much profit I earn in one day? Four thousand rubles! If I close my factory for Shabbos, I will lose a fortune. I simply cannot do it."

"Let me warn you, then," responded the *Chofetz Chaim*, "that if you do not close your factory for Shabbos, you may lose *all* your possessions. The Torah states, 'Work may be done for six days.' Why does the Torah tell us to work for six days? If the main point of the verse is to instruct us to observe the Shabbos, it need only have said, 'The seventh day shall be holy for you — a day of complete rest [designated] for Hashem.'

"This is meant to teach us," answered the *Chofetz Chaim*, "that a person's entire livelihood is dependent upon his Shabbos observance. If you do not keep Shabbos then you will have no work to do on the remaining six days of the week!"

"Do you really think," said the man derisively, "that I will close my factory just because of a verse in the Torah? I refuse!"

The man ignored the *Chofetz Chaim*'s warning and continued to desecrate the Shabbos in his factory. But a short while later, the Russian government confiscated everything he owned, and he was left a destitute pauper.

וּבַיּוֹם הַשְּׁבִיעִי יִהְיֶה לָכֶם קֹדֶשׁ שַׁבַּת שַׁבָּתוֹן לַה׳

"But the seventh day will be holy for you — a day of complete rest [designated] for Hashem" (35:2)

How wonderful and beloved is the *mitzvah* of Shabbos, remarked R' Simchah Bunim of P'shischa. It is unique in that once the holy Shabbos arrives, man is automatically and effortlessly carried into the *mitzvah*, and from then until *motzaei Shabbos*, he does not take leave of the *mitzvah* for even one moment.

This is as the verse states, "But the seventh day will be holy for you — a day of complete rest [designated] for Hashem" — even without any effort on man's part, Shabbos will be holy for him!

שַׁבַּת שַׁבָּתוֹן לַה׳

"A day of complete rest [designated] for Hashem" (35:2)

The *Chofetz Chaim* once visited the city of St. Petersburg. The Jews of the city gathered to greet the *gadol hador* and to catch a glimpse of his holy face, thereby fulfilling the words of the *Navi*, "And your eyes will behold your teachers" (*Yeshayah* 30:20).

Among the large crowd were several wealthy men who wished to receive a blessing from the *Chofetz Chaim*. One of them approached him and handed him a substantial donation for his yeshivah in Radin.

The *Chofetz Chaim* took the man's hand and began to weep bitterly. "This special hand," cried the *Chofetz Chaim*, "gives so generously to *tzedakah*. How can it desecrate the holy Shabbos?"

The *Chofetz Chaim* held the man's hand for several minutes while his tears continued to fall. Eventually, the tears penetrated the wealthy man's heart, and he, too, began to weep.

"*Rebbe*," said the man, "I give you my word that from now on I will observe the Shabbos. But please permit me to do work just on this coming Shabbos so I can finish a few matters."

"My dear child," said the *Chofetz Chaim* with much emotion, "if Shabbos belonged to me, I would allow you to do whatever you wish. Shabbos, however, belongs to Hashem, the King of kings, so I am unable to permit even a moment of Shabbos desecration."

The wealthy man accepted the *Chofetz Chaim's* words, and, from that day on, he became a fully observant, *shomer Shabbos* Jew.

ॐ

כָּל־הָעֹשֶׂה בוֹ מְלָאכָה יוּמָת:

"Whoever does work on [this day] shall be put to death" (35:2)

R' Yisrael Salanter gathered his students and delivered a fiery discourse, rebuking them over the Shabbos desecration that was becoming rampant among the businessmen in the city.

The students were surprised that R' Salanter's words were being directed at them. "*Rebbe*," one of the students asked, "what does the businessmen's Shabbos desecration have to do with us? It is *they* who are lax in observing the Shabbos, not us. Why are you rebuking us and not them?"

"You are mistaken," responded R' Salanter. "For we have *everything* to do with their Shabbos desecration! If we were more meticulous in our *mitzvah* performance, these businessmen would not desecrate Shabbos. We must make every effort to improve our own *mitzvah* observance and then it will bring an end to the desecration of Shabbos."

ॐ

קְחוּ מֵאִתְּכֶם תְּרוּמָה לַה'

"Take from yourselves a selected contribution for Hashem" (35:5)

R' Yaakov and R' Yosef were the trustees of the *tzedakah* funds in the city of Minsk. They were well known for their righteousness and honesty.

On one occasion, R' Chaim of Volozhin paid a visit to Minsk in order to raise funds for his yeshivah. R' Chaim was invited to be R' Yaakov's guest.

"Allow me to go from house to house," offered R' Yaakov, "and I will collect whatever the *Rav* needs. How much money does the *Rav* wish to raise for his yeshivah?"

"Four thousand rubles," replied R' Chaim. "I know that it is a large sum of money, but Hashem will be with you, and with His help you will be successful."

After about a month, R' Yaakov presented the full amount to R' Chaim.

R' Chaim thanked his host for his hospitality and for his extraordinary assistance, and he returned home.

Some time later, both R' Yaakov and R' Yosef appeared before R' Chaim for a *din Torah*.

"I have a claim against R' Yaakov," began R' Yosef. "We are usually partners in all the *mitzvos* we do, yet when the *Rav* came to our city to collect for his yeshivah, R' Yaakov gave him the entire sum out of his own pocket, and he left me out of the important *mitzvah*.

"I demand," concluded R' Yosef, "that he accept half of the sum from me so that I, too, could have a share in the *mitzvah*!"

R' Chaim turned to R' Yaakov and asked, "If all the money you gave me came from your own pocket, then why didn't you give it to me immediately? Why was it necessary to wait an entire month?"

"The *yetzer hara*," answered R' Yaakov, "fights so fiercely against those who wish to give *tzedakah*. I faced a very difficult battle. The *yetzer hara* came to me with a barrage of excuses and reasons why I should refrain from giving you the money: 'Don't give,' 'Don't rush into it,' 'Give yourself some time before you hand over such a large sum of money,' and other such arguments.

"Only after a month had passed," continued R' Yaakov, "was I able to defeat the *yetzer hara* — with Hashem's help, of course — and give you the money."

R' Chaim enjoyed the *tzaddik*'s response. "You have enabled me to understand the meaning of a verse," said R' Chaim to R' Yaakov. "The Torah says, 'Take from *yourselves* a selected contribution for Hashem.' Whenever someone thinks of giving *tzedakah*, he faces such an intense battle with the *yetzer hara* that, when he finally gives the donation, it is as if he has given a portion of his very being. Fortunate is the person who fulfills this lofty *mitzvah* and merits defeating the *yetzer hara*."

כֹּל נְדִיב לִבּוֹ יְבִיאֶהָ
"Every generous person shall bring it" (35:5)

A benefactor donated a large plot of land for R' Meir Shapiro's yeshivah, Yeshivas Chachmei Lublin. At the ceremony for the laying of the cornerstone of the building, the benefactor was accorded great honor and seated at the head table reserved for the distinguished guests.

Sitting next to the man was R' Yisrael of Chortkov, who turned to him and said, "I do not envy you over this *mitzvah* because it will lead to great honor. I do envy you, however, for the *mitzvah* that you performed secretly, the one that lead to this one (see *Avos* 4:2). For that must have been a flawless *mitzvah* if it was capable of leading to a *mitzvah* as great as this one."

❧

כֹּל נְדִיב לִבּוֹ יְבִיאֶהָ אֵת תְּרוּמַת ה'
"Every generous person shall bring it, as the gift for Hashem" (35:5)

R' Shraga Feivel Frank was famous for his selflessness and generosity. He gave freely to the poor his whole life.

On one occasion, he crossed the bridge that connected the cities of Kovno and Aleksot. When he arrived at the other side, he happened to see a wagon driver searching for something in the bushes.

"What did you lose?" asked the rabbi.

"I lost a large sum of money — 25 rubles," answered the man sadly. "I am a very poor man," he continued, "and now I don't know how I will support my family."

"Would you be able to identify the money if it was found?" asked the rabbi. "Was it marked in any way?"

"It certainly was," answered the man. "The money was wrapped in a red piece of cloth."

"You are quite fortunate," replied the rabbi. "Just before I saw you I found 25 rubles wrapped in a piece of red cloth. I put the money in my pouch and tossed the cloth into the river. Here is your money." And with that, R' Frank handed the wagon driver 25 rubles.

The wagon driver was overjoyed that his money had been found. He thanked R' Frank and went home. R' Frank then thanked Hashem for enabling him to perform such a precious *mitzvah*.

וַיָּבֹאוּ כָל־אִישׁ אֲשֶׁר־נְשָׂאוֹ לִבּוֹ וְכֹל אֲשֶׁר
נָדְבָה רוּחוֹ אֹתוֹ הֵבִיאוּ אֶת־תְּרוּמַת ה'

"Every man who felt inspired came. Also, all those who felt generous brought their selected contribution" (35:21)

The *Chida* (R' Chaim Yosef Azulai) offered a beautiful interpretation to this verse:

People are often inspired to do a certain *mitzvah*, but by the time they are ready to actually do the *mitzvah*, they lose their fervor and do less than they had originally thought of doing.

For instance, when a man hears about a destitute family that desperately needs financial assistance, he begins imagining the family's plight. His heart becomes filled with compassion, and he tells himself that he is going to give them a large sum of money for *tzedakah*. Yet as time passes, and he becomes accustomed to the idea of helping the needy family, he loses his enthusiasm. Though he may yet give them *tzedakah*, it will probably not be the same amount that he originally intended to give.

The *Mishkan*, however, was the exception to this rule. The Torah praises the contributors to the *Mishkan* and says, "Every man who felt inspired came. Also, *all those who felt generous brought their selected contribution.*" That is, the Jewish people did not allow their initial inspiration for donating to the *Mishkan* dissipate; they gave exactly what they had originally intended to give.

וְכָל־אִשָּׁה חַכְמַת־לֵב בְּיָדֶיהָ טָווּ וַיָּבִיאוּ מַטְוֶה

"Every wise-hearted woman spun [the threads] by hand, and they then brought the spun threads" (35:25)

On one occasion, several outstanding scholars gathered in the house of R' Chaim of Volozhin to exchange Torah thoughts.

"Rabbeinu," asked one of the students, "it states in this week's *parashah*, 'Every wise-hearted woman spun [the threads] by hand, and they then brought the spun threads.' Now, according to *halachah*, any item a woman produces belongs to her husband. How, then, was it possible for the women to donate the yarn they made if it didn't belong to them?"

While the *talmidei chachamim* were still puzzling over the difficult question, R' Chaim's mother, *Rebbetzin* Rivkah, who had overheard the question, presented an answer of her own.

"Why is it," she began, "that a woman's handiwork belongs to her husband? It is only because the husband is responsible to provide for her and sustain her, so *Chazal* gave him her handiwork as compensation.

"In the wilderness, however, none of the husbands had to provide for their wives, as they all had *manna* from heaven. There was therefore no reason why the wives would have to give their handiwork to their husbands. Consequently, the women could give the yarn they had made to the *Mishkan* — it was theirs to give!

וַיְמַלֵּא אֹתוֹ רוּחַ אֱלֹקִים בְּחָכְמָה בִּתְבוּנָה וּבְדַעַת

"He has endowed him with a Divine spirit, with wisdom, understanding, and knowledge" (35:31)

The *Midrash Rabbah* states that Betzalel must have already possessed an extraordinary degree of wisdom even before he was blessed, for Hashem does not bestow wisdom upon an individual unless he is already wise. This is as the verse states, "He gives wisdom to the wise" (*Daniel* 2:21).

To what can this be compared? To a man who wanted to buy wine, oil, or honey, and walked into a store with an empty jug in hand. If the storekeeper is intelligent, he does not have to ask the customer which of the three he wants to purchase. All he needs to do is smell the man's jug; if it gives off the scent of wine, then he has come to purchase wine. If, however, the scent is that of honey, then he has come to buy honey.

So it is with wisdom. When Hashem sees a person that has some wisdom, He fills him with more!

⁂

וַיַּעַשׂ בְּצַלְאֵל אֶת־הָאָרֹן עֲצֵי שִׁטִּים

"Betzalel made the Ark of acacia wood" (37:1)

It is interesting to note that throughout the Torah's description of the construction of the *Mishkan's* vessels, Betzalel's name does not appear. For example, the Torah states, "Every wise-hearted *person*"; "*He* made the planks"; and, "*He* made the *Menorah*" — but there is no mention of Betzalel. Only when the Torah describes the making of the Ark does it mention Betzalel, as the verse states: "Betzalel made the Ark of acacia wood."

Why is Betzalel's name mentioned specifically in connection with the Ark, asked the *Meshech Chochmah* (R' Meir Simchah HaKohen of Dvinsk), but not with any of the other vessels?

We are taught, he answered, that new vessels were made for the first and second *Beis HaMikdash*. For example, when Shlomo *HaMelech* built the first *Beis HaMikdash*, he made ten new menorahs. Similarly, in the second *Beis HaMikdash*, the menorah was initially made of wood, then of silver, and finally it was replaced with a menorah made of gold.

The only sanctified vessel that was never replaced was the Ark. There was only one Ark that was used in the first *Beis HaMikdash* — the one Betzalel built. Then it was hidden and it has remained hidden since then (there was no Ark at all in the second *Beis HaMikdash*). But with Hashem's help, when the third *Beis HaMikdash* will be built, the Ark that Betzalel made will be restored. Since the other vessels would eventually be made by other people, the Torah could not write that they were made by Betzalel. The only vessel of which the Torah could state that it was made by Betzalel, and the statement would remain true forever, was the Ark.

PARASHAS PEKUDEI

אֵלֶּה פְקוּדֵי הַמִּשְׁכָּן מִשְׁכַּן הָעֵדֻת

"These are the accounts of the Dwelling,
the Dwelling of the Testimony " (38:21)

R abbeinu Bechaya points out that the numerical value of the words "HaMishkan," "Mishkan," and "Ha'eidus" correspond to the total number of years that the first Beis HaMikdash, second Beis HaMikdash, and Mishkan stood:

The numerical value of Mishkan is four hundred and ten, alluding to the four hundred and ten years that the first Beis HaMikdash stood.

The numerical value of the word HaMishkan (415) plus the five letters that are used to spell HaMishkan (hei, mem, shin, kaf, and nun) equals four hundred and twenty. This alludes to the second Beis HaMikdash, which stood for four hundred and twenty years.

The numerical value of Ha'eidus is four hundred and seventy-nine. The alludes to the Mishkan Ha'eidus, which stood for four hundred and seventy-nine years.

אֵלֶּה פְקוּדֵי הַמִּשְׁכָּן מִשְׁכַּן הָעֵדֻת

"These are the accounts of the Dwelling,
the Dwelling of the Testimony " (38:21)

I n Maseches Yoma (21b), Chazal enumerate five items that were present in the first Beis HaMikdash but were lacking in the second:
1) The Aron Ha'eidus (the Ark)
2) The Ner Tamid (the Lamp that burned continuously)
3) The Divine Presence
4) Divine Inspiration
5) The ability to inquire of the Urim V'Tumim

This statement of Chazal, said the Chasam Sofer, is alluded to in the verse, "Eileh fekudei haMishkan Mishkan Ha'eidus." The word "haMishkan," containing a hei (numerical value, 5) at the beginning, alludes to the first *Beis HaMikdash* which possessed these *five* attributes. The word "*Mishkan*," however, alludes to the second *Beis HaMikdash* which lacked these five items.

જીબ્રજ

אֵלֶּה פְקוּדֵי הַמִּשְׁכָּן מִשְׁכַּן הָעֵדֻת

"These are the accounts of the Dwelling, the Dwelling of the Testimony " (38:21)

Rashi explains that the word *Mishkan* is stated twice in order to allude to the *Beis HaMikdash* which was taken as collateral (*mashkon*) both times it was destroyed for the sins of the Jewish nation.

How, asked the Dubno *Maggid*, did Rashi know that this verse was meant to hint at the idea of collateral?

The *maggid* answered through the following parable:

Two customers were shopping in a jewelry store. One of the customers was wealthy, and he was purchasing jewelry so it would be used by his family members. The other customer, however, was not a wealthy man at all. He had earned a slight profit from his business and he was afraid of squandering his money. So he decided to use his profits to buy gold jewelry, which he would bring home and hide for safekeeping.

The difference between these two individuals, said the *maggid*, is that when the wealthy man arrives home, he will immediately present his family with the beautiful jewelry he has bought. In contrast, the first thing the other fellow does when he comes home is record his acquisition in a ledger. He will record exactly what he bought and how much he paid for it, and then he will conceal it in a secure place. If he ever needs some money, he will take the jewelry out of safekeeping and use it as collateral to secure himself a loan.

So, too, concluded the *maggid*, in regard to the *Mishkan*. By recording all the details of the *Mishkan* and listing the exact number of beams, pillars, and bars, etc., the Torah gave us a clue that the *Mishkan* would one day be used as collateral.

מִשְׁכַּן הָעֵדֻת
"The Dwelling of the Testimony" (38:21)

Why, asked the Malbim (R' Meir Leibush Malbim), is the Mishkan referred to as the "Dwelling of *Testimony*"?

In the *pesukim* that follow, answered the Malbim, the Torah gives us an accounting of the vast amounts of gold, silver, and other materials that were used in the construction of the *Mishkan*. It records how much was donated toward the *Mishkan's* construction and how much was put to use.

The *Mishkan* itself was the best evidence that there was absolutely no dishonesty in relation to the *Mishkan's* construction, and that every last donation was accounted for and put to use. For it is inconceivable that the Divine Presence would ever dwell in a place that was tainted with corruption. If any of the donations had been misappropriated, the Divine Presence would never have rested there.

בְּיַד אִיתָמָר בֶּן־אַהֲרֹן הַכֹּהֵן:
"Under the direction of Isamar, son of Aharon the Kohen" (38:21)

The *Midrash Rabbah* records the ruling that all matters that pertain to the public's money (such as a *tzedakah* fund) must be conducted by at least two trustees. This is why even Moshe *Rabbeinu*, whom Hashem trusted, asked Isamar to join him in managing the *Mishkan's* funds.

R' Leib, known as the *Shpoler Zeide*, was the *gabbai tzedakah* of his town. He dispensed his own money freely to the poor and unfortunate and, in fact, to anybody who asked for a donation. He never investigated people to see if they were honest or not; he just gave.

Several members of the community once approached him and said, "*Rebbe*, we thought you would want to know that some of the people who come collecting from you are imposters. They dress and act like paupers, but they are really thieves."

"I am aware of this," answered the *tzaddik*, "but it is worthwhile for me to give to them as well. For there are times when a broken-hearted Jew will ask me to pray for him, and I gladly do so. But sometimes the Gates of Mercy in Heaven are locked. What do I do then? I summon my thieves and — being the experts that they are — they break open the locks for me!"

וַיְהִי מְאַת כִּכַּר הַכֶּסֶף לָצֶקֶת אֵת אַדְנֵי הַקֹּדֶשׁ ...
מְאַת אֲדָנִים לִמְאַת הַכִּכָּר כִּכָּר לָאָדֶן:

"The hundred kikar of silver were used for casting the bases ... one hundred bases (adanim) from one hundred kikar — one kikar per base" (38:27)

There is a significant connection, noted the *Chiddushei HaRim* (R' Yitzchak Meir of Gur), between the one hundred sockets that were used in the *Mishkan* and the one hundred blessings that a Jew is required to recite every day. Just as the sockets formed the foundation upon which the *Mishkan* rested, so, too, the one hundred blessings that we recite each day form the foundation upon which the life of a Jew rests.

The word "*adan* (socket)," added the *rebbe*, is similar to the word "*adon* (master)." For by reciting one hundred blessings each day, a Jew declares that Hashem is the Master of the entire universe.

וַיְבָרֶךְ אֹתָם מֹשֶׁה:
"And Moshe blessed them" (39:43)

R' Yitzchak was a wealthy Jew who lived in Volozhin. He was also a noteworthy *talmid chacham* who was very meticulous in his *mitzvah* performance.

Because of his business, he would often go on extended trips. Every time he returned from his travels, he would bring home expensive gifts for his family.

One day, as R' Yitzchak was preparing to embark on a long voyage, his wife asked him to bring home a complete set of the Talmud instead of gifts for the family. In those days, an entire set of Talmud was extremely expensive, but he, nevertheless, acceded to her request. R' Yitzchak kept his word, and, when he returned home, he brought with him a beautiful, brand-new set of the Talmud.

In order to benefit the public, R' Yitzchak and his wife decided to loan out various tractates of the Talmud, giving people the opportunity to increase their Torah knowledge. While R' Yitzchak was away on business, his wife managed the lending of their Talmud.

On one occasion, the great *Sha'agas Aryeh* (R' Aryeh Leib of Metz) came to Volozhin for a visit. When he arrived, he was told that in the home of a certain R' Yitzchak there was an entire set of Talmud, and that his family gladly lent out volumes of it to Torah scholars. When the *Sha'agas Aryeh* heard this, he went straight to R' Yitzchak's home.

R' Yitzchak's wife felt very privileged that she could help the great scholar, and she made him the following offer: "You need not trouble yourself to come here each time you need to exchange a volume. Whenever you need a different volume, I will send it with a messenger directly to the *Rav*'s place of lodging." For the duration of the *Sha'agas Aryeh*'s visit in Volozhin, she indeed sent to his lodgings whatever tractate he needed.

Before departing from Volozhin, the *Sha'agas Aryeh* stopped by the home of R' Yitzchak and blessed both him and his wife: "I bless you," said the *gaon*, "that you should merit having two sons who will illuminate the eyes of the Jewish people with their Torah! May the first son merit teaching the Talmud to the masses, and may the second one be so fluent in the entire Torah that he will not even need a set of the Talmud for reference."

The *Sha'agas Aryeh*'s blessing came true; R' Yitzchak and his wife were indeed granted two sons. The first was the legendary R' Chaim of Volozhin who founded the Volozhin Yeshivah and merited teaching Torah to generations of students. The second son was R' Zalman of Volozhin who mastered the entire Torah until he knew it all by heart.

וַיַּעַל הַנֵּרֹת לִפְנֵי ה'

"He lit the lamps before Hashem" (40:25)

In the city where R' Aryeh Leib HaKohen (author of the *Ketzos HaChoshen*) lived, there was a certain wealthy individual who performed countless acts of *tzedakah* and *chesed*. There was only one flaw with the way he did these *mitzvos*: whenever he did a good deed, he insisted that it be publicized to as many people as possible.

R' Aryeh Leib approached the man with hopes of inspiring him to perform *mitzvos* for the sake of Heaven alone: "A *mitzvah*," he said, "should not be performed with the desire of acquiring honor. Rather, it should be done only for the sake of Heaven."

"What is so wrong with my ways?" asked the man. "Does Shlomo HaMelech not state (*Mishlei* 6:23), "For a commandment is a lamp and the Torah is light"? Since a *mitzvah* is compared to a lamp, what difference does it make *how* the lamp gets lit? Regardless of how I light it, or why I light it, I have fulfilled the *mitzvah*."

"You are right," answered R' Aryeh Leib, "that a *mitzvah* is compared to a lamp. However, the Torah also states, "He lit the lamps *before Hashem*" — our *mitzvah* "lamps" must be lit only "before Hashem," and not for the sake of receiving any kind of honor or prestige!"

VAYIKRA

PARASHAS VAYIKRA

וַיִּקְרָא

"Vayikra — He called" (1:1)

THERE IS A COMMONLY ASKED QUESTION REGARDING THE WORD, "Vayikra" in this parashah: Why is it spelled with a small alef ?

The word "Vayikra" begins the sefer that deals with sacrificial offerings. The main purpose of bringing sacrifices is to bring atonement to a person who sinned. But that is only accomplished if the person regrets his previous misdeeds and repents wholeheartedly for what he has done.

The mussar masters have taught us that the trait of haughtiness lies at the root of all sin. A humble and subdued person does not sin easily, but one whose heart is filled with pride and arrogance pays little heed to rebuke, so he will inevitably succumb to sin.

The letter alef stands for the word, ani, I. "Vayikra" is spelled here with a small alef to teach us that if we make our ani small — if we make ourselves small and act with humility — then we will avoid sin and we will have no need to bring sacrificial offerings.

וַיִּקְרָא אֶל־מֹשֶׁה

"He called to Moshe" (1:1)

The Midrash Rabbah illustrates this verse with a parable: There once was a king who commanded his servant to build him a magnificent palace. The servant fulfilled the king's order and constructed an impressive palace that was lavishly decorated and beautifully furnished.

The servant engraved the king's name and royal emblem on all the pillars of the palace and on all the furnishings and vessels in the palace.

When the king entered his palace, he was overwhelmed by its beauty. Then he was surprised and delighted to see that his name and emblem had been engraved on all the pillars and vessels.

My loyal servant, thought the king, has gone to so much effort just to please me. Yet here I am, sitting in my glorious palace, while he sits in his chamber in the courtyard — that's not very nice of me.

"Summon my servant," ordered the king, "and he shall sit together with me in my palace!"

So it was with Moshe *Rabbeinu* and the *Mishkan*. Moshe erected the *Mishkan* and all its vessels, and on each item he marked: "As Hashem commanded Moshe."

Said the Holy One: "My servant Moshe has displayed so much honor toward Me, for he has set My Name on each and every part of the *Mishkan*. Should he now be left outside?" Immediately, "He called to Moshe."

❧

וַיִּקְרָא אֶל־מֹשֶׁה וַיְדַבֵּר ה׳ אֵלָיו

"He called to Moshe, and Hashem spoke to him" (1:1)

Why is the word, "*Vayikra*" written with a small *alef*? asked R' Simchah Bunim of P'shischa.

The verse comes to teach us, answered the *rebbe*, about the extraordinary humility of Moshe *Rabbeinu*. Even when he was engaged in conversation with Hashem, the King of the entire world, Moshe remained the most humble of men.

To what can this be compared? asked the *rebbe*. To a man who had scaled an enormous mountain and managed to reach its peak. Standing atop the mountain and looking about, he could get the impression that he towers over all those around him. However, if he is a wise man, he will realize that he is not tall at all, nor does his elevated position point to any personal greatness. For it is the mountain upon which he is standing that is tall. He knows that he has not grown any taller and that he is still small compared to all the mountains around him.

This is the secret to Moshe *Rabbeinu*'s humility, explained the *rebbe*. For even though he had achieved great heights, so much so that Hashem was calling him in order to speak with him, he nonetheless remained humble, as he did not attribute any of his greatness to his own personal strengths.

אָדָם כִּי־יַקְרִיב מִכֶּם קָרְבָּן לַה'

"When a man among you wishes to bring an offering before Hashem" (1:2)

Why was it necessary, asked the Alshich *HaKadosh* (R' Moshe Alshich), for the verse to include the word "*mikem*"? The verse need only have stated, "When a man brings an offering to Hashem."

The answer, said the Alshich, is as follows: It is incumbent upon the person bringing the offering to remember that the animal which is soon to be offered is coming in his stead. When the animal is slaughtered, he must keep in mind that *he* was deserving of being slaughtered. As the blood of the animal is sprinkled, let him contemplate the fact that it was *his* blood that deserved to be sprinkled.

The word "*mikem*" means, "among you," but it also means, "from your own beings." Thus the verse can be read as follows, "When a man brings an offering to Hashem from your own beings (*mikem*)" — for it is as if the person bringing the *korban* is being offered to Hashem.

∗◌∗

וְשִׁסַּע אֹתוֹ בִכְנָפָיו לֹא יַבְדִּיל

"He shall then tear it apart, with its feathers still attached, without splitting it completely" (1:17)

The *Midrash Rabbah* states that even though the feathers of a bird are repulsive to some people, they should nevertheless be included in this offering, for the offering of a poor person beautifies the *Mizbe'ach*.

On one occasion, King Agrippas wished to bring one *thousand* burnt offerings in a single day. He sent a messenger to the *Kohen Gadol*, instructing him not to bring any sacrificial offerings from other people on that day, aside from his own.

Later that day, a poor man holding two pigeons approached the *Kohen* and requested that he sacrifice them for him.

"I'm afraid I will not be able to help you," responded the *Kohen*, "for the king has given specific orders that no offering other than his own be brought today."

"My master, the *Kohen Gadol*," said the pauper, "I am but a poor man. Each day, I catch four pigeons; I use two of them as sacrificial offerings and save the other two to feed my family. By refusing to sacrifice my offering today, you will be preventing me from earning a livelihood tomorrow. For it is in the merit of this *korban* that I receive my sustenance."

The poor man's emotional plea touched the *Kohen Gadol*, and he agreed to sacrifice the man's pigeons.

That same day, King Agrippas had a dream in which a man appeared before him and told him, "Know that a poor man has preceded you!" The dream disturbed Agrippas, so he went directly to the *Kohen*. "Tell me," he asked the *Kohen*, "did you sacrifice anyone else's offering today?"

The *Kohen Gadol* admitted that he had, and he told him about the pauper. When the king heard why the *Kohen* had accepted the other man's sacrifice, he praised the *Kohen*: "You did the right thing!"

וְנֶפֶשׁ כִּי־תַקְרִיב קָרְבַּן מִנְחָה לַה׳

"When a soul wishes to bring a meal-offering before Hashem" (2:1)

Rashi comments that the word "soul" was not used with reference to any other offering besides the meal-offering. This is because the meal-offering is the *korban* of a poor person, about which Hashem says, "Although it is a modest offering, I consider it as though he has offered his very soul."

The *Midrash Rabbah* relates a story of a poor woman who brought a handful of flour as a meal-offering. When the *Kohen* saw what she had brought, he said derisively, "Look at what she has to offer! Is there even enough here for an offering?"

That same day the *Kohen* was told in a dream, "Do not mock this poor woman, for this *korban* that she has brought before Hashem is considered as though she had offered her own soul."

נֶפֶשׁ כִּי־תֶחֱטָא בִשְׁגָגָה מִכֹּל מִצְוֹת
ה' אֲשֶׁר לֹא תֵעָשֶׂינָה וְעָשָׂה מֵאַחַת מֵהֵנָּה:

"If a person unintentionally transgresses one of any of Hashem's commandments that may not be done, and does one of them" (4:2)

An individual is required to repent and bring a sin-offering even for an unintentional transgression.

This is difficult, noted the Alshich *HaKadosh* (R' Moshe Alshich), for there are certain unintentional transgressions which are completely out of a person's control. For example, if a man was walking in the street and, suddenly, something frightened him and he jumped back a step. As a result, he stepped on, and broke, his friend's vessel. What could he have done to prevent this from happening? Nothing, apparently. How can he be held responsible in such a case?

When a man consistently keeps Hashem's *mitzvos*, answered the Alshich, Hashem protects him from all mishap. For instance, if a person is always careful not to allow any food of questionable *kashrus* status into his mouth, then Hashem will see to it that he will never unintentionally eat anything forbidden. Similarly, a person who is always mindful of other people's property will not unintentionally sin with money that does not belong to him.

This idea, concluded the Alshich, is alluded to in the following verse: "If a person unintentionally transgresses ..." — When does a person come to sin unintentionally? When he "does one of them" — when he has previously committed the sin *intentionally*.

אֲשֶׁר נָשִׂיא יֶחֱטָא

"When a ruler sins ..." (4:22)

R' Shmelke of Nikolsburg once admonished the leaders of his community. He exhorted them to engage in heartfelt repentance and to increase their level of fear of Heaven so that the townspeople would learn from their good example.

"But *Rebbe*," replied one of the men, "throughout your life you have been steeped in fear of Heaven and repentance, yet no one has learned from your ways. Why should they learn from us if they have not learned from you?"

"In this week's *parashah*," answered the *rebbe*, "it states, 'When (*asher*) a ruler sins.' *Chazal* (*Horayos* 10b) expound on the word '*asher*': 'Fortunate (*ashrei*) is the generation whose ruler brings a *korban* to earn atonement.'

"There is an apparent difficulty in this remark," continued the *rebbe*. "For there is another verse, above, that begins the same way: 'If (*asher*) the anointed *Kohen* will sin ..."(*Vayikra* 4:3), yet there *Chazal* do not comment, 'fortunate is the generation whose *Kohen Gadol* ... brings an atonement.' What is the difference between the *Kohen Gadol* and the leader?

"The answer," said the *rebbe*, "is as follows: A *Kohen Gadol* is comparable to a *rebbe*, and a ruler is comparable to a community leader.

"When the *Kohen Gadol* repents, what does the nation say? 'Of course he is repenting. After all, he is the *Kohen Gadol* and our great *Rebbe*. If he doesn't pour out his heart in heartfelt repentance, who will?'

"But when it is the *Nasi*, the ruler, that repents," concluded R' Shmelke, "then the nation says, 'Fortunate is the generation that has such a leader' — and they learn from his ways."

וְהָיָה כִי־יֶאְשַׁם לְאַחַת מֵאֵלֶּה וְהִתְוַדָּה אֲשֶׁר חָטָא עָלֶיהָ:

"When he is guilty of one of these sins, he shall confess what he has sinned" (5:5)

Several close disciples of R' Yisrael Salanter related that R' Yisrael once forgot to check his pockets on *erev Shabbos*, as *Chazal* had instructed: "A person is required to examine his clothing on *erev Shabbos* just before dark, for he may forget himself and go out (*Shabbos* 12a)." Later, on Shabbos, he found a small piece of paper in one of his pockets.

R' Salanter confessed over this infraction for the next fifteen years!

וְהֵבִיא אַיִל תָּמִים ... אֶל־הַכֹּהֵן וְכִפֶּר עָלָיו הַכֹּהֵן
עַל שִׁגְגָתוֹ אֲשֶׁר־שָׁגַג וְהוּא לֹא־יָדַע וְנִסְלַח לוֹ:

"He shall bring a perfect ram ... to the Kohen; and the Kohen shall make an atonement for him — for the inadvertent sin he may have committed — and he will be forgiven" (5:18)

This offering is called the "*asham talui*" (a guilt-offering in case of doubt), as the individual does not know with certainty whether or not he has actually violated a prohibition.

Why is a ram brought as an *asham talui?* asked the Kotzker *Rebbe* (R' Menachem Mendel of Kotzk). A ram is a relatively expensive animal, and since we are not even certain that the man committed any sin, why not let him bring a less-expensive animal?

I say, answered the Kotzker, that it is specifically because *it is* a case of doubt that he is obligated to bring a more expensive animal. For when an individual knows that he has committed a sin, the mere knowledge of it causes him great suffering and leads him to regret his wrongdoing. The anguish that he experiences as a result of having committed a sin actually serves as a partial atonement for the misdeed.

However, when an individual is not sure whether he has sinned or not, then he is at least deficient in paying attention to his actions. He must correct his ways and become more aware of what he does.

It is specifically such a person that must bring an expensive offering.

וְהֵשִׁיב אֶת־הַגְּזֵלָה אֲשֶׁר גָּזָל

"He shall return the article that he stole" (5:23)

Gedolei Yisrael have always exercised great caution when dealing with the money of others, so that they would not be guilty of the severe transgression of theft.

One *erev Shabbos*, when R' Isser Zalman Meltzer returned from the *mikveh*, he suddenly realized that he had used two clothing cubbies at the *mikveh*.

Perhaps I took someone else's space, thought R' Meltzer. *I might very well owe the mikveh attendant twice the amount that I usually pay!*

One of his family members saw how much the matter was troubling R' Meltzer, so he offered to go to the *mikveh* and pay the attendant for the extra cubby.

"It is *I* who must go," replied R' Meltzer. "For the *halachah* states explicitly that one who steals from his fellow must not only repay him, but he must verbally appease him as well. The responsibility to appease the attendant is my responsibility alone."

Parashas Tzav

צַו אֶת־אַהֲרֹן
"Command Aharon" (6:2)

RASHI EXPLAINS THAT THE EXPRESSION "COMMAND" IS ONE OF URGing. Since the verse is dealing with a situation where there is a loss of money involved, it is necessary to urge, for people are reluctant to let money out of their pockets.

R' Yisrael Salanter was traveling to a distant city. On the way, he passed a small town and decided to rest in one of the local inns.

The innkeeper, sensing that his guest was a *ben Torah*, approached R' Salanter and asked: "Excuse me," said the innkeeper, "but would you happen to be a *shochet*? You see, I have a cow in the barn, and I have set it aside to be slaughtered. The problem is that we don't have a *shochet* in our town. I usually take whatever needs to be slaughtered to the neighboring town and have it slaughtered there, but if you are a *shochet*, then you could save me a trip."

"No," responded R' Salanter, "I am not a *shochet*."

About an hour later, R' Salanter approached the innkeeper and asked, "Perhaps you would be kind enough to lend me one ruble?"

"Give you a loan?" replied the innkeeper in surprise. "But I don't even know you! How can I trust you to pay me back?"

"Listen to what you are saying," said R' Salanter. "When it came to loaning me money — even an amount as small as *one* ruble — you would not trust me as I am a stranger to you. Yet when you wanted to slaughter your cow, you were prepared to rely on me though you have absolutely no idea who I am. *Shechitah* involves many *halachos*. Why were you so sure that I possess enough fear of Heaven to be a proper *shochet*?"

צַו אֶת־אַהֲרֹן
"Command Aharon" (6:2)

R ashi cites the following statement of *Chazal*: "R' Shimon said: Scripture must especially urge in a situation where there is a loss of [a money] pouch (*kis*)."

Chazal have taught us, said the *Chiddushei HaRim* (R' Yitzchak Meir of Gur), that the *korban olah* (the burnt-offering) atones for an individual's sinful thoughts.

If we would consider the matter, continued the *rebbe*, we would realize that each one of our limbs has been given a "protective covering" to protect it from sinning. For example, a person has the ability to shut his eyelids, which will prevent him from gazing at what he should not see. He can close his lips tightly to guard himself from consuming forbidden foods. Similarly, he can seal off his ears to avoid hearing a word of *lashon hara* or *rechilus*.

But how is it possible for a person to guard himself from thinking improper thoughts? Can one's mind be "covered"?

This is why R' Shimon stated, "Scripture must especially urge in a situation where there is a loss of *kis* (money pouch)." The word, *kis* resembles the word, "*kisui* (cover)." R' Shimon is telling us, then, that if a person wishes to protect his limb that lacks a "cover" — his mind — from improper thoughts then he will need to "urge himself." He will need an extra measure of self-motivation to keep his mind pure.

צַו אֶת־אַהֲרֹן
"Command Aharon" (6:2)

R ashi explains that the expression "Command" always implies urging, for now and for future generations.

The *Chofetz Chaim* was known to invest much effort in distributing the *sefarim* that he authored. He journeyed far and wide, braving uneven dirt roads and an assortment of difficult travel conditions. Bitter cold, rain, and snow would not deter this *tzaddik* from spreading and glorifying the Torah.

Several of his close disciples once asked him, "Why does the *Rav* go to such great lengths to sell his *sefarim*?"

"You know," responded the *Chofetz Chaim*, "that the noblemen go on hunting expeditions. How much toil, effort, and money do these individuals invest in this trivial sport, just to entrap one deer (*tzvi*), one bear (*dov*), or a single wolf (*zev*)!

"I, too," remarked the *Chofetz Chaim*, "am willing to invest much effort in the hope that I will succeed in drawing one R' Tzvi, one R' Dov, or one R' Zev closer to the service of Hashem."

צַו אֶת־אַהֲרֹן
"Command Aharon" (6:2)

Rashi explains that the expression "Command" is one of urging. Since the verse is dealing with a situation where there is a loss of money involved, it is necessary to urge, for people are reluctant to let money out of their pockets.

R' Levi Yitzchak of Berdichev once rebuked one of the wealthy Jews in his town for ignoring the plight of the needy.

"It is important for you to realize," said the *rebbe*, "that the *mitzvah* of giving *tzedakah* is a very great *mitzvah*, and it has the power to atone for one's sins."

"I have a much cheaper way to atone for my sins!" replied the brazen man. "*Chazal* (*Yoma* 86b) have learned from the verse, 'And let our lips substitute for bulls' (*Hoshea* 14:3), that nowadays prayer has taken the place of sacrificial offerings. I pray every day, so all of my sins are forgiven!"

"I am afraid that you are mistaken," answered R' Levi Yitzchak. "For when *Chazal* stated that prayer has taken the place of sacrificial offerings, they were referring to the *tamid*-offering alone. However, those offerings that atoned for an individual's sins, such as the *korban* chatas (sin-offering), have not been replaced by prayer but *tzedakah*. This is as the verse states, 'Redeem your sin through *tzedakah*' (*Daniel* 4:24). Give an abundance of *tzedakah*, and then Heaven will forgive your iniquity."

❧

וְאֵשׁ הַמִּזְבֵּחַ תּוּקַד בּוֹ:

"And the fire of the [incense] altar shall be lit with it" (6:2)

The greatness of the *Sefas Emes* (R' Yehudah Leib Alter of Gur) was already apparent from the time he was a youth.

On one occasion, the young R' Yehudah Leib approached his grandfather, the *Chiddushei HaRim* (R' Yitzchak Meir of Gur), and offered an interpretation of the verse, "And the fire of the altar shall be lit with it (*bo*)."

"This verse," said the *Sefas Emes*, "refers not only to the fire that burned atop the altar, but also to the fire that burned within the heart of the *Kohen*; 'The fire of the altar shall be lit *in him* (*bo*)' — his heart must be aflame in his service of Hashem."

The *Chiddushei HaRim* was delighted by the words of his grandson. He turned to the people around him and said, "Did you hear that? I am positive that this boy will grow one day to guide the masses in their service of Hashem."

❧

אֵשׁ ... תּוּקַד עַל־הַמִּזְבֵּחַ לֹא תִכְבֶּה:

"The fire ... on the altar must not be extinguished" (6:6)

The holy Torah has been compared to the Eternal Flame; it is kept burning by the diligence of those who ponder it day and night.

From his earliest youth until his old age, the *B'nei Yissachar* (R' Tzvi Elimelech of Dinov) was a paradigm of diligence, of someone who never stops studying the Torah.

It was his custom to lead the prayers on the *Yamim Nora'im*. Amazingly, he used to recite all the prayers *by heart*.

"How does the *Rebbe* know the entire *Yamim Nora'im* liturgy by heart?" asked one of his followers.

"When I was a youth," explained the *B'nei Yissachar*, "I suffered from very severe pains in my eyes. The doctors warned my parents that if I did not stop straining my eyes from my studies, then I would very likely lose my eyesight altogether. The doctor's warning, however, did not deter me — I simply could not stop studying Torah."

"When my father saw that I was not complying with the doctor's orders, he sent me from the house for several days to keep me away from my *sefarim*. That, too, was of little use, as I managed to get hold of *sefarim* outside my house. I continued my reading, often when it was already dark..."

"Finally, when he saw that he had no other option, my father locked me in a dark warehouse filled with wood. There, he thought, my eyes would finally get the rest they needed."

"But that did not help either. For I searched and rummaged through everything in the warehouse until I finally found an old *Yamim Nora'im machzor*. Since that was the only *sefer* I had, I sat down and reviewed it until I had memorized all of the prayers."

אֵשׁ ... תּוּקַד עַל־הַמִּזְבֵּחַ לֹא תִכְבֶּה:

"The fire ... on the altar must not be extinguished" (6:6)

The residents of Yerushalayim witnessed exceptional self-sacrifice for Torah study on the part of their *rav*, R' Tzvi Pesach Frank.

In 1948, the Jordanian Army barraged the city of Yerushalayim with a downpour of bombs and explosive shells. The city's inhabitants hurried to their bomb shelters, as did the *rav* of Yerushalayim, R' Tzvi Pesach Frank, who sat in a corner, bent over his *sefarim*.

People sat huddled together, as the sounds of explosions and thunderous blasts filled the air.

Finding that his learning was being disturbed by the tumultuous atmosphere that had been generated by the nervousness of the people around him, R' Frank requested to leave the bomb shelter and return to his home — there he would be able to learn Torah undisturbed.

" But *Rabbeinu*," said the people, "it is literally life threatening to leave the shelter!"

"The Torah," asserted R' Frank, "protects and saves!" And with that, he left the bomb shelter and went up to his room.

The *rav* sat in his room and learned with astounding diligence.

Some time later, a shell struck the house, and some of its fragments penetrated the shutters of R' Frank's room. But the *rav* was completely engrossed in his learning, and he did not even notice what had happened.

"I am not sure," commented the *rav* afterwards, "but I think there were some flashes of light that skipped around the room."

בִּמְקוֹם אֲשֶׁר תִּשָּׁחֵט הָעֹלָה תִּשָּׁחֵט הַחַטָּאת

"In the same place where the burnt-offering is slaughtered, so shall the sin-offering be slaughtered" (6:18)

O ur Sages have taught us, remarked R' Yisrael Salanter, that the burnt-offering atones a person for sinful thoughts (but not physically committed), while the sin-offering atones for sins that a person has unintentionally committed.

You should be aware, he continued, that sinful *thoughts* ultimately lead to sinful *acts*! This is intimated in the verse, "In the same place where the burnt-offering is slaughtered, so shall the sin-offering be slaughtered." That is, when somebody is guilty of thinking of some sin, he will likely commit an actual sin *in the same area* of observance, and he will need the atonement of a sin-offering.

זֹאת הַתּוֹרָה לָעֹלָה לַמִּנְחָה וְלַחַטָּאת וְלָאָשָׁם ...

"These, then, are the laws of the burnt-offering, the meal-offering, the sin-offering, and the guilt-offering ..." (7:37)

R' Baruch of Mezibuzh expounded this verse as follows: At times, an individual will learn Torah with the right intentions — completely for the sake of Heaven. Yet at other times he may learn Torah with improper intentions — for the sake of honor or for some other selfish motive.

The verse can therefore be explained as follows: "*Zos haTorah*" — If an individual learns Torah for the sake of Heaven, then it is considered as lofty as a "burnt-offering or a meal-offering." But if his motivations are not pure, then it is regarded as "the sin-offering, and the guilt-offering."

❧❀☙

זֹאת הַתּוֹרָה לָעֹלָה לַמִּנְחָה וְלַחַטָּאת וְלָאָשָׁם ...

"These, then, are the laws of the burnt-offering, the meal-offering, the sin-offering, and the guilt-offering ..." (7:37)

The Midrash Rabbah records a parable by R' Acha: A king conquered a province, and was making his grand entrance. The king entered the province first, followed by his powerful soldiers who were the heroes of the war.

"I am terrified by our new government," said one of the province's inhabitants to his friend. "Just look at the soldiers that the king has brought with him!"

"You needn't fear," responded his friend. "If you do as the king wants and you obey his laws, the soldiers will not harm you in any way."

So it was with the Jewish people. When they first heard the portion of the Torah dealing with the sacrificial offerings, they were frightened that they would not be able to keep all the laws of the sacrifices properly. So Moshe *Rabbeinu* told them, "Engage yourselves in Torah study, and you will have no reason to fear the sacrificial offerings."

❧❀☙

וַיֹּאמֶר מֹשֶׁה אֶל־הָעֵדָה זֶה הַדָּבָר אֲשֶׁר־צִוָּה ה' לַעֲשׂוֹת:
וַיַּקְרֵב מֹשֶׁה אֶת אַהֲרֹן וְאֶת־בָּנָיו וַיִּרְחַץ אֹתָם בַּמָּיִם:

"Moshe then said to the congregation, 'This is the procedure that Hashem commanded [me] to do.' Moshe then drew Aharon and his sons near, and he bathed them in water" (8:5-6)

When the time arrived for R' Elimelech of Lizhensk to reveal his greatness to the public, his brother, the holy R' Zusia, requested to be his attendant. But R' Elimelech refused his offer.

"Why do you not permit me to serve you?" asked R' Zusia. "We find that even Moshe *Rabbeinu* served his brother Aharon as well as his sons, as the verse states: Moshe then drew Aharon and his sons near, and he bathed them in water.'"

"That is exactly why I will not allow it!" responded R' Elimelech. "For the previous verse states: Moshe then said to the congregation, 'This is the procedure that Hashem commanded [me] to do.' This shows us that Moshe made an effort to inform the Jewish people that Hashem had *commanded* him to attend to Aharon and his sons — but if not for that, he would have been forbidden to do so."

Parashas Shemini

וַיִּקְרְבוּ כָּל־הָעֵדָה וַיַּעַמְדוּ לִפְנֵי ה':

"The entire community then approached and stood before Hashem" (9:5)

THE *ARI HAKADOSH*, R' YITZCHAK LURIA, USED TO SAY THAT BEFORE an individual accepts the sovereignty of Heaven upon himself, he must first accept upon himself to fulfill the *mitzvah* of, "You shall love your fellow as yourself."

This is alluded to in the verse, "The entire community then approached and stood before Hashem" — first "the entire community" united, and only then did they step forward "before Hashem."

וַיֹּאמֶר מֹשֶׁה אֶל־אַהֲרֹן קְרַב אֶל־הַמִּזְבֵּחַ

"Moshe then said to Aharon, 'Draw near to the altar'" (9:7)

Rashi explains that Aharon was embarrassed and afraid to approach the altar. Moshe therefore said to him, "Why are you embarrassed? This is what you were selected for."

The *Ba'al Shem Tov* elucidated Rashi's words. Moshe was saying to Aharon: Why are you embarrassed? It is specifically due to the fact that you possess the character trait of humility and that you feel ashamed before Hashem that you were chosen to be the *Kohen* — "This is what you were selected for!"

⁂

וַיָּבֹא מֹשֶׁה וְאַהֲרֹן אֶל־אֹהֶל מוֹעֵד וַיֵּצְאוּ
וַיְבָרֲכוּ אֶת־הָעָם וַיֵּרָא כְבוֹד־ה' אֶל־כָּל־הָעָם:

*"Moshe and Aharon then entered the Tent
of Meeting, and they came out and they
blessed the people, and the glory of Hashem
was then revealed to the people" (9:23)*

Rashi comments that when Aharon saw that all of the offerings had been brought and yet the Divine Presence still had not descended to Israel, he was distressed and said, "I know that the Holy One, Blessed is He, is angry with me, and it is because of me that the Divine Presence has not descended to Israel."

Thereupon, Moshe and Aharon entered the Tent of Meeting to pray for mercy, and the Divine Presence descended to Israel.

We ought to learn from Aharon's behavior, say our *mussar* masters. When the Divine Presence did not descend, he did not blame others for the Divine Presence not coming down. He blamed only himself. We, too, should not blame others when problems arise. Instead, we should examine our own deeds and strive to improve them.

To what can this be compared? To a group of paupers who were chatting about their *shul.*

"You know," began one of the poor men, "in the wealthy people's *shul*, on *Simchas Torah*, they give out choice wine between each *hakafah.*"

His friend responded with a sigh. "Well, of course — they're wealthy. But if we wanted to do the same for our *shul*, where would we get wine from? After all, we are paupers —"

"I have an idea!" said a third man. "Let's put an empty barrel in the corner of the *shul*. Every day, we will each pour a small shot glass of wine into the barrel; when Simchas Torah comes around, we will have a full barrel of wine!"

The men agreed and began to carry out their plan.

On Simchas Torah the barrel was opened up. When the men peered inside, they saw that, much to their dismay, the barrel was not filled with wine — but with water. What a disappointment!

They all stared at one another, but no one said a word, as each one of them knew that he was guilty of pouring water into the barrel instead of wine.

Now the truth emerged. They each had the same thought: *My friend will pour wine into the barrel. What would be so terrible if I pour in some water instead? I'm sure no one will even notice!* This continued until the barrel became full of water.

The same idea can be applied to man. Everybody is aware of just how important it is to rectify one's character traits. Yet each person thinks, *Let my friend correct his flaws first and then I will correct mine.*

וַתֵּצֵא אֵשׁ מִלִּפְנֵי ה' וַתֹּאכַל אוֹתָם וַיָּמֻתוּ לִפְנֵי ה':

"A fire came forth from before Hashem and consumed them, and they died before Hashem" (10:2)

The *Midrash* lists several reasons why Nadav and Avihu were punished. One reason, states the *Midrash*, is because they did not marry. In addition, the *Midrash* says that they "would walk behind Moshe and Aharon and say: When will these two elders pass away, so that you and I will lead the generation?"

These reasons, explained the Vilna *Gaon*, are not two separate reasons but two parts of one single reason.

If Nadav and Avihu had wished not to marry because they wanted to study Torah undisturbed, that would have been fine. However, since they followed Moshe and Aharon, waiting for the time when they would be the leaders of the Jewish people, it was clear that they were not intending to study Torah. Thus they deserved their punishment for both reasons combined.

וּלֲהַבְדִּיל בֵּין הַקֹּדֶשׁ וּבֵין הַחֹל וּבֵין הַטָּמֵא
וּבֵין הַטָּהוֹר: וּלְהוֹרֹת אֶת־בְּנֵי יִשְׂרָאֵל

"In order to distinguish between the sacred and the profane, and between the contaminated and the pure, and to teach the Children of Israel" (10:10-11)

C hazal (*Pesachim* 3b) relate that two students were sitting before Hillel the Elder.

One of them asked Hillel, "Why do we pick grapes using vessels that are ritually pure (*be'taharah*), and we do not pick olives with vessels that are ritually pure?"

The other one asked, "Why do we pick grapes using vessels that are ritually pure, and we pick olives with vessels that are ritually impure (*b'tumah*)?"

The two students had posed the identical question, yet the first student was careful to express it in a more refined manner.

"I am confident," responded Hillel, "that the first student, who spoke in a refined manner, will become a Torah giant and will be an important *halachic* authority in Israel."

After a short while, the first student did indeed become famous — he was none other than R' Yochanan ben Zakkai, who disseminated *halachic* rulings in Israel.

This story, said the Vilna *Gaon*, is hinted at in the verse, "In order to distinguish between the sacred and the profane, and between the contaminated and the pure, and to teach the Children of Israel." A person who is careful to speak properly, distinguishing between speech that is sacred and profane, contaminated and pure, will eventually become a teacher of halachic rulings in Israel.

אַךְ אֶת־זֶה לֹא תֹאכְלוּ

"But this is what you shall not eat" (11:4)

A n amazing incident transpired in Vilna that quickly became the talk of the city.

An hour before candle-lighting one *erev Shabbos*, a question regarding the *kashrus* of a chicken had arisen in the home of Reb Chaim the tailor.

As Reb Chaim's neighbor was none other than the *Gaon* of Vilna, he quickly sent one of his children to the sage to ask him whether the chicken was permissible to eat or not. It was not the *Gaon's* custom to respond to halachic inquiries, but since the matter was urgent, he decided to reply. He examined the chicken and ruled that it was, in fact, forbidden for consumption.

Reb Chaim's wife, who was unaware that her husband had already received a ruling from the Vilna *Gaon*, sent another one of her sons to R' Shmuel, the *rav* of Vilna, in order to determine the chicken's status. Her son hurried to the home of R' Shmuel, who ruled that the chicken was kosher!

When his wife relayed the ruling she had received from R' Shmuel, Reb Chaim was thrown into a state of confusion and did not know what to do. In a panic, he ran to R' Shmuel and told the *rav* what had occurred.

R' Shmuel stood by his ruling. "The chicken is perfectly kosher!" he maintained. "And to prove it to you, both I and the *Gaon* will come to your home Shabbos night and taste the chicken!"

That night, R' Shmuel visited the *Gaon* and said, "My master and teacher, I am like dust beneath your feet. However, this community has chosen me as their *rav*, and since I have ruled that the chicken is kosher, I humbly request that you come with me to Reb Chaim's house, where we will both taste from the chicken."

The *Gaon* , in his great humility, agreed with R' Shmuel, and they went together to the home of Reb Chaim.

Reb Chaim was very moved by the visit of these two great guests, and his wife proceeded to serve the food, including the plate of chicken.

But just as she put the plate of chicken on the table, the chandelier that had been suspended over the table suddenly came crashing down directly atop the bowl of food. The candles melted into the food, making the chicken totally inedible.

In this way, the *Gaon* was saved from eating something which was not kosher. For Hashem protects *tzaddikim* from stumbling, as the verse states, "He guards the steps of His devout ones" (*I Shmuel* 2:9).

כִּי־מַפְרִיס פַּרְסָה הוּא ...
וְהוּא גֵּרָה לֹא־יִגָּר טָמֵא הוּא לָכֶם:

"For its hoof is split ... but it does not chew its cud — it is unclean to you" (11:7)

On one occasion, R' Meir of Premishlan went to the home of a wealthy, but stingy, Jew and requested a donation for a worthy charity.

"Please forgive me," responded the wealthy man, "but I am truly pressed for time as I am in a rush to get to the *beis midrash*!"

"You should know," said R' Meir, "that it is about people such as yourself, that the verse states, 'For its hoof is split ... but it does not chew its cud — it is unclean to you.'

"'For its hoof is split' — A person's footsteps do not mean very much, even if they are taking him to the *beis midrash* if "it does not chew its cud (*v'hu geirah lo yigar*)" — if he does not set aside (*mei-gir*) a certain amount of his money for *tzedakah*. About such an individual it can be stated, "*tamei hu lachem*," he is unclean to you!

וְאֶת הַחֲסִידָה
"The chasidah" (11:19)

"Why is its name *chasidah* (literally meaning 'kind one')?" asks Rashi. "Because it does kindness with its companions with food."

According to the Ramban, said the *Chiddushei HaRim* (R' Yitzchak Meir Alter of Gur), the reason why the nonkosher birds are not kosher is because of their cruel nature. If so, the *chasidah* should have been a kosher-type bird; after all, it bestows kindness upon its companions!

The *chasidah* acts kindly toward its *companions*, answered the *rebbe*, but it does not act kindly toward anyone else. This is why it is considered not kosher.

אַל־תְּשַׁקְּצוּ אֶת־נַפְשֹׁתֵיכֶם בְּכָל־הַשֶּׁרֶץ
הַשֹּׁרֵץ וְלֹא תִטַּמְּאוּ בָּהֶם וְנִטְמֵתֶם בָּם:

"Do not make yourselves abhorrent with all the low-creeping creatures that crawl; and do not make yourselves impure with them [by eating them], for then you will be further defiled through them" (11:43)

In *Maseches Yoma* (39a), *Chazal* state that the word *"v'nitmeisem"* is related to the word *"timtum"* (obstruction). When someone eats non-kosher food, his heart and soul become "obstructed" until he loses his sensitivity to anything Jewish.

This is comparable, said the *Chofetz Chaim*, to a storeowner who sold fine, expensive perfumes. One day, he entered a tannery and inhaled the foul odor that permeated the air. As someone who was accustomed to sweet fragrances, the smell of the hides was too much for him to bear, so he quickly left the shop.

Some time later, his financial situation deteriorated, and he was forced to sell his perfume store. He went looking for some means of earning a livelihood, and, in desperation, he took a job at a tannery. At first, it was very difficult for him to work there; the smell of the hides made him nauseous and dizzy. However, he slowly grew accustomed to the foul odor. Eventually, he stopped noticing it altogether.

The same thing applies to forbidden foods, remarked the *Chofetz Chaim*. Man's soul is refined and taken from the highest realm; it is not accustomed to eating that which is forbidden. One who partakes of such food, however, slowly gets used to it, until his heart and soul become completely numb and sealed. The Torah therefore commands, "Do not make yourselves abhorrent with all the low-creeping creatures that crawl; and do not make yourselves impure with them [by eating them], for then you will be further defiled through them" — Do not eat that which is forbidden, or even of a questionable status, lest you slowly grow accustomed to it.

לְהַבְדִּיל בֵּין הַטָּמֵא וּבֵין הַטָּהֹר וּבֵין הַחַיָּה
הַנֶּאֱכֶלֶת וּבֵין הַחַיָּה אֲשֶׁר לֹא תֵאָכֵל:

*"To distinguish between what is impure and pure, and
between the living creature that may be eaten and the
living creature that must not be eaten" (11:47)*

The Gemara in *Maseches Yoma* (82b) relates a story about a
pregnant woman who smelled the aroma of a delicious dish and
began to crave it. That day was Yom Kippur, however, and her
acquaintances did not know what to do: on the one hand, it was the
fast-day of Yom Kippur; but, on the other hand, if the woman would
refrain from eating, it could possibly be dangerous for the fetus.

They came before R' Yehudah HaNasi and consulted him as to what
should be done. "Whisper in the woman's ear," said R' Yehudah, "that
today is Yom Kippur; perhaps it will settle her mind."

They followed his instructions and the woman calmed down.

A similar incident occurred with a different pregnant woman on
Yom Kippur. R' Chanina was approached and asked what measures
should be taken. He, too, advised to whisper in the woman's ear that
it was Yom Kippur.

This time, however, the woman was not relieved by their words.
Only once she was given a taste of the dish did her cravings subside.

Each woman gave birth to a son who would eventually become
famous — one for his righteousness and one for his wickedness.

The first woman gave birth to R' Yochanan ben Nafcha who would
eventually become one of the greatest of *Amora'im*.

The second woman, who tasted from the dish on Yom Kippur,
gave birth to a son, Shabsai. He became known as "Shabsai the
fruit-hoarder" because he hoarded fruits in order to force the prices
to rise exorbitantly.

These stories, noted R' Akiva Eiger, are hinted to in the following
verse: "To distinguish between what is impure and pure, and between
the living creature (*chayah*) that may be eaten and the living creature
that must not be eaten." A woman that has recently given birth is
referred to as a "*chayah*." With this in mind, we may read the verse
as follows: "To distinguish between what is impure and pure" — in
order to distinguish between a child who will be virtuous or not, look
at the difference "between the *chayah* that eats and the *chayah* that
will not eat" — see whether or not the mother ate on Yom Kippur.

וּבַיּוֹם הַשְּׁמִינִי יִמּוֹל בְּשַׂר עָרְלָתוֹ:

"On the eighth day, the flesh of his foreskin shall be circumcised" (12:3)

THE *MIDRASH* RELATES THAT THE ROMAN EMPEROR APPROACHED R' Tanchuma and said, "Come and let us be as one nation, Romans and Jews!"

"Gladly," responded R' Tanchuma, "But we Jews are circumcised and are therefore unable to resemble you; circumcise yourselves and you will resemble us."

"You have spoken well," said the emperor. "But you are well aware, of course, that all those who triumph in a debate with the emperor are thrown into the lion's den!"

The emperor's men took hold of R' Tanchuma and cast him into the den that was occupied by hungry lions looking for prey.

Amazingly, the lions remained crouched in their places and did not harm R' Tanchuma in any way.

Among those who witnessed the miracle was a Jewish heretic, who tried minimizing the miracle. "The lions must not be hungry," he said to the king. "That is why they haven't devoured him."

"If that is the case," responded the king, "then let us place you inside the cage and see if you are correct."

The wicked heretic froze in terror, but the emperor's men grabbed him and flung him into the lion's den. The lions pounced upon him and devoured him, while R' Tanchuma left the emperor's palace with prominence and honor.

וּבַיּוֹם הַשְּׁמִינִי יִמּוֹל בְּשַׂר עָרְלָתוֹ:

"On the eighth day, the flesh of his foreskin shall be circumcised" (12:3)

A t the *bris milah* ceremony, it is customary to bless the infant, "Just as he has entered into the covenant, so may he enter into the Torah, the marriage canopy, and good deeds."

R' Betzalel HaKohen of Vilna was recognized as a child prodigy. His name spread throughout the city as a Torah expert with a razor-sharp intellect.

Though he was yet young, the *shadchanim* of the city spoke highly of him, and by the time he reached the age of 12, he married.

At the meal following the *tena'im* ceremony, one of the scholars who was present got up to speak, and he said, "At a *bris milah* we bless the infant, 'Just as he has entered into the covenant, so may he enter into the Torah, the marriage canopy, and good deeds.' But the sequence of this blessing does not appear to be correct. For a child first enters the stage of 'good deeds' — when he becomes a bar-mitzvah — and only afterwards enters the wedding canopy. Why, then, is the order reversed?

"Our intent upon blessing the infant," he continued, "is that he should become so great in Torah scholarship that all will seek him for a son-in-law, so that he will enter the wedding canopy even before he reaches the age of bar-mitzvah."

וּבַיּוֹם הַשְּׁמִינִי יִמּוֹל בְּשַׂר עָרְלָתוֹ:

"On the eighth day, the flesh of his foreskin shall be circumcised" (12:3)

W hat is the meaning of the words, "Just as he has entered into the covenant"? asked R' Menachem Mendel of Kotzk. The child did not "enter" the *bris* on his own volition; it was his parents who entered him!

Rather, said the *rebbe*, we mean the following: Just as the infant entered into this tremendous *mitzvah* without the slightest feeling of haughtiness over the fact that he was fulfilling it, so, too, should he continue to perform *mitzvos* without feeling any conceit. Every *mitzvah* he performs should be solely for the purpose of fulfilling the will of his Creator!

וּבַיּוֹם הַשְּׁמִינִי יִמּוֹל בְּשַׂר עָרְלָתוֹ:

"On the eighth day, the flesh of his foreskin shall be circumcised" (12:3)

The grandson of the Brisker *Rav* (R' Yitzchak Zev HaLevi Soloveitchik) was circumcised in the *rav*'s home.

After the *bris*, the *mohel* approached the *rav* and exclaimed, "*Baruch Hashem* that I have merited performing the *mitzvah* of *bris milah*; all the more so, in the *rav*'s home and on one of his grandchildren!"

"What do you mean?" asked the *rav*. "Do you really think that a *bris* performed in my home and on one of my grandchildren bears more importance than any other *bris*?"

"To what can it be compared?" continued the *rav*. "To a teacher of young schoolchildren who received a paltry salary and remained a destitute pauper his entire life.

"One day the teacher remarked, 'If I owned all of Rothschild's vaults, I would be wealthier than him!'

"'What do you mean?' someone asked him.

"'It's very simple,' he answered. 'Though our vaults would equal one another, I would still prove the wealthier man, as I *also* receive my meager salary from serving as a school teacher.'

"The same thing applies to a *bris milah*," concluded the Brisker *Rav*. "It is such a monumental *mitzvah* that the lineage of the infant lacks any significance in comparison."

וְרָאָה הַכֹּהֵן אֶת־הַנֶּגַע ... נֶגַע צָרַעַת הוּא

"The Kohen shall look at the mark... it is a mark of tzara'as" (13:3)

Our Sages in *Maseches Arachin* (16a) have taught us that *tzara'as* is a punishment for speaking *lashon hara*, slander.

It is for this reason, commented R' Yisrael Salanter, that the Torah portion that deals with *tzara'as* appears in the Torah adjacent to the portion of kosher and nonkosher foods. People are very meticulous about the *kashrus* of the food they put into their mouths. Here the Torah is teaching us that people should be just as careful about what they allow to come *out* of their mouths as they are about what they let *in* to their mouths.

✻❂✻

נֶגַע צָרַעַת כִּי תִהְיֶה בְּאָדָם וְהוּבָא אֶל־הַכֹּהֵן:

"If a mark of tzara'as appears on a person, he shall be brought to the Kohen" (13:9)

The *Midrash Rabbah* relates a story about a *Kohen* who used to examine individuals afflicted with *tzara'as*. The *Kohen* was extremely poor, however, and he was desperate for a means to earn a livelihood.

Perhaps, thought the *Kohen*, *I should leave Eretz Yisrael and seek my fortune abroad. It is much easier to make a comfortable living overseas.*

The *Kohen* discussed his plans with his wife, and he said to her, "People often come to me to examine their *tzara'as* marks, and I feel bad leaving them. Let me teach you how to examine these marks, so that while I'm away, you will take my place and perform the necessary examinations."

His wife agreed, and the *Kohen* began to teach her the laws of *tzara'as*.

"When a person comes to be examined," instructed the *Kohen*, "make sure to observe his hair. It is important for you to know that each strand of a person's hair grows from a separate opening, and each one is nourished from its own follicle. If you see that the openings around the hairs have dried out, then you can be sure that the person has *tzara'as*."

"Listen to what you are saying!" responded his wife. "If *HaKadosh Baruch Hu* has provided each hair with a wellspring from which to draw its sustenance, how much more so you, His very handiwork. Hashem will most certainly provide you with a livelihood! Why must you wander so far away, and search for a livelihood in *chutz la'aretz*?"

The *Kohen* heeded his wife's profound words and remained at home.

כֻּלּוֹ הָפַךְ לָבָן טָהוֹר הוּא:

"If he has turned completely white, he remains pure" (13:13)

R' Yochanan in *Maseches Sanhedrin* (98a) taught, "[*Mashiach*,] the son of David, will only come to a generation that is either entirely meritorious or entirely guilty."

This statement is difficult to understand, noted the *Chasam Sofer* (R' Moshe Sofer). For while it is easily understood why a generation that is entirely meritorious would be worthy of receiving *Mashiach*, on what basis would a thoroughly guilty generation receive him?

We find a similar difficulty in the verse, "If he has turned completely white, he remains pure." If a small affliction is considered impure, why is it considered pure when it covers the *metzora's* entire body?

We can answer both questions with one answer. Skin afflictions come upon an individual in order to inspire him to repent for his misdeeds. Now, if his entire body has turned white, he will definitely be humbled to repent completely and sincerely. There is therefore no need to declare him impure.

The same applies to a generation that is completely guilty. The way to awaken a generation that is full of sin is not with reproach but by sending them *Mashiach ben David*. Then they will return to Hashem in complete repentance.

הוּא בָדָד יֵשֵׁב מִחוּץ לַמַּחֲנֶה מוֹשָׁבוֹ:

"He shall live alone, his dwelling place being outside the camp" (13:46)

Rashi explains why the *metzora* must live in isolation: "Through *lashon hara* he caused a parting between a man and his wife and between a man and his colleague — so too shall he be set apart from everyone else."

A terrible plague had broken out in Vilna. As is customary during periods of misfortune, the people of the city began examining their deeds in order to repent wholeheartedly.

There were some individuals, however, who examined the deeds of others instead of their own.

One such person approached R' Yisrael Salanter and related to him how his neighbor was a sinner who should be encouraged to leave his sinful ways.

"I'm sure you are aware," replied R' Salanter, "of *Chazal's* statement in *Maseches Arachin* (16a), that *tzara'as* was brought about by the sin of *lashon hara*!

"The Torah states regarding the *metzora*, 'He shall live alone, his dwelling place being outside the camp.' The individual who spoke negatively about his neighbor now sits alone, outside the camp without any neighbors. Now he will have the time to examine some of his *own* faults."

וְהַבֶּגֶד כִּי־יִהְיֶה בוֹ נֶגַע צָרָעַת ...

"If a garment has a mark of tzara'as on it ..." (13:47)

Clothing, remarked the *Chofetz Chaim*, is one of the catalysts in bringing about sins that result in *tzara'as*.

When a person dresses lavishly it is inevitable that haughtiness will find its way into his heart. It will also spark feelings of jealousy in the heart of his fellow man, and from jealousy stems hatred and *lashon hara* — for which the punishment is *tzara'as*.

How we must strive to emulate the traits of Yaakov *Avinu*, concluded the *Chofetz Chaim*, for Yaakov asked Hashem for "bread to eat and clothes to wear" (*Bereishis* 28:20) — he wanted clothing only for the purpose of *wearing*, not for the purpose of adorning himself!

זֹאת תִּהְיֶה תּוֹרַת הַמְּצֹרָע

"This shall be the law of the metzora" (14:2)

WHY, ASKED R' SHMUEL OF SOCHOTCHOV, DOES THE VERSE state, "This *shall be* the law of the *metzora*," and not, "This *is* the law of the *metzora*"?

The *tzara'as* affliction, answered the *rebbe*, is brought about by the sin of haughtiness (see *Arachin* 16a). Once he is afflicted, however, and individuals begin to distance themselves from him, he feels contrite and humbled.

But this feeling of humility must accompany him for the rest of his life. Even after he is healed, let him not return to his previous state of arrogance; rather, he must ingrain the lesson he has learned as a *metzora* and remain humble until his very last day.

זֹאת תִּהְיֶה תּוֹרַת הַמְּצֹרָע

"This shall be the law of the metzora" (14:2)

Our Sages have taught us that *tzara'as* is caused by transgressing the severe sin of speaking *lashon hara*.

R' Levi Yitzchak of Berdichev was walking down the street when he overheard a man speaking evil of another Jew in front of a group of people.

"Can it be, *Reb Yid*," asked R' Levi Yitzchak in astonishment, "that you are not wary of slandering the *tefillin* of *HaKadosh Baruch Hu*?"

"What does the *Rebbe* mean?" asked the man.

"I am referring," answered R' Levi Yitzchak, "to the Gemara in *Maseches Berachos* (6a) which states that inside Hashem's *tefillin* it is written, 'And who is like Your people Israel?'"

זֹאת תִּהְיֶה תּוֹרַת הַמְצֹרָע בְּיוֹם טָהֳרָתוֹ וְהוּבָא אֶל־הַכֹּהֵן:

"This shall be the law of the metzora on the day of his purification: He shall be brought to the Kohen ..." (14:2)

In *Maseches Arachin* (15b), *Chazal* state that the word, "*metzora,*" is a combination of the words, "*motzi shem ra*" (one who "expresses a negative reputation" to others).

Once a person has been declared a *metzora*, remarked the *Chofetz Chaim*, if he wishes to regain his spiritual cleanliness, he must approach the *Kohen*. Only when the *Kohen* has declared that the *metzora* is pure will he regain his former, pure status. The reason for this is as follows: Since it was his *speech* that caused his *lashon hara*, he can only be purified through the *speech* of the *Kohen*, who pronounces him "*tahor.*"

To what can this be compared? To a young child who visited his relative who worked in a factory. When the child arrived at the factory, he looked around and saw an enormous hall filled with a wide array of machinery.

"How many machines are in this factory?" asked the child.

"There are exactly two hundred and forty-eight machines!" answered the relative. "Here, look. This machine spins threads, this machine cuts them, and this one rolls them ..." The relative continued to enumerate each machine in the factory. Suddenly, the child spotted a machine in the corner of the hall; it was a large machine surrounded by fences and warning signs cautioning people not to approach.

"What does that huge machine in the corner do?" asked the child.

"This machine," responded the relative, "controls all of the other machines in the factory. It is therefore the most important machine of them all and requires special attention. If this machine were to stop working, the entire factory would have to shut down!"

The same thing applies to man, said the *Chofetz Chaim*. Man possesses two hundred and forty-eight limbs and organs, but the most important one of them all is the tongue.

The tongue determines the way all the other organs operate, as the verse states, "Death and life are in the power of the tongue" (*Mishlei* 18:21).

If a person utilizes his tongue properly — that is, to learn Torah — then it has a positive effect on all his other limbs and organs as well.

But if he lacks the sense to use his tongue for beneficial purposes, and uses it instead to speak *lashon hara*, then his entire body is influenced negatively!

❧❀❧

זֹאת תִּהְיֶה תּוֹרַת הַמְּצֹרָע בְּיוֹם טָהֳרָתוֹ וְהוּבָא אֶל־הַכֹּהֵן: ...

"This shall be the law of the metzora on the day of his purification: He shall be brought to the Kohen ..." (14:2)

People have a tendency to make light of the sin of *lashon hara*, said the Dubno *Maggid*. They say to themselves, "What are mere words? I am not harming my friend in any way by simply speaking about him."

The Torah therefore requires that the *metzora* be brought to the *Kohen*, in order for him to witness what man's speech is capable of doing. With one word, the *Kohen* defines the status of the *metzora*, making him either pure or impure — such is the power of man's words!

❧❀❧

וְצִוָּה הַכֹּהֵן וְלָקַח לַמִּטַּהֵר שְׁתֵּי־צִפֳּרִים חַיּוֹת טְהֹרוֹת ...

"The Kohen shall then order that someone take for the person being purified two live, ritually pure birds ..." (14:4)

Rashi explains that since *tzara'as* comes about because of *lashon hara*, the person being purified must bring two birds, for birds "constantly twitter with chirping sounds."

The *Talmud Yerushalmi* (*Berachos* 1:2) cites the words of R' Shimon bar Yochai, "If I would have been standing on *Har Sinai* at the time the Torah was given to the Jewish people, I would have requested before Hashem that He create two mouths for man. One mouth would be for the purpose of toiling in Torah study, and the second would be for the purpose of allowing him to speak about his ordinary needs."

Later, R' Shimon bar Yochai changed his mind, and he said, "If the world cannot withstand man's slander when he has only one mouth, how much more so would this be the case if he had two mouths!"

וְעֵץ אֶרֶז וּשְׁנִי תוֹלַעַת וְאֵזֹב:

"... a piece of cedar wood, of thread of scarlet [wool], and [a bunch of] hyssop" (14:4)

Rashi explains that cedar wood was required for the *metzora's* purification, as it alludes to the fact that afflictions of *tzara'as* are caused by haughtiness.

Gedolei Yisrael of all times have devised various strategies in order to protect themselves against the trait of haughtiness. R' Zusia of Anipoli once used a very novel strategy:

R' Zusia was extremely poor and had no means to earn a livelihood. When his daughter came of age, he lacked the necessary funds to marry her off. His family urged him to make an effort at securing the money needed for his daughter to marry, but R' Zusia placed his trust in Hashem and did not worry about it at all.

One day, R' Zusia went to see his *rebbe*, the *Maggid* of Mezirich.

"I know that you lack the money to marry off your daughter," said the *maggid*. "Here is 500 rubles; may Heaven help you find a suitable *chasan*."

On his way home, R' Zusia took up lodging in an inn. Suddenly he heard sounds of commotion and bitter weeping.

R' Zusia approached the innkeeper. "What happened?" he asked.

"An orphaned girl was about to be married," he replied, "but, immediately prior to the *chupah*, her mother discovered that she had lost the dowry money — the 500 rubles that she had collected with so much effort was gone.

"The *chasan*," continued the innkeeper, "who was also an impoverished orphan, let them know that if he did not receive the dowry prior to the *chupah*, then he would not go through with the marriage."

R' Zusia made his way into the room where the people had gathered and announced, "*Rabosai*, I have found the money."

Now the tumult turned from one of sorrow to one of joy. The crowd was so relieved and happy that the wedding would proceed on time after all!

R' Zusia, however, informed everyone that he would like 50 rubles as compensation for his efforts. The people were shocked by R' Zusia's request. "Are you not ashamed?" they yelled. "Is there no mercy in your heart for an orphaned *kallah*?"

But R' Zusia stood firm in his request — 50 rubles for the money's return.

The people finally took R' Zusia by force to the *rav* of the town, who ruled that the entire sum of money must be returned at once, without a cent going to R' Zusia. R' Zusia handed over the money and was expelled from the town in utter disgrace and shame.

Several days later, word of the incident reached the ears of the *maggid*. He summoned R' Zusia and asked him, "Why did you act in such a manner? Could it truly be?"

"When I saw the orphaned *kallah's* misery," responded R' Zusia, "I took pity on her and immediately decided to give her the entire sum of money. However, when I entered my room to get the money, the *yetzer hara* began to put various ideas into my head: 'Zusia,' he said, 'You are as great as Avraham *Avinu*,' and other such thoughts.

"'Do you want me to succumb to haughtiness?' I asked my *yetzer hara*. 'I'll show you! You will yet see how they will take the money from me and banish me from the town in disgrace.' And that's just what happened."

... וְעֵץ אֶרֶז וּשְׁנִי תוֹלַעַת וְאֵזֹב:

"... a piece of cedar wood, of thread of scarlet [wool], and [a bunch of] hyssop" (14:4)

Rashi explains that cedar wood was required for the *metzora's* purification, alluding to the fact that afflictions of *tzara'as* come because of haughtiness. Crimson wool and hyssop served as reminders that his remedy lay in lowering himself like a worm ("*tola'as*," means both "dyed wool," as in our verse, and "worm") and like hyssop — a low-growing shrub.

Throughout the generations, *Gedolei Yisrael* have always possessed the outstanding trait of humility.

When R' Akiva Eiger visited the city of Warsaw, he was met by all of the distinguished members of the city as well as many of its inhabitants, who accorded him the honor that was befitting a *Gadol b'Yisrael*.

R' Eiger, however, sat bent over in his coach, weeping bitterly.

"Why is the *rav* crying?" asked one of his students.

"I am crying," answered R' Eiger, "over the fact that our generation is so lacking in *talmidei chachamim* that people actually consider *me* to be a *talmid chacham*."

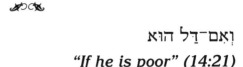

וְאִם־דַּל הוּא

"If he is poor" (14:21)

The offerings of a wealthy man and that of a poor man, remarked the *Chofetz Chaim*, are not equal. A wealthy man brings an offering in accord with his wealth, while a poor man brings an offering that is within his means.

The Mishnah in *Maseches Nega'im* (14:12) states that a wealthy *metzora* who brings a poor man's offering does not fulfill his obligation with that offering.

The same thing applies, said the *Chofetz Chaim*, to a Jew's spirituality. A person must put forth the utmost effort when it comes to serving Hashem, and he must utilize the potential that Hashem has granted him. For example, Hashem demands much more from a *talmid chacham* than from someone who is ignorant in Torah learning. Each individual must harness his *own* potential and level to its maximum.

There are times when you pray or study Torah and you think to yourself, "I may not be totally focused during my prayers and learning, but compared to my friend, I am far superior."

This is a grave error. The friend may fall into the category of a spiritually "poor man" — perhaps he never learned how to pray properly; perhaps he has worries that gnaw at his piece of mind; or perhaps the friend does not possess the same intellectual capabilities that you do.

Your friend's deeds may appear inferior to your own, but Hashem, Who knows and understands the hearts of every man, sees that your friend is praying and studying Torah to the best of his ability, thereby satisfying that which is required of him. It may very well be that it is you who are the inferior one!

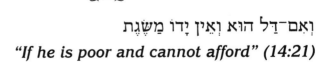

וְאִם־דַּל הוּא וְאֵין יָדוֹ מַשֶּׂגֶת

"If he is poor and cannot afford" (14:21)

In the city of Slonim lived a wealthy man who was "stricken" with a severe case of stinginess. His miserliness even extended to himself;

he refrained from eating any more than the bare minimum which he needed to sustain himself, and he routinely wore clothing that was old and tattered. He looked like one of the city's poor.

On one occasion, the rabbi of Slonim, R' Eizel Charif, asked the man to contribute a certain amount of money toward a worthy cause. The man, however, offered various excuses as to why he would be unable to be of assistance.

"Now I understand a Gemara in *Maseches Kiddushin*," commented R' Charif. "The Gemara (48b) states, 'A wealthy man who is found to be a poor man and a poor man who is found to be a wealthy man are not betrothed." That is, if a man betroths a woman who is under the impression that he is wealthy when in fact he was poor, or, the opposite — she thought he was poor and in fact he is wealthy — then the betrothal is null and void as it was performed under false pretenses.

"There is an apparent difficulty here," continued the rabbi. "Why is the betrothal invalid if she thought he was poor and it turns out that he is a wealthy man? What disadvantage could there to having wealth?

"Rather," answered R' Charif, "the Gemara is dealing with a wealthy man who is stingy even when it comes to his own provisions. He is wealthy but he gives off the impression that he is impoverished. Such a betrothal was certainly performed under false pretenses."

⋘◈⋙

וְהִגִּיד לַכֹּהֵן לֵאמֹר כְּנֶגַע נִרְאָה לִי בַּבָּיִת:

"He shall tell the Kohen, saying: There appears to me to be something like a [tzara'as] mark on my house" (14:35)

R' Mordechai of Pintchov, one of the prime disciples of the Chozeh of Lublin, lived his whole life in abject poverty.

Whenever he traveled to visit the Chozeh, his wife instructed him to describe their predicament to the *tzaddik* and request that he pray on their behalf. R' Mordechai, however, would take one step into his holy *rebbe's* room and immediately begin discussing holy issues with the *rebbe*. Each time he went, he completely forgot about his difficult financial situation.

Finally, his wife joined him on one of his trips to the rebbe in order to personally relate their predicament to the *tzaddik*.

After she tearfully described their difficult situation, the Chozeh turned to R' Mordechei and asked, "Why have you never told me about this before?"

"I figured that the *Rebbe* already knew about it through Divine Inspiration," answered R' Mordechai.

"When the Torah deals with the *tzara'as* affliction," answered the Chozeh, "it states, 'If a person will have on the skin of his flesh a *se'is*, or a *sapachas* … he shall be brought to Aharon the *Kohen*' (*Vayikra* 13:2). He does not have to say anything at all; he must simply approach the *Kohen*.

"But when the Torah deals with afflictions that come upon a person's home, then it states, 'He shall tell the *Kohen*, saying: There appears to me to be something like a [*tzara'as*] mark on my house.' When it comes to matters of the home, it is not enough simply to approach the *Kohen*; rather, one must relate the issue explicitly!"

PARASHAS ACHAREI MOS

וַיְדַבֵּר ה' אֶל־מֹשֶׁה אַחֲרֵי מוֹת שְׁנֵי בְּנֵי אַהֲרֹן

"Hashem spoke to Moshe after the death of Aharon's two sons" (16:1)

WHY, ASKS RASHI, DOES THE VERSE STATE, "HASHEM SPOKE TO Moshe *after the death of Aaron's two sons*"? Why not simply say, "Hashem spoke to Moshe"?

To answer the question, Rashi quotes R' Elazar ben Azaryah's parable: A sick man called for a doctor. The doctor instructed him, "Do not eat cold food, and do not lie in a damp, chilly place."

Then a second doctor came and told the man, "Do not eat cold food, and do not lie in a damp, chilly place, so that you will not die like so-and-so did."

By alluding to somebody who died as a result of not taking these precautions, the second doctor was more successful than the first at rousing the man to take care of himself.

This is why, explains Rashi, the verse states "after the death of Aharon's two sons." It was in order to give Aharon an extra measure of motivation to keep the laws enumerated in this portion.

בְּזֹאת יָבֹא אַהֲרֹן אֶל־הַקֹּדֶשׁ

"With this shall Aharon come into the Sanctuary" (16:3)

In the "*U'nesaneh Tokef*" prayer that we recite on the *Yamim Nora'im*, we say, "But repentance, prayer, and charity remove the evil of the decree." Almost all *machzorim* have the words "*tzom*" (fasting), "*kol*" (voice), and "*mamon*" (money) printed directly above the words "repentance, prayer, and charity."

The numerical value of the words, "*tzom*," "*kol*," and "*mamon*," each equal one hundred and thirty-six.

By adding the three words together, one gets the number four hundred and eight, the exact numerical value of the word, "*zos*."

This is an allusion to the aforementioned verse, "With this (*b'zos*) shall Aharon come into the Sanctuary." When the Jews sincerely repent, engage in heartfelt prayer, and give generously to charity, then the three combine to produce "*zos*." Then when the *Kohen Gadol* enters the Sanctuary as a messenger of the Jewish nation, his prayer is accepted, and the Jewish people receive their atonement.

בְּזֹאת יָבֹא אַהֲרֹן אֶל־הַקֹּדֶשׁ

"With this shall Aharon come into the Sanctuary" (16:3)

The Jewish nation was ravaged with brutal and horrible pogroms in the year 5408 (1648; the year commonly referred to as "*tach*," the numerical equivalent of 408). Jews all over the world shook the Heavens with their prayers for an imminent redemption.

"I am quite certain," remarked the great kabbalist, R' Shimshon of Ostropoli, "that we will indeed be redeemed this year, for the verse states, 'With this (*b'zos*) shall Aharon come into the Sanctuary.' The numerical value of '*b'zos*' is four hundred and eight, '*tach*!'"

When the year had passed and the redemption had not arrived, R' Shabsai Cohen (known as the "*Shach*") sent out a proclamation which stated, "The verse says, 'This emanated from Hashem; it is wondrous in our eyes. This is the day Hashem has made' (*Tehillim* 118: 23,24). 'This (*zos*) emanated from Hashem' – The year '*tach*' was destined by Hashem – 'it is wondrous in our eyes' – to be the year that we would witness the wonderful redemption of the Jewish nation. However, 'Today is the day Hashem has made' – we failed to repent as hinted to by the word, 'today.' For *Chazal* recount in *Maseches Sanhedrin* (98a) that R' Yehoshua ben Levi asked Eliyahu *HaNavi*: 'When will *Mashiach* come?' 'Today!' replied Eliyahu. Later, Eliyahu explained that he was referring to the verse, '*Even today*, if we but heed His call.' When we repent wholeheartedly, we will be worthy of redemption.

"In our times as well," concluded the *Shach*, "we lacked the merit of repentance, which would have enabled us to have been redeemed this past year!"

לְאֹהֶל מוֹעֵד הַשֹּׁכֵן אִתָּם בְּתוֹךְ טֻמְאֹתָם:

"[The Divine Presence] dwells with them amidst their impurity" (16:16)

Even though they are impure, explains Rashi, the Divine Presence is among them.

The Apter *Rav*'s (R' Avraham Yehoshua Heschel of Apt) arrival in a certain town sparked a dispute between two of the townspeople; each one wanted the merit of hosting the *tzaddik*. Both of them were quite wealthy and well known throughout the town for their negative character traits – one was known for his arrogance, and the other for not being particularly scrupulous in his *mitzvah* performance.

The *rebbe* – much to the surprise of his *chassidim* – chose to lodge in the home of the man who wasn't careful in his performance of *mitzvos*.

The Apter *Rav* saw that his *chassidim* were puzzled by his decision, so he explained: "When it comes to sinners, the Torah states, '[The Divine Presence] dwells with them amidst their impurity' — despite their impurity, the Divine Presence still rests among them. Now, if it is befitting for the Holy One, Blessed is He, to dwell in their midst, then it is most certainly fitting for me to do so.

"But about the arrogant individual, Hashem says, 'He and I cannot dwell together (*Sotah* 5a)!' If the Holy One is not willing to dwell in such a place, then neither am I."

⋙⋘

בַּחֹדֶשׁ הַשְּׁבִיעִי בֶּעָשׂוֹר לַחֹדֶשׁ תְּעַנּוּ אֶת־נַפְשֹׁתֵיכֶם

"In the seventh month, on the tenth of the month, you shall afflict yourselves" (16:29)

When R' Avraham of Sochotchov was 5 years old, his father told him on Yom Kippur to go home after *Shacharis* and eat. When he returned to *shul*, his father asked him whether he had recited *Kiddush* before eating. "No," responded the boy, "I did not recite *Kiddush*. The truth is that I did give the matter some thought, and I decided that it was not the correct thing to do. For while a minor is not required to observe the *mitzvos*, it is nonetheless customary for children to keep the *mitzvos* as training for when they grow up.

"I therefore did not make *Kiddush*," said the boy. "Since when I grow older I will fast all day, there was no need for me to be educated in this particular *mitzvah*."

⋙⋘

וְשָׁפַךְ אֶת־דָּמוֹ וְכִסָּהוּ בֶּעָפָר:

"He shall let its blood spill and cover it with earth" (17:13)

Aside from being a Torah genius, R' Baruch Zeldowitz was also well known for his extraordinary wealth and generosity; his hand was always open to the poor and needy. He was particularly fond of donating money to the Volozhin Yeshivah, where he had studied in his youth.

On one occasion, R' Baruch was sitting in his room with a distinguished merchant, engaged in an important business deal. Suddenly, an older gentleman burst into the room and, without even saying, "*Shalom aleichem*," he announced, "I am the fund-raiser for the Volozhin Yeshivah, and I have come to request a donation."

R' Baruch reprimanded the man for his behavior. "Why did you enter without permission?" he asked. "Is it proper to just barge into another man's home?"

The fund-raiser was offended and left the room.

Upon concluding the business deal, R' Baruch regretted that he had offended the fund-raiser, so he apologized to him.

"There is a special *mitzvah* in the Torah," began R' Baruch, "known as '*kisui hadam*' (covering the blood). When a person slaughters a bird or a *chayah* (animal) he is required to cover its blood with dust. The Gemara (*Chullin* 88b) rules that if a person is traveling in the desert and he has no dust with which to cover the animal's blood, then he can grind a gold coin into dust and use it to fulfill the *mitzvah*. For even gold, says the Gemara, is called 'earth.'"

With that, R' Baruch removed a gold coin from his pocket and handed it to the fund-raiser. "I embarrassed you," he continued, "and the Torah views that as if I had spilled your blood. Here is a gold coin for *kisui hadam*."

In addition, R' Baruch gave the Volozhin Yeshivah a large donation, as was his custom.

⯎⯏

וּשְׁמַרְתֶּם אֶת־חֻקֹּתַי וְאֶת־מִשְׁפָּטַי אֲשֶׁר
יַעֲשֶׂה אֹתָם הָאָדָם וָחַי בָּהֶם

"You shall keep My statutes and My laws which a person shall do and thereby live" (18:5)

The *Chofetz Chaim* told the following true anecdote in relation to this verse: There was an annual fair which lasted for four weeks in one of the neighboring towns of Grodno.

Despite the fact that the residents of the town had to work very hard during the fair, they nonetheless eagerly anticipated its arrival, as it was their main source of livelihood for the entire year.

One year, the *Chofetz Chaim* happened to be in the town at the time the fair was taking place. While he was there, he overheard a Jewish worker sigh and remark, "*Oy!* When will this fair finally be over, so that I will be able to get some rest!"

When the owner of the store heard his worker's words, he rebuked him harshly: "You fool! I wish the fair would last for much longer. Yes, we are tired, but later we will be able to rest and enjoy our profits."

These words made a deep impression upon the *Chofetz Chaim*. He would often repeat this story, and he would add: "Do you hear these words? It is worthwhile for a Jewish worker to lose sleep and go without food, as long as he will later enjoy his earnings.

"Life," concluded the *Chofetz Chaim*, "is similar to a fair. It is incumbent upon each individual to serve his Creator untiringly and unceasingly in this world, so that he will be able to enjoy the reward that is reserved for *tzaddikim* in *Olam Haba*."

וּשְׁמַרְתֶּם אֶת־חֻקֹּתַי וְאֶת־מִשְׁפָּטַי אֲשֶׁר
יַעֲשֶׂה אֹתָם הָאָדָם וָחַי בָּהֶם

"You shall keep My statutes and My laws which a person shall do and thereby live" (18:5)

If a person faithfully keeps the *mitzvos*, his reward is guaranteed by Hashem – he will "thereby live"!

Over the years, *Yerushalayim* was the home to many distinguished *gabbaei tzedakah*. One of the *gabba'im* was a man by the name of R' Yechezkel, who, on one occasion, was involved in collecting money for a poor orphaned *kallah*.

On his way through the city, he came to the house of R' Yosef, who was known to be a very wealthy individual. R' Yechezkel knocked on the front door of the lavish home, and, a moment later, R' Yosef himself opened the door. By the somber look on R' Yosef's face, R' Yechezkel knew that something was wrong.

"What happened?" asked R' Yechezkel.

"Please forgive me for not being able to help you at the moment," said R' Yosef. "You see, my son is gravely ill, and the doctors know of no cure for his illness."

"Dear sir," replied R' Yechezkel, "listen to me. Every morning, we say in the *Shacharis* prayer, 'These are the precepts whose fruits a person enjoys in this world but whose principal remains intact for him in the World to Come ... visiting the sick, providing for a bride, escorting the dead.' By placing the *mitzvah* of 'providing for a bride' in between 'visiting the sick' and 'escorting the dead,' our Sages are teaching us that the *mitzvah* of providing for a bride has the power to protect a person from harm. In particular, it is beneficial for healing the sick."

R' Yosef understood what his friend R' Yechezkel was telling him. He stepped into an adjoining room and a short while later he returned with the entire amount of money that R' Yechezkel needed to assist the *kallah*.

In just a few hours the son's condition improved significantly, and a short while later he rose from his sickbed, completely recovered!

וּשְׁמַרְתֶּם אֶת־חֻקֹּתַי וְאֶת־מִשְׁפָּטַי אֲשֶׁר
יַעֲשֶׂה אֹתָם הָאָדָם וָחַי בָּהֶם אֲנִי ה'

"You shall keep My statutes and My laws which a person shall do and thereby live — I am Hashem" (18:5)

R ashi explains: "'And thereby live' — In the World to Come. 'I am Hashem' — [Who is] faithful to pay reward."

Chazal state in *Maseches Sanhedrin* (90a), "All of Israel has a share in the World to Come!"

This statement of *Chazal*, remarked the *Chofetz Chaim*, presents us with an apparent difficulty. For we are taught in *Maseches Megillah* (28b), "He who studies Torah laws every day has the assurance that he will be in the World to Come." If all of Israel has a share in the World to Come, why does the Gemara imply that it is only those who study Torah laws who will merit a share in the World to Come?

The answer, said the *Chofetz Chaim*, can be understood with the following parable: There was a wealthy man who arranged a lavish wedding for his son. He wanted the rabbi of the town to attend, so he dispatched a messenger to extend a personal invitation to the rabbi. When the rabbi arrived at the wedding, the wealthy man went out to greet him and, in a display of great respect, requested that he sit with the other distinguished guests. There, he was served the choicest foods and the finest beverages that were available at the wedding.

One of the poor residents of the town heard of the extravagant wedding taking place. No one invited him, but this was a wedding he did not want to miss, so he hurried to the hall. However, when he arrived, the wealthy man did not greet him, nor did anyone offer him a seat. He simply stood in a corner and helped himself to some of the leftover food.

It is certainly true, concluded the *Chofetz Chaim*, that all of Israel has a share in the World to Come. However, it is the Jews who learn the Torah's laws each and every day who will be considered "invited" guests, worthy of being seated in an area of prominence!

∗∞∗

אֶת־כָּל־הַתּוֹעֵבֹת הָאֵל עָשׂוּ אַנְשֵׁי־
הָאָרֶץ אֲשֶׁר לִפְנֵיכֶם וַתִּטְמָא הָאָרֶץ:

"For the people who were in the land before you committed all these abominable acts, and the land thus became defiled" (18:27)

The *Rema* (R' Moshe Isserles) explained this verse by way of a parable: A father purchased an expensive and beautiful garment for his beloved son. The son, however, was not careful with the garment and he soiled it.

If the son had been careful not to sit in a dirty area, he could have defended himself before his father with the claim that the garment was so fine and delicate that it stained easily, and he should therefore not be held accountable.

But since the son sat in an area that was so muddy and full of dirt that even a coarse and inexpensive garment would have been stained, he has absolutely no way of excusing himself.

The same thing applies to the Jewish people, said the *Rema*. The Jewish nation is Hashem's precious and only son, blessed with souls so fine and delicate that even the slightest sin is capable of leaving a stain. They can therefore claim before Hashem that it is the soul's delicate nature that is responsible for its stain.

But if the Jewish people commit sins that are so severe that they are capable of contaminating even unrefined gentiles — as the verse states, "For the people who were in the land before you committed all these abominable acts, and the land thus became defiled" — then they will have absolutely no way of defending themselves before their Father in Heaven.

PARASHAS KEDOSHIM

לֹא תִּגְנֹבוּ

"You shall not steal" (19:11)

R' NOSSON ADLER, THE *REBBE* OF THE *CHASAM SOFER*, WAS ONCE standing at the window of his home. Suddenly, he noticed a thief removing a bundle of wood from the storage house in his yard.

R' Adler quickly ran outside and chased after the thief, shouting, "R' *Yid*! How fortunate you are that Heaven has allowed me to witness your deed! For now I am able to declare my wood ownerless, and you will not be in violation of 'You shall not steal'!"

The thief, taken aback at the sight of the great R' Adler standing alongside him, hurled the bundle of wood off his shoulder.

"R' *Yid*," remarked R' Adler, "you have now enabled me to merit performing an additional *mitzvah*, namely, 'You must pick it up with him' (*Devarim* 22:4)."

With that, R' Adler lifted up the bundle of wood and placed it on the shoulders of the stunned thief.

לֹא תִּגְנֹבוּ וְלֹא־תְכַחֲשׁוּ וְלֹא־תְשַׁקְּרוּ אִישׁ בַּעֲמִיתוֹ:

"You shall not steal, you shall not deny falsely, and you shall not lie to one another" (19:11)

A scholarly and God-fearing *shochet* appeared before R' Yisrael Salanter and informed the *rav* of his intention to leave his profession.

"I cannot bear the great responsibility that comes along with being a *shochet*," he said. "Perhaps a Jew will come to eat nonkosher meat because of my error, God forbid."

"What do you intend to occupy yourself with instead?" asked R' Salanter.

"I intend to open a small store and try my hand at business," was the *shochet's* response.

"You should know," said R' Salanter, "that there is only one prohibition associated with *shechitah* — the prohibition of *neveilah*, of providing a person with meat that wasn't slaughtered according to the dictates of *halachah*.

"But in a business," continued R' Salanter, "one must be wary of many transgressions: 'You shall not steal,' 'you shall not covet,' 'you shall not cheat,' 'each of you shall not aggrieve one another,' 'you shall not deny falsely,' and 'you shall not lie to one another,' to name but a few.

"All these transgressions," concluded R' Salanter, "do not worry you?"

וְלֹא־תְשַׁקְּרוּ אִישׁ בַּעֲמִיתוֹ:

"You shall not lie to one another" (19:11)

Chazal state in *Maseches Makkos* (24), "'And he speaks the truth within his heart' (*Tehillim* 15:2) — [this verse can be applied to someone] like R' Safra.

How did R' Safra merit having this verse ascribed to himself? By the way he once acted. R' Safra wished to sell an item in his possession. He placed the item in front of him and waited for a potential customer. A man approached him and asked, "Will you sell me your merchandise for 100 *zehuvim*?"

R' Safra happened to be reciting *Shema* at the time, so he sat quietly and did not respond.

It must be that R' Safra wants more money, thought the customer, *and this is why he is not answering me.* He therefore raised his offer. "Will you sell it to me for 200 *zehuvim*?" he asked.

Once again, R' Safra just sat in silence.

The customer made a final proposal. "Perhaps you will sell it for 300 *zehuvim*?"

R' Safra continued to sit quietly, not uttering a word. The man turned around and walked away.

Suddenly, the man noticed that R' Safra was pursuing him. "Are you interested in purchasing this item?" asked R' Safra.

"Indeed, I am," replied the man, as he handed R' Safra 300 *zehuvim*.

R' Safra returned 200 *zehuvim* to the man and said, "I am prepared to sell you this item for the original amount that you had offered me. At the time, I was in the middle of reciting *Shema* and was therefore unable to respond. But since I had already decided to accept your first offer of 100 *zehuvim*, I will not take even a *perutah* more!"

וְלֹא־תְשַׁקְּרוּ אִישׁ בַּעֲמִיתוֹ:

"You shall not lie to one another" (19:11)

E verything in the world can be imitated, remarked the *Kotzker Rebbe*, R' Menachem Mendel of Kotzk: everything, that is, except for the truth. As soon as truth is imitated, it stops being truth but falsehood.

וְלִפְנֵי עִוֵּר לֹא תִתֵּן מִכְשֹׁל

"And you shall not place a stumbling block before the blind" (19:14)

T he *Chofetz Chaim* traveled to many communities to sell his *sefarim*, thereby spreading Torah to the masses. One of his journeys took him to a small town, where he decided to spend Shabbos.

The *Chofetz Chaim* approached the rabbi of the town before Shabbos and asked if he could deposit, for the duration of Shabbos, the money that he had earned through selling his *sefarim*. The rabbi agreed, and the *Chofetz Chaim* thanked him and left.

On Sunday, as the *Chofetz Chaim* was leaving the town, the rabbi caught up with him and rebuked him for forgetting to collect his deposit.

"I did not forget about it at all," said the *Chofetz Chaim*. "Rather, I had not adhered to the words of our Sages in *Maseches Bava Metzia* (75b), who taught that it is forbidden to lend money to another person without witnesses watching the transaction. For if there are no witnesses to prove that the loan ever took place, it is possible that the borrower might come to covet the money in his possession and take it for himself. The one who gave the loan would thus be guilty of placing 'a stumbling block before the blind.'

"I did not want to violate this precept, so I renounced my rights to the money and gave it to you as a gift."

The rabbi nevertheless tried to return the money to the *Chofetz Chaim*, but the *Chofetz Chaim* adamantly refused to accept it, saying, "The money is yours, and if I take it from you, I will be accepting a gift, about which it has been stated, 'But one who hates gifts will live' (*Mishlei* 15:27)."

Only after much urging on the part of the rabbi did the *Chofetz Chaim* finally agree to take his money back.

וְיָרֵאתָ מֵאֱלֹקֶיךָ אֲנִי ה':

"You shall fear your God — I am Hashem" (19:14)

R' Baruch of Mezibuzh once remarked, "I am terribly frightened of one Cossack; how much more so would I fear passing between two rows of five hundred Cossacks, each one holding a leather whip and ready to strike me.

"Yet this terror," concluded the *rebbe*, "does not even come close to my fear of violating one of the Torah's prohibitions!"

בְּצֶדֶק תִּשְׁפֹּט עֲמִיתֶךָ:

"You shall judge your fellowman justly" (19:15)

R ashi comments: "'You shall judge your fellowman justly' – Judge your friend favorably."

A Jew holding an envelope containing a large sum of money visited the home of R' Avraham Shag. He wished to deposit the envelope with the great rabbi, and wanted to know if he would agree to look after it for him.

R' Shag agreed and wrote the man's name on the envelope. He forgot, however, to place it inside the drawer where he normally put the money that was deposited with him. Instead, he placed the envelope inside a *sefer* that he happened to be studying at the time.

A long time later, the man came to reclaim his money. R' Shag opened his drawer and searched inside but the envelope was not there. The *rav* suspected that his housekeeper had stolen the money but in order not to embarrass her, he borrowed money from a relative and repaid the man in full.

R' Shag revealed his suspicion to no one but his wife so that she should watch the housekeeper more closely.

One day, as R' Shag was preparing for Pesach, the envelope with the missing money fell out of one of the *sefarim* he was cleaning.

The *rav* now felt horrible that he had suspected his innocent house-keeper; he called her and asked for her forgiveness.

Even though she wholeheartedly forgave R' Shag, he did not have peace of mind until he gave her a blessing that she should bear children.

That very year, after being childless for fifteen years, the house-keeper gave birth to a daughter.

בְּצֶדֶק תִּשְׁפֹּט עֲמִיתֶךָ:

"You shall judge your fellowman justly" (19:15)

R ashi comments: "'You shall judge your fellowman justly' – Judge your friend favorably."

R' Shimon Sofer (author of *Michtav Sofer*) once participated in an assembly intended to fortify dedication to Torah. Many rabbis attend-ed this assembly, as did many distinguished laymen from various communities.

R' Sofer addressed the audience. "*Morai v'rabosai*," said the *rav*. "At this monumental gathering, I would like to display something extraordinary that I inherited from my illustrious father, the *Chasam Sofer*. He, in turn inherited it from his ancestors. In fact, this priceless object dates back to the era when the *Beis HaMikdash* stood. It is an actual *shekel hakodesh* that was used in the *Beis HaMikdash*!"

With great excitement, the people at the gathering began passing it around, so that everyone could get a closer look. But after a few min-utes, the priceless coin disappeared!

"Where is the coin?" everyone asked. "Where could it have gone?"

R' Sofer stood up and emotionally addressed the audience, "There is no doubt that each and every Jew assembled here today is honest and upright. However, it is possible that someone may have placed the *shekel* in his pocket by mistake. I therefore ask you to please check your pockets carefully; perhaps one of you will discover the coin inside."

Everyone checked his pockets, but the coin was not found.

"As the *shekel* has not yet been located," continued R' Sofer, "I regrettably must request that each person check the pockets of the person next to him."

Suddenly, a voice from the far end of the auditorium was heard saying, "I will absolutely not permit it!" The startled crowd looked around to see who had spoken. They soon realized that the speaker had been an elderly Jew who had been one of the most prominent students of the great *Chasam Sofer*.

"I will not allow you to search my pockets!" he repeated.

The people began whispering to one another. Why would this man be opposed to having his pockets searched? the people wondered. Was this not a clear indication that he was the one who stole the coin?

Realizing that he was suspected of stealing the precious *shekel*, the elderly man rose, and with tears in his eyes, addressed the crowd, "I beg of you; just wait another fifteen minutes. If the coin is not found in that time, I will agree to whatever you ask."

At that moment, the waiter burst into the room with the *shekel* in his hand! "While I was discarding the scraps that I had cleared off the tables," he explained, "I suddenly noticed the coin in the garbage."

All eyes were now on the elderly man, who was asked why he had been opposed to having his pockets checked.

"You all know," he said, "that I was a student of the *Chasam Sofer*. It just so happens that I *also* own a priceless coin of the same type, and I have it here with me today. When I heard that the *rav* was displaying his coin, out of honor for him, I did not reveal that I also own one.

"When the coin disappeared," continued the elderly man, "I knew that if my pocket would be checked, my coin would have been discovered, and I would be held culpable. This, in turn, would have resulted in a *chillul Hashem*, as people would have thought me, an elderly Jew, to be a thief. I therefore implored you to wait several minutes, during which I prayed to Hashem that the coin would be found."

R' Shimon rose and proclaimed, "How great are the words of our Sages, who have stated, 'Judge your friend favorably.'"

לֹא־תִקֹּם וְלֹא־תִטֹּר אֶת־בְּנֵי עַמֶּךָ

"You shall not take revenge and you shall not bear a grudge against the members of your people" (19:18)

There are times, said the *Chofetz Chaim*, that a man grows angry with a friend who did not do him a particular favor. Such feelings are completely unjustified.

To what can this be compared? To a man who was walking down the street, looking for his friend. As he passed people in the street, he would ask them, "Have you seen my friend, perhaps?"

"Try looking for him in the town square," he was told. "There are many people gathered there; maybe your friend will be among them."

He went to the town square, searched for his friend, yet he did not find his friend.

Would it even occur to him to feel anger toward those individuals who directed him to the town square? Of course not! He realizes that he must simply continue his search.

The same thing applies to the prohibitions of taking revenge and bearing a grudge, said the *Chofetz Chaim*. We are forbidden to feel anger toward a friend who did not do us a favor. What reason can there be to be angry with him? Hashem obviously did not designate him as the one who would bestow this particular kindness upon us. We must simply turn to someone else, and place our request with him; perhaps he is the one who will be able to assist us. If a person accustoms himself to constantly thinking in this manner, he will never bear a grudge or feel the need to take revenge.

וְאָהַבְתָּ לְרֵעֲךָ כָּמוֹךָ

"You shall love your fellow as yourself" (19:18)

R' Nosson Adler was once honored with being a *sandak* at a *bris milah* that was being held far away from his home.

Despite the freezing weather, R' Adler traveled the long distance and merited to perform the lofty *mitzvah*.

When the *bris* had concluded, the participants were alarmed to discover that R' Adler had disappeared!

They frantically searched for him until they finally found him standing outside, trembling from the cold and guarding the horse that was hitched to the wagon that he had traveled in.

"*Rebbe*," asked the host in bewilderment, "why does the *rav* prefer the bitter cold over my warm house? Has the *rav* found something wrong with my home, God forbid?"

"*Chas v'shalom*," replied R' Adler. "I simply had mercy on the wagon driver who had to remain outside with his horse while I enjoyed the comfort of a warm home. After the ceremony, I presented him with the option of trading places for a short while."

The members of the household went inside, only to find the wagon driver sleeping soundly in front of the warm oven. R' Adler, however, did not permit them to wake him. Only after one of the family members insisted that he take over the *rav*'s post guarding the horse did he finally relent and return inside.

וְאָהַבְתָּ לְרֵעֲךָ כָּמוֹךָ

"You shall love your fellow as yourself" (19:18)

A widow waited for R' Moshe Feinstein outside his yeshivah. When the great sage appeared, she approached him and complained that her son who attended his yeshivah was not receiving proper supervision.

R' Feinstein listened to the woman with an attentive ear and assured her that there was no reason to worry. As their conversation came to a close, the car that took R' Feinstein home each day pulled up in front of the yeshivah.

"Take the woman home instead," requested R' Feinstein. "She is a widow. I will walk home."

וְאָהַבְתָּ לְרֵעֲךָ כָּמוֹךָ

"You shall love your fellow as yourself" (19:18)

The son of R' Dovid of Lelov had taken ill. The *chassidim* of Lelov assembled to pray and recite *Tehillim*, hoping to bring about his son's recovery.

A short while later, the *rebbe*'s son recovered completely.

The *chassidim* entered their *rebbe*'s study expecting to find him in a happy mood. Much to their disappointment, however, the *rebbe* was sitting and weeping bitterly.

"*Rebbe*," asked the *chassidim*, "why are you crying?"

"When my son took ill," answered the *rebbe*, "I witnessed the tremendous self-sacrifice on the part of the community, how you all gathered in the *shuls* to pray and beg Hashem for His mercy. You fulfilled the *mitzvah* of visiting the sick, and lent a hand in every possible way, only in order to lighten the suffering of my sick son.

"But why is it," cried out the *rebbe*, "that people were only inspired to act this way when the sick person happened to be my son? Why do people not organize special prayer assemblies whenever any Jew takes ill? Why have we forgotten the Torah's commandment of, 'You shall love your fellow as yourself'? This is why I am crying!"

Parashas Emor

וְלֹא תְחַלְּלוּ אֶת־שֵׁם קָדְשִׁי וְנִקְדַּשְׁתִּי בְּתוֹךְ בְּנֵי יִשְׂרָאֵל

"You must not desecrate My Holy Name. I shall be sanctified among the Children of Israel" (22:32)

THROUGHOUT HIS LIFE, THE *CHOFETZ CHAIM* WENT TO GREAT LENGTHS to avoid causing a *chillul Hashem*. He was once rushing to the railway station in order to catch the train departing to Vilna. As he hurried down the street, an unfamiliar man approached him and asked if he would be willing to be the tenth man in a *minyan* that was taking place in the house of a mourner.

Despite the fact that he had already *davened*, the *Chofetz Chaim* nonetheless acceded to the man's request. While he would miss his train, it was far more important to him not to bring about a *chillul Hashem*.

אֵלֶּה הֵם מוֹעֲדָי: שֵׁשֶׁת יָמִים תֵּעָשֶׂה
מְלָאכָה וּבַיּוֹם הַשְּׁבִיעִי שַׁבַּת שַׁבָּתוֹן

**"These are My appointed festivals. For six days
work may be done, but on the seventh day there
shall be a complete cessation of work" (23:2-3)**

I n these verses, said the Vilna *Gaon*, we find an allusion to the festivals on which it is permissible to do *melachah* (creative activity) for
the sake of preparing food.

"For six days work may be done" — There are six festival days on
which the Torah permits cooking food. They are: The first day of
Sukkos, Shemini Atzeres, the first day of Pesach, the seventh day of
Pesach, Shavuos, and the first day of Rosh Hashanah (the second day
of Rosh Hashanah is a rabbinical ordinance).

"But on the seventh day" — On Yom Kippur, however, it is forbidden to perform *melachah* for the purpose of preparing food. This is the
reason the Torah refers to it as "a *complete* cessation of work."

בֶּעָשׂוֹר לַחֹדֶשׁ הַשְּׁבִיעִי הַזֶּה יוֹם הַכִּפֻּרִים הוּא
מִקְרָא־קֹדֶשׁ יִהְיֶה לָכֶם וְעִנִּיתֶם אֶת־נַפְשֹׁתֵיכֶם

**"On the tenth of this seventh month is the Day
of Atonement. It shall be designated for you for
holiness and you shall afflict yourselves" (23:27)**

C hazal state (*Yoma* 81b) that whoever eats on the ninth of Tishrei
is considered as if he fasted on both the ninth *and* the tenth.

R' Levi Yitzchak of Berdichev arrived in *shul* shortly before the *Kol
Nidrei* service. Surprisingly, instead of sitting in his seat, he began to
search beneath each and every bench in the *shul*, as if trying to find
a lost object.

After he had concluded his search, the *tzaddik* approached the *amud*,
lifted his eyes to the Heavens, and exclaimed, "Master of the World! Look
down from the Heavens and see, 'Who is like Your people, Israel'!

"What would have happened if you had commanded the heathens
to eat and drink on *erev Yom Kippur*? How many of them would be

rolling around the streets in a drunken stupor? How many of them would be found beneath the benches and tables?

"But the Children of Israel," continued the *rebbe*, "are Your holy people! You have commanded them to eat on the ninth of Tishrei, yet here they stand like angels, draped in their *talleisim*, filled with fear and dread over the awesome day that shall soon be upon them. There is not one Jew who can be found lying beneath a bench or a table. Please, Hashem, grant the Jewish people a complete atonement!"

❦

וּלְקַחְתֶּם לָכֶם ...

"You shall take from what is yours..." (23:40)

Proper intentions are extremely important when performing a *mitzvah*, remarked the Ba'al Shem Tov. A person must make sure that his intentions are solely for the sake of Heaven and not for the sake of earning honor or any other motive.

For example, when a person goes looking to purchase a beautiful *esrog* for Sukkos, he must investigate his true motives. Is his intention purely for the sake of honoring Heaven or is he merely interested in displaying his magnificent *esrog* before an admiring crowd?

This is alluded to in the acronym of the verse: "*Al tevo'eini regel ga'avah* ("Let not the foot of arrogance come to me" — *Tehillim* 36:12)," which spells "*esrog*."

❦

וּלְקַחְתֶּם לָכֶם בַּיּוֹם הָרִאשׁוֹן פְּרִי עֵץ הָדָר

"On the first day, you shall take from what is yours, a fruit of a citron tree" (23:40)

R' Mordechai of Nesh'chiz lived in dire poverty his whole life. Even so, he severely limited his spending throughout the year, eating the barest minimum, just so he could afford to purchase a beautiful *esrog* for Sukkos.

One year he managed to save up more money than he ever had. He set out to the market on *erev Sukkos* in good spirits, eager to purchase a lovely *esrog*.

On his way, R' Mordechai noticed a Jew sitting on the road and weeping bitterly. "Why are you crying?" asked the *rebbe.*

"A great misfortune has struck me," answered the man. "You see, I am a wagon driver by profession. This morning, however, my horse suddenly died. I am left without a horse and without a livelihood. That is why I am weeping."

R' Mordechai removed the bundle of money that had been intended for the purchase of an *esrog* and handed it to the man.

"Here you go, my dear Jew; go and buy yourself a new horse."

R' Mordechai returned home absolutely elated.

"Where is your *esrog*?" asked his family.

"This year, I will not buy an *esrog*!" responded R' Mordechai.

"You're not buying an *esrog*?" asked his family in shock. "On what will you recite a *berachah*?"

"This year," answered the *tzaddik*, "all Jews will recite a blessing over an *esrog*. I, however, will recite a blessing over a horse."

$$\mathscr{A}\!\!\mathscr{D}\!\mathscr{C}\!\!\mathscr{R}$$

וּלְקַחְתֶּם לָכֶם בַּיּוֹם הָרִאשׁוֹן פְּרִי עֵץ הָדָר ...

"On the first day, you shall take from what is yours, a fruit of a citron tree..." (23:40)

The Vilna *Gaon* had a great love for the *mitzvah* of the four species. Year after year, Vilna's vendors streamed to the *Gaon's* house with choice *esrogim*, and he would select the one he thought was the nicest.

One year, a vendor showed the *Gaon* an exquisite *esrog*. The *Gaon* was very impressed and was willing to pay its full price.

"I do not wish to sell the *esrog* for money," responded the vendor. "Rather, I desire the reward that you will garner for performing the *mitzvah* of the four species."

"I readily agree," said the *Gaon*. "I will take the *esrog*, and you will receive my reward."

All those who visited the *Gaon* that *Sukkos* saw him savoring his beautiful *esrog* to a far greater degree than in previous years.

To calm their curiosity, the *Gaon* explained: "Throughout my entire life, I have yearned to fulfill the words of our Sages (*Avos* 1:3): 'Be like servants who serve their master not for the sake of receiving a reward.' A person must not serve Hashem simply in order to receive a reward. This is extremely difficult, however, as we are constantly aware that we will receive a reward each time we perform a *mitzvah*. But this year, I was given the opportunity to perform a *mitzvah* with full knowledge that I would not be receiving any reward for doing so!

"I am so fortunate to have merited such an opportunity. This is why you find me so overjoyed."

פְּרִי עֵץ הָדָר
"A fruit of a citron tree" (23:40)

R' Yechiel Michel of Z'lochev was poverty stricken and had no means to earn a livelihood. One year, on *erev Sukkos*, he had no money with which to buy an *esrog*. What did he do? He owned a beautiful pair of *tefillin*, which he had received as an inheritance from his illustrious father, the *Maggid* of Drohovitz. He sold the *tefillin* and, with the money he received, purchased a beautiful *esrog*.

With his *esrog* in hand, R' Yechiel Michel returned home in good spirits.

Upon entering his house, he was greeted by his wife. "Why are you so happy?" she asked him. "We're so poor, we don't even have bread to eat—"

"Look at this," said R' Yechiel Michel, as he lifted up his beautiful *esrog*. "It is this exquisite *esrog* that Hashem has sent me which brings me such happiness."

"Where did you get the money to buy such an *esrog*?" asked his wife.

"I sold the *tefillin* that I inherited from my father," answered the *rebbe*. "I then took the money and bought the *esrog*."

"What?" asked his wife in astonishment. "You sold your precious *tefillin* — for an *esrog*?"

In a fit of anger, his wife quickly snatched the *esrog*, bit off the *pitom*, and hurled it to the floor.

As he stared down at the *esrog* which was now unfit for use, R' Yechiel Michel thought, *I have neither my tefillin nor an esrog. What could the yetzer hara want from me? Perhaps he wants me to become angry. I refuse to do so! He will not cause me to succumb to the trait of anger!*

That night, his father appeared to him in a dream, and said, "You should know, my son, that selling your beautiful *tefillin* in order to purchase an *esrog* had a very great effect in Heaven. Conquering your anger, however, had an even greater effect."

בַּסֻּכֹּת תֵּשְׁבוּ שִׁבְעַת יָמִים

"You shall dwell in thatched-roof huts for a seven-day period" (23:42)

The governor of Berlin was once invited to the home of R' Tzvi Hirsch Levine, the *rav* of Berlin, on the Seder night.

The governor sat at the beautifully set table, and listened carefully as the youngest son asked, "How is this night different from all other nights?"

The governor then turned to R' Levine. "I have a question to ask you," he said. "Why do you ask, 'How is this night different,' tonight, as you sit at a table which is so beautifully set with fancy dishes and cutlery? Would it not be more appropriate to pose such a question on Sukkos, when you leave your homes and venture into a dilapidated *sukkah*?"

"Jews," answered R' Levine, "are not strangers to hardship. Every generation has seen Jew-haters attempt to annihilate us, and we have been expelled from our homes many times.

"Therefore, when we sit in our temporary dwelling on Sukkos, the child is not the least bit amazed, as it does not strike him as being out of the ordinary. It is specifically when we sit at a table that is adorned with such splendor that he begins to wonder, 'Why is this night different from all other nights?'"

בַּסֻּכֹּת תֵּשְׁבוּ שִׁבְעַת יָמִים

"You shall dwell in thatched-roof huts for a seven-day period" (23:42)

There are three types of *sukkos* that are acceptable according to the dictates of *halachah*: (1) a *sukkah* with four walls; (2) a *sukkah* with three walls; (3) a *sukkah* with two complete walls and a third wall the size of a *tefach*.

These three *sukkos*, remarked the Vilna *Gaon*, are alluded to in the letters that spell the word "*sukkah*":

The letter *samech* (ס) is enclosed on all four sides – an allusion to a *sukkah* with four walls.

The letter *chaf* (כ) is enclosed on three sides – an allusion to a *sukkah* with three walls.

The letter *hei* (ה) is enclosed from two sides and has a short leg – an allusion to a *sukkah* with two complete walls and a third the size of a *tefach*.

✦✦✦

בַּסֻּכֹּת תֵּשְׁבוּ שִׁבְעַת יָמִים

"You shall dwell in thatched-roof huts for a seven-day period" (23:42)

R' Dovid of Lelov had a unique *sukkah* that was made of wood and engraved with the emblems of the twelve tribes of Israel.

Every year, scores of Yerushalayim's Jews would go to see the *rebbe*'s magnificent *sukkah*.

One year, word spread that R' Dovid had built an ordinary *sukkah*! Why was this year any different from years past?

No one knew, and R' Dovid did not reveal his motives. The matter remained an absolute mystery, until a poor tailor divulged the secret.

R' Zalman was a destitute tailor who lived in a run-down hut at the edge of the city. The previous winter had been particularly difficult. Biting winds had howled outside, and bitter cold had made living conditions unbearable.

The freezing weather took its effect on R' Zalman's son who developed pneumonia. When the doctor arrived to examine him, he was horrified at the condition of the house. "Light a fire in your oven and heat your home!" he exclaimed. "If you don't, your son's situation will surely worsen."

What shall I do? thought R' Zalman. *Where will I obtain enough money to purchase wood to heat my home?* Suddenly an idea came to him. *I will go and speak with R' Dovid. Maybe he can help me.*

R' Zalman donned his tattered overcoat and, fighting the powerful winds, made his way to the *rebbe*'s house.

"What do you need, R' Zalman?" asked the *rebbe*. "What has brought you to my home on such a stormy night?"

"Please help me, *Rebbe*," pleaded R' Zalman. "My son is stricken with pneumonia, and I lack the money to buy wood in order to heat my home."

R' Dovid listened sympathetically to the tailor's misfortune, and his forehead was wrinkled in concern. Suddenly his eyes lit up. "Wait," he said. "I don't have any money, but I do have wood."

R' Dovid took a saw and cut the wood used to build his *sukkah*. When he finished, he piled up all the wood, and placed it before R' Zalman.

"Here you are," said the *rebbe*. "Go and heat your home, and may Hashem send your son a complete recovery."

Parashas Behar

וְשָׁבְתָה הָאָרֶץ שַׁבָּת לַה':

"The land shall observe a Sabbath rest for Hashem" (25:2)

R' Aharon Rokeach of Belz was a holy man. He was completely dedicated to Divine service, and his mind was constantly filled will elevated and holy thoughts.

One day, he summoned his attendant and requested that he hire a gardener to cultivate the garden in his courtyard.

The members of the *rebbe*'s household were astounded by this strange request. Why was the *rebbe*, who lived every day of his life with exalted sanctity, suddenly concerned over the garden's aesthetics? Despite their bewilderment, they nevertheless hurried to do his bidding.

On *erev Rosh Hashanah*, the *rebbe* instructed his attendant to inform the gardener that today would be his final day of work, as the coming year would be a *shemittah* year.

The *rebbe*'s pure intentions were now fully understood. Everything he had done was simply in order to practice the *mitzvah* of *shemittah*!

שָׂדְךָ לֹא תִזְרָע וְכַרְמְךָ לֹא תִזְמֹר:
"You must not sow your field nor prune your vineyard" (25:4)

T he *Chazon Ish* (R' Avraham Yeshayahu Karelitz) was known as one of the biggest proponents of *shemittah* observance in *Eretz Yisrael*. A rabbi once approached him and attempted to persuade him to rule more leniently regarding the laws of *shemittah*.

"There is certainly room to be lenient," claimed the rabbi. "After all, in our times, *shemittah* is only a rabbinical decree."

"There are many prohibitions," said the *Chazon Ish* with much emotion, "that are 'only' of rabbinical decree. But do we have any notion of the depth of *Chazal's* thinking that we can appreciate the severity of a rabbinical prohibition? After all, a person is required to give up all that he owns just so that he won't transgress their holy words, God forbid!"

וְסָפַרְתָּ לְךָ שֶׁבַע שַׁבְּתֹת שָׁנִים שֶׁבַע שָׁנִים שֶׁבַע פְּעָמִים וְהָיוּ לְךָ יְמֵי שֶׁבַע שַׁבְּתֹת הַשָּׁנִים תֵּשַׁע וְאַרְבָּעִים שָׁנָה:
"You shall count for yourself seven cycles of sabbatical years, seven times seven years; the period of the seven cycles of sabbatical years will be for you forty-nine years" (25:8)

W hy, asked the Dubno *Maggid*, did the Torah elaborate by enu- merating the number of years that comprise the seven cycles of sabbatical years? It would have been sufficient to simply write, "You shall count for yourself seven cycles of sabbatical years."

To what can this be compared? asked the *maggid*. To a poor man who spent his entire life going from door to door collecting money. On one occasion, he boasted to his friends about the large amount of money he had managed to amass.

"What are you boasting about?" asked one of his friends. "All these years, you have gone from one home to another and have grown accustomed to counting each *perutah* you receive. You may have col- lected many *perutos*, but if you were to exchange them for gold *dinarim*, you would see that you don't have all that much money."

So it is with man, concluded the *maggid*. A man believes that he has a long life ahead of him, as he calculates his life span according to months and years; he will spend seventy years in this world, maybe even eighty. Thinking in such a manner leads one to believe that he controls his life and his home.

But if a person reflects on how many *shemittos* he has to live and, all the more so, how many *yovels* (cycles of fifty years) he will spend in this world, he will immediately arrive at the stark realization that he is not a landlord but a mere sojourner passing through the world.

ക

וְכִי־תִמְכְּרוּ מִמְכָּר לַעֲמִיתֶךָ אוֹ קָנֹה
מִיַּד עֲמִיתֶךָ אַל־תּוֹנוּ אִישׁ אֶת־אָחִיו:

"When you sell something to your fellowman
or buy from your fellowman, you must not
cheat each other" (25:14)

R' Shraga Feivel Frank earned his livelihood by working in a shop selling leather hides. One day, a Jewish merchant who wished to purchase a large number of hides visited his store.

"How much of a discount am I entitled to?" asked the merchant. "After all, I am purchasing a considerable number of hides from you."

"I do not give discounts," answered R' Frank. "I have a set price, and I do not bargain, regardless of how many hides are being bought. By all means, go to other dealers and see if you can get a better price." With that, he handed the merchant the addresses of several other dealers in town.

After looking into the prices that the other shops were charging, the merchant realized that R' Frank's prices were indeed the lowest. He therefore returned to his store.

"I will sell you as many hides as you want," said R' Frank to the merchant, "and I will also give you the discount that you initially requested."

"Discount?" asked the merchant in surprise. "But a short while ago you told me that you don't give discounts!"

"After you left my store," said R' Frank, "I thought, *He does want to buy a substantial quantity of merchandise, why should he not deserve a discount?*

"Since I had already decided to give you a discount, I will not change my mind — the discount is yours!"

וְלֹא תוֹנוּ אִישׁ אֶת־עֲמִיתוֹ

"You must not cheat one another" (25:17)

The trait of truthfulness was firmly embedded into the character of the *Chofetz Chaim.*

On one occasion, he arrived in a town and was scheduled to address the townspeople. When he came to the *shul* where he would be speaking, he noticed a sign promoting his upcoming lecture. In addition to providing details as to when and where the speech was going to be held, it also referred to the *Chofetz Chaim* as the author of the *Mishnah Berurah.*

At that time, only the first volume of the *Mishnah Berurah* had been printed. The *Chofetz Chaim* viewed this as a form of deceiving the congregation. He, therefore, quickly removed his pen from his pocket, and added several words to the sign: "At present, only one volume of the *Mishnah Berurah* (until *siman* 128) has been printed. God willing, the remaining volumes will be published at a later date."

וְלֹא תוֹנוּ אִישׁ אֶת־עֲמִיתוֹ וְיָרֵאתָ מֵאֱלֹקֶיךָ

"No man among you may mislead his fellowman, and you shall fear your God" (25:17)

According to the simple meaning of the verse, remarked R' Simchah Bunim of P'shischa, the Torah is only prohibiting an individual from deceiving his fellowman. An individual of true piety, however, will go beyond the letter of the law and refrain from deceiving *himself* as well.

וְכִי תֹאמְרוּ מַה־נֹּאכַל בַּשָּׁנָה הַשְּׁבִיעִת

"If you ask, 'What will we eat in
the seventh year?'" (25:20)

The year 5719 (1958-1959) was a *shemittah* year. With the encouragement of the great *Chazon Ish* (R' Avraham Yeshayahu Karelitz), a special committee was formed in order to assist *shemittah*-observant Jews. The committee exerted much effort in supplying permissible produce. Despite their endeavors, however, there was a noticeable shortage of onions.

One morning, an ownerless cargo ship sailed into the Jaffa seaport. Amazingly, the ship was fully stocked — with onions!

After a thorough investigation, it turned out that the ship was an Egyptian carrier that had been on its way to Egypt. The captain had made a navigational error and had mistakenly sailed the ship into Jaffa. When he realized that they were nearing the coast of Israel, he and his crew abandoned the ship in a panic.

That year, there were plenty of onions for the *shemittah*-observing farmers — "The strong warriors who do His bidding, to obey the voice of His word (*Tehillim* 103:20)."

וְכִי תֹאמְרוּ מַה־נֹּאכַל בַּשָּׁנָה הַשְּׁבִיעִת ... וְצִוִּיתִי אֶת־בִּרְכָתִי
לָכֶם בַּשָּׁנָה הַשִּׁשִּׁית וְעָשָׂת אֶת־הַתְּבוּאָה לִשְׁלֹשׁ הַשָּׁנִים:

"If you ask, 'What will we eat in the seventh
year ... I will then order My blessing for you in the
sixth year, and [the land] will yield produce
sufficient for the three-year period" (25: 20-21)

Komemius was one of the first settlements in Israel to properly fulfill the *mitzvah* of *shemittah*, and it merited witnessing the actualization of the verse, "I will order My blessing for you ..."

The agency that had been granted jurisdiction over the fields and orchards in Israel at that time sent its representatives to try and persuade the farmers in Komemius not to observe *shemittah*. "If you will not work your fields," they charged, "what will you eat?"

Toward the end of the year 5732 (1972), shortly before Rosh Hashanah of the coming *shemittah* year, the members of the agency were astonished to see that Komemius had produced exactly three times their yearly yield!

They approached R' Binyamin Mendelson, the rabbi of Komemius, and asked him to explain this phenomenon.

"Nothing extraordinary has transpired," responded R' Mendelson. "The Torah clearly assures those who observe *shemittah*, 'If you ask, "What will we eat in the seventh year?" ... I will then order My blessing for you in the sixth year, and [the land] will yield produce sufficient for the three-year period.' Hashem is telling us not to worry about what we will eat during the seventh year, the *shemittah* year, for He will provide us with three times the amount we normally receive, and it will suffice for the sixth, seventh, and eighth years."

כִּי־יָמוּךְ אָחִיךְ
"If your brother becomes poor" (25:25)

R' Avraham Yehoshua Heschel, the *rebbe* of Kapishnitz, once visited the home of one of his *chassidim* who was known to be wealthy. The *rebbe* knocked on the door and waited for a response.

The *chassid* opened his door, and was taken aback by the sight of the holy *rebbe* standing at his doorstep. "Why did the *rebbe* have to trouble himself to come to my home?" asked the wealthy man. "The *Rebbe* could have summoned me and I would have come at once."

"It is I who needs you," answered the *rebbe*, "and this is why I have come."

"How can I be of assistance?" asked the man.

"I know of a certain family," replied the *rebbe*, "that is in desperate need of help. The husband is without work, the wife takes care of the young children, and, to add to their hardship, they have a son who is ill and requires special medical attention. Their expenses are well beyond their means."

"But *Rebbe*," said the wealthy man, "did this necessitate you having to exert yourself by traveling to my home? Why did the *rebbe* not simply send me a messenger, and I would have gladly given whatever sum of money that was needed!"

"This particular request is of great importance to me," responded the *Rebbe*. "It was therefore essential that I come to your home personally."

"I am prepared to give as much money as necessary!" exclaimed the man. "To whom shall I send this money?"

"Send the money," answered the *rebbe*, "to your brother."

≈

אַל־תִּקַּח מֵאִתּוֹ נֶשֶׁךְ וְתַרְבִּית וְיָרֵאתָ מֵאֱלֹקֶיךָ

"Do not take from him interest of any kind, and you shall fear your God" (25:36)

The sin of charging interest is so severe that *Chazal* have included one who transgresses this prohibition among those who forfeit their portion in the World to Come.

One of the wealthy men of Posen was a moneylender who turned a blind eye to the prohibition against charging interest. When the man passed away, the *chevrah kaddisha* requested that his family pay an extremely high sum of money for a burial plot.

The man's family was furious. On what basis were they being charged such an extraordinarily high price? They took their case before the *rav* of Posen, R' Akiva Eiger.

"The amount we are being forced to pay," claimed the family, "is several times more than the amount paid by everyone else. What entitles the *chevrah kaddisha* to demand such an exorbitant fee?"

"We Jews believe in the resurrection of the dead," responded R' Eiger. "This is why everyone must pay a certain amount for their plot. The deceased, however, loaned money and transgressed the prohibition of charging interest. *Chazal* tell us that one who charges interest loses his portion in the World to Come. It stands to reason then, that the deceased will not be resurrected along with everyone else, so he therefore will need his burial plot for a much longer period of time. The higher price is entirely just."

PARASHAS BECHUKOSAI

אִם־בְּחֻקֹּתַי תֵּלֵכוּ ...

"If you pursue My statutes ..." (26:3)

RASHI EXPLAINS: "'IF YOU PURSUE MY STATUTES' – TO LABOR IN [THE study of] the Torah."

The degree of toil which R' Chaim Shmulevitz invested in his Torah study was legendary. His entire life was spent delving into the Torah's depths with every last bit of energy he possessed so that he could arrive at a clear understanding of its sanctified words. There were times when after eating breakfast, he would begin learning without pause — for thirty straight hours!

R' Chaim was not feeling well one day, and he suddenly fainted. The members of his household rushed to help him, and with Hashem's help, he eventually came to. He rested in bed for about half an hour without moving, and he was unable to speak.

He then got up and declared that he was ready to deliver his *shiur*.

"When did you have time to review your *shiur*?" asked his family in surprise. "You were lying unconscious!"

"Yes I was," replied R' Chaim. "But after I had regained consciousness and lay down, incapable of speaking with anyone, I took the opportunity to review the *shiur* by memory."

אִם־בְּחֻקֹּתַי תֵּלֵכוּ ...

"If you pursue My statutes ..." (26:3)

A student of the *Chasam Sofer* (R' Moshe Sofer) approached his *rebbe* and posed the following question: "*Rebbe*," asked the student, "what is the secret to your success in Torah study?"

"I became a *talmid chacham*," answered the *Chasam Sofer*, "in five minutes."

The student was puzzled by his *rebbe*'s words. "Five minutes?" he asked in amazement. "How is it possible to become a *talmid chacham* in only five short minutes?"

"The minutes I was referring to," explained the *Chasam Sofer*, "were the five-minute periods that most people don't take advantage of: five minutes standing in line, five minutes waiting for somebody.... If a person is careful not to waste these precious moments and utilizes them for the sake of studying Torah, they will eventually add up to a very significant amount of time. This is the way to become a *talmid chacham!*"

In a similar vein, a story is related about how the Vilna *Gaon*'s travels once took him to the city of Meretz. The city's inhabitants were excited to have the distinguished guest in their midst. When they discovered where the *Gaon* had taken up lodging, they immediately set out to get a glimpse of this exalted Jew. In their overwhelming desire to see him, the people carried ladders with them. They leaned the ladders against the house, and took turns ascending and peering through the *Gaon*'s window, so that they could see him poring over his *sefarim* studying Torah.

The *Goan* hardly slept at night because he did not want to squander his precious time sleeping when it could be used for studying Torah. That night, however, he slept ten more minutes than he usually did.

When the *Gaon* awoke, he was distressed at having lost those valuable moments.

On his way home from his travels, the *Gaon* once again stopped off at the city of Meretz. This time, however, he slept ten minutes less than he usually did in order to rectify the other night.

אִם־בְּחֻקֹּתַי תֵּלֵכוּ ...
"If you pursue My statutes ..." (26:3)

A kollel student approached the *Chofetz Chaim* and poured his heart out before the *tzaddik*.

"*Rebbe*," said the dejected man, "I have been studying Torah for many years now — I did not stop learning after getting married. I invest all my strength into my learning, yet I have never seen any success from my endeavors. Why, I have still not acquired a profound understanding of the Torah, nor do I comprehend one halachic issue!"

"Do not despair," reassured the *Chofetz Chaim*. "Was a Jew commanded to be a *gaon*? Certainly not! All the Torah commands us is that we labor when studying it. If you labor and exert yourself in your Torah study, then you are indeed fortunate, for you are assured of eventually seeing tremendous blessing in your Torah study!"

וְאֶת־מִצְוֹתַי תִּשְׁמְרוּ ...

"And keep My commandments ..." (26:3)

One morning, a student of R' Eliyahu Lopian entered his *rebbe*'s room in order to bring him breakfast. The student noticed that his *rebbe* was fatigued. "Why is the *Rav* so exhausted?" asked the student.

"It is my practice to rise before dawn," answered R' Lopian.

"Why does the *Rav* deem it necessary to wake up so early," his student continued to ask, "when *davening* in the yeshivah does not begin until 7 o' clock?"

"The Gemara teaches us," explained R' Lopian, "that when a person is summoned to appear before the Heavenly court, he will be asked, 'Did you observe the Torah and its *mitzvos*?'

"Undoubtedly, every person will claim that they adhered to all of the Torah's commandments.

"But then," said R' Lopian, "a *Shulchan Aruch* will be opened before him, and he will be asked regarding each and every *se'if* (paragraph), 'Did you fulfill what is what is written in this *se'if*? Did you fulfill this law?'

"The very first *se'if* in the *Shulchan Aruch*," concluded R' Lopian, "states as follows: 'One should be strong like a lion to arise in the morning for the service of his Creator — that *he* should awaken the morning.' The *Shulchan Aruch* is instructing us to arise before dawn. I certainly do not want to be embarrassed right away, not having fulfilled the very first law in the *Shulchan Aruch*! This is why I am accustomed to rising before sunrise."

וְאֶת־מִצְוֹתַי תִּשְׁמְרוּ ...

"And keep My commandments ..." (26:3)

R' Moshe Feinstein's piety was legendary. The following story illustrates, albeit to a very small degree, just how careful R' Feinstein was when it came to adhering to the dictates of *halachah*.

He was once invited to a rabbinical gathering at which he was scheduled to speak. As he was walking down the corridors that led to the auditorium, he noticed an individual in the middle of the *Shemoneh Esrei* prayer.

The only way to reach the auditorium was by passing in front of that individual, yet R' Feinstein stopped and did not continue, as the *halachah* dictates that it is forbidden to pass in front of a person who is in the middle of *Shemoneh Esrei*.

Those who were escorting him tried to persuade him to continue walking toward the auditorium. "There are many people waiting to hear the *Rav* speak," they said. "Perhaps just this once the *Rav* could permit himself to pass before a person who is in the middle of *Shemoneh Esrei*."

"Do you not see?" R' Feinstein asked them. "There is a wall in front of me! How can I possibly continue walking?"

וַאֲכַלְתֶּם לַחְמְכֶם לָשֹׂבַע
"You will eat your food to satisfaction" (26:5)

Says Rashi: "'You will eat your food to satisfaction' — A person will eat a small amount, and it will become blessed in his stomach."

Why, asked R' Moshe of Biala, does Rashi interpret Hashem's blessing for satiety as meaning that a man will eat a small amount, and it will become blessed inside of him? Why can't the blessing mean that they will have an abundance of food and that is how they will eat to satisfaction?

From here we learn, answered the *rebbe*, that even if a person is showered with blessing and prosperity, he should not overindulge in the pleasures that this world has to offer. Rather, he should be content with little, as the Ramban explains the verse, "You shall be holy": "Sanctify yourselves with that which is permitted to you."

וּפָנִיתִי אֲלֵיכֶם
"I will turn My attention toward you" (26:9)

Rashi explains that Hashem was saying to the Jewish people, "I will turn away from all of My concerns in order to pay your reward."

There are instances when Hashem rewards the wicked in this world for the good deeds they have done. But the Jewish people will receive their reward in the World to Come. When the time comes, Hashem, as it were, will *turn* His attention *away* from rewarding the wicked to give the Jewish people their due reward.

There is a parable, said the *Chofetz Chaim*, that can help us understand why the wicked receive their reward in this world:

A wealthy man employed dozens of workers in his factory.

The wealthy man had an only daughter who was engaged to be married. As the wedding drew nearer, he thought, *I should definitely invite my workers to my daughter's wedding. However, it would not be appropriate for them to sit together with my friends and other distinguished guests.*

What did he do? The day before the wedding, he set up large tables in his house and invited all of his workers to a special feast. "Come," he said to them, "and rejoice with me at my daughter's wedding."

The wealthy man's neighbor passed by the house and was surprised to see the lavish feast that he had arranged for his workers. *Are these workers more esteemed than all of his other friends and acquaintances, that he has prepared an exclusive feast just for them?* thought the neighbor.

The neighbor was unaware, however, that the workers were not invited to a private feast because of their importance but precisely because of their unimportance — because he did *not* want them at his daughter's wedding along with the distinguished guests.

The same thing applies to the wicked, explained the *Chofetz Chaim*. They get rewarded in this world specifically because they are not welcome in the World to Come.

וְזָכַרְתִּי אֶת־בְּרִיתִי יַעֲקוֹב וְאַף אֶת־בְּרִיתִי
יִצְחָק וְאַף אֶת־בְּרִיתִי אַבְרָהָם אֶזְכֹּר

**"I will recall My covenant with Yaakov
and also My covenant with Yitzchak, and also
My covenant with Avraham I will recall" (26:42)**

This verse presents two difficulties, noted the Dubno *Maggid*: (1) Why does this verse appear in the middle of the portion of the Admonitions? 2) Why are the Forefathers listed here in reverse order:

Yaakov, then Yitzchak, and last, Avraham?

Both questions, said the *maggid*, can be resolved with the following parable: Two individuals accused of theft were brought before a judge. The judge asked the first man for his name and his father's name. When the judge heard who is father was, he said, "I knew your father well. He was a thief just like you. More than once he was brought before me to be tried. I sentence you to three years in prison as a punishment for your crime."

The second man was also asked for both his name and his father's name.

When the judge heard who this man's father was he replied, "I knew your father as well. He was a very great rabbi and *tzaddik*. I hereby sentence you to four years in prison."

"Why," asked the second defendant, "are you being more stringent with me than with my friend?"

"Your friend," responded the judge, "was raised in a family of thieves. The 'education' he received was how to be crooked and dishonest. You, on the other hand, come from a family of rabbis and were educated properly. You deserve a more severe penalty, for you should have known better!"

The prosecutor then stood up and said, "Your honor, in my opinion the man deserves an even stricter sentence. For it was not only his father that was a rabbi; his grandfather and great-grandfather were all distinguished rabbis as well."

So it is in our case, concluded the *maggid*. Why does this verse come in the middle of the Admonitions? Because it, too, is part of the rebuke for the Children of Israel. How can the Jewish nation sin when they herald from the great Yaakov? But they are not only the children of Yaakov, but also the grandchildren of Yaakov's father, Yitzchak, and his grandfather, Avraham. To hail from such greatness, and yet sin, demands a very harsh punishment indeed!

וְזָכַרְתִּי אֶת־בְּרִיתִי יַעֲקוֹב וְאַף אֶת־בְּרִיתִי
יִצְחָק וְאַף אֶת־בְּרִיתִי אַבְרָהָם אֶזְכֹּר

*"I will recall My covenant with Yaakov and
also My covenant with Yitzchak,
and also My covenant with Avraham
I will recall" (26:42)*

Why are the Forefathers listed in reverse order? asked R' Shmelke of Nikolsburg.

*Chaza*l have taught us, answered the *rebbe*, that "The world depends on three things – on Torah study, on the service [of God], and on kind deeds" (*Avos* 1:2).

Each one of the Forefathers was noted for a different character trait. Yaakov embodied Torah study. He was "a wholesome man abiding in tents" (*Bereishis* 25:27) who studied Torah in the yeshivah of Shem and Ever. Yitzchak, who had been bound to an altar, represented service of Hashem. Avraham, the paradigm of hospitality, represented the trait of kindness.

The order in which the verse lists the Forefathers — Yaakov, Yitzchak, and Avraham – corresponds to the order utilized by *Chazal* to enumerate the three things which the world depends upon — first "Torah," then "service of God," and finally, "kindness."

BAMIDBAR

Parashas Bamidbar

וַיְדַבֵּר ה' אֶל־מֹשֶׁה בְּמִדְבַּר סִינַי

"Hashem spoke to Moshe in the Wilderness of Sinai" (1:1)

T HE *MIDRASH RABBAH* CITES THE WORDS OF *CHAZAL*: "WITH THREE things was the Torah given: with fire, with water, and with wilderness .... And why was it given with these three things? Rather, just as these things are free for all mankind, so are the words of Torah free ... as the verse states, 'Ho, everyone who is thirsty, go to the water'" (*Yeshayahu* 55:1).

Fire, water, and wilderness, remarked the Dubno *Maggid*, symbolize the three qualities needed by anyone who wishes to grow great in Torah.

Fire: The individual's Divine service must be aflame within him.

Water: The person must thirst for words of Torah just as one thirsts for water.

Wilderness: He must be content with little and as free of materialism as the wilderness. This is as *Chazal* state in *Pirkei Avos* (6:4), "This is the way of the Torah: Eat bread with salt, drink water in small measure, sleep on the ground, live a life of deprivation — but toil in the Torah!"

וַיְדַבֵּר ה' אֶל־מֹשֶׁה בְּמִדְבַּר סִינַי

"Hashem spoke to Moshe in the Wilderness of Sinai" (1:1)

C *hazal* relate that when the Jews came to the wilderness of Sinai, they were a united people, as the verse states, "*vayichan sham Yisrael neged hahar*" ("And Israel encamped there, opposite the mountain"— *Shemos* 19:2). *Chazal* point out that the word "*vayichan*" is in the singular form, indicating that at that point the Jewish people were one cohesive unit. Because they were united, they merited receiving the Torah.

The first verse of *Bamidbar*, noted the *Chida* (R' Chaim Yosef David Azulai), contains an allusion to the Jews' unity while they were at Sinai. For the words *"b'Midbar Sinai"* and *"b'shalom"* ("in peace") have the same numerical value (378)!

Furthermore, said the *Chida*, most years we read *Parashas Bamidbar* on the Shabbos before Shavuos — the festival of the giving of the Torah. This should remind us to increase our unity and the performance of *mitzvos bein adam l'chavero* (*mitzvos* that pertain to man and his fellow) during this time so that we will thereby merit receiving the Torah.

וַיְדַבֵּר ה' אֶל־מֹשֶׁה בְּמִדְבַּר סִינַי
"Hashem spoke to Moshe in the Wilderness of Sinai" (1:1)

R' Meir Shapiro, the *rosh yeshivah* of Yeshivas Chachmei Lublin, once addressed a large audience. "HaKadosh Baruch Hu," he began, "gave the Jewish people the Torah on condition that they would continue to fulfill its commandments even if it required self-sacrifice on their part.

"*Chazal* state in the *Midrash Rabbah*," he continued, "'With three things was the Torah given: with fire, with water, and with wilderness.'

"'Fire' is an allusion to the self-sacrifice of Avraham *Avinu*, who was cast into the fiery furnace because of his belief in Hashem.

"'Water' alludes to the extraordinary act of Nachshon ben Aminadav, who was the first to jump into the Sea of Reeds in order to sanctify Hashem's Name.

"'Wilderness' is an allusion to the self-sacrifice of our ancestors who traveled in the desert for forty years with complete faith in Hashem."

וְאִתְּכֶם יִהְיוּ אִישׁ אִישׁ לַמַּטֶּה אִישׁ רֹאשׁ לְבֵית־אֲבֹתָיו הוּא:
"With you shall be one man for each tribe, the man being the head of his ancestral house" (1:4)

When R' Dov Ber of Mezritch was a young boy, a terrible fire broke out in his town. The houses, which were constructed of wood, were consumed within moments, as the fire blazed without mercy.

His mother barely managed to save him and his siblings from their burning home. Once they reached safety, she burst into bitter sobbing.

"Mother," asked young Dov Ber, "why are you weeping? Is a wooden house and wooden furniture worth shedding tears over?"

"My son," replied his mother, "I am not crying on account of our house or our furniture. I weep over the precious family tree that was lost ... that family tree listed all of our holy and special ancestors."

"Do not weep," said Dov Ber. "For I guarantee you that when I get older, with God's help, I will begin a new family tree of distinguished lineage."

וְאִתְּכֶם יִהְיוּ ... אִישׁ רֹאשׁ לְבֵית־אֲבֹתָיו הוּא:
"With you shall be ... the head of his ancestral house" (1:4)

R' Tzvi Hirsch of Riminov's parents died when he was about 10 years old. His relatives were very poor and could not support him. They felt they had no choice but to send the youngster to work as an apprentice to a simple tailor.

Many years later, when he had already become a renowned *tzaddik*, R' Tzvi Hirsch sat among his *chassidim* and remarked, "I did not merit learning anything from my father, as I was orphaned at a young age. From the tailor, however, I learned two very important lessons: (1) not to ruin new items; (2) to try as much as possible to mend old ones."

אֵלֶּה קְרוּאֵי הָעֵדָה
"These were the summoned ones of the community" (1:16)

Rashi explains that they were called "the summoned ones" because they were summoned for every matter of importance.

The Vilna *Gaon* and the leaders of Vilna's community had reached an agreement that they would not invite the *Gaon* to their meetings unless they planned to institute a new regulation.

One day, they decided to implement a new regulation: *Chazal* have ruled (*Bava Metzia* 71a) that one is obligated to provide for the needy of his own city before providing for the needy of other cities. That being the case, Vilna's communal leaders wanted to forbid *tzedakah* collectors from other cities from making their rounds in Vilna.

A meeting was scheduled and the *Gaon* was invited to attend.

After listening to the details of the regulation that they wished to ratify, the *Gaon* rose to his feet and said, "Why have you invited me to this meeting? We had agreed that I would only be asked to attend meetings at which new regulations would be adopted."

"Is this not a new regulation?" asked the communal leaders.

"No, it is a very old one," responded the Vilna *Gaon*. "It has existed since the times of Sodom and Amorah!"

וְאַתָּה הַפְקֵד אֶת־הַלְוִיִּם
"Now you, appoint the Levi'im" (1:50)

During a year of horrible famine, the poor and unfortunate of Brisk approached R' Chaim Soloveitchik in a state of terrible distress. "*Rebbe*," they said, "please help us! Some of the city's leaders are acting very cruelly toward us and are not helping us. *Rebbe*, if no one comes to our aid in this time of famine, we will die of starvation!"

R' Chaim summoned the city's leaders. When they arrived, he began by quoting a Gemara in *Maseches Bava Basra* (8a): The Gemara tells us that during a year of famine, R' Yonasan ben Amram came before Rebbe (R' Yehudah HaNasi) and asked him for food.

"'Do you learn Torah?' asked Rebbe.

"'No,' replied R' Yonasan.

"Rebbe continued to inquire of him, 'Do you learn Mishnah?'

"Once again, R' Yonasan responded in the negative.

"'If that is so,' asked Rebbe, 'how can I provide for you?'

"'Provide for me (*parneseini*) like the dog and the raven,' replied R' Yonasan.

"Now I would like to ask you," said R' Chaim, "why would R' Yonasan want Rebbe to provide for him in the same way as dogs and ravens? Dogs and ravens are cruel animals!

"In truth," answered R' Chaim, "the community leaders were giving to all those in need. But in order to minimize the embarrassment of Torah scholars, who would be forced to stand together in line with ignoramuses, two lines were set up. The simpletons stood on line to receive their rations from the community leaders and the Torah scholars stood on line before Rebbe.

"This is why," continued R' Chaim, "when R' Yonasan ben Amram came before Rebbe, Rebbe asked him whether he had studied or not. He wanted to know if the man standing before him was on the correct line."

"When R' Yonasan replied that he was unknowledgeable in both Torah and Mishnah, Rebbe asked him, 'How can I provide for you?' — You are standing in the wrong line. Rebbe was telling the man that 'It is not I who is meant to provide for you, but the community leaders.'

"R' Yonasan therefore responded, 'My providers (*parneseini*) — the ones who are supposed to provide for me — are treating me cruelly, "like the dog and the raven." I therefore beseech *you*, Rebbe, please provide for me!'"

וְאֵלֶּה תּוֹלְדֹת אַהֲרֹן וּמֹשֶׁה ...
"These are the offspring of Aharon and Moshe ..." (3:1)

Rashi comments that the verse states, "These are the offspring of Aharon and Moshe," yet the Torah lists only Aharon's sons. Why are Aharon's sons also referred to as *Moshe's* offspring?

This is because Moshe taught Aharon's children Torah, answers Rashi. This teaches us that whoever teaches his friend's son Torah is viewed by the Torah as if he had fathered him.

Even at the young age of 5, the *Rebbe* R' Heschel of Cracow was already known as a prodigy, and many scholars enjoyed discussing Torah matters with him.

"Please enlighten me," said one of the scholars. "Rashi teaches us that 'whoever teaches his friend's son Torah is viewed by the Torah as if he had fathered him.'

"Yet in *Maseches Bava Metzia*, *Chazal* state that the honor that one must show his teacher is greater than the honor he must show his father. For his father only brought him to this world, while his teacher — by teaching him Torah — brings him to the World to Come as well.

"So perhaps you can tell me," he continued, "which is greater: the honor that one must demonstrate for a teacher, or the honor that one must demonstrate for a parent?"

The young R' Heschel thought for a brief moment and then replied, "The honor that should be accorded the teacher is certainly greater, as he has enabled his student to earn a share in the World to Come. When Rashi says that 'whoever teaches his friend's son Torah is viewed by the Torah as if he had fathered him,' he means to say that it is as if he fathered him *and* taught him Torah!"

וְאֵלֶּה תּוֹלְדֹת אַהֲרֹן וּמֹשֶׁה

"These are the offspring of Aharon and Moshe" (3:1)

The students of R' Eliezer Yehudah Finkel, the *rosh yeshivah* of Mir, were as dear to him as his own sons, and whenever they visited his home, he requested that they share words of Torah with him.

One day, a student whom he had not seen in many years arrived at his home. R' Finkel was delighted to see him, and he asked him to relate a novel Torah thought that he had recently formulated.

The student complied and began to speak words of Torah, but he was unexpectedly interrupted by R' Finkel.

"Please forgive me, my dear student," said the *rosh yeshivah*. "But I asked you for a *new* Torah thought, and you are presently repeating something which I heard from you thirty-five years ago."

הַקְרֵב אֶת־מַטֵּה לֵוִי וְהַעֲמַדְתָּ אֹתוֹ
לִפְנֵי אַהֲרֹן הַכֹּהֵן וְשֵׁרְתוּ אֹתוֹ:

"Bring the tribe of Levi near and present them before Aharon the Kohen, and they shall serve him" (3:6)

The *Midrash Rabbah* expounds on this verse, "Thus it is written, 'A righteous man will flourish like a date palm, like a cedar in Lebanon he will grow tall. Planted in the house of Hashem' (*Tehillim* 92:13)."

There are two types of *tzaddikim* in the world, remarked the *Ba'al Shem Tov*. There are *tzaddikim* who serve Hashem with all their limbs, yet they remain secluded inside their homes and do not influence students with the bounty of good that they possess.

Other *tzaddikim*, on the other hand, actively try to draw their fellow Jews closer to their Father in Heaven.

A *tzaddik* of the first sort is compared to a cedar, a tree of towering stature, yet one that bears no fruit.

A *tzaddik* of the second sort is compared to a date palm, which is also a tall tree, yet one that bears fruit for others to enjoy.

Chazal compared the tribe of Levi to a date palm because they stood before Aharon and served him. By *serving* Aharon they were exemplary role models for the Jewish nation to emulate, and they succeeded in drawing their brethren closer to Divine service.

PARASHAS NASSO

אִישׁ אוֹ־אִשָּׁה כִּי יַעֲשׂוּ מִכָּל־חַטֹּאת הָאָדָם ...

וְהִתְוַדּוּ אֶת־חַטָּאתָם ... וְנָתַן לַאֲשֶׁר אָשַׁם לוֹ:

"A man or woman who commits any
of man's sins ... they shall confess their sin
... he shall make restitution for his guilt" (5:6-7)

O NE *EREV* YOM KIPPUR, R' MOSHE CHAGIZ DELIVERED A *DERASHAH* IN which he said: "In *Parashas Nasso* it states, 'A man or woman ... *they* shall confess ... *he* shall make restitution for his guilt.' The verse begins in the singular, switches to the plural, and then concludes by reverting to the singular. This is to teach us that all Jews form one nation and we are all responsible for one another.

"'They shall confess' — on Yom Kippur, an individual is not only required to confess his own sins but even the sins of his fellow Jew.

"To what can this be compared? To a group of individuals who set sail together on a large and magnificent ship. Each one of the passengers received his own quarters for the duration of the trip.

"When they had reached the very heart of the sea, one of the passengers began to drill a hole in the wall of the ship.

"'What are you doing?' yelled his friends. 'You are going to sink the ship!'

"'Why is this any concern of yours?' he asked them. 'I am making a hole in *my* quarters, not yours.'

"All Jews are responsible for one another," concluded R' Chagiz. "If one Jew sins, the entire Jewish nation is held accountable.

"It is incumbent upon every Jew to keep this great responsibility in mind."

וְאִישׁ אֶת־קֳדָשָׁיו לוֹ יִהְיוּ
"A man's holy items shall remain his" (5:10)

To what can this be compared, asked the *Chofetz Chaim*? To a king who summoned his servant, Reuven, to appear before him.

Reuven was filled with dread and thought, *Why has the king summoned me? Perhaps someone has slandered me and falsely accused me of committing some crime.*

Reuven approached his trusted friend, Shimon, and asked him to accompany him to the king's courtyard; yet Shimon refused!

What shall I do? thought Reuven. *Shimon, my closest friend, has refused to join me; I will go and ask Levi. True, Levi is not my best friend, but perhaps my plea will sway him enough that he will accompany me.*

"I am prepared to join you," replied Levi, "but I am afraid of entering the king's palace. I will accompany you to the king's courtyard, and then I will have to part from you."

Left with little choice, Reuven approached Yehudah, whom he hardly knew.

Surprisingly, it was Yehudah who agreed to join Reuven on his visit to the king. He agreed to enter the palace and to intercede on Reuven's behalf.

When a person departs from this world, concluded the *Chofetz Chaim*, and is summoned to appear before *HaKadosh Baruch Hu*, the King of all kings, his closest "friend" — the gold and silver that took so much effort to amass — will refuse to accompany him.

His sons and daughters escort him partway, but they will not enter the king's palace.

Only the *mitzvos* and good deeds that he performed during his life — the things he appreciated least — will be the ones to accompany him all the way to the Throne of Glory. Only they will plead on his behalf!

This is as the verse states, "A man's holy items" — the *mitzvos* and holy deeds that a man has done throughout his life — "shall remain his" — only they will remain with him to intervene on his behalf after passing from this world.

אִישׁ אֲשֶׁר־יִתֵּן לַכֹּהֵן לוֹ יִהְיֶה:

"And what a man gives to the Kohen shall be his" (5:10)

R' Zalman Sorotzkin related the following story to a group of students:

A certain Jew, who was a highly regarded adviser to the king of Poland, was very successful in his business, and he eventually grew quite rich. Despite his wealth and high position, he remained a God-fearing Jew and a true servant of Hashem.

There were, however, several officers in the king's court who envied the Jew, and they devised a wicked scheme. They told the king that all of the Jew's wealth had been stolen from the Royal Treasury.

The king, who very much respected the Jewish adviser, did not believe a word of the officers' libel. He yielded to their pressure, however, and summoned the Jew for an interrogation.

"What is the value of your entire fortune?" the king asked him.

The Jew reported an amount that was approximately a tenth of his assets.

Realizing that the Jew's answer was far from accurate, the king deduced that the Jew was hiding the truth from him. In a fit of rage, he ordered that the Jew's property be confiscated and placed in the Royal Treasury and that the Jew be thrown into prison. After the Jew's property was confiscated, it was even more apparent to the king that, indeed, the Jew had lied to him.

On the day of the trial, the king asked the Jew, "Why did you lie and conceal the true value of your estate from me?"

"Your highness," answered the Jew, "all of my words were true! I am accustomed to giving a tenth of my income to *tzedakah*. I then record the amount that I gave in a special notepad. When you inquired what I owned, I told you the amount listed in my notepad, for those are my true assets that cannot be taken away from me!

"This is as it states in our holy Torah," concluded the Jew, "'And what a man gives to the *Kohen* shall be his.'"

The sincere words of the Jew made a favorable impression upon the king, and he released him from prison and reinstated him, making him the highest-ranking officer in the kingdom.

אִישׁ אֲשֶׁר־יִתֵּן לַכֹּהֵן לוֹ יִהְיֶה:

"And what a man gives to the Kohen shall be his" (5:10)

To what can this be compared? asked the *Chofetz Chaim*. To a poor man who decided to travel to a distant land and try his hand at business.

He took leave of his home and traveled to faraway Africa. It was extremely hot in Africa, and as a result, there was very little for the cattle to graze on. This, in turn, meant that the animals produced very little milk; and, consequently, milk was an expensive item. The poor man wisely began to sell milk, and, in a short while, he earned a fortune. Despite his success, he chose not to return home; rather, he stayed in Africa and continued his business dealings.

After several years, he received a letter from his wife, asking him to return home. The man thought, *"It is worthwhile for me to purchase a large amount of milk and ship it to my hometown in order to sell it there and earn a large profit.* And so he did.

Before he boarded the ship, he was approached by a diamond dealer, who offered to sell him diamonds for presents to his family.

"Diamonds," said the man, "I can buy anywhere. I am better off spending my money on milk."

After much persuading on the part of the merchant, the man agreed to buy a few diamonds with the little money he had left.

When he arrived at his home, he was heartbroken to discover that all the milk he had taken with him had spoiled and was now worthless.

"For *this* I suffered so many years in your absence?" yelled his embittered wife.

The man stood there in utter humiliation. Years of effort and struggle had evaporated overnight.

He suddenly remembered the few diamonds he had bought before boarding the ship. The man took the diamonds and sold them, and with the money he received, he and his family managed to live comfortably for many years to come.

We can only imagine how much the man regretted not buying more diamonds!

Man, concluded the *Chofetz Chaim*, comes down to this world to perform *mitzvos*. Yet he spends most of his days trying to amass material goods — goods that have absolutely no value in the World to Come.

When he stands before the Heavenly court, he will be asked, "Give a detailed accounting of your deeds!" But he will just stand there, shame faced and speechless. Suddenly, he will recall the little amount of money he once gave to *tzedakah*, the sick people that he was kind enough to visit, and so on. It is those meritorious deeds that will earn him a reward in the World to Come.

How great will his anguish be, however, over not spending more time amassing *mitzvos* and good deeds!

אִישׁ אוֹ־אִשָּׁה כִּי יַפְלִא לִנְדֹּר נֶדֶר נָזִיר לְהַזִּיר לַה':

"A man or woman who distinguishes himself [or herself] by taking a Nazirite vow of abstinence for the sake of Hashem" (6:2)

The Gemara in *Maseches Nedarim* (9b) quotes the words of Shimon *HaTzaddik* who related the following story: On one occasion, a *nazir* from the south of *Eretz Yisrael* came before him. He had beautiful eyes, he was very handsome, and the locks of his hair were arranged into curls.

"My son," asked Shimon *HaTzaddik*, "why do you want to destroy your beautiful hair?" [On the day that a *nazir's* term has been completed, he is required to shave his head — see *Bamidbar* 6:1.]

"I was a shepherd," he replied. "One day, I was going to draw water from the spring, and I caught a glimpse of my reflection in the water. My *yetzer hara* sought to drive me from the world! I said to him, 'Wicked one! Why do you become haughty in a world that is not yours? Do you attempt to glorify yourself in a man whose end is worms and maggots?' I immediately vowed to shave my hair for the honor of Heaven!"

Upon hearing the *nazir's* story, Shimon *HaTzaddik* rose and kissed him on the head, saying, "May it be His will that there be more *nezirim* like you in Israel!"

When the shepherd saw his visage in the water, asked the Steipler *Gaon* (R' Yaakov Yisrael Kanievsky), which sin did the *yetzer hara* entice him to commit?

From the shepherd's response to his *yetzer hara*, answered the Steipler, "Why do you become haughty in a world that is not yours?" we understand that the *yetzer hara* wished to make him succumb to the sin of arrogance.

In most cases, continued the Steipler, when a person realizes that he possesses a quality that his friends do not have, he is immediately filled with pride, and he imagines that he is the best person in the world. He becomes convinced that all must pay him tribute.

But *why* does the *yetzer hara* try to plant arrogance into the heart of every man, and why is this looked upon as an attempt to drive a person from the world?

The answer is that when haughtiness enters a person's heart, the Divine Presence immediately departs! Then, once the Divine Presence leaves him, he remains a prisoner to his *yetzer hara* and amenable to all the *yetzer's* whims.

⚘⚘⚘

אִישׁ אוֹ־אִשָּׁה כִּי יַפְלִא לִנְדֹּר נֶדֶר נָזִיר לְהַזִּיר לַה':

"A man or woman who distinguishes himself [or herself] by taking a Nazirite vow of abstinence for the sake of Hashem" (6:2)

"Why," asks Rashi, "was the Torah portion of the *nazir* put adjacent to the portion of the *sotah* (a woman who deviated from moral behavior)? To tell you that anyone who sees a *sotah* in her disgrace should take upon himself to abstain from wine [by becoming a *nazir*]."

Whenever a person sees something improper, he must think, *Why has Heaven shown this impure thing to me?* He must do some serious soul-searching and attempt to strengthen himself in his Divine service.

R' Yisrael Salanter once caught a bad cold. The first day of his illness, he spent the entire day worrying.

"Why is the *Rav* so worried?" asked one of his close disciples. "*Baruch Hashem*, it's just a cold and it will not pose any serious threat to your health."

"It is not my health that concerns me," responded R' Salanter. "I worry over what it states in *Mishlei*, 'Colds and traps are in the path of the stubborn' (*Mishlei* 22:5).

"This verse is evidence that I was stricken with a cold on account of possessing the terrible trait of stubbornness."

Only once evening had arrived and R' Salanter had thoroughly examined his deeds without finding the trait of stubbornness within himself was his mind put to rest.

וְכִפֶּר עָלָיו מֵאֲשֶׁר חָטָא עַל־הַנָּפֶשׁ

"And he shall provide him atonement for having sinned through a dead person" (6:11)

When the *nazir's* term has been completed, he brings a sin-offering because his vow of *nezirus* prevented him from performing several *mitzvos*. For example, he was unable to escort the dead, for he was forbidden to become ritually impure; and he could not recite *Kiddush* on a cup of wine, as he had accepted upon himself to abstain from drinking wine. R' Meir Yechiel Halstuck of Ostrovtze fasted frequently and engaged in much self-affliction.

"*Rebbe*," asked one of his *chassidim*, "we find that the *nazir* is obligated to bring a sin-offering because 'he pained himself [by abstaining] from wine' (*Nazir* 19a). Similarly, *Chazal* state in *Maseches Ta'anis* (11a), 'Anyone who sits in fasting is called a sinner'! How, then, does the *Rebbe* permit himself to fast?"

"A very good question, indeed," replied the *Rebbe*. "But you will notice, however, that the Gemara does not say, 'Anyone who fasts,' but rather 'Anyone who *sits* in fasting.' In other words, an individual who weakens himself by fasting and therefore remains sitting in his place, unable to reach lofty levels in his service of Hashem — this is the person whom *Chazal* have called a sinner!"

וְכִפֶּר עָלָיו מֵאֲשֶׁר חָטָא
"And he shall provide him atonement for having sinned" (6:11)

Chazal ask in *Maseches Ta'anis* (11a): "Which person has he sinned against? Rather, it is because he pained himself [by abstaining] from wine."

He is therefore required to bring a sin-offering on the day that his term of *nezirus* has been completed.

A story is told of a young married man who approached R' Yisrael of Rizhin and requested ordination.

"*Rebbe*," said the man, "besides the Torah that I have studied, I also afflict myself. The only beverage I drink is water, and I have nails driven into the soles of my shoes in order to make walking uncomfortable. In addition, I roll around in the snow in the wintertime, and accept forty 'lashes' from the sun each day of the summer."

R' Yisrael called the young man over to the window and asked him to look outside. The young man complied, but saw nothing more than a horse rolling around in the snow.

"What does the *Rebbe* wish to show me?" asked the young man. "A horse?"

"That is exactly what I wish to show you!" replied the *Rebbe*. "This horse also drinks nothing but water, has nails driven into its hooves, rolls around in the snow, and receives many lashes from the wagon driver each and every day. Despite all that, however, he remains no more than a horse."

כֹּה תְבָרְכוּ אֶת־בְּנֵי יִשְׂרָאֵל אָמוֹר לָהֶם:
"So shall you bless the Children of Israel, saying to them" (6:23)

The word "*amor*," noted R' Levi Yitzchak of Berdichev, also means love, as the verse states, "And Hashem has loved (*he'emircha*) you today" (*Devarim* 26:18).

This is the why the verse says, "So shall you bless the Children of Israel, saying (*amor*) to them." In other words, only one who loves the Children of Israel is permitted to bless them.

בַּיּוֹם הָעֲשִׂירִי נָשִׂיא לִבְנֵי דָן
"On the tenth day, the leader
of the Children of Dan" (7:66)

Several of the Vilna *Gaon*'s students were sitting at a meal arranged in celebration of a *mitzvah*. That day was *Rosh Chodesh Nisan*, and the conversation at the table revolved around the custom to read, during the first twelve days of *Nisan*, the passages in the Torah that relate to the dedication offerings brought by the leaders of the tribes.

One of those students was R' Zalman of Volozhin, who was one of the Vilna *Gaon*'s primary disciples.

"Did you know," said R' Zalman to his friends, "that the day of the week on which we read about the tribe of Dan's offering is also the day of the week on which the following Rosh Hashanah will fall? The day of *Dan*'s offering corresponds to the day when Hashem judges (*dan*) all of mankind.

"This is also hinted to in the blessing that Yaakov *Avinu* bestowed upon Dan, as the verse states, *Dan yadin amo* — 'Dan will judge his people.'"

PARASHAS BEHA'ALOSCHA

וַיַּעַשׂ כֵּן אַהֲרֹן
"Aharon did exactly so" (8:3)

RASHI QUOTES THE *SIFREI*: "'AHARON DID EXACTLY SO' — [THIS IS stated] to tell the praise of Aharon in that he did not deviate [from the instructions]."

Why is the fact that Aharon did not deviate from Hashem's instructions considered praise? asked the Dubno *Maggid*. Every Jew knows not to second-guess the words of Hashem. Is it not obvious that Aharon would not deviate from Hashem's command?

The *maggid* answered with a parable. To what can this be compared? To three men who contracted serious illnesses and turned to a well-known physician for treatment.

The doctor prescribed identical medications and instructions to all three of them. The first man followed the doctor's instructions exactly as he had been told, and, after a short while, he recovered completely.

The second man, who had a basic knowledge of medicine, investigated the medications that were prescribed for him and took only those that he deemed would be helpful, and he remained ill.

The third man also wondered about the necessity of taking each medicine. However, he trusted the doctor who was known to be an expert. He therefore decided to take all of them, and he, too, recovered.

The Torah, concluded the Dubno *Maggid*, is the antidote that Hashem has given us in order to combat the *yetzer hara*. There are those who follow the Torah's instructions without question. Then there are others who wish to understand the reasoning behind each *mitzvah* and will only keep the ones they comprehend. Still others investigate the reasoning behind each *mitzvah,* but, in the end, keep the *mitzvos* as Hashem commanded.

The group of unquestioning Jews never falters, the group of skeptic Jews always neglects some of the *mitzvos*, and the group of inquiring Jews runs the risk of ignoring Hashem's will.

Aharon *HaKohen* never deviated from his Divine service because he never questioned Hashem's commandments — he trusted Hashem completely.

This is why the Torah praises Aharon!

וְהִבְדַּלְתָּ אֶת־הַלְוִיִּם מִתּוֹךְ בְּנֵי יִשְׂרָאֵל וְהָיוּ לִי הַלְוִיִּם:

"You shall separate the Levites from among the Children of Israel, and the Levites shall remain Mine" (8:14)

The *Yalkut Shimoni* relates a parable about a king who arranged a lavish feast for all of his servants and friends. There was, however, one friend whom he did not invite — his best friend.

This distressed the man very much, and he thought, *What have I done and how have I sinned against the king, that he should not have invited me to his feast?*

After the party and all the guests had gone home, the king dispatched a royal messenger to his friend's home. "You are invited to the royal palace," declared the messenger to the friend. "The king wishes to see you immediately."

When he arrived at the palace, the king greeted him with a big smile. "Welcome, my good friend!" said the king joyously. "You are more beloved to me than all my other acquaintances, and I have therefore arranged a special party just for you."

This is what happened with the tribe of Levi. In *Parashas Nasso*, we learned about how the leaders of each tribe brought an offering to Hashem. But the tribe of Levi did not have a leader and therefore did not bring an offering.

The members of the tribe of Levi were very pained that they had been left out, and they asked, "Why have we not merited to bring offerings as well?"

Thereupon the Holy One said to them: "It is specifically because you are so dear to Me that I have set aside a special service for you to perform in the Tent of Meeting. No laymen can come close to it!"

הֶאָנֹכִי הָרִיתִי אֵת כָּל־הָעָם הַזֶּה אִם־אָנֹכִי
יְלִדְתִּיהוּ ... מֵאַיִן לִי בָשָׂר לָתֵת לְכָל־הָעָם הַזֶּה

"Did I father this entire people or give birth to them ... From where shall I get meat to give to this entire people?" (11:12-13)

A young married man approached the *Sefas Emes* (R' Yehudah Leib of Gur) with a series of complaints against his father.

"From the day I got married," said the young man, "my father has refused to help me support my family."

The *rebbe* called upon the father and asked him, "Why do you refuse to help your son?"

"All my life," answered the father, "I have worked hard to support myself and my family. Once my children marry, however, I see no reason to concern myself regarding their livelihoods."

"Your argument is flawed," said the *rebbe*. "For when the Jewish people desired to eat meat, Moshe *Rabbeinu* claimed before Hashem, 'Did I father this entire people or give birth to them ... From where shall I get meat to give to this entire people?'

"This implies," continued the *Sefas Emes*, "that had Moshe actually given birth to the nation, he would not have been able to claim, 'From where shall I get meat?'

"That being the case," concluded the *rebbe*, "you, too, must help your son."

מִקִּבְרוֹת הַתַּאֲוָה נָסְעוּ הָעָם חֲצֵרוֹת וַיִּהְיוּ בַּחֲצֵרוֹת:
"From Kivros-hata'avah the people journeyed to Chatzeros, and they remained in Chatzeros" (11:35)

There was always a large group of *chassidim* waiting at the court of R' Menachem Mendel of Kotzk in the hope of hearing even a small *devar Torah* from their esteemed *rebbe*.

A group of *chassidim* once asked the Kotzker for a blessing.

"I know why you want my blessing," replied the *rebbe*. "You want it to save you from your desires and improper thoughts. But the answer is 'no'! This you must achieve on your own. You must first battle your desires, and only afterwards should you come to my court for a blessing.

"The verse practically says this explicitly," he continued. "'From *Kivros-hata'avah* the people journeyed to *Chatzeros* and they remained in *Chatzeros*.' First a *chassid* must bury his desires ("*likvor ta'avaso*") and only afterwards can he journey to the courtyard ("*chatzer*") of his *rebbe* and remain in his presence."

וְהָאִישׁ מֹשֶׁה עָנָו מְאֹד
"Now the man Moshe was exceedingly humble" (12:3)

A father was sitting in his car, waiting for his son. Seeing no sign of him, he stuck his head out the car window and began to call loudly, "Moshe! Moshe!"

At that very moment, R' Moshe Feinstein happened to be passing by. Hearing someone calling his name, the *gaon* walked over to the car and asked the man what he wanted.

The father was taken aback at the sight of the great R' Feinstein and began to apologize profusely, "Please forgive me, *Rabbeinu*. I certainly had no intention of calling you; rather I was calling my son. I would never think to address the *Rosh Yeshivah* in such a manner."

"Do not worry about it," answered R' Feinstein. "It has already been many years since I attributed any meaning to these things."

✺◦✺

וְהָאִישׁ מֹשֶׁה עָנָו מְאֹד מִכֹּל הָאָדָם אֲשֶׁר עַל־פְּנֵי הָאֲדָמָה:

"Now the man Moshe was exceedingly humble, more than any person on the face of the earth" (12:3)

Rashi comments: "'*Anav*' — [This means] humble and long suffering."

R' Chaim of Volozhin and his brother, R' Zalman, arrived at an inn late one night. When they entered the inn, the innkeeper spoke to them harshly and showered them with a series of insults. To make matters worse, he refused to allow them to lodge at his inn. Left with no other choice, the brothers continued their journey in the dark of night.

Suddenly, R' Chaim noticed that R' Zalman was weeping bitterly.

"Why are you crying?" asked R' Chaim. "Is it because the innkeeper offended you? Believe me, I paid no attention to a word he said."

"Heaven forbid," answered R' Zalman. "I am not shedding tears on account of the verbal abuse we endured. However, when the innkeeper insulted us, I was hurt ever so slightly by his words. The fact that it bothered me at all is what I am upset about now. Why have I not merited reaching the lofty level of, 'Those who are insulted and do not insult others perform [*mitzvos*] with love, and are happy with suffering ...'? (*Yoma* 23a, *Gittin* 36b). Why was I not happy when the innkeeper insulted me? This is why I cry!"

וְהָאִישׁ מֹשֶׁה עָנָו מְאֹד מִכֹּל הָאָדָם אֲשֶׁר עַל־פְּנֵי הָאֲדָמָה:

"Now the man Moshe was exceedingly humble, more than any person on the face of the earth" (12:3)

R' Naftali Amsterdam was known to be one of the greatest disciples of R' Yisrael Salanter. Throughout his life, he expended much effort in concealing his Torah greatness from others. While he held a rabbinical post, he, nonetheless, refused to deliver *derashos*, claiming to be unfit for the task.

Another example of his humility is that he always entered *shul* holding a *sefer* in his hand. "The congregation is standing in honor of the *sefer*," he would say.

One Purim, R' Amsterdam hosted R' Yaakov Yechiel Weinberg (the *Seridei Aish*) for the festive meal.

At one point during the meal, R' Amsterdam began praising his friends, fellow students of R' Yisrael Salanter, by telling R' Weinberg what R' Salanter used to say about each one of them.

"And what did R' Salanter have to say about you?" asked R' Weinberg.

R' Amsterdam gave a piercing look at his guest and said, "Do you think that just because today is Purim you are permitted to make fun of an old man? I am nothing compared to them; I simply stood alongside them when our great teacher would deliver his *derashos*! Oh, they acted graciously toward me, but it was only out of pity for such a lowly person as myself—"

"But are you not famous throughout the city and its surrounding?" asked R' Weinberg.

"That is only due to the merit of R' Salanter," replied R' Amsterdam. "For everyone errs and considers me one of his *talmidim*.

"And how have I gotten to be so well known? I will tell you: My wife bakes beautiful challahs in honor of the Shabbos. All of the women see them and are amazed; they then praise the *Rebbetzin* who, as is her way, begins to relate my praise to them — despite the fact that I am truly not worthy of it."

וְהָאִישׁ מֹשֶׁה עָנָו מְאֹד מִכֹּל הָאָדָם אֲשֶׁר עַל־פְּנֵי הָאֲדָמָה:

"Now the man Moshe was exceedingly humble, more than any person on the face of the earth" (12:3)

Many distinguished rabbis had gathered in Berlin for an important assembly. Among them sat the great R' Elchanan Wasserman, author of the classic work, *Kovetz Shiurim.*

When R' Wasserman was about to address the audience, R' Yaakov Yechiel Weinberg quickly preceded him and, before the entire crowd, recited the blessing that is said upon seeing an outstanding Torah scholar, "Blessed are You, Hashem, our God, King of the universe, Who has apportioned of His knowledge to those who fear Him."

R' Wasserman was shocked by what R' Weinberg had done, and he leaped from his place, yelling, "No! Absolutely not!"

His protests were of no use, however, for the entire audience rose to their feet and recited the blessing as well.

On another occasion, R' Wasserman took part in an assembly meant to strengthen religious observance. One of the speakers began his speech with the words, "*Rabbosai*, do you have any idea who is in your midst?"

When he heard the speaker's words, R' Wasserman immediately got up and ran from the room as if he was fleeing from a fire.

וַיִּצְעַק מֹשֶׁה אֶל־ה' לֵאמֹר אֵ-ל נָא רְפָא נָא לָהּ:

"Moshe cried out to Hashem, saying, "Please, God, heal her now" (12:13)

Chazal relate the following story in *Maseches Berachos* (34a): One of R' Eliezer's students stepped before the ark to lead the prayer services. The student prayed very slowly, so the prayers were being drawn out excessively.

The other students said to R' Eliezer, "Our teacher, this person prays for so long."

He said to them, "Does he spend more time praying than Moshe *Rabbeinu*, about whom it is written, 'I threw myself down before Hashem for the forty days and the forty nights' (*Devarim* 9:25)?"

On another occasion, a different student went down before the ark in the presence of R' Eliezer, but this student prayed very quickly.

This time the students said to R' Eliezer, "Our teacher, this person prays too fast."

He said to them, "Are his prayers shorter than those of Moshe *Rabbeinu*, about whom it is written, 'Moshe cried out to Hashem, saying: Please, God, heal her now'?"

אֶ-ל נָא רְפָא נָא לָה:

"Please, God, heal her now" (12:13)

R' Meir Yechiel of Ostrovtze once met with the *Imrei Emes* (R' Avraham Mordechai of Gur). R' Meir Yechiel, who was quite ill at the time, asked the *Imrei Emes* to pray for his complete recovery using his name and his mother's name, as is customary.

"In *Maseches Berachos* (34a)," questioned the *Imrei Emes*, "*Chazal* state that anyone who beseeches mercy on the part of his friend need not mention his friend's name; for when Moshe *Rabbeinu* prayed for Miriam, he did not mention her name, as the verse states, 'Please, God, heal her now.' That being the case, why did you tell me your name?"

"What the Gemara means to say," answered R' Meir Yechiel, "is that it is not necessary to mention the friend's and mother's names *explicitly*; rather, one can *allude* to them he if likes, for we find that the numerical value of the words, *"refa na,"* (332) is equal to that of *"Miriam, Yocheved"*!

PARASHAS SHELACH

וַיַּעֲלוּ בַנֶּגֶב וַיָּבֹא עַד־חֶבְרוֹן

"They went up through the south and he came as far as Chevron" (13:22)

RASHI EXPLAINS WHY THE VERSE BEGINS IN THE PLURAL, STATING, "*They* went up," but concludes in the singular, "*he* came." This is to allude to the fact that Kalev alone went to Chevron to pray over the graves of the Patriarchs, so that he should not be persuaded by his companions to join their plan.

Throughout the generations, Jews have maintained the practice of praying at the graves of *tzaddikim*. In particular, they appreciated the power of prayers recited at *Me'aras HaMachpelah*, the gravesite of our holy Forefathers.

One year during the rule of the Turks in *Eretz Yisrael*, there was a severe drought. All the land's inhabitants — Jews and gentiles alike — prayed for rain, but none fell.

When the gravity of the situation increased, the Turkish pasha called on the rabbis of Jerusalem and gave them the following order: "Go and pray to your God that He send rain. If it does not rain, you will be severely punished!"

The rabbis were very frightened by this demand and knew they would need special assistance in their prayers. They therefore asked the pasha for special permission to pray inside *Me'aras HaMachpelah*, which, at the time, was off limits to Jews.

The pasha handed the keys to the cave to the rabbis of Jerusalem, and they went directly to Chevron.

Upon reaching *Me'aras HaMachpelah*, they unlocked the gate of the cave and went down five steps. They stopped there and began reciting *Tehillim* with great fervor. When they concluded the first book of *Tehillim*, they went outside to see if the skies had darkened with clouds. The sun, however, was still shining brightly.

They descended another five steps and tearfully recited the second book of *Tehillim*, begging Hashem for mercy. Still, the sun continued to beat down on the land.

The rabbis descended yet another five steps and recited the third book of *Tehillim*. Amazingly, the sky turned gray and rain began to fall!

They remained inside *Ma'aras HaMachpelah* for some time and continued to pray — not for rain but for the ultimate redemption.

But just then, before the rabbis were able to conclude their prayers, a strong wind began to blow and it literally pushed them outside the cave.

The rabbis understood that Hashem had forced them to stop praying in that holy site because the time of redemption had not yet arrived.

∗◦∗

וְאַתֶּם אַל־תִּירְאוּ אֶת־עַם הָאָרֶץ ... סָר צִלָּם מֵעֲלֵיהֶם וַה׳ אִתָּנוּ
"You need not fear the local people ... Their protection has departed from them and Hashem is with us" (14:9)

To what can this be compared, asked the *Sefas Emes* (R' Yehudah Leib Alter of Gur)? To a man walking alone in the dark, whose imagination gets the best of him. Conjuring up frightening thoughts of what might lay hidden within the darkness, he thinks that he sees and hears all sorts of treacherous things. However, as he gets closer to the dreaded shapes and forms, he realizes that they are no more than shadows.

Similarly, Yehoshua and Kalev said to the spies: "You say that you saw large, fortified cities and the sons of the giants? 'You need not fear the local people .... Their protection (*tzilam*) has departed from them and Hashem is with us.'

"'You need not fear the local people' — be courageous and go there; then you will see that 'their *shadow* (*tzilam*) has departed from them' — all of this was no more than a frightening shadow. It seems very real, but it is only a mere illusion. 'Hashem is with us' — anyone who truly trusts in Hashem, has nothing to fear!"

פֹּקֵד עֲוֹן אָבוֹת עַל־בָּנִים עַל־שִׁלֵּשִׁים וְעַל־רִבֵּעִים:

"He reckons the fathers' transgression to the sons' account, up to the third and fourth generations" (14:18)

In explaining how children can be punished for the sins of their parents, R' Berechiah *HaNakdan* recounts the following parable: A hungry wolf met a fox and desired to devour it.

"Why would you want to devour me?" asked the sly fox. "I am thin and have few bones .... Go and devour a fat-fleshed human, and you will enjoy the feast."

"I cannot devour a human," replied the wolf, "as the verse states, 'Of every beast I will demand it'" (*Bereishis* 9:5). [This verse warns beasts against killing people — see Rashi there.]

The fox cackled and said, "You have nothing to fear, for you will not receive the punishment — but your children, as the verse says, 'He reckons the fathers' transgression to the sons' account.'"

The wolf was persuaded by the fox, and it began to search for a human. On the way, it fell into a trap laid by hunters. The wolf began yelling for help. When the fox heard the calls of the wolf, it carefully approached the wolf.

"You liar!" screamed the wolf. "Did you not say that only my children would get punished for my sins?"

"Fool that you are," replied the fox. "You are also not getting punished on account of your own sins, but for the sins of *your* fathers."

"How could that be?" screamed the fox, "Why would I suffer for what others have done?"

"And why did you set out to devour humans?" queried the fox. "Was it not because you were counting on the fact that it would be your children who would suffer for your sins? Since you felt it was fair that your children bear your sins, it is only fitting that you bear your fathers' sins!"

A child, concluded R' Berechiah, is only punished for his father's sins if he is guilty of the same sins. This is because an individual's punishment is meted out measure for measure. When someone emulates the sinful ways of his father, without concern that his children will receive punishment on account of his sins, he, too, gets punished for the sins of *his* fathers.

If this is true of the negative, how much more so is it true of the positive: when a righteous son follows in the ways of a righteous father, he will certainly be rewarded for the good deeds of his father!

סְלַח־נָא לַעֲוֹן הָעָם הַזֶּה כְּגֹדֶל חַסְדֶּךָ

"Please forgive the transgression of this people as befits the greatness of Your kindness" (14:19)

R' Dovid Moshe of Chortkov once said the following on the night of Yom Kippur: "Master of the World! Indeed, we are full of transgressions, but You are full of mercy! However, even if our sins are severe and numerous, how few they are in comparison to Your abundant mercy, for Your mercy and kindness are limitless.

"Forgive and pardon Your nation Israel on the Day of Judgment — "as befits the greatness of Your kindness!'"

אַל־תַּעֲלוּ כִּי אֵין ה' בְּקִרְבְּכֶם

"Do not ascend, for Hashem is not in your midst!" (14:42)

Why, asked the Dubno *Maggid*, did Moshe tell the Jewish people not to ascend; had they not already completely repented?

The answer, said the *maggid*, can be explained with the following parable: A certain individual climbed to prominence. This man had an only daughter who had come of age, and he wished to marry her off. Matchmakers came before him and presented him with two possible matches. The first young man came from a wealthy family, but was an *am ha'aretz*. The other young man was the son of a great Torah scholar and was himself a *talmid chacham* with impeccable character traits.

The father chose the second boy for his daughter, but he made one stipulation with the boy's father; namely, that he present his daughter with a set of diamond earrings.

"I cannot afford to buy such expensive jewelry," replied the boy's father.

"In that case," said the girl's father to the matchmaker, "I prefer the son of the wealthy man for my daughter. He will certainly not deprive my daughter of the gifts she so deserves."

"What have you done?" asked his friends. "The son of the wealthy man is an *am ha'aretz*! You have exchanged gold for feathers."

The girl's father saw his mistake, so he approached the matchmaker once again and requested that he arrange the match between his daughter and the *talmid chacham* after all. This time, however, the boy's father rejected the match.

"If he was willing to marry off his daughter to an *am ha'aretz* just for some jewelry," he said, "then it is clear that he does not value Torah or character development in the least. I therefore do not want my son to marry his daughter!"

The same applied to the spies, concluded the Dubno *Maggid*. If after returning from *Eretz Yisrael* they still stood firm in their notions and cared about the low price of fish in Egypt, then it is clear that their minds were still unrefined and that they were completely insensitive to the holiness of *Eretz Yisrael*. If that is the case, they are not yet ready and worthy of entering the Land.

৵১৵

דַּבֵּר אֶל־בְּנֵי יִשְׂרָאֵל וְאָמַרְתָּ אֲלֵהֶם וְעָשׂוּ לָהֶם צִיצִת

"Speak to the Children of Israel and say to them that they shall make for themselves tzitzis" (15:38)

C hazal point out that the double expression of "speak" and "say" is coming to urge adults to take care that their little children also wear *tzitzis*.

In the house of R' Yisrael of Rihin it was customary for children ages one month and up to wear *tzitzis*.

One day, when R' Yisrael's son, R' David Moshe (who would later be renowned as the great R' David Moshe of Chortkov), was but an infant lying in his crib, he suddenly started crying hysterically, and no one could pacify him. This alarmed the *rebbetzin*, so she entered her husband's study to seek his advice.

"Please go and check the *tzitzis* that the baby is wearing," said the *rebbe*.

The *rebbetzin* hurried to the baby and saw that one of the strings on his *tzitzis* had gotten caught on a hook in the crib and had torn. She removed the invalid pair of *tzitzis* and replaced them with a new, kosher pair — and the baby's crying stopped instantly.

דַּבֵּר אֶל־בְּנֵי יִשְׂרָאֵל וְאָמַרְתָּ אֲלֵהֶם וְעָשׂוּ לָהֶם צִיצִת

"Speak to the Children of Israel and say to them that they shall make for themselves tzitzis" (15:38)

For many years, R' Mordechai of Nesh'chiz yearned to own a pair of *tzitzis* made in *Eretz Yisrael*. There were not many people traveling to *Eretz Yisrael* in those days, and the *rebbe*, therefore, had no one to purchase the *tzitzis* for him. Yet one day, one of his *chassidim* returned from a visit to the Holy Land with a gift for the *rebbe* — a beautiful new pair of *tzitzis*.

R' Mordechai was delighted to receive the *tzitzis*, and he immediately handed them to one of his students in order to fashion a neck hole.

The student folded the *tzitzis* in order to cut the hole, but instead of folding it once, he folded it twice so that when he cut the cloth, he accidentally made *two* holes.

The student was horrified by what he had done and did not know what he would say to the *rebbe*. When he entered the *rebbe*'s study, however, with the *tzitzis* in hand, the *rebbe* said warmly, "My dear student, why are you so frightened? Two holes are exactly what my *tzitzis* needed! One hole is for putting the *tzitzis* over my head, and the other hole is to see if R' Mordechai will get angry."

וְעָשׂוּ לָהֶם צִיצִת

"That they shall make for themselves tzitzis" (15:38)

Before departing from the world, the Vilna *Gaon* took hold of his *tzitzis*, and, with much emotion, he said: "How difficult it is for me to take leave of this world. By performing one small *mitzvah* — such as the inexpensive *mitzvah* of *tzitzis* — a person can reach such sublime levels to the point of being worthy of basking in the glory of the Divine Presence. But where can one find such a thing in the World of Truth? There, even if a person exerts every last drop of effort, he cannot reach such levels."

וּרְאִיתֶם אֹתוֹ וּזְכַרְתֶּם אֶת־כָּל־מִצְוֹת ה'

"That you may see it and remember all Hashem's commandments" (15:39)

It is true, remarked the *Chofetz Chaim*, that the *mitzvah* of *tzitzis* reminds an individual of all the *mitzvos*. But it only does so if that person has previously studied the laws pertaining to each of the *mitzvos*. However, if one has never studied them in the first place, then of what use is a reminder?

To what can this be compared? To an experienced merchant who travels to a trade fair. On the way, he occasionally glances at a list of all the items he intends to buy, adding and subtracting items as he sees fit. Such is the way of an experienced merchant.

A person that lacks experience, however, and has never been to a fair, has no idea of what to buy or where to buy it. What good would a list do him? He could stare at it from morning until night and still not know what to purchase.

So it is, concluded the *Chofetz Chaim*, with the person who has never studied the laws pertaining to the *mitzvos* — what good will remembering them do if he has no idea how to fulfill them?

וְלֹא־תָתוּרוּ אַחֲרֵי לְבַבְכֶם וְאַחֲרֵי עֵינֵיכֶם

"You must not explore after your heart and after your eyes" (15:39)

R' Zundel of Salant's extraordinary eyesight was well known throughout Jerusalem — not his physical vision but his spiritual one. His ability to see matters of holiness was astounding.

By merely looking at a vessel that was purchased from gentiles, he could tell whether or not it had been immersed in a *mikveh*.

When he was asked how he had merited attaining such a penetrating gaze, he responded, "There is nothing wondrous about it. Anyone who guards his eyes from seeing forbidden sights can easily gain this ability."

אֲנִי ה' אֱלֹקֵיכֶם אֲשֶׁר הוֹצֵאתִי
אֶתְכֶם מֵאֶרֶץ מִצְרַיִם ... אֲנִי ה' אֱלֹקֵיכֶם:

*"I am Hashem, your God, Who took you out of the
land of Egypt ... I am Hashem, your God" (15:41)*

When R' Shneur Zalman of Liadi was young, the scholars of his town enjoyed engaging him in Torah discussions.

"Please tell me," one scholar asked the young prodigy, "where is there a verse in the Torah which begins and ends with the same three words?"

"The verse appears," replied the young boy, "in a place where Moshe *Rabbeinu* did not say *emes* (truth)."

"What? Moshe *Rabbeinu* did not say the *emes?*" wondered the bystanders.

"Indeed, he did not," answered young Shneur Zalman. "In the passage dealing with the *mitzvah* of *tzitzis*, we find a verse that begins and ends with the three words, 'I [am] Hashem, [your] God.' When we recite the *Shema*, we say this passage and add the word, '*emes.*' Moshe *Rabbeinu*, however, did not say the word, '*emes*,' but rather ended with the words, 'I am Hashem, your God.'"

PARASHAS KORACH

וַיִּקַּח קֹרַח
"Korach ... separated himself" (16:1)

RASHI EXPLAINS: "'KORACH ... SEPARATED HIMSELF' — HE TOOK himself off to one side to be separate from the assembly [of Israel] ...."

Korach had many outstanding qualities, noted R' Simchah Bunim of P'shischa. He hailed from a distinguished family, was a *talmid chacham*, possessed extraordinary wealth, and was a very wise man. Someone who has that many qualities stands a good chance of eventually being appointed as a leader.

So why did he not merit this? Because he "separated himself"! He did not wait patiently for the moment when he would be called upon to lead the people; rather, he tried to seize greatness for himself.

He was therefore punished measure for measure, said the *rebbe*, as the verse states: "The earth opened its mouth and swallowed them" before their time to be buried in the ground had arrived.

וַיִּקַּח קֹרַח בֶּן־יִצְהָר בֶּן־קְהָת בֶּן־לֵוִי
"Korach, the son of Yitzhar, the son of Kehas, the son of Levi," (16:1)

Rashi points out that in this verse that lists Korach's lineage, "It does not mention [that Levi was] *the son of Yaakov* because [Yaakov] prayed for mercy that his name should not be mentioned in connection with their quarrels, as it is said, 'Let my honor not be included in their congregation' (*Bereishis* 49:6)."

A story is related of two men who appeared before R' Eliyahu Klatzkin, the *rav* of Lublin, in a *din Torah*. One of the litigants began by telling the *rav* that he has very distinguished lineage.

Upon hearing his words, R' Klatzkin retorted, "In *Parashas Korach*, Rashi explains that Yaakov *Avinu* 'prayed for mercy' that his name not be mentioned with regard to a dispute.

"What form of mercy is this exactly?" continued the *rav*. "In fact, would not the opposite have been more merciful? From the standpoint of mercy, Yaakov should have requested that his name *be* mentioned so that his merit serve as protection for his grandchildren!

"Rather," answered R' Klatzkin, "the fact that his name was not mentioned was true mercy. For when a person hails from such a prominent family and nevertheless acts inappropriately, the punishment he incurs is far more severe."

וַיִּקַּח קֹרַח בֶּן־יִצְהָר בֶּן־קְהָת בֶּן־לֵוִי וְדָתָן וַאֲבִירָם

"Korach, the son of Yitzhar, the son of Kehas, the son of Levi, separated himself, together with Dasan and Aviram" (16:1)

Chazal state in *Pirkei Avos* (5:20), "Any dispute that is for the sake of Heaven will have a constructive outcome; but one that is not for the sake of Heaven will not have a constructive outcome. What sort of dispute was for the sake of Heaven? — The dispute between Hillel and Shammai. And which was not for the sake of Heaven? — The dispute between Korach and his entire company."

Why, asked R' Yonason Eybeschutz, does the Mishnah state, "The dispute between Korach and his entire company"? Wasn't the dispute between Korach and Moshe?

From here we learn, said R' Eybeschutz, that the dispute was not between Korach and Moshe at all; rather, it was really between Korach and his assembly, as each one of them was vying for leadership and power! Moshe *Rabbeinu*, however, did not take up their quarrel; on the contrary, he tried his utmost to appease them so as not to carry on a dispute that would eventually lead to disastrous results.

קְרִאֵי מוֹעֵד אַנְשֵׁי־שֵׁם:

"Those summoned for meeting, men of renown" (16:2)

The *Midrash Tanchuma* states that although the verse does not explicitly mention these men by name, they can be identified through the hints included in this portion.

To what can this be compared? asks the *Midrash*. To a boy from an upstanding family who was discovered stealing the belongings of another person. The owner of the items did not want to publicize the boy's name, as this would bring shame to the boy's family. He therefore provided hints of the boy's identity instead.

When he was asked, "Who is the thief?" He replied, "The thief is rather tall; he has pleasant-looking teeth, black hair, and a fine-looking nose ..."

Once he described the thief, everyone realized exactly who it was.

In the *sefer She'eris Menachem* by R' Tzvi Morgenstern, the author writes that we can learn a valuable lesson from this *Midrash*. Even though the one being described is a thief and a criminal, when we provide signs and describe his features, we only give a positive and noteworthy description. We describe his pleasant-looking teeth, his fine-looking nose, etc.

We see the same thing in our verse. Though the Torah is discussing men of dispute, they are nonetheless described in a favorable light, as the verse states, "Those summoned for meeting, men of renown."

✼✼✼

וּמַדּוּעַ תִּתְנַשְּׂאוּ עַל־קְהַל ה׳

"Why do you elevate yourselves over Hashem's congregation?" (16:3)

Such is the nature of a dispute that is not for the sake of Heaven, noted R' Simchah Bunim of P'shischa. It blinds the eyes and closes the hearts of the quarrelers, so that they lose their common sense. For the Torah testifies about Moshe *Rabbeinu*: "Now the man Moshe was exceedingly humble, more than any person on the face of the earth." How could anyone possibly accuse him of possessing the contemptible trait of arrogance? Yet this is exactly what Korach and his assembly did, as the verse states, "Why do you exalt yourselves over the congregation of Hashem?"

Rather, this is the way of strife; the power of impurity that accompanies it totally corrupts an individual's intellect.

בֹּקֶר וְיֹדַע ה' אֶת־אֲשֶׁר־לוֹ וְאֶת־הַקָּדוֹשׁ
וְהִקְרִיב אֵלָיו וְאֵת אֲשֶׁר יִבְחַר־בּוֹ יַקְרִיב אֵלָיו:

*"In the morning, Hashem will make known
those who are designated for His [service] and
those who are holy [for the priesthood], and He will
bring them near to Himself; and the one He chooses
He will bring near to [serve] Him" (16:5)*

In the city of Lvov resided a young scholar who desperately wished to be appointed *dayan* (judge) of the city. He therefore coerced many of Lvov's residents into selecting him as their *dayan*.

When word of the young man's actions reached the rabbi of Lvov, R' Yaakov Meshulem Ornstein, he invited the man to his study.

"As you are quite a luminary," began R' Ornstein, "I am sure that you remember a simple verse from the *Chumash*. Perhaps you can enlighten me: "Why does the verse repeat itself: 'Hashem will make known those who are designated for His [service] and those who are holy [for the priesthood], and *He will bring them near to Himself*; and the one He chooses (*yivchar*) He *will bring near to [serve] Him*'"?

The young man stood silently, not knowing what to respond.

"Let me tell you what the answer is," said the *rav*. "Korach and his followers made the following claim before Moshe: 'The entire community, all of them, are holy' — we are all just as scholarly as you are, and we are worthy of leadership as well — 'so why do you elevate yourselves?'

"Moshe therefore replied, 'Hashem will make known those who are designated for His [service] and those who are holy [for the priesthood], and He will bring them near to Himself' — In truth, each and every one of us is holy and adequately suited to have Hashem draw us close to a position of leadership. But this is not sufficient, however, for a leader must fulfill another requirement; that of 'and the one *who is chosen* (*yibacheir*) He will bring near to [serve] Him' — the members of the congregation must choose him willingly, and not be forced to do so."

וַיַּקְרֵב אֹתְךָ וְאֶת־כָּל־אַחֶיךָ בְנֵי־לֵוִי אִתָּךְ וּבִקַּשְׁתֶּם גַּם־כְּהֻנָּה:

*"And He drew you near, and all your brethren, the sons of
Levi, with you — yet you seek priesthood as well!" (16:10)*

The Dubno *Maggid* explained this verse by way of a parable: A
king appointed a number of his servants to work his fields; each
servant was responsible for one field.

"Your highness," said one of the servants, "I would like to request
that you place several more fields under my authority."

"Why are you requesting additional fields?" asked the king, "You
earn a set wage and it makes absolutely no difference whether you
take care of one field or several fields. You must therefore be scheming to steal my land's produce! If that is the case, not only will you not
receive any additional fields, but I also demand that you return the
original field that I placed under your care!"

So it was with Korach, concluded the Dubno *Maggid*. When Korach
requested the priesthood even though he was already a Levi, this was
a sure sign that he was a wicked man who simply wished to satisfy his
desires. That being the case, he also lost his status as a Levi.

וַיִּשְׁלַח מֹשֶׁה לִקְרֹא לְדָתָן וְלַאֲבִירָם
*"Moshe sent [a messenger] to
summon Dasan and Aviram" (16:12)*

Rashi quotes the Gemara in *Maseches Sanhedrin* (110a): "From
here [we see] that we do not keep up a dispute. For Moshe went
after them [that is, he sought them out], to restore harmony with them
with words of peace."

One day, one of the townspeople of Kosov appeared in the home of
R' Menachem Mendel of Kosov. The man was known to be a violent
person who regularly schemed evil against the city's inhabitants. More
than once he even harassed the *rebbe* himself.

How shocked the *chassidim* were, therefore, when their *rebbe*
greeted the man with a smile and asked him, "How can I assist you,
my friend?"

"I have a daughter of marriageable age," said the man with tears in his eyes. "Through great effort, I found her a suitable *chasan*, but I do not have the means to pay the dowry which I have promised him."

R' Menachem Mendel opened his desk drawer and said, "Here you go! Take as much money as you need from this drawer. May Hashem help you marry off your daughter in the right time!"

The man thanked the *rebbe* profusely and left the room in good spirits.

After he had left, the *rebbe*'s brother, R' Yitzchak, entered his room. "Can it be that one is required to be so giving?" he asked R' Menachem Mendel. "Why, the *rebbe* is so impoverished that store-owners even refuse to sell his wife food on credit! Yet to this *rasha* the Rebbe gives all of his money!"

"Yes!" responded the *rebbe* emphatically. "Indeed, the *yetzer hara* already preceded you with this claim, but I did not heed him, *baruch Hashem*, and I gave the man the *tzedakah* he needed.

"This violent man," concluded the *rebbe*, "has become my friend in just one day."

לֹא חֲמוֹר אֶחָד מֵהֶם נָשָׂאתִי
"I have not taken even a single donkey of theirs" (16:15)

In his youth, the *Chazon Ish*, R' Avraham Yeshayahu Karelitz, was asked to rule on the kosher status of a cow that had been slaughtered in a nearby town.

He walked on foot to the town, examined the cow, and ruled that it was kosher.

As he turned to leave, the butcher requested that he wait until they ordered a coach to take him home.

The *Chazon Ish* would not hear of it and said, "In *Parashas Korach* it states, 'I have not taken even a single donkey of theirs.' What does this mean? Is it even conceivable that Moshe *Rabbeinu* would break into another man's stable and steal his donkey?

"Rather," answered the *Chazon Ish*, "Moshe *Rabbeinu* was apparently invited to rule on a halachic matter, and he was offered a donkey that would transport him back to his home. But Moshe *Rabbeinu* did not accept even this small gift. *That* was his greatness.

"*Ma'aseh avos siman l'banim*' (the conduct of the Forefathers is a sign for their children)," remarked the *Chazon Ish*. "I, too, cannot accept your offer."

✥

וְאִם־בְּרִיאָה יִבְרָא ה' וּפָצְתָה הָאֲדָמָה אֶת־פִּיהָ וּבָלְעָה אֹתָם
"But if Hashem will create a phenomenon, and the earth opens its mouth and swallows them" (16:30)

Rashi cites the Gemara in *Maseches Sanhedrin* (110a): "If the mouth of the earth is a creation from the six days of Creation," said Moshe *Rabbeinu*, "then fine. But if not, may Hashem create one!"

Why, asked the *Chasam Sofer* (R' Moshe Sofer), did Moshe *Rabbeinu* have any doubt as to whether or not the mouth of the earth had been created during the six days of Creation? For *Chazal* (*Avos* 5:8) state explicitly, "Ten things were created on *erev Shabbos* at twilight. They are: The mouth of the earth ...." How, then, could Moshe have overlooked this Mishnah?

One of the ten things enumerated by *Chazal*, answered the *Chasam Sofer*, was "Moshe's grave." This grave, whose location is unknown, was also created at twilight of that *erev Shabbos*.

The Holy One therefore concealed all ten things from Moshe so that he would not hear of his own passing. Thus, Moshe had to request, "If the mouth of the earth is a creation from the six days of Creation, then fine. But if not, may Hashem create one!"

PARASHAS CHUKAS

זֹאת חֻקַּת הַתּוֹרָה

"This is the statute of the Torah" (19:2)

RASHI EXPLAINS THAT THE SUBJECT OF THE *PARAH ADUMAH* (RED COW) is referred to as "statute" (*chukah*) because this *mitzvah* "is a decree [issued] by Me; you have no right to reflect upon it!" That is, *parah adumah* is a decree that you may not question.

R' Eliyahu Meisels, the *rav* of Lodz, had taken upon himself the task of collecting money for a certain young man in dire straits.

He turned to one of the wealthy, but miserly, men of Lodz to contribute toward the cause. After much urging on the part of R' Meisels, the wealthy man yielded and gave him a considerable sum for *tzedakah*.

But then the wealthy man began boasting about his act of kindness, and he spared no effort publicizing what he had done.

The young man who had been the recipient of the *tzedakah* was humiliated by having his situation made so public. In his distress, he asked R' Meisels to speak to the wealthy man and request that he cease talking about his act of *tzedakah*.

The *rav* invited the arrogant fellow to his home and rebuked him for the anguish he had caused the young man. He then added the following thought: "In the Torah's passage dealing with the *parah adumah*, Rashi explains that it is called a 'statute' because this *mitzvah* 'is a decree [issued] by Me; you have no right to reflect upon it!'

"The same applies to the *mitzvah* of *tzedakah*," concluded the *rav*. "Before the person gives *tzedakah*, he must think, *It is a decree issued by Me* — this is the will of Hashem! However, once he has given the *tzedakah*, 'you have no right to reflect upon it' — it is forbidden to give *tzedakah* and afterwards reflect upon how much he gave and to whom, for such thoughts may lead to haughtiness."

זֹאת חֻקַּת הַתּוֹרָה
"This is the statute of the Torah" (19:2)

Regarding the *mitzvah* of the *parah adumah*, Shlomo *HaMelech*, the wisest of all men said, "I thought I could become wise, but it is beyond me" (*Koheles* 7:23).

To what can this be compared? asked the Dubno *Maggid* — To a rich villager who wished to travel to the end of the world.

He did not leave it as a dream; he set out to do it! He equipped a wagon with two strong, able-bodied horses, and he took along provisions for the trip.

He and his servant climbed aboard the wagon, and set out for the end of the world.

The wealthy man traveled three hundred *parsos* on the first day of the journey, and as evening set in, he decided to stop at a hotel to get some rest.

At the hotel, the wealthy man dined with the other guests and took part in their conversation. The main topic was everyone's experiences on their journey. Each guest related the purpose behind his trip, how far he had traveled that day, and how much further he had yet to travel.

The wealthy man jumped to his feet. "I am journeying to the end of the world," he proclaimed excitedly, "and I have already traveled three hundred *parsos!*"

The guests enjoyed a hearty laugh. "You fool!" they said. "Don't you know that the world is round? You are not getting any closer to your destination, for no matter how far you travel, you will still be just as far from the 'end of the world' as when you started out."

Shlomo *HaMelech* wished to understand the secrets of the Torah, concluded the Dubno *Maggid*, but the more he learned, the more he realized that the Torah contains far more depth than can be fathomed. He therefore stated, "I thought I could become wise, but it is beyond me"!

זֹאת חֻקַּת הַתּוֹרָה
"This is the statute of the Torah" (19:2)

The *Targum Onkelos* renders this verse: "*Da gezeiras oraisa*" ("This is a decree of the Torah").

The *Magen Avraham* (*siman* 580) relates that in France in the year 5004 (1244), a wicked decree was cast, ordering the burning of the *Talmud Bavli*.

On the Friday of the week that *Parashas Chukas* was to be read, a large fire was lit in the center of Paris and 24 wagons carrying hundreds of volumes of the Talmud were unloaded into the flames.

In commemoration of that bitter day, the Sages of the time established it as a day of fasting for all future generations.

Usually, fast days are set to mark certain dates of the month, but this fast day was set by the Rabbis to be marked on a particular day of the week — the Friday before *parashas Chukas*. They did this because they had been shown in a dream the verse, "This is the statute of the Torah," as well as Onkelos' Aramaic translation, "This is a decree of the Torah." This told them that the calamity was directly connected to *parashas Chukas*. They therefore enacted that all subsequent generations fast specifically on the Friday before *Parashas Chukas* is read.

זֹאת חֻקַּת הַתּוֹרָה
"This is the statute of the Torah" (19:2)

R' Yonasan Eybeschutz once saw a heretic eating nonkosher food. When the man saw that the *rav* had noticed him, he felt uncomfortable, so he said, "I would like the *rav* to understand that I completely adhere to the Torah's ethical commandments, for I am able to comprehend the logic behind them. It is only the *chukim*, which I do not comprehend, that I do not observe."

"In *Sefer Tehillim* (50:16-18)," responded R' Eybeschutz, "it states: 'But to the wicked, God said, "To what purpose do you recount My decrees (*chukai*) and bear My covenant upon your lips?" For you hate discipline and you threw My words behind you. If you saw a thief you agreed to be with him, and with adulterers was your lot.'

"'But to the wicked, God said, "To what purpose do you recount My decrees?"' — Why do you tell tales, claiming that it is only the *chukim*, which you do not understand, that you opt not to adhere to?

"'For you hate discipline' — In truth, you hate even the ethical commandments of the Torah!

---

* Though most textbooks record that the burning took place in 5002 (1242), the *Magen Avraham* clearly writes that it was in 5004 (1244).

"'And you threw My words behind you' — Together with the *chukim*, you have also disregarded all of the other *mitzvos* of the Torah.

"'If you saw a thief you agreed to be with him, and with adulterers was your lot'!"

זֹאת הַתּוֹרָה אָדָם כִּי־יָמוּת בְּאֹהֶל ...
"This is the law: If a man dies in a tent ..." (19:14)

Reish Lakish in *Maseches Berachos* (42b) taught: "From where do we know that words of Torah will endure only in one who kills himself over it [that is, it endures only in someone who dedicates himself completely to its study]? — From the verse, 'This is the law (*Zos haTorah*): If a man dies in a tent.'"

To what can this be compared? asked the *Chofetz Chaim*. To a successful storeowner who was patronized by customers from all the surrounding cities.

At all hours of the day, he was occupied with his business; even the nighttime afforded him no rest, as he would stay awake making calculations and organizing his merchandise for the next day. He was so busy, that he was never able to find the time to pray with a *minyan*.

The years passed, and the storeowner grew older. His beard had already turned white. One day, he began to worry: He was aging and his strength was not what it used to be. His time to leave this world would soon arrive, and there was not much time left to prepare "provisions" — in the form of Torah and good deeds — for his journey to the World to Come.

The following day, the storeowner rose early and set out for *shul*. He joined the *minyan* and prayed with great intensity. When he had finished praying, he sat down to study Torah for about two hours.

Though negative thoughts tried entering his mind — such as, "What will be with my many customers?" and, "Perhaps people will choose to purchase from a different store?" — he quickly pushed these thoughts aside, telling himself, "What good will my customers do me in the World to Come?"

Finally, he headed for his store. When he arrived, his wife was waiting for him. "Why are you so late? What happened to you?" she complained. "Where were you? Many customers came by the store today, but when they saw that you were not here, they simply turned and walked away."

"Tell me, please," he said to his wife, "what would you have done if my time had come to depart from this world? Would you then come to me with questions, demanding to know where I was? Would you still tell me that I should be in the store, serving customers?

"When I sit and study Torah in the *beis midrash*, consider it as if I am no longer alive. Then, when I return to the store after several hours, think of it as if I have risen for *techiyas hameisim* (Resurrection of the Dead)!"

❧◈☙

זֹאת הַתּוֹרָה אָדָם כִּי־יָמוּת בְּאֹהֶל ...
"This is the law: If a man dies in a tent ..." (19:14)

R' Efraim Zalman Margolios was known to be an extraordinary Torah genius. He was also famous for his wealth, as he engaged in many successful business ventures.

Several merchants once visited his home with a business proposition they wished to share with him. At that moment, however, R' Margolios was sitting in his study and toiling over a difficult piece of Gemara; he therefore refused to meet with them.

"This matter is urgent and cannot be delayed," said one of the merchants to the *rebbetzin*. "Please tell the *rav* that if he refuses to meet with us, he stands to lose a fortune!"

The *rebbetzin* entered the *rav's* study and related the merchant's words.

"In *Parashas Chukas*," R' Margolios replied, "it states, 'This is the law (*zos haTorah*): If a man dies in a tent.' When a person is engaged in the study of Torah, he must make himself like a dead person in relation to worldly matters — I am therefore not willing to meet with the merchants at this time!"

The merchants went on their way, and, indeed, as a result of not taking them up on their offer, R' Margolios lost thousands of *zehuvim* in profit.

"Praiseworthy is my lot," said the *rav* with genuine joy, "for today I merited to pay thousands of *zehuvim* for a single page of Gemara!"

שִׁמְעוּ־נָא הַמֹּרִים

"Listen now, O rebels'" (20:10)

Rashi explains that the word *hamorim* means, "Fools; those who instruct their teachers."

Why, asked the *Imrei Emes* (R' Avraham Mordechai of Gur), did Rashi have to provide us with two interpretations of the word, *hamorim*?

These two interpretations, answered the *rebbe*, are actually one. *Chazal* have taught us in *Pirkei Avos* (4:1) "Who is wise? He who learns from every person." We see from here that one who does not possess the desire to learn is certainly not considered wise; rather, such an individual is a fool.

But worst of all is a person who wishes to teach his teachers. Believing himself to be of superior intellect, he has no desire to learn from anyone — and there can be no greater fool than that!

We are now in a position to understand Rashi's words. Rashi explained that "*hamorim*" means "the fools." Now, why are they considered fools to begin with? Because "they instruct their teachers."

וַיִּשְׁלַח מַלְאָךְ וַיֹּצִאֵנוּ מִמִּצְרָיִם

"He sent a malach who took us out of Egypt" (20:16)

Moshe *Rabbeinu*, in an attempt to persuade the king of Edom to allow the Jews to pass through his land, told the king that the Holy One had sent a *malach* (an angel) to take the Jews out of Egypt. Who was this *malach*? It was Moshe *Rabbeinu* himself.

Could it truly be, asked R' Zalman Sorotzkin, that Moshe *Rabbeinu*, the most humble of men, would actually refer to himself as a *malach*?

This can be compared, said R' Sorotzkin, to a rabbi of a city who was walking along the road. Suddenly, he noticed a Jewish villager traveling in a wagon that was being drawn by both a horse and a cow!

The rabbi rebuked the villager, "Are you not aware that what you are doing is forbidden by the Torah?" he asked. "Every second spent on that wagon is a violation of the prohibition of *kilayim* (forbidden mixtures)!"

The villager pretended not to hear the rabbi and continued on his way.

"You should be aware," warned the rabbi, "that I am a rabbi of a city. If you do not bring the wagon to a halt immediately, I will have you excommunicated!" The villager was frightened by the rabbi's threat, and he stopped the wagon and untied the animals.

Moshe *Rabbeinu*, explained R' Sorotzkin, wished to strike fear in the heart of Edom's king. He therefore related how Hashem had sent a "*malach*" to take the Jewish nation out of Egypt — perhaps this way the heathen would take him seriously!

❧⊙❀

וַיְמָאֵן אֱדוֹם נְתֹן אֶת־יִשְׂרָאֵל עֲבֹר בִּגְבֻלוֹ וַיֵּט יִשְׂרָאֵל מֵעָלָיו:

"Edom thus refused to allow Israel to pass through his territory, so Israel turned away from him" (20:21)

One of the *chassidim* of R' Yisrael of Rizhin, an individual who worked as a *shochet* (slaughterer), was known to be a miser who refused to give *tzedakah* or host guests in his home.

One day, the *shochet* paid his *rebbe* a visit. Upon entering R' Yisrael's study, the *rebbe* commented, "*Chazal* state that a person who is born under the *mazal* (constellation) of *ma'adim* ("the Red Planet," Mars) will be a spiller of blood. Such a person can therefore become either a *shochet* or, God forbid, a murderer.

"Praiseworthy is the one who merits becoming a *shochet* and enables the Jews to eat kosher meat!

"The *shochet*, however, must go about his task with intentions that are purely for the sake of performing a *mitzvah* and not for the sake of cruelty. He must therefore be steeped in the *mitzvah* of *hachnasas orchim* (showing hospitality to guests), in order to strengthen the trait of mercy within him.

"But a *shochet* who refuses to host guests," continued the *rebbe*, "must be suspected of possessing the nature of a murderer, and he must be removed from the *shechitah* profession!

"We find an allusion to this in the verse," concluded R' Yisrael. 'Edom thus refused to allow Israel to pass through his territory' — If one whose *mazal* is 'adom' (red) refuses to permit a Jew to pass through his territory, then 'Israel turned away from him' — then we must distance ourselves from him and remove him from his post."

וּמִמִּדְבָּר מַתָּנָה:
"A gift from the Wilderness" (21:18)

A man entered the study of R' Yisrael of Rizhin to ask the *tzaddik* for a blessing. He placed a note with his name on the *rebbe*'s desk so his name could be included in the *rebbe*'s prayer. He also placed a considerable sum of money on the *rebbe*'s desk as a *pidyon nefesh* (money customarily given to a *rebbe* when seeking a blessing from him).

R' Yisrael picked up the note but refused to accept the money.

"Why will the *rebbe* not take this man's *pidyon nefesh*?" asked his attendant.

"The Torah states, 'A gift from the Wilderness.' The Wilderness symbolizes uprightness and honesty, as *Chazal* (*Sanhedrin* 49a) expound on the verse, 'And he [Yoav] was buried in his house in the Wilderness — Just as a Wilderness is free from robbery and immoral behavior, so too was Yoav's house free from robbery and immoral behavior.'

"'A gift from the Wilderness,'" explained R' Yisrael, "is a gift that bears the qualities of the Wilderness — uprightness and honesty. That is the only type of gift I am willing to accept.

"I sense," concluded the *rebbe*, "that *this* money was earned in a fashion that was less than honorable."

עַל־כֵּן יֹאמְרוּ הַמּשְׁלִים בֹּאוּ חֶשְׁבּוֹן
"Regarding this the poets would say: Come to Cheshbon" (21:27)

In *Maseches Bava Basra* (78b), *Chazal* expound on this verse as follows: "'Regarding this *hamoshlim* would say' — This refers to those who rule (*hamoshlim*) over their *yetzer hara*. 'Come to Cheshbon' — Come and let us make a calculation (*chesbon*) of world importance." This teaches us that it is incumbent upon each individual to evaluate his deeds in order to determine whether or not he is acting properly.

R' Yitzchak Blaser, one of the primary figures in the Mussar movement, was approached by members of his community who requested that the *rav* rouse them with words of inspiration in light of the upcoming High Holy days.

"Allow me to draw a parable," he began. "A caravan lost its way in a forest. For a week the travelers wandered around aimlessly, unable to find their way out. Suddenly, the men saw a lone figure walking in the distance. They quickly made their way toward him and asked him to show them the way out of the forest.

"'My brothers and friends,' replied the man, 'you have been roaming this forest for only a week; I, however, have already been lost for *several* weeks. Let us try to find the way out of here together, perhaps then we will be successful.'

"'But there is one area in which I can be of assistance,' continued the man, 'I will tell you the paths that I have already tried, and we will know not to mistakenly tread them again.'

"This applies to our own situation as well," said R' Blaser with great humility. "I am just as lost as you are; only more so, for I am old and have already been lost for many years. Yet my experience can be of benefit, as I will be able to enlighten you as to things that I have seen in my life which I have investigated and found to be trivial and meaningless!

"You can trust me on those matters that it would not be worth your while to try those things.

"Come, let us search together for the path that leads to complete repentance!"

PARASHAS BALAK

וַיִּשְׁלַח מַלְאָכִים אֶל־בִּלְעָם בֶּן־בְּעוֹר
"He sent messengers to Bilam the son of Beor" (22:5)

"IF YOU ASK," COMMENTS RASHI, "WHY DID THE HOLY ONE LET HIS DIVINE Presence rest upon so wicked a heathen, [I reply that] it was in order that the heathen nations should have no excuse to say, 'If we had prophets, we would have changed for the better.' [The Holy One] therefore established a prophet for them, yet this [prophet] broke down the [moral] fence of the world." This is difficult to understand, noted R' Simchah Bunim of P'shischa. For the heathens could still claim that while the Jews had a righteous prophet such as Moshe, *their* prophet was full of conceit, envy, and wickedness. Had Hashem given them a prophet like Moshe, they could assert, they would have repented. If so, of what use was it to give them a prophet such as Bilam?

"To answer this question," said R' Simchah Bunim, "I will tell you a story that once happened to me: I once developed an eye illness, so I sought an expert doctor to treat it. I was advised to see a certain doctor who cured every illness by utilizing *segulos* (spiritual remedies).

"When I heard that," continued the *rebbe*, "I thought the following: Ideally, any Jew that is stricken with an ailment should go exclusively to his *rebbe* and request that he pray for his complete recovery. However, *Chazal* (*Berachos* 60a) have expounded on the verse, 'And he shall provide for healing' (*Shemos* 21:19) — 'From here [we see] that a doctor was given permission to heal.' It is therefore permissible to go to a doctor. Now, the verse is speaking about a regular doctor, one who treats his patients with standard medical procedures. But if somebody is prepared to visit a doctor who treats his patients with *segulos*, then the person would do better by going to the *tzaddik* of the generation, such as the *Maggid* of Koznitz, and asking him to supplicate to Hashem on his behalf.

"The nations of the world," concluded R' Simchah Bunim, "believed in neither Hashem nor His servant, Moshe; He therefore gave them a prophet from their own people whom they would believe. Since they did believe in Bilam, they were no longer able to contend that they did not believe in Moshe; for once they believed in Bilam, they were certainly better off believing in Moshe."

בִּי לוּ יֶשׁ־חֶרֶב בְּיָדִי כִּי עַתָּה הֲרַגְתִּיךְ:

"If only there were a sword in my hand I would have killed you now!" (22:29)

To what can this be compared? asks the Midrash — To a doctor who had become famous for his ability to cure any illness with divinations and incantations.

He once received an emergency call, requesting him to come to the aid of an individual who had been bitten by a snake. Along the way, he spotted a lizard standing on the road, and he searched for a stick in order to kill it. The bystanders who witnessed the doctor's actions began to laugh heartily, and they said mockingly, "If you cannot over-power a lizard without the help of a stick, then how will you be able to cure a snakebite with your tongue?"

So said the she-donkey to Bilam: "If you are unable to kill me with-out wielding a sword in your hand, then how will you be able to uproot an entire nation with your tongue?"

❧

וַתֹּאמֶר הָאָתוֹן אֶל־בִּלְעָם הֲלוֹא אָנֹכִי
אֲתֹנְךָ אֲשֶׁר־רָכַבְתָּ עָלַי מֵעוֹדְךָ עַד־הַיּוֹם הַזֶּה

*"The she-donkey replied to Bilam, 'Am I not
your she-donkey, upon which you have
ridden all your life until this day?' (22:30)*

R' Yitzchak of Ponevezh (commonly referred to as R' Itzele Ponevezher) was on his way to attend a very important assem-bly. Upon arriving there, he noticed that the laymen — the wealthy laymen in particular — were in the midst of argument as to which one of them would be the first to speak. Each one claimed that he was of more distinguished standing and should therefore be accorded the honor of opening the assembly.

R' Itzele listened to their claims and calmed them down. He then said, "Listen, gentlemen, and I will tell you a story: The donkeys once came before the Holy One with a claim: 'Master of the World, why are we different from all other wild animals? All other wild animals eat and drink and have no master. Domesticated animals also wander around all day without any labor to perform and in total peace; and, at night, they sleep soundly. But as for us, we perform oppressive labor day and night, not to mention all the beatings we regularly receive.'

"'Our request,' continued the donkeys, 'is that You at least give us a tongue that will enable us to persuade our master to have mercy on us.'

"And indeed," said R' Itzele, "Hashem granted their request on one occasion and granted a tongue — that is, the power of speech — to Bilam's she-donkey.

"And this donkey, instead of presenting its claims, began to give an account of its esteemed standing, as it said, 'Am I not your she-donkey, upon which you have ridden all your life until this day?'

"Its power of speech was immediately taken away, for if it is boasting about its prominence that it uses its tongue, then it is better for it to remain silent."

הֶן־עָם לְבָדָד יִשְׁכֹּן וּבַגּוֹיִם לֹא יִתְחַשָּׁב:

"Behold! They are a people that will dwell in solitude and not be reckoned among the nations" (23:9)

O ne *erev Shabbos*, R' Yisrael *Ba'al Shem Tov* was returning from the *mikveh* when he suddenly heard a loud commotion coming from the other end of the street.

The noise was coming from a group of gentiles merrily parading down the street in a drunken stupor. They were stretched out to the full width of the street, and the *Ba'al Shem Tov* was afraid that they might touch him as they passed by. He therefore pressed himself up against the wall as much as possible and waited for them to walk by. As they passed, he heard one of the gentiles say to his friend, "Ivan, be careful that this Jew doesn't touch you and contaminate you."

The *Ba'al Shem Tov* smiled and said to his *chassidim*, "I now understand the following verse: 'Behold! They are a people that will dwell in solitude' — The Jewish nation is 'alone' as a holy nation, for they are 'not ... reckoned among the nations' — the nations of the world themselves do not consider the Jews to be a nation, so they distance themselves from the Jews."

הֶן־עָם לְבָדָד יִשְׁכֹּן וּבַגּוֹיִם לֹא יִתְחַשָּׁב:

"Behold! They are a people that will dwell in solitude and not be reckoned among the nations" (23:9)

T he *Midrash Rabbah* states that each Hebrew letter has a partner except for the letters *hei* and *nun*.

For example, the partner of the letter *alef* is the letter *tes*. When their numerical values are added together they equal ten.

The partner of the letter *beis* is the letter *ches*. When added together, they also equal ten. This pattern repeats itself until the letter *hei*, whose partner is the *hei* itself.

The partner of the letter *yud* is the letter *tzaddi*. When their numerical values are added together they equal one hundred.

The partner of the letter *chaf* is the letter *fei*. They also equal one hundred when added together. This pattern repeats itself until the letter *nun*, whose partner is the *nun* itself.

"**Hein**"— In other words, just as the letters *hei* and *nun* (which spell the word "*hein*") remain alone, without partners, so too, the Jewish nation "will dwell in solitude and not be reckoned among the nations."

לֹא־הִבִּיט אָוֶן בְּיַעֲקֹב
"He perceived no iniquity in Yaakov" (23:21)

R' Levi Yitzchak of Berdichev remarked: Hashem, to Whom everything is revealed and known, does not look at the sins of a Jew, as the verse states, "He does not look (*lo hibit*) at the iniquity in Yaakov."

If this is the way of Hashem, how much more so is it forbidden for us — flesh and blood — to look at the sins of another Jew! We, too, must cling to this lofty trait of, "He does not look (*lo hibit*) at the iniquity in Yaakov."

לֹא־הִבִּיט אָוֶן בְּיַעֲקֹב וְלֹא־רָאָה עָמָל בְּיִשְׂרָאֵל
"He perceived no iniquity in Yaakov,
and saw no perversity in Israel" (23:21)

It is well known, said R' Zusia of Anipoli, that a good angel is created every time a Jew performs *mitzvah* and that an evil angel is created every time he sins, God forbid.

"I tell you," exclaimed the *rebbe*, "that the Jews are a holy people! For I have seen the angels that have been created by their good deeds and I have also seen the ones created by their sins. All the angels created by their transgressions are imperfect and flawed — for a Jew never sins wholeheartedly! At the moment of transgression, he is inevitably filled with shame and remorse over his actions. Such a sin can create no more than a crippled and deficient angel."

⚜

כִּי לֹא־נַחַשׁ בְּיַעֲקֹב וְלֹא־קֶסֶם בְּיִשְׂרָאֵל

כָּעֵת יֵאָמֵר לְיַעֲקֹב וּלְיִשְׂרָאֵל מַה־פָּעַל אֵ־ל:

"There is no divination in Yaakov and no sorcery in Yisrael. [There will again be] a time like this, when it will be asked of Yaakov and Yisrael, 'What has God wrought?'" (23:23)

To what can this be compared? asked the Dubno *Maggid* — to a commander of an army who heard that in a faraway land there was a wise man who produced a unique ointment. What made this ointment so special was that it had the power to protect from weapons of war all those who used it; neither arrow nor sword could inflict any damage on one who was anointed with it.

The commander decided to purchase this amazing ointment, so he traveled to the faraway land and bought the ointment at a very high price.

On his journey home, he was assailed by a band of thieves. They shot arrows at him, but having previously smeared himself with the ointment, he was impervious to any bodily harm.

Frightened by the sight of a man upon whom arrows had no effect, the thieves turned to flee. The commander, however, called to them and said, "Please wait! Do not be frightened. Come here and I will serve wine and delicacies in your honor."

"Why are you treating us in such a manner?" asked the incredulous thieves. "Why, just a moment ago we attempted to murder you and now you repay us with kindness?"

"You did me a very great service," replied the commander. "For I purchased an extraordinary ointment, capable of protecting the one who wears it from injury. Throughout the trip, however, I was concerned that perhaps I had been swindled and the ointment was a hoax. Yet I feared putting it to the test, lest it turn out to be exactly that. Now that you have attacked me and I have not been injured, I am certain that the ointment is legitimate. Thanks to you, I will now be able to fearlessly face all my foes!"

So it was with the Jewish nation, explained the Dubno *Maggid*. Throughout the generations, the Jewish people had been aware that "there is no divination in Yaakov and no sorcery in Yisrael." Sorcerers have no influence upon the Jewish people, as we see that Yaakov dwelled in the house of Lavan the Aramean, who attempted to deceive him with his sorcery, but was unable to do so. Despite knowing that they were impervious to sorcery, they were nonetheless wary of actually putting themselves in a predicament where they would be forced to rely on this invincibility.

So when Balak sent Bilam to curse the Jewish nation and harm them with his sorcery, but was unsuccessful, Hashem told Balak, "You have done the Children of Israel a very great favor. For now My children know with certainty that they will not be harmed by either sorcery or divination!"

৶৹৻

יֵאָמֵר לְיַעֲקֹב וּלְיִשְׂרָאֵל מַה־פָּעַל אֵ-ל: הֶן־עָם כְּלָבִיא יָקוּם

"It will be asked of Yaakov and Yisrael,
'What has God wrought?' Here is a people
that rises like a lioness" (23: 23-24)

A delegation of rabbis headed by R' Yitzchak Elchanan Spektor went to appeal before a high-ranking Russian official that he annul several harsh decrees that had been imposed on the Jews.

"There is but one issue that puzzles me," remarked the official's deputy, who was a known and open anti-Semite (and the person who had formulated the cruel edicts). "Why was the Jewish nation created? What purpose do they serve?"

"When I hear your words," replied R' Yitzchak Elchanan, "my heart is filled with pure elation."

"Elation?" asked the officer in surprise. "Why do my deputy's words bring you such joy?"

"The Torah states," answered R' Yitzchak Elchanan, "'*It will be asked of Yaakov and Yisrael, "What has God wrought?"*'" — when a Jew-hater arises and asks, 'Why did Hashem create the Jewish nation?' It is a sign that the continuation of the verse will be fulfilled; namely, *'Here is a people that rises like a lioness'* — which is a hint that the time of redemption will soon arrive."

הֶן־עָם כְּלָבִיא יָקוּם וְכַאֲרִי יִתְנַשָּׂא לֹא יִשְׁכַּב עַד־יֹאכַל טֶרֶף

"Here is a people that rises like a lioness, and like a lion, raises itself. They do not lie down until they consume their prey" (23:24)

The *Shulchan Aruch* begins with the following words: "One should strengthen himself like a lion to get up in the morning for the service of his Creator." The *Rema* (R' Moshe Isserles) adds the following, "Even in private and when one is lying on his bed, he should be cognizant before Whom he lies."

The *Rema*, remarked R' Meir of Premishlan, is giving us sound advice! What will enable us to strengthen ourselves like lions in the morning? If *at night*, an individual is aware before Whom he is lying, then in the morning he will be able to strengthen himself to rise like a lion!

This idea, concluded the *rebbe*, is alluded to in the following verse, "Here is a people that *rises like a lioness*, and like a lion, raises itself. They do not *lie down* until they consume their prey."

PARASHAS PINCHAS

לָכֵן אֱמֹר הִנְנִי נֹתֵן לוֹ אֶת־בְּרִיתִי שָׁלוֹם:
"Therefore, say: Behold, I give him My covenant of peace" (25:12)

WHY, ASKED R' YITZCHAK OF VOLOZHIN, WAS MOSHE COMmanded to personally inform Pinchas about the reward he was to receive on account of his great deed?

This can be compared, said R' Yitzchak, to a commander in an army that was in the midst of a brutal war with a cruel and ferocious enemy. At one point during the war, the commander made a major tactical error, which led to the deaths of many soldiers and almost brought about their defeat. Their situation looked hopeless. But then, all of a sudden, a relatively unknown soldier performed a heroic deed that turned the tide of the war and sent the enemy running for their lives.

The king summoned the commander and asked him to personally present the soldier with a medal of honor for his brave act.

Similarly, explained R' Yitzchak, Moshe *Rabbeinu* was instructed to personally inform Pinchas about the reward he was to receive for his brave act that stopped the plague from raging among the Jews.

בְּנֵי יִשָׂשכָר לְמִשְׁפְּחֹתָם תּוֹלָע מִשְׁפַּחַת
הַתּוֹלָעִי לְפֻוָה מִשְׁפַּחַת הַפּוּנִי: לְיָשׁוּב
מִשְׁפַּחַת הַיָּשֻׁבִי לְשִׁמְרֹן מִשְׁפַּחַת הַשִׁמְרֹנִי:
"The descendants of Yissachar, by their families were: Tola, the Tola'i family; of Puvah, the Puni family; of Yashuv, the Yashuvi family; of Shimron, the Shimroni family" (26:23-24)

Yissachar was blessed by Yaakov *Avinu*, "Yissachar is a strong boned donkey," because he carried the yoke of Torah upon himself like a donkey carries a heavy load on its back. Thus the members of the tribe of Yissachar were Torah scholars who taught halachic rulings to all the other tribes. In particular, they were the ones who knew the calculations necessary for setting the months and declaring the leap years in the Jewish calendar, as the verse states: "The children of Yissachar [are] men with understanding of the times" (*I Divrei HaYamim* 12:33).

The *Ohr HaChaim* (R' Chaim ben Attar) sees in the names of Yissachar and his sons allusions to their greatness in Torah and to their refined character.

"Yissachar" — *Yeish sechar* (There is reward)! The true reward is bestowed in the World to Come, and it is reserved for those who study the Torah and fulfill its *mitzvos*.

"Tola" — The Torah endures only in one who is humble and makes himself like a lowly *tola'as* (worm).

"Puvah" — Puvah is similar to the word "*peh*" (mouth); man must use his mouth to speak about Torah. Also, the letter *nun* was added to their family name, Puni, hinting to the fact that one must keep his mouth clear (*lifnos*) from speaking about meaningless things.

"Yashuv" — A person must sit (*lasheves*) in a yeshivah and refrain from occupying himself with trivialities.

"Shimron" — A person must take great care (*lihishamer*) to avoid desecrating the Name of Hashem.

לְיֵצֶר מִשְׁפַּחַת הַיִּצְרִי לְשִׁלֵּם מִשְׁפַּחַת הַשִּׁלֵמִי:
"Of Yetzer, the Yitzri family; of Shilem, the Shilemi family" (26:49)

This verse, said the *Chofetz Chaim*, can be expounded upon in the following manner:

"Of Yetzer" — One who succumbs to the lure of the *yetzer hara* will immediately find himself in the company of the "the Yitzri family" — the members of the *yetzer hara's* family are all more than ready to help him along the path of wickedness. "Of Shilem" — But one who strives for perfection (*sheleimus*) will find himself in the company of "the Shilemi family" — those who fear Heaven and have achieved spiritual perfection will help him along the upright path.

"In the path that a man wishes to go, he is led" (*Makkos* 10b)!

אָבִינוּ מֵת בַּמִּדְבָּר וְהוּא לֹא־הָיָה בְּתוֹךְ הָעֵדָה
הַנּוֹעָדִים עַל־ה'... וַיַּקְרֵב מֹשֶׁה אֶת־מִשְׁפָּטָן לִפְנֵי ה':

"Our father died in the Wilderness, but he was not among the assembly who protested against Hashem ... And Moshe brought their claim before Hashem" (27:3-5)

T wo men appeared R' Yosef Babad (author of *Minchas Chinuch*) for a *din Torah*. When they began to speak, they reminded the *rav* that at one point they had been part of a close circle of the *rav*'s friends who prevented a potential quarrel that was about to break out against him.

"And why have you come before me today?" he asked them.

"We have come for a *din Torah*. We would like the *Rav* to pass judgment in our case," they responded.

"I am afraid that I will be unable to do so," declared R' Babad. "For when the daughters of Tzlafchad appeared before Moshe *Rabbeinu*, they began by telling him, 'Our father died in the Wilderness, but he was not among the assembly [of Korach's group] who protested against Hashem.' They then continued with a claim for a portion of the land. After hearing their initial words, however, Moshe *Rabbeinu* did not wish to decide their case, because he feared that he would no longer be able to judge their case objectively. The Torah therefore states, 'And Moshe brought their claim before Hashem!'"

יִפְקֹד ה'... אִישׁ עַל־הָעֵדָה:... וְלֹא תִהְיֶה
עֲדַת ה' כַּצֹּאן אֲשֶׁר אֵין־לָהֶם רֹעֶה:

"May Hashem ... appoint a man over the assembly. ... Let Hashem's assembly not be like sheep that have no shepherd" (27:16-17)

G edolei Yisrael have always exhibited the utmost concern and devotion for their students, similar to the concern a shepherd demonstrates for his flock of sheep.

One day, a former disciple of the *Chofetz Chaim* approached his *rebbe*. Weeping bitterly, he told the *Chofetz Chaim* that doctors had diagnosed him with a grave illness which they did not know how to treat.

The *Chofetz Chaim* listened to his student and said, "Do not worry. I will give you some advice — but on one condition. You must never reveal the advice that I am about to give you to another soul!"

The student agreed to the stipulation. The *Chofetz Chaim* continued, "Go to Rabbi So-and-so, and tell him about your predicament. He will bless you to have a complete recovery, and, with Hashem's help, you will recuperate!"

The student did just as the *Chofetz Chaim* instructed. He visited the scholar whom his *rebbe* had mentioned and, before long, he miraculously recovered.

Some twenty years later, this student's sister-in-law contracted the same illness that he had suffered from so long ago. However, the student kept his word and did not reveal the secret of how he had recovered.

But when her condition deteriorated, the student told his wife what had happened to him twenty years earlier.

Shortly thereafter, the student once again began suffering from the illness. Frightened, he told his wife that he had to journey to his *rebbe* for a second time.

Upon arriving in Radin, he entered the home of the *Chofetz Chaim*, who by then was old and frail. He had not forgotten his student, however, and greeted him warmly and affectionately.

"*Rebbe*," began the student, "I am sick once again, and I have come to request the *Rav*'s blessing for a speedy recovery."

"I wish I could help you," responded the *Chofetz Chaim*. "But what can I do at this point? When you had taken ill the first time, I was much younger and I fasted forty days in order for you to get better. But now I am elderly and cannot fast as I once did."

יִפְקֹד ה'... אִישׁ עַל־הָעֵדָה: ...וְלֹא תִהְיֶה
עֲדַת ה' כַּצֹּאן אֲשֶׁר אֵין־לָהֶם רֹעֶה:

*"May Hashem ... appoint a man over the
assembly. ... Let Hashem's assembly not
be like sheep that have no shepherd" (27:16-17)*

A terrible epidemic had broken out in the city of Warsaw; many Jews contracted the disease and had to be admitted into the city's hospitals.

On *erev Yom Kippur*, word spread that the *rav* of Warsaw, R' Shlomo Zalman Lipschitz (author of *Chemdas Shlomo*), had requested all Jews who worked in the hospitals not to attend the Yom Kippur prayer services, as he did not want the many patients to be left without proper care.

Prior to the *Kol Nidrei* service on Yom Kippur night, a massive crowd gathered in R' Lipschitz's *beis midrash*. The only one absent was the *rav* himself.

After waiting for quite some time, a messenger was dispatched to the *rav*'s home in order to find out the reason behind his delay.

Upon returning, the messenger told the congregation that the *rav* was not at home; in fact, no one knew his whereabouts. A search party was dispatched, and they began to look throughout the city for the missing *rav*. Finally, he was located in the hospital — where he was tending to the many patients.

"On my way to *shul*," related the *rav*, "I decided to check whether the hospital staff had complied with my instructions. When I realized that many of them had left the hospital in order to attend the prayer services, I remained here to lend a hand."

יִפְקֹד ה'... אִישׁ עַל־הָעֵדָה: ...וְלֹא תִהְיֶה
עֲדַת ה' כַּצֹּאן אֲשֶׁר אֵין־לָהֶם רֹעֶה:

"May Hashem ... appoint a man over the assembly. ... Let Hashem's assembly not be like sheep that have no shepherd" (27:16-17)

R' Yehudah Asad had received word that on Pesach night, as the Jews would be sitting around their Seder tables, a band of rioters and murderers were planning to attack the city.

R' Asad requested all Jews to conduct their Seder in the local *shul*, and the congregation readily complied. That night, everyone ate in *shul* together with R' Asad, who sat at the head of the table and conducted the Seder with utmost serenity.

Suddenly, one of the non-Jewish residents of the town burst into the shul and announced that the rioters were quickly approaching the town.

"Stay where you are," said R' Asad to the frightened congregation, "and I will go out to greet them!" The *rav* grabbed a *shofar* from the drawer beneath the *Aron Kodesh* and went out into the street.

Adorned in his white *kittel*, R' Yehudah went out alone to meet the bandits. As soon as he saw them, he stopped, raised the *shofar* to his lips, and began to blow.

When the rioters saw R' Asad, they were filled with dread. A great tumult erupted among them, and they fled for their lives, trampling one another under the hoofs of their horses.

וְנָתַתָּה מֵהוֹדְךָ עָלָיו

"Invest him with some of your splendor" (27:20)

Chazal (*Bava Basra* 75a) expound on this verse, "'Some of your splendor' — but not *all* of your splendor! The elders of that generation said that the face of Moshe resembled the sun and the face of Yehoshua resembled the moon. Woe to such shame; woe to such disgrace."

Should the fact that Yehoshua's face shined like the moon, asked the *Chofetz Chaim*, be a cause of shame and disgrace?

To what can this be compared? he continued — to an individual who heard that a mine full of precious gems had been discovered in a faraway land, and that anyone who wished to dig for gems was free to do so.

The man decided to make the trip and dig for the precious stones, but he felt that he would be better off having a friend accompany him for the lengthy journey.

He appealed to many of his friends, but they all refused, as each one was deterred by the prospect of enduring such a time-consuming trip. Finally, one of them agreed, and the two traveled together.

After several years, they returned home carrying a precious load. They sold their gems and made a fortune.

"Such a pity," remarked his friends, "that we did not agree to travel with him, for if we had, we could have been as wealthy as they are."

The elders of the generation, concluded the *Chofetz Chaim*, had similar feelings. Seeing how Yehoshua had risen to greatness caused them great anguish, as he had been one of them. But because he remained in the presence of Moshe *Rabbeinu*, he soared to great heights. They therefore thought, *If only we would have attended to Moshe, we, too, would have merited achieving such greatness. We are therefore to blame ourselves for not having merited such a lofty level.*

"Woe to such shame; woe to such disgrace!"

וְנָתַתָּה מֵהוֹדְךָ עָלָיו
"Invest him with some of your splendor" (27:20)

Why, asked the Vilna *Gaon*, was it only the elders who exclaimed, "Woe to such shame; woe to such disgrace"? Was the younger generation unable to perceive the distinction between Moshe and Yehoshua?

Rather, answered the *Gaon*, everyone certainly saw the difference between Moshe and Yehoshua. The younger generation, however, thought, *Perhaps the reason that Moshe Rabbeinu is greater than Yehoshua lies in the fact that Moshe is older than he is, but when Moshe was younger he, too, appeared as Yehoshua does now.*

This is why *Chazal* said that it was the elders who had made the comment, for the elders were old enough to remember what Moshe

Rabbeinu was like when he was Yehoshua's age, and they understood just how great the difference was between the two of them.

יוֹם תְּרוּעָה יִהְיֶה לָכֶם:

"It shall be a day of sounding the shofar for you" (29:1)

R' Yisrael *Ba'al Shem Tov* called upon his disciple, R' Zev Kitzis, and told him, "R' Zev, with Hashem's help, you will be our *ba'al tokea* (*shofar* blower) for Rosh Hashanah this year!"

R' Zev began to prepare himself for the holy day. He made a list of all of the sanctified intentions that one should have during the blowing of the *shofar*, intentions that he had learned from his *rebbe*, the *Ba'al Shem Tov*. He then placed the special piece of paper between the pages of his *machzor*.

When the time to blow the *shofar* arrived, R' Zev approached the *bimah* and flipped through the pages of his *machzor* — but the list was not there! R' Zev was brokenhearted, and hot tears streamed from his eyes — tears of anguish that he would not be able to blow the *shofar* with the special intentions.

In such a state did R' Zev sound the *shofar*; He blowed and wept, blowed and wept again …

After the prayers had concluded, the *Ba'al Shem Tov* announced before his *chassidim*, "You should know that R' Zev's *shofar* blowing split open heavens!"

Then, to R' Zev he said, "All the sacred intentions we possess can be compared to a key — it will fit the keyhole of one gate but not another. If the key doesn't fit, the gate wil remain locked. A broken heart, however, can be compared to an ax that is capable of splitting open any gate and partition in the world. This is as the verse states, 'A heart that is broken and humbled, O God, You will not despise'" (*Tehillim* 51:19)!

יוֹם תְּרוּעָה יִהְיֶה לָכֶם:

"It shall be a day of sounding the shofar for you" (29:1)

As is well known, said R' Yitzchak Blaser, when the Satan hears the *shofar* sound on Rosh Hashanah, he immediately grows frightened and confused and thinks, *Perhaps Mashiach is coming now.*

But, noted R' Blaser, the Satan hears the blowing of the *shofar* year after year and *Mashiach* has not yet arrived — why is he still so frightened by the sound?

Every year, answered R' Blaser, the Satan suspects that perhaps the Jews have repented and have become worthy of receiving *Mashiach.* This is why he worries so!

There is a lesson we should learn from this, concluded R' Blaser; namely, that one must never despair and think, *So many years have passed. Many High Holy Days and shofar soundings have passed as well — and I still have not merited repenting for my misdeeds. Perhaps there is no hope for me, God forbid.*

The person should banish this foreign thought from his heart and rouse himself to repentance with renewed vigor, year after year!

PARASHAS MATOS

וַיְדַבֵּר מֹשֶׁה אֶל־רָאשֵׁי הַמַּטּוֹת לִבְנֵי יִשְׂרָאֵל לֵאמֹר ...

"Moshe spoke to the heads of the tribes of the Children of Israel, saying ..." (30:2)

RASHI EXPLAINS THAT MOSHE *RABBEINU* ACCORDED HONOR TO THE princes by teaching them first, and only afterwards did he teach all the rest of the Children of Israel.

In a certain town, the leader of the community was a strong-willed man whose prominent position led him to pursue honor endlessly. If he felt that a member of the community was not showing him the proper amount of respect, he would go out of his way to make the person's life miserable.

Word of the community leader's behavior reached R' Yisrael of Rizhin, and the *tzaddik* sent him a message stating that he wished to see him.

When the man appeared before R' Yisrael, the *rebbe* rebuked him and said, "There is only a single case in the Torah in which we find that honor was shown to a leader. When was that? When Moshe *Rabbeinu* taught the laws pertaining to vows; he accorded honor to the princes by teaching them first, and only afterwards did he teach the rest of the Jewish people.

"Any other type of illusory honor is strictly forbidden! All the more so is it forbidden for a community leader to pursue honor, as he serves as a role model for the entire congregation."

אִישׁ כִּי־יִדֹּר נֶדֶר
"If a man takes a vow to Hashem" (30:3)

In his youth, R' Yaakov Meshulam Ornstein (known as the *Yeshuos Yaakov* after his work by that title) was known as a very gifted child. By the time he was 12 years old, the rich men of his city vied with each other to claim him as a son-in-law.

On one occasion, one of these men sent a great Torah scholar to test the boy to see if he was indeed as brilliant as he was rumored to be.

When they met, the boy extended his hand and offered the scholar the customary "*Shalom aleichem.*"

"Perhaps you would be able to tell me," asked the scholar, "a *pilpul* (a sharp-witted Torah discourse) regarding the expression, '*Shalom aleichem.*'"

"Certainly," he responded. "Let me ask you a question: Why is it that when two individuals meet, one of them says, '*Shalom aleichem,*' while the other responds, '*Aleichem Shalom*'?

"The answer," said the boy, "is as follows: In *Maseches Nedarim* (10a), *Chazal* state that one who takes a vow should not say, 'For Hashem is this vow,' for perhaps he will die in the middle of saying his words and will have uttered Hashem's Name in vain. Rather, he should say, 'This vow is for Hashem.'

"*Shalom,*' continued the boy, "is one of the Names of Hashem. It would therefore stand to reason that one should not be permitted to say, '*Shalom aleichem,*' for he might die in the middle of saying the greeting and he will have pronounced Hashem's Name in vain. However, *Chazal* have stated elsewhere, 'One who precedes his friend in offering him "*Shalom,*" has his days and years extended.' This is why the one who greets his friend first is permitted to say, '*Shalom aleichem*' — as he took the initiative to greet his friend, he need not fear that he will die midsentence, for he is rewarded by having his years lengthened. His friend, however, must respond, '*Aleichem Shalom.*'"

⤞⤝

לֹא יַחֵל דְּבָרוֹ כְּכָל־הַיֹּצֵא מִפִּיו יַעֲשֶׂה:
"He shall not desecrate his word; according to whatever comes from his mouth shall he do" (30:3)

R' Yehoshua Leib Diskin once attended a eulogy for one of his students who had passed away. At the conclusion of the eulogy, the customary "*Keil malei rachamim*" was recited and then the crowd dispersed, each person going his separate way.

R' Diskin approached the *gabbai* of the *shul* and handed him a coin *l'ilui nishmas* (for elevating the soul) of the departed. "I am giving this coin on behalf of all the people who had been present at the eulogy," said R' Diskin, "because when the *chazan* recites the *Kel malei rachamim* prayer, he says 'for the entire congregation vows to contribute to charity in order to elevate his soul.' Since the people took a vow, I fear that there may be some among them who will forget to fulfill what they accepted upon themselves. I am therefore giving on behalf of the entire congregation."

⤞⤝

לֹא יַחֵל דְּבָרוֹ כְּכָל־הַיֹּצֵא מִפִּיו יַעֲשֶׂה:
"He shall not desecrate his word; according to whatever comes from his mouth shall he do" (30:3)

Explains Rashi: "'*Lo yacheil devaro*' — [This has the same meaning] as 'he shall not profane (*yechalel*) his word' [that is], he shall not make his words mundane."

On this verse, R' Menachem Mendel of Kosov remarked: When an individual is careful to speak only of holy matters and consistently avoids speaking of mundane matters, then Hashem rewards him by fulfilling the man's blessings or prayers. Thus *Chazal* assert, "A *tzaddik* decrees and *HaKadosh Baruch Hu* fulfills."

This idea, concluded the *rebbe*, is hinted at in the verse, "*Lo yacheil devaro*" — A person who does not make his words profane merits reaching the level where, "according to whatever comes from his mouth *He* will do" — A *tzaddik* decrees and *HaKadosh Baruch Hu* fulfills.

ֆ⊃Ց₭

וַיִּקְצֹף מֹשֶׁה עַל פְּקוּדֵי הֶחָיִל
"Moshe was angry with the commanders of the army" (31:14)

C hazal (*Pesachim* 66b) expound on this verse, "Any person who becomes angry — if he is a wise man, his wisdom will desert him."

The Sages of Israel have always taken great care not to become angry.

It is said that the *Alter* of Kelm (R' Simchah Zissel Ziv) made it a personal rule not to grow angry — regardless of the circumstances — unless he first put on a special garment that he reserved for such occasions.

"This approach works very well," explained the *Alter*. "For when a person has to stop to put on a special garment before he allows himself to become completely enraged — by the time he has donned the garment, his anger will have subsided, and his calm will have been restored."

ֆ⊃Ց₭

אַךְ אֶת־הַזָּהָב וְאֶת־הַכֶּסֶף ... כָּל־דָּבָר
אֲשֶׁר־יָבֹא בָאֵשׁ תַּעֲבִירוּ בָאֵשׁ וְטָהֵר
"Only the gold and the silver... everything that comes into the fire — you shall pass through the fire and it will be purified" (31:22-23)

C hazal derived the laws of *hagalas keilim* (purging nonkosher utensils) from these verses.

The word *Ach*, "only," teaches us that the utensil must be thoroughly cleaned from any rust or other substance that may be clinging to it, until nothing but the gold and silver remains.

From the next verse we learn that every utensil must be purified in the manner that it was used, as it states, "Everything that comes into the fire — you shall pass through the fire." Thus if a utensil was primarily used on the fire, its purification is also with fire.

From here, noted the *Chofetz Chaim*, we learn how a person should go about cleansing himself of the sins he has committed. He must first clean himself from any refuse that may be clinging to him; that is, he must regret his misdeeds and completely separate himself from sin.

He must then repent in the exact manner as he had sinned. If he sinned with fervor, he must return to Hashem with utmost fervor. If he sinned publicly, he must repent publicly. If he sinned with his mouth, he must accept upon himself from now on to speak words of Torah.

Only then, concluded the *Chofetz Chaim*, will he reach the level where he "will be purified"!

כָּל־דָּבָר אֲשֶׁר־יָבֹא בָאֵשׁ תַּעֲבִירוּ בָאֵשׁ וְטָהֵר

"Everything that comes into the fire — you shall pass through the fire and it will be purified" (31:23)

There are two kinds of fire, said the *Chida* (R' Chaim Yosef David Azulai). There is the fire of the *yetzer hara* which burns inside a man's bones and tempts him to sin. But, then, there is the fire of the Torah — a fire of holiness and purity.

Chazal state in *Maseches Kiddushin* (30b), "I have created the *yetzer hara*, and I have created Torah as its antidote." The only way for a person to combat his *yetzer hara* is by studying the holy Torah. Through Torah study an individual can save himself and vanquish his *yetzer hara*.

This, concluded the *Chida*, is alluded to in the following verse, "Everything that comes into the fire" of the *yetzer hara*, "you shall pass through the fire" of the Torah, "and it will be purified"!

וַאֲנַחְנוּ נֵחָלֵץ חֻשִׁים לִפְנֵי בְּנֵי יִשְׂרָאֵל

"We will arm ourselves and go as an advance guard before the Children of Israel" (32:17)

The *Sefas Emes* (R' Yehudah Leib of Gur) grew up in the home of his esteemed grandfather, the *Chiddushei HaRim* (R' Yitzchak Meir of Gur).

One night, young Yehudah Leib continued his Torah study through the night. Only at dawn did he finally get into bed in order to take a brief nap.

Early that morning, the *Chiddushei HaRim* entered his grandson's room and was dismayed to see him still sleeping. He woke the boy from his deep slumber and admonished him for sleeping until such a late hour instead of rising with alacrity to serve Hashem.

Yehudah Leib listened to his grandfather's reproach, and when he finished speaking, he explained to his grandfather that he had slept late only as a result of learning diligently throughout the night.

"Why did you not tell me this right away?" asked the *Chiddushei HaRim*. "If I would have known that, I would have not have offered you such harsh rebuke."

"In *Parashas Matos*," answered the boy, "we learn about how Moshe reprimanded the children of Gad and the children of Reuven. After Moshe had concluded his reproof, they answered him, 'We will arm ourselves and go as an advance guard before the Children of Israel.'

"At first glance, this seems difficult," continued young Yehudah Leib. "If all along their intention was to go up and fight, then why did they permit Moshe to rebuke them so harshly? The moment Moshe began his criticism, they should have related what their true motives were!

"Rather," he answered, "the children of Gad and the children of Reuven were delighted to have an opportunity to hear words of rebuke from Moshe *Rabbeinu*. Is hearing reproof from such a holy *tzaddik* something to give up easily? They were not about to pass up such a golden opportunity.

"The same applies to me as well," said R' Yehudah Leib. "If I would have revealed that I had studied Torah the entire night, I would not have merited to hear Grandfather's wonderful words of reproof."

וִהְיִיתֶם נְקִיִּם מֵה' וּמֵיִשְׂרָאֵל
"Then you will be free of any obligation before Hashem and Israel" (32:22)

A student of the *Chofetz Chaim* had agreed to serve as the rabbi of a small city, and he now turned to his *rebbe* for advice on how he should lead his community.

The *Chofetz Chaim* responded: "The verse states, 'Then you will be free of any obligation before Hashem and Israel' — a rabbi's first responsibility is to ensure that his flock keep the Torah and *mitzvos* properly, and only afterwards should he concern himself with its physical needs.

"Anybody," concluded the *Chofetz Chaim*, "who, in order to find favor in the eyes of his community, reverses this sequence will not succeed at either endeavor!"

וִהְיִיתֶם נְקִיִּם מֵה' וּמֵיִשְׂרָאֵל
"Then you will be free of any obligation before Hashem and Israel" (32:22)

A wealthy childless woman approached the *rav* of the city of Budapest. In her hand was a large sum of money — 400 *zehuvim* — and she asked the *rav* to accept it on condition that he would pray for her to bear a child.

"I will give you some advice," responded the *rav*. "Send the money to R' Yosef Chaim Sonnenfeld, the *rav* of Yerushalayim. He is a great *tzaddik* and Hashem will surely listen to his prayers and grant you a child."

The woman accepted his advice and sent the money to the *rav* of Yerushalayim.

Several weeks later, the husband of the woman approached the *rav* of Budapest. "Why did you send the money without my knowledge?" he asked angrily. "I demand that you send a letter to the *rav* of Yerushalayim requesting that my money be returned at once."

The *rav* was upset by the husband's demand, and said, "I will give you the entire sum of money from my own pocket, just as long as I do not have to ask R' Sonnenfeld to return the money!"

As they continued to discuss the matter, the postman arrived with an envelope for the *rav*.

The *rav* opened the envelope and was astounded to see that it contained a letter from R' Sonnenfeld and 400 *zehuvim*!

The letter read as follows: "I received your letter along with four hundred *zehuvim*. But since you wrote that a woman gave you the money, I fear that she may have done so without the consent of her husband .... I am therefore sending the money to you, and I request that you return it to the woman as quickly as possible.

"This, of course, did not prevent me from fulfilling her request, and I have prayed on the woman's behalf.

"May it be His will," concluded R' Sonnenfeld, "that the prayers will be accepted by our Father in Heaven."

PARASHAS MASEI

אֵלֶּה מַסְעֵי בְנֵי־יִשְׂרָאֵל

"These are the journeys of the Children of Israel" (33:1)

THIS VERSE ALLUDES TO THE FOUR EXILES THAT THE JEWISH NATION would endure:

Eileh — *Edom* (Rome)
Masei — *Madai* and *Paras* (Medes and Persia)
Bnei — *Bavel* (Babylonia)
Yisrael — *Yavan* (Greece)

אֵלֶּה מַסְעֵי בְנֵי-יִשְׂרָאֵל אֲשֶׁר יָצְאוּ מֵאֶרֶץ מִצְרַיִם ...
"These are the journeys of the Children of Israel, who had left Egypt ..." (33:1)

Why, asks Rashi, was it necessary to enumerate all of the different journeys?

To answer this question, Rashi quotes the words of the *Midrash Tanchuma*: "This can be compared to the case of a king whose son was ill and he took him to a distant place to cure him. Once they started back, his father began to enumerate all the stages [of their journey], saying to [his son], 'Here we slept. Here we felt cold. Here you had a headache, etc.'"

What is the *nimshal* (the application) of this parable? asked the *Imrei Emes* (R' Avraham Mordechai of Gur). Is the Torah merely telling us that the Jews rested or cooled themselves in these places? Isn't it obvious that they had to do these things? What, then, is the *Midrash* coming to teach us by listing the places where they slept or felt cold?

These verses and *Chazal's* parable, answered the *rebbe*, have deep meaning and contain hidden admonishments: "Here we slept" — This is an allusion to the time of the Giving of the Torah. For on that monumental morning when the Torah was to be given, the Jewish nation overslept.

"Here we felt cold" — This alludes to when Amalek "cooled down" the Jewish nation's enthusiasm for serving Hashem, as the verse states, "That he happened (*karcha*, "made you cold") upon you on the way" (*Devarim* 25:18).

"Here you had a headache (*chashasta es roshecha*)" — This is an allusion to the sin of the Golden Calf, when the Jewish people had uncertainties (*chashashos*) regarding the whereabouts of their leader (*rosh*), Moshe *Rabbeinu*.

This is why, concluded the *rebbe*, the Torah specified each journey, in order that the Jewish nation should remember what transpired at each place and repent wholeheartedly.

וַיִּסְעוּ מִקִּבְרֹת הַתַּאֲוָה וַיַּחֲנוּ בַּחֲצֵרֹת:

"They journeyed from Kivros-hata'avah and camped in Chatzeros" (33:17)

From this verse, remarked R' Yitzchak of Vorka, we learn that for an individual to break the *yetzer hara* within him, he must constantly recall the fact that this world is but a temporary one intended to be utilized in preparation for the World to Come.

This is hinted in the verse: "They left *Kivros-hata'avah*" — how will one be able to bury (*likvor*) his lust (*ta'avah*) and subdue his *yetzer hara*? By remembering that this world is no more than "*Chatzeros*," a yard (*chatzer*) in front of a house, a hallway leading to a palace.

A person who ingrains this thought in his heart, said the *rebbe*, will triumph in his war against the *yetzer hara*.

וַיִּסְעוּ מֵחֲצֵרֹת וַיַּחֲנוּ בְּרִתְמָה:

"They journeyed from Chatzeros and camped in Rismah" (33:18)

Says Rashi, "[*Rismah* was called by this name] because of the slanderous speech of the Spies, as it says (*Tehillim* 120:3-4), 'What will a treacherous tongue give to you, or gain for you? Sharp arrows of a warrior with coals of juniper (*resamim*)?'"

Gedolei Yisrael have always exercised the utmost caution so as not to violate the grave sin of speaking *lashon hara*.

A special fund was established in Vilna in order to financially assist Torah scholars. Part of this fund was set aside to cover the weekly expenses of the Vilna *Gaon* and was delivered to him once a week with a special messenger.

One day, however, the messenger succumbed to temptation and decided to take the *Gaon*'s money for himself. On his way to the *Gaon*'s house, he simply pocketed the money and kept on walking. The theft continued week after week.

The *Gaon* did not utter a word of the matter to anyone, even though the money had been his family's main source of livelihood. Now impoverished, they were literally starving for bread.

Several weeks turned into several *years*, and the money had still not made its way to the *Gaon*'s house! This continued until the messenger — lying on his deathbed full of guilt — admitted having abused his post by not delivering the money to the Vilna *Gaon* for several years!

זֹאת הָאָרֶץ אֲשֶׁר תִּפֹּל לָכֶם בְּנַחֲלָה

"This is the land that shall fall to you as an inheritance" (34:2)

To what can this be compared? asks the *Midrash Rabbah* — To a king who owned slaves and maidservants. One day, the king met another king and said to him, "I own slaves and maidservants and you also own slaves and maidservants; come, and we will marry my slaves to your maidservants and my maidservants to your slaves."

Some time later, the king thought, *Why must I marry my slaves and maidservants to his slaves and maidservants? I can marry my own slaves and maidservants to one another.*

So, too, Hashem, as it were, said: "The land is Mine and the Nation of Israel is Mine as well. It is best that I bequeath My land to My nation!" [The verse] therefore says, "This is the land that shall fall to you as an inheritance."

זֹאת הָאָרֶץ אֲשֶׁר תִּפֹּל לָכֶם בְּנַחֲלָה

"This is the land that shall fall to you as an inheritance" (34:2)

Chazal (*Sanhedrin* 91a) relate that on one occasion the people of Africa had the Jews tried before Alexander Macedonia.

"The Land of Canaan is ours!" claimed the Africans. "For the Torah refers to the Land of Israel as 'the Land of Canaan,' and Canaan was our father."

An elderly man by the name of Geviha ben Pesisa said to the Sages of Israel, "Grant me permission and I will deliberate with them before the king. If they defeat me, you can say to them, 'You have defeated but a simple man from among us.' If I defeat them, however, you can say to them, 'The Torah of Moshe *Rabbeinu* defeated you!'"

The Sages agreed and granted him permission.

"What is your proof that the Land of Canaan is yours?" asked Geviha ben Pesisa.

"From the Torah!" they answered him.

"I will also bring a proof from the Torah," replied Geviha, "for the verse states (*Bereishis* 9:25), 'Cursed is Canaan; a slave of slaves shall he be to his brothers.' If so," he continued, "please tell me — if a slave somehow acquired property, to whom would it belong? To the master! Therefore, the land is ours. Furthermore, *you owe us* compensation for all the years that you have neglected to work for us."

"Answer them!" ordered Alexander Macedonia.

"Give us three days time," said the Africans, "and then we will respond."

The king granted them the requested time. They searched, but were unable to find an answer. They immediately fled, leaving behind their fields and vineyards that they had planted. That year was a *Shemittah* year. As the Jews were forbidden to work their fields, they were in need of food. Now that the Africans had abandoned their planted fields, the Jews' problem was solved.

וְלֹא־תַחֲנִיפוּ אֶת־הָאָרֶץ אֲשֶׁר אַתֶּם בָּהּ
"Do not pollute the land in which you are" (35:33)

From this verse, says the *Sifri*, we derive an admonition against the prohibition of engaging in flattery (*chanifah*). Indeed, *Gedolei Yisrael* would not display an ounce of flattery when it came to ensuring the principles of our holy Torah.

One of the wealthy individuals of Slutsk arranged a lavish celebration for his son upon his reaching the age of bar mitzvah.

He rented a magnificent stagecoach, boarded it, and traveled to the home of the city's *rav*, R' Yosef Dov Soloveitchik (the *Beis HaLevi*), in order to personally escort him to the *simchah* (festive occasion).

When he arrived at the *rav*'s house, he entered and, with great honor and reverence, extended him an invitation.

"Which Torah topic will the young man be speaking about?" asked R' Soloveitchik. (It is customary for a bar mitzvah boy to present a *derashah*, a discourse, on a particular Torah topic.)

The man appeared somewhat bewildered. "Which topic?" he asked. "Why, the boy will not be speaking at all. Doesn't the *rav* realize that the times have changed and that a *derashah* is no longer customary?"

"A bar mitzvah celebration that doesn't include a *derashah* from the bar mitzvah boy is no more than a session of levity!" exclaimed the *rav*. "I am therefore not willing to attend!"

The rich man was dumbfounded and did know what to respond.

At the same time, there was a simple man waiting to speak with R' Soloveitchik. This man's son was also celebrating his bar mitzvah that day. The man had come only to receive the great *rav*'s blessing. But now that he heard what the *rav* had said, he summoned the nerve to ask, "Perhaps the *Rav* would be willing to participate in the bar mitzvah celebration of *my* son; he studies Torah diligently and will even be presenting a *derashah* in honor of the occasion."

"With you I will go!" exclaimed R' Soloveitchik. With that, he rose from his chair and put on his coat.

"But *Rav*," said the wealthy man, "the guests are waiting — what will I tell them?"

"Tell them," replied the *rav*, "that I do not attend bar mitzvah celebrations at which the young man does not speak words of Torah!"

Humiliated, the wealthy man returned home and related to his guests what had transpired in R' Soloveitchik's house. His rich friends were furious, and they audaciously decided to take revenge against the *rav*.

They therefore warned the city's inhabitants that under no circumstances was anyone to rent R' Soloveitchik a place to live. Anyone found to have done so would be dealt with severely!

The next day, the *rav*'s landlord approached him and nervously told him that he had been threatened to either evict the *rav* or suffer the consequences.

"Do not worry," responded R' Soloveitchik. "I will leave willingly." Indeed, the *rav* moved out of his house and was left without a roof over his head.

When the non-Jewish governor of Slutsk — a great admirer of R' Soloveitchik — heard about the *rav*'s predicament, he immediately sent word to him that *he* would give the *rav* a luxurious ten-room house free of charge!

The *rav* considered accepting the offer but decided that it would be a *chilul Hashem* to accept the gentile's offer. He therefore collected his belongings and left the city of Slutsk forever.

✍︎

וְלֹא־תַחֲנִיפוּ אֶת־הָאָרֶץ אֲשֶׁר אַתֶּם בָּהּ

"Do not pollute the land in which you are" (35:33)

R' Moshe Yitzchak the well-known *darshan*, the *Maggid* of Kelm, did not refrain from offering rebuke when the situation demanded it, and he did not display partiality to anybody.

In those days, there were two wealthy salt dealers living in Kelm. They sold two types of salt in their store: one was the standard white salt and the other was called "red salt." It was a salt of higher quality, called "red" because of its reddish tint.

In order to make more money, these storeowners used to deceitfully mix small quantities of red dye with the white salt, giving customers the impression that they were actually purchasing red salt.

When the *maggid* discovered their scheme, he went to the salt dealers and rebuked them for their fraud.

"I want you to know," said the *maggid* to the storeowners, "that I will personally stand at the threshold of your shops and warn potential customers."

When their disgraceful behavior became public knowledge, the storeowners decided to take revenge against the *maggid*. They therefore slandered him to the authorities in an attempt to ruin his reputation. Shortly thereafter, the *maggid* was arrested by the authorities on the charge of treason, and he was thrown into prison.

A few days later, the prison warden met up with his good friend, the post-office manager. At one point during their conversation, the warden told his friend about the new prisoner that was suspected of treason.

"R' Moshe Yitzchak is suspected of treason?" cried out the post-office manager in shock. "It simply cannot be!

"Let me tell you who R' Moshe Yitzchak is," he continued. "From time to time he enters the post office and buys several stamps. Yet immediately after purchasing them, he tears them up! When I realized what he does, I approached him and asked him to explain his bizarre behavior.

"'It's really very simple,' he answered me. 'There are times that I send mail with private messengers instead of the official postal service. Doing so might be considered stealing from the government who has established an official mail service. I therefore purchase stamps worth the cost of shipping of my packages, and then I tear them up; this way, the government does not lose any income on account of my actions.'

"Could such an upright individual," added the post-office manager, "possibly be suspected of treason?"

The warden was very impressed by the story, and he freed R' Moshe Yitzchak that very day.

וְלֹא־תַחֲנִיפוּ אֶת־הָאָרֶץ אֲשֶׁר אַתֶּם בָּהּ
"Do not pollute the land in which you are" (35:33)

R' Chaim Ozer Grodzinski was once sent to prison as a result of a vicious libel.

When he was in jail, the lawyer who had been appointed to defend him visited him. The lawyer told R' Grodzinski that he was capable of having him released. But then the lawyer suddenly noticed that R' Grodzinski was not even looking at him.

"Why are you not looking at me?" he asked.

"I am not looking a you," replied R' Grodzinski, "because it is forbidden to look at the face of a wicked person!"

The lawyer was amazed at the prisoner's trait of truthfulness, and he related to the judge what had occurred. "Think about it," he told the judge. "Here I am, I have the power to save him from imprisonment, yet he refuses to look at me, upholding his principles. Such an honest person certainly cannot be guilty of the vile slander said about him!"

The judge took the lawyer's words to heart and released the *rav* immediately.

HAFTARAH OF PARASHAS MASEI

הַהֵימִיר גּוֹי אֱלֹקִים וְהֵמָּה לֹא אֱלֹקִים
וְעַמִּי הֵמִיר כְּבוֹדוֹ בְּלוֹא יוֹעִיל:

*"Has a nation [ever] exchanged its gods, though they
are not [genuine] gods? Yet My people has exchanged
its Glory for something of no avail" (Yirmiyahu 2:11)*

TO WHAT CAN THIS BE COMPARED, ASKED THE DUBNO *MAGGID*? To
a young married man whose father-in-law attempted to persuade him to leave yeshivah and enter the business world.
He gave him a substantial sum of money and sent him to the fair to
purchase merchandise.

The young man, who knew nothing at all about business, returned
from the fair with several wagons full of toothpicks.

"You good-for-nothing!" screamed the father-in-law in despair.
"What have you done? You won't be able to sell such merchandise in
seventy years! Go back to your yeshivah and study Torah!"

Several years later, the father-in-law once again tried to convince
him to try his hand at business. Like before, he gave him a large sum
of money and sent him to the big fair, this time with plenty of warn-
ings not to buy toothpicks.

The son-in-law looked around the fair and thought, *Which merchandise is a worthwhile investment?"*

With the month being *Elul* and Rosh Hashanah not far away, the
young man reasoned that it would be wise to purchase a massive
stock of *shofars.*

The father-in-law was not particularly pleased when he saw what
his son-in-law had bought. "How impractical can you be?" he yelled.
"What have you done? You've purchased enough *shofars* to last until
Mashiach arrives and sounds his!"

What will I do now? thought the father-in-law. In desperation, he
turned to a shrewd businessman and related his son-in-law's blun-
ders. He handed over the stock of toothpicks and said, "Sell or
trade this merchandise as you see fit; just save whatever you can of
my money."

He then turned to a second businessman and gave him the massive stock of *shofars* in order that he exchange them for merchandise that would be easier to sell.

Maybe at least one of them will succeed at getting rid of these goods, thought the father-in-law.

Several days later, the two businessmen met in a hotel and told each other about the merchandise they were carrying with them.

"I would like to exchange *shofars*," said one of them. "And I would like to exchange toothpicks," said the other.

"Let us exchange goods with each other!" they said.

They each returned happily to the father-in-law, and told him how successful they were in their endeavors: one had traded *shofars* for toothpicks, while the other had traded toothpicks for *shofars*.

When the son-in-law heard about their transaction, he turned to his father-in-law and asked, "Why were you so angry at me? You yourself have made a business error!"

"What should *I* have done?" responded the father-in-law. "What more could be expected with such poor merchandise to sell? You, however, had the option of buying the finest merchandise available, but, instead, you chose the *worst* merchandise available!"

The heathens, concluded the Dubno *Maggid*, can exchange their gods with one another, wooden gods for stone gods and so on, for such exchanges incur neither gain nor loss.

The Jewish nation, on the other hand, "Has exchanged its Glory for something of no avail" — they exchanged the Living God for gods of wood and stone!

DEVARIM

PARASHAS DEVARIM

אֵלֶּה הַדְּבָרִים
"These are the words" (1:1)

THE WORD *HADEVARIM*, SAID THE *CHIDA* (R' YOSEF DAVID AZULAI), can also be read *hadabarim*, "the leaders."

Furthermore, the numerical value of the word *"eileh"* is thirty-six, alluding to the thirty-six *tzaddikim* that Hashem plants in every generation and in whose merit the world continues to exist. As *Chazal* state in *Maseches Sukkah* (45b), "Abaye says: There are never less than thirty-six righteous people in the world who greet the Divine Presence each day."

Who are these "leaders" to whom the verse refers? The thirty-six greatest *tzaddikim* of every generation.

❧◦❧

אֵלֶּה הַדְּבָרִים אֲשֶׁר דִּבֶּר מֹשֶׁה אֶל־כָּל־יִשְׂרָאֵל
"These are the words that Moshe spoke to all Israel" (1:1)

WHY, asked the *Megaleh Amukos* (R' Nosson Nota Shapira), does the verse state, "... that Moshe spoke to *all* Israel," and not simply, "... that Moshe spoke to Israel"?

The acronym of the word, *eileh*, he answered, is *"avak lashon hara"* ("the dust of evil speech" — subtle types of slander).

Chazal state in *Maseches Bava Basra* (165b), "Most individuals transgress the sin of theft, a small minority transgress the sin of illicit relations, but all transgress the sin of *avak lashon hara*." The grave sin of *lashon hara* is a sin that all of Israel might come to transgress, so *all Jews* must be cautioned of the danger it presents. The verse therefore states, "These are the words that Moshe spoke to *all* Israel."

אֵלֶּה הַדְּבָרִים אֲשֶׁר דִּבֶּר מֹשֶׁה אֶל־כָּל־יִשְׂרָאֵל

"These are the words that Moshe spoke to all Israel" (1:1)

On this verse, Rashi comments: "Because these are words of rebuke, and he is here listing all the places where they provoked the Omnipresent, he therefore expressed these matters vaguely and referred to them only through allusion—out of Israel's honor."

On one occasion, a *darshan* visited the city of Berdichev and proceeded to deliver a fiery *derashah* in which he harshly rebuked the congregation.

Among the people who came to hear the speaker was the consummate defender of the Jewish people, R' Levi Yitzchak of Berdichev. When the *darshan* finished speaking, R' Levi Yitzchak approached him and told him, "Now that you have admonished the congregation for their sins against their Father in Heaven, the time has come to beseech Our Father in Heaven to have mercy on His nation that suffers so horribly in this long and brutal exile. Let us pray to Hashem until we arouse His mercy for His people.

"Moshe *Rabbeinu* only uttered words of reproach," continued the *rebbe*, "when he was speaking to the Jewish people, as the verse states, 'These are the words that Moshe spoke to all Israel.' And even then, he only intimated and hinted his reproof.

"But when Moshe spoke to the Holy One, he did not mention the sins of the Jewish people. On the contrary, when he spoke to the Holy One, he lauded them and spoke highly of their fine character traits, in order to evoke Hashem's mercy for His nation."

❦

אֵלֶּה הַדְּבָרִים אֲשֶׁר דִּבֶּר מֹשֶׁה אֶל־כָּל־יִשְׂרָאֵל

"These are the words that Moshe spoke to all Israel" (1:1)

The *Yalkut Shimoni* states in relation to this verse: "This teaches us that they were all capable of enduring reproof."

The *Ba'al Shem Tov* was residing in a certain town for Shabbos. A *maggid* was scheduled to speak in the *shul*. As soon as the *maggid* ascended the podium, he began to offer harsh rebuke to the audience.

When the *Ba'al Shem Tov* heard the words of the *maggid*, he stood up and left the *shul*.

When the audience saw that the *Ba'al Shem Tov* had left, they too, walked out, and the *maggid* was forced to end his lecture early.

Afterwards, the *maggid* approached the *Ba'al Shem Tov* and asked him why he had walked out of his *derashah*.

"Is it possible," responded the *Ba'al Shem Tov*, "for a Jew to stand in a *shul* before a holy congregation and speak *lashon hara* against the Jewish people?

"Do you have any idea how beloved the Jewish nation is to Hashem?" he continued. "Consider the Jew who has spent his entire day in the marketplace trying to earn a living. As sunset draws near, he suddenly remembers, '*Oy!* I am late for *Minchah!*' and he runs to *shul* and prays. Let us say that the quality of his prayer was not very high, still, do you have any idea just how great an influence such a prayer has in Heaven?

"At that moment, all of the *Seraphim* and *Ofanim* start to tremble."

שְׁמֹעַ בֵּין־אֲחֵיכֶם וּשְׁפַטְתֶּם צֶדֶק
"Listen [to every dispute] among your brethren, and judge honestly" (1:16)

Even as a child, R' Yonasan Eybeschutz was recognized for his brilliance. When he reached the age of 13 and became a barmitzvah, he was approached by one of the finest scholars in his town, who asked him, "Please tell me; it is well known that a child possesses a *yetzer hara* from the day he enters the world but that he does not obtain a *yetzer tov* until he turns 13. That being the case, how were you able to surmount your *yetzer hara* all these years?"

"In this week's *parashah* it states," answered the young R' Eybeschutz, "'Listen [to every dispute] among your brethren, and judge honestly.' From this verse, *Chazal* (*Sanhedrin* 7b) derive that a judge may not listen to the testimony of one of the litigants before the other one has arrived.

"I simply acted according to the words of *Chazal!*" responded R' Eybeschutz. "Whenever my *yetzer hara* would begin to state his claims before me, I would tell him, 'Wait until the second litigant — the *yetzer tov* — arrives! Only after you have both presented your claims will I decide which one of you is correct!'"

✿❀✿

שָׁמֹעַ בֵּין־אֲחֵיכֶם וּשְׁפַטְתֶּם צֶדֶק בֵּין־אִישׁ וּבֵין־אָחִיו וּבֵין גֵּרוֹ:

"Listen [to every dispute] among your brethren, and judge honestly between each man and his brother or his litigant" (1:16)

A merchant purchased a large quantity of wine in Hungary and, with the help of his assistant, transported it to Prague. On *erev Shabbos*, they stopped at an inn and began to prepare for Shabbos. The assistant wanted to protect his money from being stolen, so he hid his money among the barrels of wine.

His mind was so preoccupied with hiding the money, however, that he did not notice that his employer, the merchant, had followed him and saw where the money was hidden. After the assistant walked away, the merchant came in and stole the money.

On *motza'ei Shabbos*, the assistant returned for the money, but lo! it was gone!

He quickly concluded that the merchant must have been the thief, and he had him summoned to a *din Torah* before R' Yechezkel Landau of Prague (the *Noda B'Yehudah*).

When the merchant arrived at R' Landau's home, he began to shout, "Is this how my assistant repays me for all the good that I have bestowed upon him all these years — by calling me a thief?"

"Please forgive me, sir," said the *rav*. "I can clearly see that you are an upstanding and upright individual. I certainly do not suspect that you stole the money; rather, it was surely one of the gentile wagon drivers who perpetrated the crime."

"The *rav* must be correct," agreed the merchant happily.

"That being the case," concluded R' Landau, "you are completely absolved from paying your assistant anything at all, and you are free to return home. However ... you are required to pour out all of the wine in your possession."

"Pour out all of my wine?" yelled the merchant, "Whatever for? I will incur a tremendous loss!"

"I understand," replied the *rav*. "But if indeed it was a gentile who made off with your money, it is likely that he touched one of your wine barrels in the process, giving the wine the status of *yayin nesech*! [Wine of an idol-worshiper, from which it is forbidden to derive benefit.] All of the wine is therefore prohibited to you, and it must be spilled out accordingly!"

When the merchant heard the ruling, he began to cry and immediately admitted his guilt, saying that he was prepared to return the money.

"I do not believe you!" responded R' Landau. "For *Chazal* state, 'A person cannot establish himself to be a wicked person.' If a person admits to committing a certain sin, we do not believe him. Besides, how do I know that you are not simply trying to save your wine?"

The merchant began to provide proof that he was the actual thief, but the *rav* was unwilling to believe him unless he would go to the town *shul* and swear publicly that he was the thief. In addition, he would have to agree to pay a fine that would be determined by R' Landau.

The merchant agreed and acted accordingly, and only then did the *rav* permit his wine for use.

וּשְׁפַטְתֶּם צֶדֶק בֵּין־אִישׁ וּבֵין־אָחִיו וּבֵין גֵּרוֹ:
"And judge honestly between each man and his brother or his litigant" (1:16)

Two men appeared before R' Yechezkel Landau in a *din Torah*. One man was dressed like a simple wagon driver, the other was clad in regal attire.

The first individual tearfully related his account of what had happened to him:

"I am a wheat merchant from a distant city, and I wanted to sell my wheat in Prague. I therefore hired a wagon driver to help me transport the wheat.

"But," the man continued, "in the middle of our trip, the wagon driver attacked me and stole all of my money. In addition, he even forced me to switch my clothing with him. Once I was dressed as a poor wagon driver, he forced me to drive the horse-drawn wagon into Prague.

"When we arrived in Prague," cried the merchant, "the wagon driver pretended that *he* was the successful merchant. Now I am left without a *perutah* in my pocket, and no one believes a word I say."

R' Landau turned to the lavishly dressed man. "And what have you to say?" he asked.

"This man has unfortunately lost his mind," he replied. "For two days now, he has followed me around the city, demanding his money."

The *rav* thoroughly interrogated the two men, but each one stood firm in his claim.

"Come back tomorrow morning," he told them. "At that time, I will provide you with a ruling."

After the men left, R' Landau called his attendant and instructed him not to allow the men into his study the next day, no matter what the circumstances might be.

The next day, the men arrived and attempted to enter the *rav's* study. "I apologize," said the attendant. "But you may not enter the *rav*'s study; he is very busy at the moment."

The two men sat down to wait. One hour passed, and then two, but R' Landau's door remained shut. The afternoon had arrived and there was absolutely no indication that the *rav* was coming out any time soon. It was as if he had completely forgotten about them.

The sun had set and the men had grown tired. Suddenly, the door to the study opened, and in a loud voice, R' Landau announced, "The wagon driver may enter!"

Eager to finally enter the *rav's* study, the man in the elegant attire rose to his feet and hurriedly walked toward the door.

"You wicked man!" exclaimed R' Landau. "You are the true wagon driver; you are a thief! Return this man's money at once!"

כַּקָּטֹן כַּגָּדֹל תִּשְׁמָעוּן
"Listen to the great and small alike" (1:17)

Rashi explains: "A case involving the value of a *perutah* [the least valuable of coins] shall be as dear to you as a case [involving the value] of 100 *maneh*."

Gedolei Yisrael have always been extra cautious when dealing with money that belongs to others, so as not to violate the grave sin of stealing.

R' Elchanan Wasserman was once traveling in a wagon that was headed for Vilna. One of the yeshivah students also wished to travel to

Vilna, but he couldn't afford the fare. What did he do? He walked until he was outside the city and waited for the wagon to pass by. When it did, he hopped aboard the wagon, and, with the help of several of the passengers, climbed inside without the wagon driver noticing.

When R' Wasserman saw this, he asked the passengers, "What permission did you have to help this young man board the wagon without paying?"

"The driver probably doesn't mind," they replied.

"The question here is not merely one of monetary law," explained R' Wasserman. "The issue is not whether this young man was permitted to do what he did or not. The question is far more severe: Will you all be sentenced to the flames of *Gehinnom* for stealing a *perutah* or not?"

לֹא תָגוּרוּ מִפְּנֵי־אִישׁ
"You shall not fear any man" (1:17)

A disagreement once broke out in the city of Radin, and it eventually escalated into a bitter feud. The situation deteriorated to such a degree that the two parties actually raised their hands against each other.

The *Chofetz Chaim* tried his utmost to settle the dispute and declared that anyone who would so much as lift a hand against his fellow Jew would be excommunicated.

One of the men involved in the fight was a strong and arrogant individual who paid no heed to the *Chofetz Chaim*'s pronouncement and once again struck at a member of the opposing camp. He even had the audacity to state that whoever would try to excommunicate him would pay a dear price.

Because of the man's violent nature, the leaders of the community were reluctant to excommunicate him. The *Chofetz Chaim*, however, was not afraid to do so. He ascended the *bimah* and proclaimed, "As the Torah exhorts us, 'You shall not fear any man,' I hereby excommunicate so-and-so until he repents!"

When the man heard the *Chofetz Chaim*'s announcement, he became frightened and immediately repented.

וַיִּיטַב בְּעֵינַי הַדָּבָר וָאֶקַּח מִכֶּם שְׁנֵים עָשָׂר אֲנָשִׁים

"I approved and appointed twelve men" (1:23)

If sending spies was good in Moshe's eyes, asks Rashi, why did he rebuke the Jewish people for doing so?

Rashi answers this question by way of a parable: There once was a man who asked his friend to sell him his donkey, and the owner of the donkey agreed.

The first man then asked, "Would you agree to let me try it first?"

"Yes!" he answered.

"Can I try it on the mountains and the hills?" he then asked.

"To this, as well, I agree," he replied.

The seller is agreeing to all of my requests, thought the buyer. *The donkey must be in perfect condition, otherwise he would not be so willing.*

With that, he handed the money to the owner, and said, "Give me your donkey. I have no need to try it!"

Similarly, Moshe agreed to send spies as he thought, *When they see that I am not refusing their request, they will understand that the land is good and flawless.*

But the Jews did not retract their request and nevertheless insisted on sending spies. That is why Moshe rebuked them

PARASHAS VA'ESCHANAN

וָאֶתְחַנַּן אֶל־ה'

"I implored Hashem" (3:23)

THE MIDRASH STATES THAT MOSHE OFFERED FIVE HUNDRED AND FIF-teen prayers to Hashem in order to be allowed to enter the Land! This is alluded to in the word "*Va'eschanan*," whose numerical value is five hundred and fifteen.

Not only does the word "*Va'eschanan*" equal five hundred and fifteen, noted the *Chasam Sofer* (R' Moshe Sofer), but so does the word "*tefillah*" (prayer).

Furthermore, if we add twenty-six — the numerical value of the ineffable Name of Hashem (*yud, hei, vav, hei*) — to the number five hundred and fifteen, we will get five hundred and forty-one — the numerical value of the word *Yisrael*!

❧

לֹא תֹסִפוּ עַל־הַדָּבָר אֲשֶׁר אָנֹכִי מְצַוֶּה אֶתְכֶם
וְלֹא תִגְרְעוּ מִמֶּנּוּ לִשְׁמֹר אֶת־מִצְוֹת ה'

"You must not add to the word that I command you, nor subtract from it, so as to safeguard the commandments of Hashem" (4:2)

To what can this be compared? asked R' Yonasan Eybeschutz — to an individual who became ill and developed a stomachache.

When the doctor examined him, he immediately saw which illness the man was suffering from and prescribed the appropriate medication for treating the ailment.

"Take one spoon of this medicine in the morning and another at night," he instructed the patient.

When the man obtained the medicine, he was overjoyed. *I will soon be healed*, he thought.

He quickly opened the cap and gulped down all the medicine in the bottle!

Needless to say, the man seriously harmed himself by drinking all of it at once.

Similarly, concluded R' Eybeschutz, just as every patient understands that he must take only the amount of medicine prescribed by his physician, so too, we must understand that we must not add or subtract from the *mitzvos* that Hashem has commanded us.

לֹא תֹסִפוּ עַל־הַדָּבָר אֲשֶׁר אָנֹכִי מְצַוֶּה אֶתְכֶם
וְלֹא תִגְרְעוּ מִמֶּנּוּ לִשְׁמֹר אֶת־מִצְוֹת ה'

**"You must not add to the word that I
command you, nor subtract from it, so as to
safeguard the commandments of Hashem" (4:2)**

The Dubno *Maggid* explained this verse by way of a parable: An individual went to his neighbor and asked to borrow a spoon. The next day, he returned the spoon he had borrowed together with another small spoon.

"Why are you giving me *two* spoons?" asked his neighbor. "I only loaned you one."

"That is correct," responded his friend. "But you see, the spoon which you had loaned me was pregnant — and it gave birth."

The neighbor realized that his friend's mind had become unstable, but he nonetheless accepted the two spoons without comment.

Several days later, the friend returned and asked to borrow a cup. The neighbor lent him the cup and, surely enough, the friend gave back not one but two cups, claiming that the cup had given birth to a smaller version. The neighbor silently accepted the two cups.

Several days passed, and the neighbor was once again approached by his friend. This time, he requested to borrow a pair of silver candlesticks. *The fool,* thought the neighbor, *will surely give me back four candlesticks. I will happily loan them to him.*

Several days later, when the neighbor saw that his candlesticks had not been returned, he complained to his friend: "Where are my silver candlesticks? Why have you not returned them?"

"I am sorry," responded the friend, "but your candlesticks have passed away."

"Passed away?" yelled the neighbor. "Who has ever heard of candlesticks passing away?"

"My dear sir," responded the friend. "Who has ever heard of a spoon or a cup that gave birth? Yet when I gave you two spoons, you took them without saying a word.

"Now if a spoon can give birth, than a candlestick can most certainly pass away."

With this, we can understand the aforementioned verse, concluded the Dubno *Maggid*. An individual must perform Hashem's *mitzvos* with utmost precision, for if he begins to add to the *mitzvos*, he will eventually come to subtract from them.

✧⌘✧

כִּי הוּא חָכְמַתְכֶם וּבִינַתְכֶם לְעֵינֵי הָעַמִּים
"For [through] this you [will be considered] wise and intelligent in the eyes of the nations" (4:6)

I n Tunis, there were two Arab farmers whose fields shared a common border. The border was marked off with a row of fruit trees.

On one occasion, one of the neighbors journeyed to another country. Upon returning home, he discovered that his neighbor had uprooted the fruit trees that had marked the boundary between the two fields, and, worse, he had stolen a significant portion of his property.

The Arab took his neighbor to the local judge in their district, but the judge did not know how to determine who was right. He therefore sent the case to a higher-ranking judge, but he too did not know how to rule. The case went from one judge to another, until it was finally brought before the king.

The king summoned the two men to hear their claims. Both men had compelling arguments, so — much to his embarrassment — the king himself could not resolve the dispute.

With no choice left, the king summoned R' Yitzchak Teib, one of the great rabbis of Tunis.

After listening to their claims, R' Teib turned to the Arab whose property had been stolen and asked, "Tell me, do you happen to own a mule?"

"Yes, I do," responded the Arab.

"Then please take me to your home," said R' Teib.

When they arrived at the Arab's house, the *rav* took hold of the mule and led it out to the field. The *rav* was about to use a fact that many people know: A mule will not enter a field that it is not familiar with.

R' Teib let go of the reins and the mule began to run freely through the field. Suddenly it came to an abrupt halt.

They walked over to where the mule had stopped, and the *rav* ordered, "Dig here. I am certain that you will find the evidence you need."

The Arab and his family began to dig, and they soon uncovered the remaining roots of the uprooted fruit trees.

"This is where the boundary was," concluded R' Teib, "and it is irrefutable proof to your claim."

Word of the case spread throughout Tunis, and all those who heard about it praised the wisdom of the Jewish rabbi.

⚜

וְנִשְׁמַרְתֶּם מְאֹד לְנַפְשֹׁתֵיכֶם
"Watch yourselves very carefully" (4:15)

As a youth, R' Yechezkel Abramsky was sent to Siberia. The cold was unbearable, and temperatures dropped to as low as 40 degrees below zero.

Wearing only light clothing, young Yechezkel stood in line along with the other Jews who had been exiled to that forsaken part of the world. They were all trembling from the cold.

"Listen, Jews!" shouted the commanding officer. "Every morning, you are to remove your shoes and run barefoot in the snow for the duration of an hour. Anyone who dares violate this order with be severely punished!"

R' Abramsky, who was a weak and frail youth, was frightened by this cruel order. Back at his warm home, his loving mother had always tended to him, dressing him in warm clothing and scarves, but now he would have to run barefoot in the snow!

He lifted his eyes to Heaven and pleaded with Hashem, "Master of the World," he said, "You have exhorted us in Your holy Torah, 'Watch yourselves very carefully.' In truth, man is usually able to take care of his health by wearing warm clothing, but here in this Siberian labor camp, we are unable to do so. We therefore cannot be held responsible for our health. I therefore beg of You, Master of the World, watch over us and protect us!"

Amazingly, throughout his entire stay in Siberia, R' Abramsky did not get sick even once.

וְשַׁבְתָּ עַד־ה׳ אֱלֹקֶיךָ וְשָׁמַעְתָּ בְּקֹלוֹ:
"You will return to Hashem, your God, and heed His voice" (4:30)

R' Yisrael Salanter was returning home very late one night. As he walked through the dark alleyways, he suddenly noticed that a light was still burning in the home of the shoemaker. He knocked on the door and entered his home.

"Why are you still sitting and working at such a late hour?" asked R' Salanter.

"As long as the candle burns," replied the shoemaker, "it is still possible to repair."

Those words made a great impression upon R' Salanter and, from then on, he repeated them on many occasions.

"Do you hear?" R' Salanter would ask. "As long as the candle burns, it is still possible to repair! As long as a person is alive and his soul is within him, he can still repent and rectify his deeds."

וְיָדַעְתָּ הַיּוֹם וַהֲשֵׁבֹתָ אֶל־לְבָבֶךָ
"You shall realize it today and impress it upon your heart" (4:39)

The *Chofetz Chaim* once traveled to the city where his *sefarim* were being printed.

When he arrived at the printing press, the *Chofetz Chaim* observed a young boy working vigorously.

"How old are you?" asked the *Chofetz Chaim*.

"Fifteen years old," was the boy's response.

"Do you earn a decent living from your work?" he asked.

"The truth is," said the boy, "I am presently not earning very much money at all, and I make just enough to cover my most basic living expenses. However, in another five or six years, after having mastered the skill of printing, I will open my own printing press. Then I will earn enough to live like a wealthy man."

The *Chofetz Chaim* was amazed by the words of this young boy, and upon returning home, he related them to a crowd that had gathered to hear him speak.

"Do you appreciate the words of this young boy?" asked the *Chofetz Chaim*. "It is worthwhile for an individual to temporarily suffer from hard labor in order to later live a life of comfort! It is worthwhile for a person to perform *mitzvos* and good deeds in this world, even if it appears difficult for him, in order to receive great reward in the World to Come. 'Today for their performance and tomorrow to receive their reward' (*Eruvin* 22a)!"

❧◊❧

אָז יַבְדִּיל מֹשֶׁה שָׁלֹשׁ עָרִים בְּעֵבֶר הַיַּרְדֵּן מִזְרָחָה
"Then Moshe set aside three cities
on the eastern side of the Jordan" (4:41)

Hashem commanded Moshe to establish six cities of refuge. If an individual killed someone without intent, he could escape to one of these cities and the relatives of the victim would not be allowed to harm him.

Of the six cities, three were located in *Eretz Yisrael* and three were located on the eastern side of the Jordan River.

Rashi comments that Moshe was aware that he would not be allowed to enter *Eretz Yisrael* and would therefore be unable to set aside the three cities of refuge of *Eretz Yisrael*. Nevertheless, he set aside the three on the eastern side of the Jordan, as he thought, *A mitzvah that has come my way — I shall fulfill.*

To what can this be compared? asked the *Chofetz Chaim* — to a young boy who was standing in the marketplace, holding a basket of apples that he wished to sell.

Suddenly, a man came over to him and began to grab the apples from the basket. Horrified, the boy screamed out with all his might, "Fellow Jews, help me!"

A wise man passed by and said to the boy, "Young man, why are you screaming? Instead of screaming, start grabbing as many apples as you can before this man leaves you with nothing."

So it is with us, remarked the *Chofetz Chaim*. There are times when a person is standing in prayer, but the *yetzer hara* refuses to leave him alone, using every means at his disposal in order to distract him. By the time this person is halfway through the prayer, he still has not been able to concentrate for even one moment.

If he is wise, he will try to "grab" the remaining words of prayer for himself, reciting them with fervent concentration. For if he does not, the *yetzer hara* will have taken the entire prayer, and he will be left with nothing.

כַּבֵּד אֶת־אָבִיךָ וְאֶת־אִמֶּךָ

"Honor your father and your mother" (5:16)

The Brisker *Rav* (R' Yitzchak Zev HaLevi Soloveitchik) was moving to a new home. When the movers arrived, they saw him standing in his room, next to a well-packed chest.

The *rav* called to one of the movers and asked, "Do you see this chest? When you carry it, please take great care that it not turn over! Carry it upright!" The mover lifted the chest, while the Brisker *Rav* observed carefully. He did not take his eyes off the chest until it reached his new home.

One of his students summoned the nerve to ask: "*Rebbe*," he began, "why did the chest have to be kept upright? What is in the chest?"

"This chest," answered the Brisker *Rav*, "contains the *chiddushei Torah* (novel Torah ideas) of may father as well as my own. Obviously, my father's *chiddushei Torah*, which are far greater than mine, are placed on top. If, God forbid," concluded the *rav*, "the mover would have turned over the box, my writings would have been on top of my father's, and that would have been a lack of respect toward my father!"

וְאָהַבְתָּ אֵת ה' אֱלֹקֶיךָ

"You shall love Hashem, your God" (6:5)

Every individual, remarked the Dubno *Maggid*, is required to love Hashem with all his heart. In order to do this, he must remove all negative and sinful thoughts from his heart.

To what can this be compared? — to a farmer who arrived in a city on the market day and quickly sold all of his merchandise.

Now that he had a large sum of money in his possession, he decided to buy himself an elegant outfit, the type customarily worn by the city dwellers. He entered a store that sold expensive silk garments, and was given one to try on. The garment seemed too small, however, as the farmer was unable to get his arm into the sleeve.

"The garment that you have given me is too small," said the farmer to the storeowner.

"The garment is exactly your size," laughed the storeowner, "but before you try it on, you must first remove your heavy farmer's outfit."

Only after a man removes all the wicked thoughts from his heart, explained the *maggid*, can there be room in his heart to love Hashem properly.

: וְאָהַבְתָּ אֵת ה' אֱלֹקֶיךָ בְּכָל־לְבָבְךָ וּבְכָל־נַפְשְׁךָ וּבְכָל־מְאֹדֶךָ

"You shall love Hashem, your God, with all your heart, with all your soul, and with all your resources" (6:5)

R' Moshe Feinstein and one of his students set out to collect money for an important public cause. After several hours, the student sensed that the elderly *tzaddik* was tired from the day's exertion. He therefore suggested that they stop for the day and return home.

"A *mitzvah* has presented itself to me," replied R' Feinstein, "and I will not allow it slip away."

The student tried a different approach: "*Rebbe*," he began, "there has not been very much time to study Torah today. Let us conclude for now and return to our Torah study."

"My dear student," responded R' Feinstein. "The Torah states, 'You shall love Hashem, your God, with all your heart, with all your soul, and with all your resources.' *Chazal* teach us that one must sacrifice everything that he has for the sake of serving Hashem — his heart, his soul, and even that which he loves with all his being.

"Now what is more beloved to me than anything else?" he continued, "Studying the holy Torah! Even this I am willing to sacrifice for a *mitzvah* that pertains to *Klal Yisrael*."

וְדִבַּרְתָּ בָּם ... וּבְלֶכְתְּךָ בַדֶּרֶךְ
"You shall speak about them ...
when you travel along the way" (6:7)

The *Chofetz Chaim* was traveling on the road late at night. Glancing over at the wagon driver, the *Chofetz Chaim* noticed that he had almost dozed off.

"Are you sleeping?" asked the *Chofetz Chaim*.

The driver replied that he was not.

"You know," continued the *Chofetz Chaim*, "it is worthwhile for every individual to memorize a certain amount of *mishnayos* by heart. For when he grows older, he may lose his eyesight and no longer be able to read from a *sefer*. If he memorizes *mishnayos*, however, he will be able to learn whenever he pleases.

"Let us now learn *mishnayos* together," said the *Chofetz Chaim* to the wagon driver. "I will read and you can listen."

The wagon driver listened as the *Chofetz Chaim* began reciting various chapters of *mishnayos* — together with the commentary of R' Ovadiah MiBartenura and the *Tosafos Yom Tov* — by heart.

The wagon driver assumed that the *tzaddik* would recite only a few chapters of *mishnayos*, but the *Chofetz Chaim* continued reciting one chapter after another until dawn had broken.

PARASHAS EIKEV

וְלֹא־תָבִיא תוֹעֵבָה אֶל־בֵּיתֶךָ
"You must not bring an abomination
into your home" (7:26)

THIS VERSE TEACHES US, NOTED R' LEVI YITZCHAK OF BERDICHEV, just how despicable the trait of arrogance truly is. It is so abhorred that one is forbidden to even allow a haughty individual to enter his home. We learn this from a verse in *Mishlei*, "Every haughty heart is the abomination of Hashem" (16:5). We, see, therefore, that a haughty individual is referred to as an "abomination," about which our verse explicitly states, "And you must not bring an abomination into your home."

וְאָכַלְתָּ וְשָׂבָעְתָּ וּבֵרַכְתָּ אֶת־ה' ...
"You will eat and be satisfied, and then you shall bless Hashem ..." (8:10)

A chassid of R' Yitzchak of Vorka came to visit him. The *chassid* was a very wealthy man, but he was known as a miser. Despite his enormous wealth, he lived his entire life subsisting on no more than black bread and salted fish, as he loathed the thought of having to spend money.

R' Yitzchak offered the man sound rebuke: "If Hashem has given you wealth," he said, "then you should live comfortably! Your meals should consist of meat, fish, and old wine!"

"Why does the *rebbe* care if this man chooses to eat like a pauper?" asked the other *chassidim*. "Is this man's diet really of such concern to the *rebbe*?"

"Do you think that it is *he* I am worried about?" responded R' Yitzchak. "Absolutely not! I am worried about the poor man who will knock on this man's door asking for food. If he will dine on meat, fish, and wine, then he will at least give the poor man black bread and salted fish. But if he himself chooses to eat like a pauper, what do you think he will give the poor man?"

הִשָּׁמֶר לְךָ פֶּן־תִּשְׁכַּח אֶת־ה' אֱלֹקֶיךָ
"Be careful that you do not forget Hashem, your God" (8:11)

R' Simchah Bunim of P'shischa entered the study of his *rebbe*, R' Yitzchak Yaakov of Lublin (the *Chozeh*, "the Seer"), and saw him pacing back and forth worriedly.

"*Rebbe*," asked R' Simchah Bunim, "why are you so worried?"

"For a brief moment," answered the *Chozeh*, "I took my mind off Hashem and thereby violated the commandment, 'Be careful that you do not forget Hashem, your God.' Oh, what shall I do?"

"*Chazal* offer the following ruling with regard to the *mitzvah* of 'forgetting,'" responded R' Simchah Bunim. "If a man forgets a bundle the size of two *se'ah* in his field, it is not included in the law of 'forgetting.' Since the bundle is so large, it is obvious that the owner will remember it and return to reclaim it. It is considered as if he never forgot it in the first place.

"The same thing applies to the *rebbe*," said R' Simchah Bunim. "A momentary lapse in thinking about Hashem cannot truly be considered as having forgotten Him. For *HaKadosh Baruch Hu* is so infinitely important that even if He is forgotten for a moment, He will immediately be remembered!"

וְאָמַרְתָּ בִּלְבָבֶךָ כֹּחִי וְעֹצֶם יָדִי עָשָׂה לִי אֶת־הַחַיִל הַזֶּה:
"And you say in your heart, 'My strength and the power of my hand amassed this wealth for me'" (8:17)

A wealthy wood merchant approached R' Chaim of Volozhin and told him that he was in danger of losing his entire fortune.

"Why is your fortune at risk?" asked R' Chaim.

The merchant related his story: "I sent a large ship carrying wood to Prussia," he explained. "The Prussian authorities, however, are not allowing my merchandise into their country. They have warned me that should the ship not turn around, they will sink the ship and all of my precious cargo along with it!"

"Do not worry!" responded R' Chaim. "You will see, Hashem's salvation comes in the blink of an eye!"

That same day, the price of wood increased significantly, and, to the merchant's good fortune, the Prussian authorities also allowed his ship to enter their country.

The overjoyed merchant ran over to R' Chaim. "*Rebbe*," he said, "today I have witnessed the hand of Divine Providence! I now realize that the government's unwillingness to allow my ship to enter their country was all for the best. For had it been permitted to enter any earlier, I would have received a lower price for my wood. Hashem saw to it, however, that my ship would not enter Prussia any earlier so that I would reap far greater profits."

"You now see the difference between a rich man and a poor man," sighed R' Chaim. "A poor man sees Hashem's guiding Hand each and every day. But a rich man, who is certain that his wealth stems from his own abilities and strengths, only notices Hashem's Providence once every few years."

וְעַתָּה יִשְׂרָאֵל מָה ה' אֱלֹקֶיךָ שֹׁאֵל מֵעִמָּךְ

"Now, O Israel, what does Hashem, your God, ask of you?" (10:12)

A former student of the *Netziv* (R' Naftali Tzvi Yehudah Berlin of Volozhin) came to visit him.

"What do you do?" asked the *Netziv*.

"*Baruch Hashem, Rebbe*," answered the student, "I am healthy and make a comfortable living." In fact, the man had become very wealthy over the years.

The conversation continued until the *Netziv* asked once again, "And what do you do?"

"*Baruch Hashem*," repeated the student a second time, "I earn a comfortable living, and my health is good —"

"I am asking you what it is that *you* do," exclaimed the *Netziv*, "and you keep responding with what Hashem is doing for you! Let me ask you again: What do you do for Hashem? Do you set aside time during the day to study Torah? Do you give the proper amount of charity ...?"

וּלְאַהֲבָה אֹתוֹ וְלַעֲבֹד אֶת־ה' אֱלֹקֶיךָ בְּכָל־לְבָבְךָ וּבְכָל־נַפְשֶׁךָ:

"To love Him, and to serve Hashem, your God, with all your heart and with all your soul" (10:12)

The *Chiddushei HaRim* (R' Yitzchak Meir Alter of Gur) met with an individual who had stolen funds designated for the public's welfare.

"Murderer!" shouted the *Chiddushei HaRim* with all his might. "Know that you are a murderer!"

"*Rebbe*," asked his *chassidim* in bewilderment. "Why do you call this man a murderer? He is a thief, not a murderer!"

"In the first section of the *Shema*," answered the *rebbe*, "it states, 'with all your heart, with all your soul, and with all your resources.' *Chazal* (*Berachos* 54a) explain that the words, 'with all your resources,' refers to an individual's money.

"Yet in the second section," continued the *rebbe*, "it states, 'with all your heart and with all your soul,' but 'with all your resources' is not mentioned. What is the reason for this discrepancy?

"In the second section," answered the *Chiddushei HaRim*, "the Torah is addressing the public, as is implied by the words, '*levavchem*' ('your heart,' plural) and '*nafshechem*' ('your soul,' plural). Why is 'with all your resources' — which refers to money — not mentioned? It is because the public's money is included in the phrase, 'with all your soul'! Money that is designated for charity and is meant to find its way into the hands of starving paupers, widows, and orphans is literally a matter of life and death! Someone who steals this money can therefore accurately be called a murderer!"

וְעָצַר אֶת־הַשָּׁמַיִם וְלֹא־יִהְיֶה מָטָר
"He will restrain the heavens so there will be no rain" (11:17)

A terrible drought had stricken the land, and not a cloud could be seen in the sky. It did not appear as if rain would fall anytime soon. *Gedolei Yisrael* therefore called upon the masses to fast and pray fervently — perhaps the harsh decree could be annulled.

In the *beis midrash* of R' Yisrael *Ba'al Shem Tov*, a very large crowd had gathered to beseech Hashem for His mercy. The *Ba'al Shem Tov* observed a simple man reciting the *Shema* with intense concentration. When he reached the verse, "He will restrain the heavens so there will be no rain," he burst into heartfelt weeping.

"Tell me," asked the *Ba'al Shem Tov* after the prayers had concluded, "what were your intentions when you said the words, 'He will restrain the heavens so there will be no rain'?"

"I am but a simple man," he responded, "and I do not pray with very lofty intentions. I simply asked Hashem to 'squeeze' (*ve'atzar*) the sky in the same manner that we squeeze olives and grapes. This way, the rain will not stay in the heavens, but will descend to the earth."

The *Ba'al Shem Tov* was amazed by the simple words of this Jew, and he told the man: "It would be fitting for rain to fall in the merit of your sincere prayer!"

Toward evening, the sky filled with clouds and rain of blessing indeed began to fall.

וְשַׂמְתֶּם אֶת־דְּבָרַי אֵלֶּה עַל־לְבַבְכֶם וְעַל נַפְשְׁכֶם
"You shall impress these words of Mine upon your hearts and upon your souls" (11:18)

During World War II, the students of the Mir Yeshivah escaped to Shanghai, China in a miraculous fashion. The few Jews that lived in Shanghai were elated to have the Mir Yeshivah in their midst, and they tried their utmost to make their stay in China as comfortable as possible. They gave them the large *shul* building for a study hall and other dwellings for living quarters.

There was a significant lack of *sefarim*, but the few volumes that the boys of the yeshivah had managed to take with them provided much satisfaction and enjoyment. One of the students had managed to bring with him a copy of the *Ketzos HaChoshen*, but much to the dismay of his fellow students, two pages of the *sefer* were missing.

When R' Chaim Shmulevitz heard of their predicament, he sat down and wrote out the two missing pages *from memory*.

After the war, R' Shmulevitz's version was compared with a printed *Ketzos* and, to everyone's amazement, the two versions were identical — down to the very last word!

וְלִמַּדְתֶּם אֹתָם אֶת־בְּנֵיכֶם לְדַבֵּר בָּם
"You shall teach them to your children so that they speak about them" (11:19)

In the summer of 5652 (1892), the Russian government decreed that all Torah institutions were required to include two hours of secular studies in their daily schedule. Any institution that failed to comply with this law would be shut down.

The *rosh yeshivah* of the Volozhin Yeshivah, R' Naftali Tzvi Yehudah Berlin (the *Netziv*), was afraid to take the responsibility for such a weighty matter upon himself. He therefore organized a gathering of *gedolei Yisrael* so they could decide together how to respond to the decree.

Most of the assembly's participants felt that there was no other choice but to add secular studies to the curriculum, but the *Beis HaLevi* (R' Yosef Dov HaLevi Soloveitchik) was of a different opinion. With tears streaming down his cheeks, he addressed the assembly:

"*Morai v'rabosai!*" he began. "While we are required to teach the holy Torah to our students, we are only obligated to transmit it in the way that the previous generations bequeathed it to us. To establish a new path of Torah study, one that incorporates secular studies as well as our holy Torah, is far too great a responsibility for us to bear. I say that we must close the doors of the yeshivah. Let the One Who has given the Torah do what He has to do!"

From here we can see, remarked the *Chofetz Chaim*, the foresight and profundity of the *gedolei hador*. For had they agreed to allow secular subjects to penetrate the yeshivah's walls, that which was primary and that which was secondary would have been reversed over the years. Secular subjects would be studied the bulk of the day, while the Torah would be relegated no more than two hours. If such a thing would have transpired, not a trace of the holy Torah would remain, God forbid.

The decision to close the Volozhin Yeshivah, however, paved the road for new pathways of Torah to develop in *yeshivos* located in Lithuania and Poland.

Indeed, concluded the *Chofetz Chaim*, the One Who has given the Torah did what He had to do.

וְלִמַּדְתֶּם אֹתָם אֶת־בְּנֵיכֶם לְדַבֵּר בָּם
**"You shall teach them to your children
so that they speak about them" (11:19)**

When the *Ridbaz* (R' Yaakov David Willowsky) was a youth, his father hired the city's finest tutor to teach him Torah. The tutor, R' Chaim Sender, used to charge one ruble a month — a high salary in those days.

The *Ridbaz's* father was a poor man who supported his family by building ovens, and he was finding it increasingly difficult to afford the tutor's wages. Yet he tried as hard as he could to pay the monthly fee, just so that his son could receive the best Torah education possible.

One winter, there was a severe shortage of bricks, making oven construction impossible. Left without a livelihood, the *Ridbaz's* father was simply unable to pay the tutor. After three months had passed, the tutor informed them that if he was not compensated, he would be forced to stop teaching the child.

His father was greatly distressed by the tutor's words. What did he do? He dismantled the oven in their own home and rebuilt it in the house of one of the wealthy men of the town. He was paid 6 rubles for his work and he immediately sent them to R' Chaim Sender, who was duly compensated for the past three months as well as the coming three months.

That winter was a difficult one, and the *Ridbaz's* home was freezing, but his parents' hearts were filled with joy knowing that their son was studying Torah and developing into a Torah scholar.

וּכְתַבְתָּם עַל־מְזוּזוֹת בֵּיתֶךָ וּבִשְׁעָרֶיךָ:

לְמַעַן יִרְבּוּ יְמֵיכֶם וִימֵי בְנֵיכֶם

"And you shall write them on the doorposts of your house and on your gates. This is so that you and your children live long lives" (11:20-21)

Upon emigrating to *Eretz Yisrael*, R' Yehoshua Leib Diskin founded an orphanage in Yerushalayim that bears his name until this very day.

On one occasion, he called upon a group of *sofrim* (scribes) to go from house to house and check all the *mezuzos* on the homes of Yerushalayim in order to make sure they were kosher.

"Your payment will be taken from the orphanage fund," he told them.

His close students were surprised. "*Rebbe,*" they asked, "Why did the *rav* tell the *sofrim* that he will pay them from the orphanage fund — is the fund not practically empty as it is?"

"In the Torah it states," answered R' Diskin, 'And you shall write them on the doorposts of your house and upon your gates.' In the very next verse it says, 'In order to prolong your days.' The *mitzvah* of *mezuzah* is rewarded with long life!

"We see, then, that there is a clear connection between the *kashrus* of a *mezuzah* and an orphanage; for if *mezuzos* are kosher, then people will live longer, guaranteeing fewer orphans in the world. This is why the *sofrim* will be paid from the orphanage fund."

PARASHAS RE'EH

בָּנִים אַתֶּם לַה׳ אֱלֹקֵיכֶם
"You are children to Hashem, your God" (14:1)

A SIMPLE MAN ONCE APPROACHED THE *CHOFETZ CHAIM* AND ASKED, "*Rebbe*, why must there be different groups of Jews in the world? For example, there are *chassidim* and there are *misnagdim*; some Jews focus primarily on prayer, others on Torah study, and yet others dedicate their Divine service on serving Hashem with joy. Why is it necessary to have so many different divisions within Judaism?"

"Why are you asking me?" questioned the *Chofetz Chaim*. "Go and ask the Russian czar why he needs so many different divisions of soldiers in his army. For instance, there are soldiers who fight on horses, soldiers who man the cannons, pilots, sailors, and infantrymen!

"The czar would undoubtedly answer," continued the *Chofetz Chaim*, "that each group of soldiers is essential for his army, for each unit contributes in a different way and serves a unique purpose. Infantrymen are not equipped with the skills necessary to wage aerial combat. A soldier adept at manning a cannon is unique in that he can target enemies that are long distances away. Even the soldiers in the army's band serve a unique purpose, as they lift the spirits of the soldiers at war."

"This is the reason," concluded the *Chofetz Chaim*, "that the Jewish people have also been divided into many different groups. Each one of the groups has its own unique characteristic and contributes in its own invaluable way to the battle against the *yetzer hara!*"

עַשֵׂר תְּעַשֵׂר אֵת כָּל־תְּבוּאַת זַרְעֶךָ
"You shall tithe the entire crop of your planting"(14:22)

The Gemara in *Maseches Ta'anis* (9a) promises: "*Aseir te'aseir — aseir bishvil shetis'asheir,*" "Tithe in order that you should become wealthy." Upon fulfilling the *mitzvah* of *ma'aser kesafim*, one should not think that he has just lost some of his wealth. The opposite is the truth; he is assured that the fulfillment of this *mitzvah* will bring him an *abundance* of wealth.

All his life, R' Chaim of Volozhin was careful to give not just a tenth but a fifth of his earnings to *tzedakah*.

On one occasion, R' Chaim was unsure whether he had given an entire fifth of his earnings to *tzedakah*, or whether he had yet to contribute 3 *zehuvim* in order to have given a fifth. After much thought, he concluded that he had, in fact, already donated the fifth, so he did not give any additional money to *tzedakah* at that time.

Later that day, R' Chaim's attendant went to draw water from the well. Much to his dismay, the bucket that he was using to draw the water fell to the bottom of the well! He tried to retrieve the bucket with the aid of an axe, but that too slipped from his hands and fell to the bottom of the well!

When the attendant related the story to R' Chaim, the *tzaddik* thought for a moment, made a calculation, and realized that the value of the bucket and the axe amounted to exactly 3 *zehuvim*.

He quickly went and gave 3 *zehuvim* to *tzedakah*. A short time later, he was informed that the bucket and the axe had been retrieved from the well!

וְכִי ... כִּי לֹא תוּכַל שְׂאֵתוֹ כִּי־יִרְחַק מִמְּךָ הַמָּקוֹם

"And if ... you are unable to carry it ...
or the place ... is too far from you" (14:24)

T he Dubno *Maggid* presented the following parable: There was once a wealthy diamond dealer, who had sent his servant to reclaim a valise filled with rare and precious gems that he had deposited with a friend.

The diamond dealer stood gazing from the window of his home, and anxiously awaited his servant's arrival. Finally, he saw his servant coming toward him. The servant seemed to be having a difficult time carrying the valise. He was sweating and breathing heavily as he carried the valise on his back.

"Woe is me," cried the diamond dealer, as he held his head in his hands. "A terrible tragedy has occurred! Thieves must have made off with my precious gems and replaced them with heavy rocks of no value. After all, someone who is carrying a valise filled with diamonds should not have to struggle so much."

"If a Jew," concluded the Dubno *Maggid*, "is '*unable to carry it*' — if he groans and sighs as he performs *mitzvos*, and he appears to be struggling beneath the yoke of Hashem's commandments — it is a sign that '*the Makom* (Hashem, the Omnipresent) ... *is too far from you.*' In other words, such an individual is apparently far from his Father in Heaven, for Hashem's pure *mitzvos* should not evoke any sigh or groan."

וְלֹא תִקְפֹּץ אֶת־יָדְךָ מֵאָחִיךָ הָאֶבְיוֹן:

"You must not ... close your hand to
your destitute brother" (15:7)

I n the city of Cracow resided an elderly, wealthy Jew, Reb Shimon. His wealth was well known to the people of Cracow; just as well known, however, was his stinginess.

All the days of his life, he did not so much as give one *perutah* to *tzedakah*. Thus his nickname: "Shimon the Miser."

One day, Reb Shimon passed away. The town's *chevrah kaddisha* decided to bury him in a disgraceful manner and lay him to rest on the outskirts of the cemetery, a place reserved for the lowly members of the town.

That *erev Shabbos*, the *rav* of Cracow, R' Yom Tov Lipman Heller (author of *Tosafos Yom Tov*), sat in his home engaged in Torah study. Suddenly, he heard a faint knock at the door. "Come in," the *rav* called out. The door opened and in walked Reb Zalman, one of the poor men of Cracow. "*Rebbe*," said Reb Zalman, "could you please help me? This week, I don't have even one *perutah* in order to buy food for Shabbos."

"What do you mean by, '*this* week'?" asked R' Heller. "What did you do until this week?"

"Until this week," answered Reb Zalman, "every *erev* Shabbos morning, I would find an envelope placed under my door containing the amount of money I need to buy food for Shabbos. Yet this morning, I checked under my door and there was no envelope! I am therefore left without any money to buy Shabbos food."

While they were conversing, there was another knock at the door. Another pauper walked in; he, too, came to ask for money for Shabbos. He was followed by another pauper and yet another…. They all had the same request: "*Rabbeinu*, please provide us with our Shabbos needs."

The wise *rav* deduced that the man who had passed away that week, an individual who everyone had thought to be a miser, was in reality a hidden *tzaddik* who had performed the *mitzvah* of *tzedakah* with utmost secrecy. Every week, Reb Shimon had apparently provided scores of Cracow's poor with the funds to acquire their Shabbos needs.

The *rav* made a public announcement: "I order the entire community to gather in the *shul* at once!"

The *rav*, wrapped in his *tallis*, ascended the podium, opened the *aron kodesh*, and declared, "We, the people of Cracow, are gathered here today in order to beg forgiveness from one of the *tzaddikim* that lived in our midst. His greatness went unnoticed by us; we denigrated him and called him, 'The Miser.'

"In the name of the entire community," cried the *rav*, "I hereby beg for total forgiveness from Reb Shimon, who was a righteous and holy Jew!"

Years later, when it came time for R' Heller to depart to his Heavenly abode, he requested from the *chevrah kaddisha* that they bury him next to the *tzaddik*, Reb Shimon.

כִּי־פָתֹחַ תִּפְתַּח אֶת־יָדְךָ לוֹ
"Rather, you shall open your hand to him" (15:8)

The Dubno *Maggid* visited the home of a wealthy individual to collect money for ransoming Jewish captives (*pidyon shevuyim*). This wealthy man was a *talmid chacham*, so the Dubno *Maggid* prefaced his words with a *d'var Torah*.

When the Dubno *Maggid* finished speaking, the man responded with a *d'var Torah* of his own which was related to the idea that the *maggid* had discussed. At this point the *maggid* wanted to direct the conversation toward the purpose of his visit, so he told the man a *d'var Torah* pertaining to the *mitzvah* of *pidyon shevuyim*. But as soon as he finished, the man, once again, countered with a *d'var Torah* of his own, also dealing with the *mitzvah* of *pidyon shevuyim*.

The *maggid* realized now that the man was trying to avoid giving him money. He therefore turned to the wealthy man and said, "Excuse me, sir. Allow me to share a parable. There was a certain individual who once traveled to a distant land. Upon investigation, he was surprised to discover that the inhabitants of the land had never heard of, nor had ever seen, an onion. So the man removed several onions from his pouch and presented them to the people as a gift. When the people tasted the onion for the first time, they were enamored by it and immediately paid him the onion's weight in gold. The visitor accepted the gold, packed his belongings, and went on his way.

Some time later, the man once again paid a visit to the faraway land. This time, he realized that the inhabitants of the land had never heard of garlic. He therefore removed some garlic from his pouch and handed it to them, in the hope of receiving gold in return.

Much to his disappointment, however, upon tasting the garlic — and thoroughly enjoying it, as well — the people gave him not gold but ... onions.

"So it is with us," concluded the Dubno *Maggid*. "I came to your home, not to hear your innovative Torah thoughts. Indeed, they are pleasant and delightful. However, I desperately need money to free Jews in captivity."

כִּי־פָתֹחַ תִּפְתַּח אֶת־יָדְךָ לוֹ ... דֵּי מַחְסֹרוֹ אֲשֶׁר יֶחְסַר לוֹ:

"Rather, you shall open your hand to him ... whatever he needs for his requirements" (15:8)

One of the premier *talmidei chachamim* in Prague, R' Zerach Eidlitz, paid a visit to the home of R' Yechezkel Landau (the *Noda B'Yehudah*).

"*Rebbe*," said R' Eidlitz, "I have lost all of my money and I remain without a penny. My debts are enormous, and my debtors refuse to relent."

"How much money do you need?" asked the *Noda B'Yehudah*.

"At present, I need 3,000 *dinarim*," responded R' Eidlitz.

The *Noda B'Yehudah* went to his cabinet, removed a purse of money, and handed it to R' Eidlitz. "Take this," said the *Noda B'Yehudah*, "it contains 3,000 *dinarim*."

R' Eidlitz thanked the *Noda B'Yehudah* profusely and went on his way in good spirits.

Some time later, the *Noda B'Yehudah*'s wife noticed that the large sum of money they had been storing in their cabinet — money that had been intended to cover the expenses for their daughter's upcoming wedding — had disappeared. In a state of panic, she immediately informed her husband of their misfortune. But the *Noda B'Yehudah* remained calm; he simply explained to his wife that he had loaned the money to R' Eidlitz.

"R' Eidlitz?" she cried. "The entire town is talking about how he has lost all of his money! How will he be able to pay us back?"

"Do not worry," responded the *Noda B'Yehudah*. "I am most certain that R' Eidlitz will pay us back on time."

The wedding date was quickly approaching, and there was still no sign of the money. One day, the *Noda B'Yehudah* received a letter requesting him to arbitrate between several bickering heirs. The father had been an extraordinary wealthy man, and, after his death, his children had simply been unable to arrive at any sort of compromise in regard to the inheritance.

The *Noda B'Yehudah* wrote down his decision, and sent it to the heirs.

Several days later, the *Noda B'Yehudah* received a response. The letter stated that the children were most grateful to the *rav* for his decision and for ironing out the differences that had come up between them. In addition to the letter, the envelope contained a sum of money as payment for the *Noda B'Yehudah*'s arbitration. The amount of money in the envelope was, amazingly, 3,000 *dinarim*!

נָתוֹן תִּתֵּן לוֹ וְלֹא־יֵרַע לְבָבְךָ בְּתִתְּךָ לוֹ
"You shall surely give him, and let your heart not feel bad when you give him" (15:10)

A poor person appeared before the *tzaddik*, R' Mendel of Rimanov. He poured his heart out before R' Mendel, sparing no detail of his difficult financial situation. The *rebbe* gave the man a substantial sum of money. Then, as the man turned to leave, the *rebbe* presented him with yet another coin.

"Why did the *rebbe* give the man *tzedakah* twice?" asked the *rebbe*'s family.

"The first time I gave him," answered R' Mendel, "it was out of sympathy, as I was very saddened by the severity of his predicament. The second time, however, was purely for the sake of fulfilling the *mitzvah* of *tzedakah*."

"We find an allusion to this in Scripture," concluded R' Mendel. "For when the Torah tells us to give charity, it uses a repetitive expression, '*Nason titein lo.*' This is to teach us that we should 'give, and give again.' The first time we give charity it should be for the sake of '*lo yeira le'vavecha,*' that our hearts should not be wicked against our friends. We must learn to feel compassion in our hearts; then Heaven will have compassion toward us.

"The second time we give, however, we should do so purely for the sake of the *mitzvah* of giving — '*b'sit'cha lo.*'"

נָתוֹן תִּתֵּן לוֹ ... כִּי בִּגְלַל הַדָּבָר הַזֶּה יְבָרֶכְךָ ה' אֱלֹקֶיךָ
"You shall surely give him ... for on account of this thing Hashem, your God, will bless you" (15:10)

The *Arizal HaKadosh*, R' Yitzchak Luria, was once sitting with his students in one of the fields neighboring Tzefas, teaching them the hidden parts of the Torah.

Suddenly, the *Arizal* interrupted his lesson, and said: "Go quickly and gather *tzedakah* for a poor man who lives in our midst! The poor man's name is R' Yaakov Altrutz and he is presently sitting at home and weeping. His cries are splitting apart the Heavens and have found their way into Hashem's innermost sanctuary. They are arousing Hashem's wrath against our entire city, for we have not shown him a proper measure of mercy.

"I hear," continued the *Arizal*, "a pronouncement being declared in Heaven, stating that a terrible plague of locusts will descend upon the city of Tzefas. We must act quickly and give him *tzedakah* — perhaps we will yet annul the harsh decree!"

They quickly collected money and sent a fellow student, R' Yitzchak HaCohen, to the house of R' Altrutz.

When R' Yitzchak arrived at the home of R' Altrutz, he found R' Altrutz sobbing bitterly. "Why are you crying?" asked R' Yitzchak.

"I am crying," answered R' Altrutz, "because my water barrel has broken, and I don't have even a single *perutah* in order to replace it."

R' Yitzchak handed him the money that had been collected from the *Arizal*'s students, and the poor man — who a moment ago had been so despondent — was now filled with joy.

When R' Yitzchak returned to the *Arizal*, his teacher informed him that the decree had, with Heaven's mercy, been annulled.

As they were speaking, a strong wind began to blow. The students looked up at the sky and were horrified to see that the wind had brought with it a swarm of locusts.

The *Arizal*, however, calmed them: "Do not worry, for the decree against Tzefas has been annulled." And, indeed, the wind carried the locusts away from Tzefas and toward the sea where they drowned.

כִּי בִּגְלַל הַדָּבָר הַזֶּה יְבָרֶכְךָ ה'
אֱלֹקֶיךָ בְּכָל־מַעֲשֶׂךָ וּבְכֹל מִשְׁלַח יָדֶךָ:
"For in return for this matter, Hashem,
your God, will bless you in all your deeds
and in your every undertaking" (15:10)

A chassid appeared before his *rebbe*, R' Meir Yechiel of Ostrovtze. He began to complain to the *rebbe* over his lack of a livelihood.

"Do you give *tzedakah*?" asked the *rebbe*.

"Certainly," responded the *chassid*. "I give *tzedakah* at every opportunity."

"In that case," advised the *rebbe*, "start a business, and Hashem will assist you, as the verse states, 'You shall surely give him ... for in return for this matter, Hashem, your God, will bless you in all your deeds and in your every undertaking.'"

"But *Rebbe*," replied the *chassid*, "my father bequeathed a textile shop to me. He always earned a large profit from the shop, yet ever since I took over the business, I have been losing money. Sometimes an entire day can pass, and not one customer will so much as enter my shop!"

"Tell me," asked the *rebbe*, "how do you occupy your time when there are no customers to serve?"

"To be honest with the *Rebbe*," answered the *chassid* sheepishly, "I just sit and do nothing at all."

"That," said the *rebbe*, "is why you are unable to earn a living. When your father was in charge of the store, he was careful not to squander a single moment. Between each customer, he would review something he had learned previously, or he would recite *Tehillim*. The *yetzer hara*, therefore, sent him many customers, in order to interrupt his learning. But you," concluded the *rebbe*, "you waste away your precious time. The *yetzer hara* has no reason to disrupt you with customers."

וְזָכַרְתָּ כִּי־עֶבֶד הָיִיתָ בְּמִצְרָיִם

"You shall remember that you were a slave in Egypt" (16:12)

To what can this be compared? asked R' Aryeh Leib of Metz (author of *Sha'agas Aryeh*) — to a king who went on a hunting trip. When he was out in the field, he happened upon a shepherd who was sitting next to his flock of sheep and playing a flute.

The king was captivated by the pleasant sounds flowing from the flute, and he found himself unable to move on. Finally, after some time had passed, the shepherd finished the melody he was playing. The king approached the shepherd and engaged him in conversation and discovered that the shepherd was very wise, full of wisdom and insight.

The king was very impressed by the shepherd, so he invited him to his palace to serve as one of his advisers. The shepherd agreed and went with the king.

From that day on, the shepherd lived in the king's palace, and he advised the king on all matters that pertained to his kingdom. In time, the shepherd rose to become one of the king's highest-ranking ministers.

The king's other ministers were filled with envy over the success of this former shepherd, and they schemed against him in order to bring about his ruination. They decided to slander him, and they informed the king that he had stolen from the palace.

The king summoned the shepherd for an interrogation, but he proved his honesty and loyalty to the king. The jealous ministers, however, still managed to persuade the king to search the former shepherd's home for possible evidence.

The king and his ministers went together to search the shepherd's quarters, but found only a modestly furnished home. They went from room to room without seeing anything suspicious, until they came to a locked door.

"What is inside this room?" asked the king.

The shepherd fell to his knees and began to plead with the king, "Your highness, I beg of you, do not ask me to show you what lies beyond this door! I am ashamed by what you will find there."

The pleas of the shepherd only strengthened the king's suspicions, and he demanded that the door be opened.

The door was opened and the king, accompanied by his ministers, entered the room. They glanced around the room and, much to their surprise, found nothing more than a flute and an old shepherd's bag.

The king and his men were bewildered.

"Your highness," explained the minister, "from the day that you invited me to dwell in your palace, I have not grown conceited or haughty over my high-ranking position because every day I make it a point to visit this room. I sit here and play my flute, recalling my days as a lowly shepherd."

The same is true of a Jew, concluded the *Sha'agas Aryeh*. When a Jew remembers that he was once a slave in Egypt, he will not become haughty. For the moment he feels the slightest bit of arrogance, he will recall his days as a lowly slave in Egypt and he will retain his humility.

וְשָׁפְטוּ אֶת־הָעָם מִשְׁפַּט־צֶדֶק:

"And they shall judge the people with righteous judgment" (16:18)

A GROUP OF WICKED INDIVIDUALS IN THE CITY OF VILNA LIBELED ONE OF the city's distinguished citizens. To ruin the man's reputation, they even hired false witnesses to substantiate their claim.

When word of the scandal reached the Vilna *Gaon*, he immediately suspected that the witnesses were hired to slander the man. He therefore requested to personally examine the "witnesses."

The witnesses appeared before the *Gaon* and related their testimony. The *Gaon* kept his eyes closed throughout their testimony and waited for them to finish. When they concluded, the *Gaon* rose to his feet and declared, "They are false witnesses!"

The imposters, terrified by the *Gaon*'s declaration, quickly admitted their guilt and revealed that they had been hired to deliver a false testimony.

The judges of the *beis din* were amazed. "How did *Rabbeinu* know that they were false witnesses?" they asked the *Gaon*.

"The answer lies in a Mishnah in *Maseches Sanhedrin* (5:4)," he replied.

"The Mishnah states that the judges first listen to the testimony of one witness. When the witness has concluded, the judges invite the second witness to testify. The Mishnah then states, 'If the words were found to correspond' then they are believed. What does 'if the words were *found* to correspond' mean? Either the testimonies match up or they do not; what need is there for the judges to figure out if the testimonies correspond?

"The reason," explained the *Gaon*, "is as follows: Every individual has his own style and approach when it comes to relating that which he has seen. Therefore, when judges hear two testimonies that differ slightly from one another, if they can find a way to reconcile them, the testimonies will be accepted in *beis din*. For although the two witnesses expressed themselves in different manners, the two testimonies are one and the same. In fact, it is a sign that the witnesses are honest.

"However, when these witnesses testified before me," concluded the *Gaon*, "there were no discrepancies between their testimonies. If two people recount the same story, using the same words, it is a clear indication that they are false witnesses!"

❦

וְשָׁפְטוּ אֶת־הָעָם מִשְׁפַּט־צֶדֶק:
"And they shall judge the people with righteous judgment" (16:18)

One day, a Jew visited R' Ber Meisels, the *rav* of Warsaw. Upon entering the *rav's* home, the man broke out in uncontrollable sobbing. "*Rebbe*," he cried, "please, help me! I am in great distress."

"Have a seat, and tell me what happened," responded R' Meisels.

"I am a merchant," began the man, "and I came to Warsaw on business matters. I arrived here this past *erev Shabbos*, and I had in my possession an extremely large sum of money — 5,000 rubles in total. I was afraid of staying at an inn, lest my money be stolen from me. I therefore asked one of my friends, one of the merchants of Warsaw, to host me for Shabbos, and he was happy to accommodate me. Just before Shabbos, I left all of my money with him for safekeeping. Sunday morning, I requested that he return the money that I had deposited with him, but he completely denied ever receiving a single penny from me."

R' Meisels summoned the friend to appear before him, and he arrived promptly. When he entered R' Meisels' study, the merchant screamed out, "You *rasha*! Return my money at once!"

"I do not understand what he wants from me," said the friend to R' Meisels. "He never gave me any money!"

"You can see for yourself," said R' Meisels to the friend, "that this man will not let you be. Give him a few rubles in order to appease him; perhaps he will leave you alone after that."

"Fine. I am prepared to give him 25 rubles, just so long as he stops harassing me."

"Twenty-five rubles?" yelled the merchant. "He stole 5,000 rubles from me!"

"Give him 100 rubles," said R' Meisels. "Then he will withdraw his claim."

"I am even willing to give him 100 rubles," declared the businessman, "simply in order that he should leave me alone."

But the merchant adamantly refused any such compromise; he demanded that every last ruble that had been stolen from him be returned.

"Let us try one last time," said R' Meisels. "Offer him 500 rubles and see if he will relent."

"If the *Rav* thinks it is a good idea," said the friend, "then I am prepared to give even 500 rubles."

"You *rasha*!" reprimanded R' Meisels. "Return his money this instant! I know you well and I am well aware of your miserly character. Just the other day, I asked you for charity on behalf of an orphaned girl who was soon to be married, and you refused to contribute even 10 rubles! Yet all of a sudden, you are ready to pay this man 500 rubles? Return his money at once!"

This frightened the crook, and he immediately returned all the stolen money.

וְלֹא־תִקַּח שֹׁחַד
"And you shall not accept a bribe" (16:19)

The *rav* of Brisk, R' Yosef Dov Soloveitchik, once met with a gentile judge who worked for the Russian civil court.

"Our laws are far superior to yours," said the judge to R' Soloveitchik. "For example, we have a law that prohibits bribery. If a judge is found to have accepted a bribe, not only is *he* penalized, but so is the one who gave him the bribe. Yet according to Jewish law, there is only a prohibition against accepting bribes, but the one who gives the bribe is not in violation of any prohibition."

"On the contrary," responded R' Soloveitchik. "It is specifically this law which points to the Torah's superiority and to its dedication to upholding justice. According to your laws, why should a judge ever fear accepting a bribe? Neither he nor the one who gave the bribe will ever admit to their guilt, as they are both afraid of being punished."

"But this is not the case when it comes to Torah law," concluded R' Soloveitchik. "Since the Torah only forbids accepting a bribe, but does not punish the one who offered it, the judge would certainly be wary of ever taking a bribe. After all, the one who gave him the bribe may decide to expose the judge for what he has done."

וְלֹא־תִקַּח שֹׁחַד
"And you shall not accept a bribe" (16:19)

The *rebbe* R' Heschel of Cracow once presided over a court case involving a disagreement between two extremely wealthy individuals. They were in the midst of a bitter dispute over a very large sum of money.

A few days before the trial, one of the wealthy men approached R' Heschel and said, "As I will be coming before the *Rav* in a few days for a *din Torah*, please see to it that justice is served." Upon concluding his words, he reached into his pocket, removed 100 *dinarim*, and placed it on R' Heschel's table. R' Heschel took the money and requested that the man return to him the following day.

After the man left, R' Heschel called his wife and asked her to prepare a large feast for their family — for all their children and grandchildren.

The next day, R' Heschel sat at his table, surrounded by his entire family. He called for their attention, and then removed the 100 *dinarim* from his pocket. He counted the money in front of them — once, twice, three times!

Naturally, his family was curious as to what he was doing and waited for his explanation. "Do you all see this money?" R' Heschel asked. "This is a bribe. I invited you here today in order that you should see for yourselves what a bribe looks like. Now that you have seen it, you will know to flee from it like fire."

R' Heschel immediately summoned the wealthy man and, when he arrived, cast the money before him and rebuked him harshly.

כִּי הַשֹּׁחַד יְעַוֵּר עֵינֵי חֲכָמִים וִיסַלֵּף דִּבְרֵי צַדִּיקִם:

"And you shall not accept a bribe, for the bribe will blind the eyes of the wise and make just words crooked" (16:19)

A plaintiff wished to bribe R' Avraham Yehoshua Heschel of Apta (the *Ohev Yisrael*). But he was unsure how to go about it; for how does one bribe a *tzaddik*? So he came up with a plan. When he was confident that no one was watching, he slipped into the room where the judges kept their personal belongings. He found the *Ohev Yisrael*'s coat and placed a substantial sum of money in its pocket.

As the *Ohev Yisrael* sat in *beis din*, he suddenly felt an unyielding urge to rule in favor of the plaintiff. He immediately adjourned the *beis din* for the day and returned home. The *Ohev Yisrael* spent that entire night in heartfelt prayer, crying out to Hashem, and begging Him to open his eyes to the truth.

The next morning the *Ohev Yisrael* discovered the sum of money in his pocket, and he immediately understood what had transpired.

"Look at the powerful influence of bribery!" exclaimed the *Ohev Yisrael*. "Even if the judge is not aware that he is in possession of it, he is still under its sway.

"Now I am able to resolve a difficulty that has bothered me for quite some time," continued the *Ohev Yisrael*. "The verse states, 'For the bribe will blind the eyes of the wise and make crooked *divrei tzaddikim*.' How can a judge who would accept a bribe be referred to as righteous?"

"The verse," answered the *Ohev Yisrael*, "must be speaking of a judge who, unbeknownst to him, had a bribe placed in his pocket. The judge remains righteous, as he was unaware that he was being bribed. Nonetheless, the bribe still has the ability to twist his words!"

כִּי הַשֹּׁחַד יְעַוֵּר עֵינֵי חֲכָמִים וִיסַלֵּף דִּבְרֵי צַדִּיקִם:

"And you shall not accept a bribe, for the bribe will blind the eyes of the wise and make just words crooked" (16:19)

The *Chofetz Chaim* offered the following insight: If a pauper tells his peers that an individual is very wealthy, it does not prove that the individual is indeed wealthy. For while this individual may appear quite well off in the poor man's eyes, in the eyes of the rest of the world he may not be considered wealthy at all.

But if a very wealthy individual tells you that a certain person is wealthy, you can be sure that he truly is wealthy.

So it is, continued the *Chofetz Chaim*, with regard to wisdom. Let us imagine for a moment that our great teacher, the Rambam, testified that a certain person is a wise man. There would be no doubt that, in fact, the man is a very wise man. Now let us envision the wisest of all men, Shlomo HaMelech, testifying about the brilliance of a particular individual. We would, undoubtedly, be positively assured of that person's immense wisdom.

It stands to reason, concluded the *Chofetz Chaim*, that if *HaKadosh Baruch Hu*, in all of His glory and splendor, attested to the great intelligence of an individual, then that individual must be brilliant beyond compare.

The verse states, "For the bribe will blind the eyes of the wise and make just words crooked." Bribery, said the *Chofetz Chaim*, is so enticing that it can blind even one whom *Hashem* refers to as wise!

❧◆❧

לֹא תָסוּר מִן־הַדָּבָר אֲשֶׁר־יַגִּידוּ לְךָ יָמִין וּשְׂמֹאל:
"You shall not deviate from the word that they will tell you, right or left" (17:11)

Rashi cites the words of the *Sifri*: "Even if he says to you about right that it is left, and about left that it is right."

Each generation is commanded to heed the words of its Torah sages. Even if it appears that their advice is incorrect, we must assume that it is *our* perspective that is inaccurate, and that the truth lies with the words of our Torah leaders.

R' Yechezkel Abramsky illustrated this idea by way of a parable: There was an individual who wished to test the eyesight of his friends. He therefore made a small mark on a board and placed it one hundred meters away from them.

"Who can see what is on the board?" he asked them.

The first friend looked at the board but saw nothing, because his vision was poor and only extended to thirty meters.

The second friend tried his luck, but he could see no further than eighty meters.

Finally, someone with stronger vision stepped up, and being able to see a full one hundred meters, he saw the small mark on the board.

"So it is with our Torah sages," said R' Abramsky. "Our sages are unique individuals to whom Hashem has granted a heightened sense of sight. Therefore, if they rule on a certain matter, and it appears to us as if they have erred, we are, nevertheless, required to heed their words — for they are able to see far more than what we can see."

תָּמִים תִּהְיֶה עִם ה' אֱלֹקֶיךָ:
"You shall be wholehearted with Hashem, your God" (18:13)

In reference to two traits alone, noted R' Pinchas of Koritz, do we find the expression, "with Hashem."

The first reference is in the verse, "You shall be wholehearted with Hashem, your God." The second is in the verse, "Walk humbly with your God" (*Michah* 6:8).

It is with regard to these two traits — wholeheartedness and humility — that a person can most easily fool the general public, convincing people that he actually possesses them. A person can act as though he has perfect trust in Hashem and can appear to shun all honor, and no one would know the truth.

This is why the verse states, "with Hashem, your God," with regard to these two traits. The Torah is teaching us that the only One Who can know whether a person is truly wholehearted or modest is "Hashem, your God."

תָּמִים תִּהְיֶה עִם ה' אֱלֹקֶיךָ:
"You shall be wholehearted with Hashem, your God" (18:13)

To what can this be compared? — R' Yisrael Salanter offered the following parable: There once was a king who sent one of his dukes on a mission to a neighboring country. "I have only one condition," said the king to the duke. "No matter what the circumstances are, you are forbidden to enter into any type of bet with an officer from that country." The duke agreed to the peculiar condition, and he went on his way.

Upon arriving at his destination, the duke was greeted by an officer of that land who engaged him in conversation:

"Your highness, the duke," said the officer. "A rumor has spread that you are a hunchback. Could such a thing be true?"

"That rumor is an absolute lie!" responded the duke. "I am not a hunchback, nor have I ever been a hunchback!"

"I am willing to wager 100,000 *dinar* that you really are a hunchback," said the officer. "Remove your shirt, and then we will be able to see whether the rumor is accurate or not!"

The duke immediately recalled the king's admonition, but then he thought, *This is a sure bet, as I am by no means a hunchback. Why should I waste an opportunity to earn 100,000 dinar?*

The duke therefore agreed to the bet and removed his shirt. When all those who were present saw that he was not a hunchback, the officer removed 100,000 *dinar* from his pouch and handed it to the duke.

When the duke returned to the palace, he approached the king and related to him what had transpired.

"Woe is me!" cried the king, clutching his head between his hands. "What have you done? You have won 100,000 *dinar*, but I have lost *500,000 dinar!* For I placed a wager with the officers of that country that they would never be able to bait you into removing your shirt!"

The same applies to a Jew, concluded R' Salanter. Let us not innovate or rationalize attempts to shirk our responsibilities as Jews. It is incumbent upon each Jew to simply follow the Torah's instructions, fulfilling its commandments with faithfulness and wholeheartedness. We do not know what is at stake!

כִּי־תֵצֵא לַמִּלְחָמָה עַל־אֹיְבֶךָ וְרָאִיתָ סוּס וָרֶכֶב
עַם רַב מִמְּךָ לֹא תִירָא מֵהֶם כִּי־ה' אֱלֹקֶיךָ עִמָּךְ

***"When you go out to war against your enemies
and see horses and chariots, and a people more
numerous than you, you must not be afraid of
them, for Hashem, your God, is with you" (20:1)***

Several fortunate students witnessed the fulfillment of this verse in
the home of the *tzaddik*, R' Yosef Yozel Horowitz (the *Alter* of
Novaradok).

During the *Alter*'s later years, a brutal war had broken out in Russia.
The battle had taken to the streets, as Russian citizens fought against
the marauding Bolsheviks.

One *motza'ei Shabbos*, the *Alter* stood with a cup of wine in hand,
ready to recite *Havdalah*.

Suddenly, sounds of gunfire and shouting filled the air, as rioters
entered the small town of Novaradok. The townspeople were in a
panic, and screams of terror could be heard emanating from the
houses. The sounds of gunfire and explosions were also clearly heard
in the *Alter*'s courtyard.

Yet to everyone's amazement, the apparent danger seemed to have
no effect on the *Alter*. With a calm and pleasant voice, the *Alter* began
reciting *Havdalah*, displaying a heart full of trust in Hashem.

The students who were present in the *Alter*'s home that *motza'ei
Shabbos* later remarked that in those incredible few moments, they
had learned what it means to truly trust in Hashem.

כִּי־תֵצֵא לַמִּלְחָמָה עַל־אֹיְבֶיךָ

"When you go out to war against your enemies" (21:10)

"**T**HE MOST DIFFICULT WAR OF ALL," REMARKED THE *CHOFETZ Chaim*, "is man's war against his *yetzer hara*."

In his youth, R' Yaakov Yisrael Kanievsky (the Steipler *Gaon*) was conscripted into the Russian army.

It was not easy serving in the Russian army. He was surrounded by numerous anti-Semites and he often had to stand guard in subzero temperatures.

Despite the difficult circumstances, the Steipler used great cunning and devised various strategies that enabled him to observe the Shabbos.

It was so cold outdoors that whoever was on guard duty was given a special, thick coat to wear during his shift. But there was only one such coat, so the soldiers took turns wearing it.

One Shabbos eve, when the Steipler came to do his guard duty, the soldier who was wearing the coat took it off and, instead of handing it to the Steipler, hung it on a tree.

The Steipler now stood trembling in the freezing cold, and he was unsure as to what he should do. It was already Shabbos, and removing an item from a tree on Shabbos is forbidden. On the other hand, without his coat he would freeze.

Five minutes, he thought. *Let me see if I can bear not wearing the coat for just five minutes. If after five minutes I feel as if I simply cannot stand the cold, then I will retrieve the coat; after all, this is a life-threatening predicament.*

Five minutes passed, as the Steipler stood shivering in the bitter cold. *Another five minutes,* he thought. *I'll wait five more minutes and then I'll get the coat.*

Another five minutes passed, then another, and yet another, until the night had passed and the guard on the next shift came to relieve him.

The Steipler had not moved from his place the entire night, nor had he transgressed any of the holy day's sanctified commandments.

The war against one's *yetzer hara* is a most difficult one. The way to emerge victorious is by devising clever strategies. Yet one should not attempt to overcome his *yetzer hara* all at once, for that will prove to be too difficult. Rather, he should progress gradually, taking a step-by-step approach, as the verse states, "Thoughts conceived in counsel will be firm; wage war with strategies" (*Mishlei* 20:18).

❧⊱⊰❧

לֹא־תִרְאֶה אֶת־שׁוֹר אָחִיךָ אוֹ אֶת־שֵׂיוֹ נִדָּחִים וְהִתְעַלַּמְתָּ מֵהֶם

"You must not see your brother's ox or sheep wandering astray and ignore them" (22:1)

One who finds a lost object is forbidden to act as if he did not see it. Rather, he is commanded to bring the object into his possession and announce that the item has been found so that the person who lost it can come and retrieve it. In this way, the finder will fulfill the *mitzvah* of *hashavas aveidah* (returning an object to its rightful owner).

Chazal (*Bava Metzia* 30a) teach us, however, that there are certain instances when one is permitted to ignore a lost object. For example, if the one who finds the object is a *talmid chacham*, and it is not befitting someone of his stature to pick it up, then he is allowed to bypass the lost item.

R' Akiva Eiger was once walking through the alleyways of Warsaw, trying to locate the home of a relative who was known to be a simple man.

An acquaintance of the sage said to him, "*Rebbe*, it is not appropriate for one as distinguished as yourself to go and seek out that relative. Are there not times when *Chazal* exhort one to, in fact, 'ignore' and overlook things?"

"There are two places in the Torah," responded R' Eiger, "where we encounter the concept of 'ignoring.' The first time is regarding the *mitzvah* to return a lost object, as the verse states, 'and ignore them.' The second time is in *Yeshayahu* (58:7), where the verse states, 'and do not ignore your kin.'

"The exemption of 'an elder for whom it is not befitting' applies only to the law of returning lost objects, but it does not apply to being close to one's relatives."

הָשֵׁב תְּשִׁיבֵם לְאָחִיךָ:
"You must return them to your brother" (22:1)

On one of his many travels, the *Alter* of Novaradok (R' Yosef Yozel Horowitz) arrived at a small town and stayed at the local inn.

On *erev Shabbos*, the *Alter* asked a fellow lodger — an individual who hailed from faraway Moscow — to lend him a clothing brush, as he wished to clean his clothing in honor of the Shabbos.

After Shabbos, when the *Alter* returned from *shul*, he immediately made his way to the man's room in order to return the brush. To the *Alter*'s dismay, however, the man had already left the inn and had gone on his way. This caused the *Alter* great distress.

The incident bothered the *Alter* for seven *years* until he met a Jew on a train ride. In the course of a conversation with him, the Jew mentioned that he was from Moscow.

"Did you say Moscow?" asked the *Alter* with joy. "Perhaps you know so-and-so?"

"Why, I most certainly do." responded the man. "Actually, I know him quite well."

"If so," said the *Alter*, "please do me a great favor, and return this brush that I borrowed from him seven years ago."

וְאִם־לֹא קָרוֹב אָחִיךָ אֵלֶיךָ וְלֹא יְדַעְתּוֹ וַאֲסַפְתּוֹ אֶל־תּוֹךְ
בֵּיתֶךָ וְהָיָה עִמְּךָ עַד דְּרֹשׁ אָחִיךָ אֹתוֹ וַהֲשֵׁבֹתוֹ לוֹ:
"But if your brother is not near you or you do not know him, you shall then bring it into your house, and it shall remain with you until your brother inquires after it, and you shall then return it to him" (22:2)

The Mishnah in *perek Eilu Metzios* of *Bava Metzia* instructs us how to deal with a lost object that has not yet been recovered by its owner. The finder is responsible for taking care of the item, so that when its owner eventually comes to retrieve it, he will find it in exactly the same condition as when he lost it.

R' Meir Michel Rabinowitz, *rav* of Shott, once went to a convalescent home in the town of Liboy.

While he was there, several of his students paid him a visit. As they entered their *rebbe*'s room, they saw R' Rabinowitz reciting *Tehillim* from what appeared to be a very old *sefer*. When the *rav* concluded saying *Tehillim*, his students watched in wonder as he gave the *sefer* a little tap and then put it aside. Their curiosity grew all the more when the *rav* picked up a pair of *tzitzis* that was lying on his bed, and began to shake them forcefully.

The students were perplexed by their *rebbe*'s behavior and asked him to share with them the motives behind his actions.

R' Rabinowitz explained: "About twenty years ago, I found this *sefer* *Tehillim* and this pair of *tzitzis*, but I was unable to locate their owner. *Chazal* tell us that one who finds a garment is required to shake it out every thirty days, in order to keep it free from dust and dirt. Similarly, one who finds a *sefer* is required to read it once every thirty days and maintain it.

"Today," concluded R' Rabinowitz, "is the thirtieth day, on which I am required to shake out the *tzitzis* and read from the *Tehillim*. I have therefore brought them here with me in order to fulfill the dictum of *Chazal*."

לֹא־תַחֲרֹשׁ בְּשׁוֹר־וּבַחֲמֹר יַחְדָּו:

"You shall not plow with an ox and a donkey together" (22:10)

R' Nosson Adler was once traveling in the company of his great disciple, the *Chasam Sofer* (R' Moshe Sofer). It was a cold winter day, and the wagon that was being pulled by two horses was barely maintaining its balance on the snow-covered roads.

Suddenly, one of the horses tumbled over and died. The remaining horse, which was now pulling the wagon on its own, simply did not have enough strength to go on. The wagon driver was left with no choice but to disembark from the wagon and travel on foot to the nearest town in order to procure an additional horse.

After some time had passed, the wagon driver made his way back to the wagon, leading — a donkey.

When R' Adler saw the donkey, he immediately descended from the wagon and began dancing with joy.

"*Rebbe*," asked the *Chasam Sofer*. "Why are you so happy?"

"Do you not see?" asked R' Adler. "The driver has brought a donkey instead of a horse! When have I ever had the chance to fulfill the *mitzvah* of 'You shall not plow with an ox and donkey together'? Sitting in my home in Frankfurt, I would never have dreamed that I would one day be so fortunate as to fulfill this commandment! Now that I have been worthy of fulfilling it, *baruch Hashem*, I am overcome with joy!"

At their behest, the driver returned to the town and, in place of the donkey, brought a horse.

לֹא תִלְבַּשׁ שַׁעַטְנֵז צֶמֶר וּפִשְׁתִּים יַחְדָּו:
"You shall not wear [a garment of] mixed fibers — wool and linen together" (22:11)

Physicians once sent R' Yisrael Salanter to a city known for its medical and rest facilities. Also visiting the city was a wealthy man, who was known to be a Torah scholar as well.

One day, R' Salanter was taking a stroll down the city's roads. Suddenly a lavish stagecoach being pulled by two strong steeds stopped alongside him. The wealthy man was inside the coach, and he extended a warm invitation to R' Salanter, asking him to join him on his excursion.

R' Salanter politely refused.

"*Rebbe*," said the wealthy man. "Does the *Rav* suspect, perhaps, that the cushions inside my stagecoach are made of *sha'atnez*? All the leading halachic authorities have already ruled that these cushions are free of *sha'atnez*!"

"It is not the *sha'atnez* that I am afraid of," responded R' Salanter. "It is haughtiness that terrifies me so!"

עַל־דְּבַר אֲשֶׁר לֹא־קִדְּמוּ אֶתְכֶם בַּלֶּחֶם וּבַמַּיִם ...
וַאֲשֶׁר שָׂכַר עָלֶיךָ אֶת־בִּלְעָם ... לְקַלְלֶךָ:

"This is because they did not greet you
with bread and water ... and because [Mo'av] hired
against you Bil'am ... to curse you" (23:5)

The Dubno *Maggid* explained this verse by way of a parable:
There was a certain villager who arrived one day in a yeshivah.
He approached the *rosh yeshivah* and explained to him that he had
come to find a suitable match for his daughter.

"I commit myself," said the man, "to supporting the young man and
providing him with all of his needs."

The *rosh yeshivah* chose a young man of exemplary character,
who also possessed an extraordinary breadth of Torah knowledge. In
time, the couple married, and they moved into the villager's home.

The morning following the wedding, the son-in-law took a seat at
the kitchen table in preparation for breakfast, but much to his surprise,
a plate containing stale bread and a glass sparsely filled with water
were placed before him.

The mild-mannered son-in-law did not say a word; slowly, he chewed
the aged bread and drank the water. That night, the situation repeated
itself; once again, he was served stale bread and water. The next day
was exactly the same as the one preceding it, and the son-in-law was
finding it increasingly difficult to continue eating in such a manner.

Finally, the son-in-law could not take it anymore; he simply
refrained from eating and eventually grew emaciated.

When the man saw that his son-in-law had stopped eating, he burst
into a terrible fit of rage. He started to scream at him: "Why do you
not eat? Did your body grow accustomed to consuming only delicacies when you were in yeshivah?"

When the father-in-law saw that his yelling had not motivated the
young man to resume eating, he hired two muscular individuals to
constantly accompany the son-in-law and make sure that he ate.
During each meal they would stand over him with straps in their
hands. Whenever the son-in-law tried pushing away the stale bread
that was placed in front of him, they whipped him.

Late one night, the son-in-law escaped from his father-in-law's
house, and made his way back to the yeshivah. Battered and bruised,

he approached the *rosh yeshivah* and told him about the nightmare he had lived through since the day he had gotten married.

The next day, the father-in-law came to the yeshivah searching for his son-in-law, but he was met by the *rosh yeshivah* instead.

"Why do you not feed your son-in-law adequately?" asked the *rosh yeshivah*.

"I will tell you the truth," responded the father-in-law. "I do not have enough money to pay for anything more than bread and water."

"Wicked man!" yelled the *rosh yeshivah*. "You do not have enough money for your son-in-law, yet for paying two guards to abuse him you do have enough money?"

This is the explanation of the verse, concluded the Dubno *Maggid*. The verse states, "Because they did not greet you with bread and water" — but, you may ask, perhaps they could not afford to do so. The verse therefore continues, "because he hired against you Bil'am ... to curse you" — when it came to hiring Bil'am to curse the Jewish people, they had no shortage of money. This proves that their refusal to provide for the Jewish people stemmed from pure wickedness.

זָכוֹר אֵת אֲשֶׁר־עָשָׂה ה' אֱלֹקֶיךָ לְמִרְיָם
"Remember what Hashem, your God, did to Miriam" (24:9)

In this verse, we are warned against speaking *lashon hara*. It is incumbent upon us to remember how Hashem afflicted Miriam with *tzara'as* as a result of her speaking *lashon hara*.

To what can this be compared? The *Chofetz Chaim* drew the following parable: There was a father who had two sons; one was brilliant while the other was average.

One day, the father observed his genius son acting haughtily, showing off his superior intellect to his friends. This behavior disturbed the father, so, in full view of his friends, he smacked the son across the face.

Several days later, the son of average intelligence also began to act as if he was superior to his friends. Upon seeing this, the father approached his son and said, "My son, if I did not spare your brother's honor when he acted as he did, I will certainly not spare *your* honor."

This, said the *Chofetz Chaim*, is how we are to understand the Torah's portrayal of Miriam's sin and her subsequent punishment.

If Miriam's greatness — the entire Jewish nation was supplied with water for forty years in the desert due to her merit — did not prevent Hashem from punishing her for speaking *lashon hara*, then how much more so will Hashem not refrain from punishing simple people like ourselves when we speak *lashon hara*.

בְּיוֹמוֹ תִתֵּן שְׂכָרוֹ

"You shall pay his wages on the day they are due" (24:15)

When R' Yosef Teomim (the *Pri Megadim*) was appointed rabbi of Frankfurt an der Oder, he ordered a new overcoat, one that was befitting a rabbi of a major congregation.

R' Teomim gave his wife money to pay for the coat, instructing her to pay the tailor as soon as he brought them the coat. She should pay him without any delay, he added, as the verse states, "You shall pay his wages on the day they are due."

Late that night, R' Teomim returned home and noticed the new coat that the tailor had made. He was quite surprised, however, to see that the money he had given his wife was still on the table.

R' Teomim deduced that his wife had forgotten to pay the tailor for his work. He therefore rushed out in the dark of night to find the tailor and pay him.

However, when he reached the home of the tailor, the tailor — who was very moved by R' Teomim's efforts — informed R' Teomim that his wife had paid for the entire coat herself.

אֶבֶן שְׁלֵמָה וָצֶדֶק יִהְיֶה־לָךְ אֵיפָה שְׁלֵמָה

"You shall have complete and accurate stone weights" (25:15)

Throughout the generations, *gedolei Yisrael* scrupulously kept the *mitzvah* of maintaining accurate weights and measures.

In a certain city, the sages decreed that a fast day be held on account of the lack of rain. The entire city fasted as the sages had ordained, but rain still did not fall.

That night, the *rav* of the city had a dream. In it, he was told that if a particular storeowner would lead the community in a prayer for rain then rain would, indeed, fall.

The next day, the *rav* gathered the entire community to pray together for rain. To everyone's surprise, he asked the storeowner to lead the services.

The storeowner declined, claiming that he was but a simple man and unfit to lead the prayers. The *rav*, however, did not relent, and he explained that it was specifically the storeowner who could come to their aid and no one else!

The storeowner left the *shul* and returned holding a pair of scales that he used to weigh his merchandise.

He approached the *bimah* and cried out, "Master of the World! The two pans of these scales parallel the two *heis* of Your Great Name! The bar parallels the *vav*, and the handle parallels the *yud*.

"Master of the World! If I have used these scales dishonestly and thereby desecrated Your Holy Name, I hereby accept upon myself whatever punishment I deserve! But if I have acted in an upright manner, then I pray that You send us rain of blessing!"

As soon as the storeowner finished his words, the sky filled with clouds, and it began to rain.

Parashas Ki Savo

אָרוּר מַכֵּה רֵעֵהוּ בַּסָּתֶר
"Cursed is he who secretly strikes his fellowman" (27:24)

RASHI EXPLAINS THAT THIS CURSE REFERS TO ONE WHO SPEAKS *lashon hara* — when someone speaks evil, he secretly "strikes" his fellowman.

The *Chofetz Chaim* was traveling in the company of a well-known rabbi on their way to performing a *mitzvah*.

After traveling for some time, they decided to rest at an inn.

The woman who owned the inn realized that her two new guests were highly esteemed rabbis, so she quickly set a table and offered them various delicacies.

When they had finished eating, she approached them and asked, "How was the meal?"

"It was excellent!" remarked the *Chofetz Chaim*. "The food was delicious."

"And how did you enjoy the food?" asked the hostess to the other rabbi.

"The food," answered the rabbi, "was certainly adequate, but it could have used a bit more salt."

Their hostess cleared the table and entered the kitchen.

As soon as she left the room, the *Chofetz Chaim* turned to the rabbi and, with sorrow in his voice, said: "All my life, I have taken the utmost care not to speak or hear words of *lashon hara*. But now that I am in your company, you have caused me to falter — I am greatly distressed that I have made this trip. I am sure that this trip was not truly for the sake of a *mitzvah*, for it is impossible that one who has set out to perform a *mitzvah* should come to violate such a grave transgression!"

"But what did I say?" asked the rabbi. "I said the food was good. I just added that the food could have used a little salt."

"You have no idea," answered the *Chofetz Chaim*, "of the incredible power of one's words. In all likelihood, the cook is a poor widow who works in this inn to support her family. I am sure that because of your comment, the hostess will go to this poor widow and tell her that the guests are complaining about her cooking. The widow, in defense of her cooking, will deny that the guests have any grounds for complaints. At that point, the hostess will become incensed and shout at her, 'Do you think the distinguished guests are lying? You are the one who is the liar!' Ultimately, the hostess, in a fit of anger, will fire the poor, unfortunate cook.

"Just look at how many sins you have committed with your words: (1) You spoke *lashon hara*; (2) you caused both the hostess and myself to hear *lashon hara*; (3) you caused the hostess to relate the words of *lashon hara* to the cook; (4) you caused the cook to lie in defense of her cooking; (5) you caused the cook terrible suffering."

"Surely you are exaggerating," said the rabbi to the *Chofetz Chaim*.

"Not in the least," responded the *Chofetz Chaim*. "Come with me and I'll show you."

The two rabbis entered the kitchen and were greeted with a sorry sight. The poor cook was standing with her head in her hands, sobbing.

The rabbi took one look at the widow, and immediately understood just how correct the *Chofetz Chaim* had been. He quickly made his way to the hostess and pleaded with her to forgive the cook and restore her to her position.

⚜

אָרוּר מַכֵּה רֵעֵהוּ בַּסָּתֶר
"Cursed is he who secretly strikes his fellowman" (27:24)

On one occasion, the *Chofetz Chaim* once traveled to another city in a coach. Also traveling on that coach was a group of animal traders who spent the entire trip discussing oxen and horses. The *Chofetz Chaim*, however, remained silent, immersed in his thoughts.

As the conversation continued, one of the businessmen began to speak in a derogatory manner about a certain individual who also made his living in the animal trade. At this point the *Chofetz Chaim* suddenly interjected:

"Gentlemen," said the *Chofetz Chaim*. "Up until now you had been carrying on a rather pleasant conversation centered around oxen and horses; why must the topic shift to human beings? Such talk involves the sin of *lashon hara!*"

The traders, who did not know that the person rebuking them was the *Chofetz Chaim*, made light of his words. The *Chofetz Chaim*, however, paid no heed to their insults.

Once they had concluded deriding the *Chofetz Chaim*, the men resumed their malicious speech.

When the *Chofetz Chaim* realized that his words were not being taken to heart, he asked the wagon driver to stop so he could get off. "It is better to leave the coach in the middle of my trip," remarked the *Chofetz Chaim*, "than to hear words of *lashon hara!*"

אָרוּר אֲשֶׁר לֹא־יָקִים אֶת־דִּבְרֵי הַתּוֹרָה־הַזֹּאת
"Cursed is he who does not uphold the words of this Torah" (27:26)

When the *gedolei Yisrael* assembled in Vienna for a historic convention (the first *Knessiah Gedolah*), scores of residents gathered in front of the house where the *Chofetz Chaim* had been staying, in order to meet the sage and receive his blessing.

Among those who were standing on line were a father and his young son. When they entered the *Chofetz Chaim*'s room, the *Chofetz Chaim* scolded the father, "I do not know why you have come to me for a blessing; if you send your son to yeshivah you will have no need for my blessing, for you will have been blessed by Heaven. Yet if you decide to send your son to a secular school, then my blessing will be of no help, as the verse states, 'Cursed is he who does not uphold the words of this Torah'!"

The father was stunned by the *Chofetz Chaim*'s words, and he trembled with much emotion.

"How did the *rav* know that I was about to send my son to a secular school?" asked the shocked father. "Indeed, the spirit of God must lie within him!"

יְקִימְךָ ה' לוֹ ... כִּי תִשְׁמֹר אֶת־מִצְוֹת ה' אֱלֹקֶיךָ
"Hashem will establish you for Himself ... if you keep the commandments of Hashem, your God" (28:9)

A poor woman once visited the home of R' Moshe Feinstein, and requested a meeting with the *rav*. "Why do you need to speak with the *rav*?" asked one of the members of R' Feinstein's family.

"I received a letter from my sister who lives in Russia," said the woman. "I would like the *rav* to translate it for me."

"For this you have come to the *rav*?" asked the relative who was obviously startled by the woman's response. "R' Feinstein cannot be bothered with such things!"

"Why not?" asked the woman. "He has been translating these letters for me for the last twenty years."

וְהָלַכְתָּ בִּדְרָכָיו:
"And follow His ways" (28:9)

The Midrash *Eliyahu Rabbah* states in relation to this verse, "'Follow His ways' — that is, the ways of Heaven. Just as the ways of Heaven are merciful, so shall you be merciful to one another."

One *erev Shabbos*, a poor individual visited the home of R' Yeshayahu Bardaki, and tearfully related how his family lacked the most basic necessities, and were unable to purchase even *challah* for Shabbos.

Since R' Bardaki himself did not have any money, he picked up one of the candlesticks that had been standing on the table, and without hesitation, gave it to the poor man.

Several weeks later, the poor man once again returned in tears, lamenting the dire poverty in his home and how his family was again unable to afford Shabbos food.

This time, R' Bardaki happily gave the poor man the second candlestick that had been standing on his table. "Please take this," said R' Bardaki. "Go and buy yourself as much Shabbos food as you need."

A short while later, the poor man once again appeared at R' Bardaki's door, asking for *tzedakah*. R' Bardaki searched his entire house for something of value, and eventually emerged with the *shtriemel* that he wore in honor of Shabbos. Without a moment's deliberation, he gave it to the poor man.

The poor man, however, was not pleased. "Every time that I come to ask you for *tzedakah*, you give me an item which I must sell in order to obtain money. When will you finally give me cash, so that I will no longer be forced to find people who are willing to buy these objects?" As he spoke, the poor man erupted into a fit of rage. He could not control himself, and, in a moment of hysteria, he actually smacked R' Bardaki across the face!

Oy! thought R' Bardaki. *If a Jew can become so enraged, who knows how deeply he must hurt inside!*

"Come with me," said R' Bardaki to the poor man. "I will come with you to collect cash for you."

וְהָלַכְתָּ בִּדְרָכָיו:
"And follow His ways" (28:9)

A widow approached R' Yosef Zundel of Salant. "Excuse me," she said, "but for the last hour, I have been looking for a water carrier. Would you like to earn a few *perutos*? Then go and draw me five pails of water, and carry them to my home." She had mistaken him for an elderly pauper.

R' Yosef Zundel happily complied and carried five pails full of water to the widow's home.

When he had completed the task, the woman attempted to pay him. R' Yosef Zundel, however, who did not want to be compensated for his work, told her that he would permit her to pay him the next time he would draw water for her.

Some time later, the widow was informed of the true identity of her "water carrier." Horrified, she ran to the house of R' Yosef Zundel and begged him for forgiveness.

"Forgiveness for what?" asked R' Yosef Zundel. "On the contrary, *I* owe you a heartfelt thanks for giving me the opportunity to utilize my body in the performance of an act of kindness!"

וְרָאוּ כָּל־עַמֵּי הָאָרֶץ כִּי שֵׁם ה' נִקְרָא עָלֶיךָ וְיָרְאוּ מִמֶּךָּ:
"And all the nations of the earth will see that Hashem's Name is displayed upon you, and they will revere you" (28:10)

In *Maseches Berachos* (6a), *Chazal* expound on the above verse: "From where do we know that *tefillin* are a source of might for Israel? — From the verse, 'And all the nations of the earth will see that Hashem's Name is displayed upon you, and they will revere you.' And it was taught: R' Eliezer HaGadol said, 'these are the *tefillin* of the head (*sheba'rosh*).'"

The *Sha'agas Aryeh* (R' Aryeh Leib from Metz) was once traveling. Throughout the trip he wore his *tallis* and *tefillin* and engaged in Torah study.

The wagon driver was also wearing his *tallis* and *tefillin* — he was praying while steering the horses.

Suddenly, a band of armed robbers jumped out from the forest and attacked the wagon; they demanded that the driver stop the wagon and hand over all of his money.

The driver was terribly frightened. "*Rebbe,*" he screamed, "we're in danger!"

The *Sha'agas Aryeh* heard the screaming coming from up front, so he stuck his head out the window to see what was happening. But when the ordinarily bold thieves took one look at the *Sha'agas Aryeh* they were overcome with fear and immediately fled!

"*Rebbe,*" asked the driver. "I am both younger and stronger than you, yet it was *you* whom the thieves were terrified of. Why did the robbers run away when they saw you?"

"The robbers did not run because of my strength," answered the *Sha'agas Aryeh*, "but because of the *tefillin* on my head!"

"But I am also wearing *tefillin,*" responded the driver. "Why did the thieves not run away from me?"

The *Sha'agas Aryeh* explained: "The Torah says, 'And all the nations of the earth will see that Hashem's Name is displayed upon you, and they will revere you.' The Gemara quotes R' Eliezer HaGadol who teaches that this verse is referring to the *tefillin* of the head (*sheba'rosh*). If you read the words of *Chazal* carefully, you will notice that *Chazal* did not say '*tefillin* she'**al** ha'rosh' ('*tefillin* that rest *on* one's head'); rather, '*tefillin* she**ba**'rosh' ('*tefillin* that are *inside* one's head'). The holiness of the *tefillin* must be absorbed *into* one's head, and then it instills fear into the nations of the world. But if the *tefillin* are simply lying *on top* of one's head, then the nations of the world do not fear us at all."

וְרָאוּ כָּל־עַמֵּי הָאָרֶץ כִּי שֵׁם ה׳ נִקְרָא עָלֶיךָ וְיָרְאוּ מִמֶּךָ׃

"And all the nations of the earth will see that Hashem's Name is displayed upon you, and they will revere you" (28:10)

The Jews of Potik were terribly frightened. The gentiles of the vicinity had libeled the Jews, accusing them of a serious crime. Now there were rioters armed with clubs gathering in the Jewish section of Potik, intent on inflicting horrible damage. A pogrom was about to begin.

The terrified Jews locked themselves inside their homes. They sealed the shutters and bolted their doors, hoping to gain some protection against the wild mob outside.

The city's *shochet*, however, was not that fortunate. The frenzied mob broke down his door, grabbed him, dragged him into the street, and began to beat him mercilessly.

When the rabbi of the city, R' Shalom Mordechai HaCohen Schwadron (known by the acronym *Maharsham*), heard what was happening to the *shochet*, he quickly put on his coat and hat and went out into the street.

The pleas of R' Schwadron's family, begging him not to put his life in danger, did not deter him. "It is my duty to try and save him!" he replied.

R' Schwadron rushed out into the street, and when the thugs caught a glimpse of him, they backed away from the *shochet*. They then approached R' Schwadron, asked for his forgiveness, and quickly left Potik!

In this manner, R' Schwadron was the very fulfillment of, "And all the nations of the earth will see that Hashem's Name is displayed upon you, and they will revere you."

וְהָיוּ חַיֶּיךָ תְּלֻאִים לְךָ מִנֶּגֶד וּפָחַדְתָּ לַיְלָה וְיוֹמָם
"Your life will hang in the balance. Night and day you will be afraid" (28:66)

R' Eliezer HaGadol in *Maseches Sotah* (48b) said: "Anyone who has bread in his basket yet says, 'What will I eat tomorrow?' is among those who have little faith."

Similarly, the *Zohar HaKadosh* (quoted in *Mishnah Berurah*, siman 157) states that it is forbidden for an individual to deprive himself in order to save food for the next day. This is in order that he should beseech Hashem each and every day for his sustenance.

During World War II, the Brisker *Rav* (R' Yitzchak Zev Soloveitchik) resided in Warsaw. The city suffered from endless bombings and its inhabitants spent their days and nights in bomb shelters.

Even in these most trying times, the Brisker *Rav* heeded the words of *Chazal* and did not leave even one morsel of that day's food for the next day. Rather, with pure faith, he trusted in Hashem that He would provide him with all that he needed.

However, when the eighth day of Tishrei arrived, the Brisker *Rav* was doubtful as to what he should do. Should he continue his practice of not leaving any food over for the next day, or, since tomorrow would be *erev Yom Kippur* — a day when it is a mitzvah to eat — would it be correct to deviate from his usual custom and leave over a piece of bread?

After much deliberation, the *gaon* decided to leave over some bread in order to fulfill the next day's *mitzvah*.

The next morning there was a knock on the Brisker *Rav*'s door. It was the owner of one of the city's bakeries, and he had something to tell the *rav*. He related how he had prepared a pot full of food for the *rav* to eat on the eve of the fast. But on the way to deliver the food, he was startled by the sounds of explosions that were shaking the city. As a result, he dropped the pot, and all the food that was in the pot fell to the ground and became soiled.

The Brisker *Rav* understood that this was a sign from Heaven that he should not have left over any bread for the next day; had he not had a lot to eat, he would have gotten the fresh food that was now ruined.

וֶהֱשִׁיבְךָ ה' מִצְרַיִם בָּאֳנִיּוֹת בַּדֶּרֶךְ
אֲשֶׁר אָמַרְתִּי לְךָ לֹא־תֹסִיף עוֹד לִרְאֹתָהּ

"Hashem will take you back to Egypt in ships, along the route about which I said to you, 'You shall never see it again'" (28:68)

Throughout his life, R' Yosef Chaim Sonnenfeld yearned desperately to emigrate to *Eretz Yisrael* and settle there. Therefore, in the year 5633 (1873), R' Sonnenfeld boarded a ship bound for the Holy Land.

Before he left, however, he bid his elderly mother and sister farewell. "If I will merit to reach *Eretz Yisrael*," said R' Sonnenfeld, "then I plan on remaining there for the rest of my life. I have no intention of ever leaving. I bless you, may you both merit to one day emigrate to *Eretz Yisrael* — then we will reunite."

After the journey had commenced, the captain of the ship announced that they would be docking temporarily in Alexandria, Egypt. After a short stay, they would resume their trip to *Eretz Yisrael*.

When R' Sonnenfeld heard that the ship was nearing the shores of Egypt, he locked himself in his cabin so that he would not violate the prohibition of, "You shall never see it again."

Only after the ship set sail from the port of Alexandria did R' Sonnenfeld emerge from his cabin. From that point on, he waited on the deck until *Eretz Yisrael* came into full view.

Approximately seven years later, R' Sonnenfeld's blessing to his family was fulfilled, when they, too, journeyed to *Eretz Yisrael* and settled in Yerushalayim, near his home.

Parashas Nitzavim

הַנִּסְתָּרֹת לַה׳ אֱלֹקֵינוּ וְהַנִּגְלֹת לָנוּ וּלְבָנֵינוּ

"The hidden [sins] are for Hashem, our God [to punish], but the revealed [sins] are our and our children's [responsibility]" (29:28)

R ASHI EXPLAINS THAT A JEW IS NOT EXPECTED TO OFFER HIS FRIEND rebuke for the sins that lie hidden within his heart, for how can he possibly know what another man is thinking? Therefore, in the case of hidden sins, Hashem exacts retribution from the sinner alone.

On the other hand, a Jew *is* expected to rebuke his fellow man for the sins he does openly. Consequently, when Jews overlook other people's misdeeds, Hashem's anger is brought upon all of them.

A terrible dispute broke out in Radin, the *Chofetz Chaim*'s hometown. Though the *Chofetz Chaim* (R' Yisrael Meir Kagan) was by now in his later years, he rushed to the *shul* and approached the *bimah*. From there, he addressed the community.

"My dear brothers!" began the *Chofetz Chaim*. "If someone would have offered me 2,000 rubles to deliver a *derashah* in *shul*, I would not have accepted it! I am not willing to sell my precious time for money. However, because of the situation, I am forced to speak. We must know that there will come a time when each and every one of us will be required to stand before the Heavenly court and give an account of all the deeds that he performed over the course of his life.

"You must be aware that strife is a very serious matter! A person may have performed scores of *mitzvos* in his life, but if he was guilty of causing or involving himself in matters of dispute, then he is like a person who tried filling a bag that had a large hole at its bottom — all the *mitzvos* he performed will be lost!

"I have no doubt that when the individuals from Radin who were involved in the dispute come before the Heavenly court, they will attempt to clear themselves by stating the following:

"'We cannot be held accountable! For in our city there lived an elderly Jew by the name of Yisrael Meir whom we deemed to be a *talmid chacham*. He saw all that was transpiring, yet he remained silent.'

"Therefore, my dear brothers," concluded the *Chofetz Chaim* in a voice filled with emotion, "I beg of you — do not mention my name before the Heavenly court!"

As these words left the mouth of the *Chofetz Chaim*, he broke down and wept bitterly, and his frail body trembled. This sight made a very powerful impression on the people of Radin, and the dispute was resolved immediately.

❧◷◈

הַנִּסְתָּרֹת לַה׳ אֱלֹקֵינוּ וְהַנִּגְלֹת לָנוּ וּלְבָנֵינוּ
"The hidden [sins] are for Hashem, our God [to punish], but the revealed [sins] are our and our children's [responsibility]" (29:28)

In *Maseches Sanhedrin* (98a), R' Yehoshua ben Levi poses a question regarding a verse dealing with the eventual redemption of the Jewish people. The verse states, "I am Hashem, in its time I will hasten it" (*Yeshayahu* 60:22). Asks R' Yehoshua ben Levi: If the redemption will ultimately occur "in its time," then how can Hashem promise the Jewish people, "I will hasten it"?

The answer, says the Gemara, is as follows: If the Jewish people will carry out the will of Hashem, then the redemption will, in fact, be hastened. But if not, then the redemption will occur at its assigned time.

Chazal's words, said the *Kesav Sofer* (R' Avraham Shmuel Binyamin Sofer, son of the *Chasam Sofer*), are alluded to in the above mentioned verse: "The hidden are for Hashem, our God" — if the Jewish people will not perform the will of Hashem, then the redemption will come at a fixed date, one that is ultimately hidden from us and known only to Hashem. However, "the revealed are our and our children's [responsibility]" — if the Jews choose to follow the will of Hashem, then the redemption will arrive immediately. The time of the redemption, therefore, can be revealed and known to the Jewish people, for it is something that can be determined by their actions.

וְשַׁבְתָּ עַד־ה' אֱלֹקֶיךָ וְשָׁמַעְתָּ בְקֹלוֹ
"You will return to Hashem, your God, and heed His voice" (30:2)

The *Chofetz Chaim* recounted an extraordinary parable to describe the most effective path to performing *teshuvah*.

A wine retailer, who wished to purchase a large amount of wine for his store, visited a wholesaler. After the wholesaler had presented the retailer with a bill for the wine he had ordered, the retailer requested whether he could have the wine on credit, as he simply did not have the funds to cover the cost at that time. He promised that he would pay the wholesaler back at a later date.

"I am afraid that I will not be able to do that," said the wholesaler to the retailer. "Several times now, I have given you wine on credit. Each time you have promised to pay me back at a later date — but you have not kept your word."

"Please, just this one time," pleaded the retailer. "Give me the wine on credit, and I assure you that I will pay you back on time! On all the previous occasions, something came up that prevented me from paying you, but this time I guarantee that I will pay on time!"

Despite all of the retailer's begging, the wholesaler remained firm in his refusal.

In the midst of their conversation, another wine retailer entered the warehouse. After listening to them for a short while, he turned to the first retailer and said, "Let me give you some advice. Why buy such a large amount of wine and incur so expensive a bill? Instead, buy a smaller amount of wine, and pay the wholesaler now."

The retailer agreed to follow the wise suggestion, and he purchased only a small amount of wine. He brought the wine back to his store, and quickly sold all of it. With his money in hand, he returned to the wholesaler and purchased another small barrel of wine. Once again, the retailer did not have much trouble selling the wine, and he immediately returned to the wholesaler to buy some more wine. This process repeated itself several times until, finally, the retailer was able to repay all of his old debts to the wholesaler.

The same is true of us, concluded the *Chofetz Chaim*. We ask Hashem to forgive us for all the sins we have committed, promising Him that we will never repeat them. However, it is clear to Him that, despite all of our promises, we will sin again.

The only choice we have is to use the retailer's approach. We must start the *teshuvah* process by repenting for one specific sin. For example, a person may choose to be more careful about violating the sin of forbidden speech. When he succeeds at surmounting that sin, he may then choose to guard his eyes from seeing that which is improper, and so on. In this way a person will gradually be able to erase the debts that he has incurred in Heaven, until he has earned the status of becoming a full-fledged *ba'al teshuvah*.

⋇⊙⋇

וּמָל ה' אֱלֹקֶיךָ אֶת־לְבָבְךָ וְאֶת־לְבַב זַרְעֶךָ לְאַהֲבָה
אֶת ה' אֱלֹקֶיךָ בְּכָל־לְבָבְךָ וּבְכָל־נַפְשְׁךָ לְמַעַן חַיֶּיךָ:

*"Hashem, your God, will then remove the layer over
your heart and your descendants' hearts, so that you
will love Hashem, your God, with your whole heart and
your entire being, in order that you may live" (30:6)*

The *Chofetz Chaim* explained this verse with a parable: The son of a king was once traveling. Suddenly, as he reached a fork in the road, a band of thieves attacked him. They were about to kill him, but, much to his good fortune, a pauper dressed in rags happened to cross that spot at that very moment. When the pauper saw the king's son being assaulted, he gathered his strength and, in a display of great bravery, succeeded to drive away the thieves, saving the king's son.

When the king heard of the pauper's heroic deed, he invited the pauper to the palace. When the pauper arrived, the king thanked him and pledged: "As a reward for having saved my son, I hereby permit you to spend an entire day in the royal treasury; you may take anything that your heart desires."

When the gates of the royal treasury were opened for the pauper, he joyously fell upon the massive piles of gold and diamonds and began gathering all that he could.

When the pauper left the royal treasury that evening, he was a changed person. In one day, he had gone from being a destitute pauper to an extraordinarily wealthy man. The next day, this former pauper began a business and, in a short time, it was a thriving enterprise. By now, he had become one of the richest men in all the land, and his former life of poverty and deprivation were all but forgotten.

Every year, on the day that he had been blessed with the good fortune of entering the royal treasury, the former pauper arranged a lavish feast. All of his friends and relatives were invited to the annual feast.

One year, in the middle of one of his great feasts, the wealthy man turned to his guests and asked, "Please tell me: Which day, do you think, was the happiest day of my entire life?"

"It must be this very day," responded the guests. "Today must be the happiest day of your life! After all, today your mansion is decorated, your servants surround you, and all of the distinguished individuals of the land accord you great honor!"

"You are mistaken," said the wealthy man. "While today is certainly one of great joy, it is only a mere remembrance of that special day when I was transformed from a lowly beggar in ragged clothing to a man of enormous wealth. *That* day was the happiest day of my life.

"On that day," he continued, "I spent the entire day in the vaults of the king's treasury. I was so engrossed in gathering riches that I felt neither hunger nor weariness. The more valuables I amassed, the more joy I reaped. I have never experienced such a blissful day as that one, nor will I ever again."

So it is with us, said the *Chofetz Chaim*. Hashem grants a person the most precious gift of all — life. Throughout his life, man has the ability to amass as many *mitzvos* and good deeds as his heart desires.

An individual who views the world from such a perspective is truly the happiest of men. The reason we don't have this perspective is because our hearts have been sealed off and clogged with our many sins.

At the End of Days, however, Hashem will remove the "layer over your heart" that prevents our hearts from gaining true understanding, and we will finally be able to appreciate the life that we have been granted. Then we will rejoice over our great fortune — that we had been given the opportunity to study Torah and amass *mitzvos*.

This is what the verse means when it states, "Hashem, your God, will then remove the layer over your heart and your descendants' hearts" — only when Hashem removes the layers that render our hearts insensitive will we be able to reach the level where we are able to "love Hashem, your God, with your whole heart and your entire being, in order that you may live." Only then will we be able to appreciate the great gift that Hashem has bestowed to each and every one of us — life!

לֹא בַשָּׁמַיִם הִוא לֵאמֹר מִי יַעֲלֶה־לָּנוּ הַשָּׁמַיְמָה וְיִקָּחֶהָ לָּנוּ

"It is not in the heavens that [you would then] say, "Who can go up to the heavens and fetch them for us" (30:12)

Commenting on this verse, Rashi quotes the Gemara in *Maseches Eruvin* (55a): "'It [the Torah] is not in the heavens' — for if it was in heaven, you would have to go up after it and learn it"!

R' Shlomo Zalman of Vilna once needed a certain *sefer*. The only problem was that there was a heavy box — so heavy that it would have taken at least three men to move it — standing directly in front of the *sefer*, making it impossible for him to reach it.

R' Shlomo Zalman paced back and forth, repeating the Gemara in *Eruvin* again and again. *Do you hear that, Shlomo Zalman?* he asked himself. *If it were in heaven, you would have to go up after it and learn it!* He repeated these words many times. Suddenly, R' Shlomo Zalman turned around and lifted the massive box *on his own*! Once it was out of his way, he took the *sefer* and delved into his Torah study.

לֹא בַשָּׁמַיִם הִוא לֵאמֹר מִי יַעֲלֶה־לָּנוּ הַשָּׁמַיְמָה וְיִקָּחֶהָ לָּנוּ

"It is not in the heavens that [you would then] say, "Who can go up to the heavens and fetch them for us" (30:12)

Throughout the generations, the Jewish people have witnessed the immeasurable love of Torah that *gedolei Yisrael* possess. Their love for Torah being as great and intense as it is, one could accurately claim that had it actually been in heaven, they would have scaled those great heights in order to obtain it.

When R' Baruch Ber Leibovitz was newly married, he resided in the city of Slutsk. One winter night, a major snowstorm hit Slutsk. Snow was falling rapidly as fierce winds howled through the trees. The temperature was well below freezing.

It was now quite late at night, and R' Baruch Ber was at home, bent over his Gemara, studying intensely. Suddenly, he heard the faint sound of footsteps in the snow, and he realized that someone was approaching his home.

R' Baruch Ber was very frightened. Who would dare walk outdoors on a night like this?

There was a light knocking on the door. R' Baruch Ber went to the door and opened it. Much to his amazement, standing at the threshold of his home was none other than the rabbi of Slutsk, R' Yaakov David Willowsky (the *Ridvaz*).

"My esteemed friend," said R' Baruch Ber, "what could have brought you to my house on a night like this?"

"Please forgive me," replied the *Ridvaz* with joy on his face. "I just came up with an amazing *chiddush* (novel Torah insight) in the commentary of the *Rif,* and I simply could not wait until the morning to share it with you."

לֹא בַשָּׁמַיִם הִוא ... וְלֹא־מֵעֵבֶר לַיָּם הִוא ...
כִּי־קָרוֹב אֵלֶיךָ הַדָּבָר מְאֹד בְּפִיךָ וּבִלְבָבְךָ לַעֲשֹׂתוֹ:

*"It is not in the heavens .... Nor is it across the sea ...
Rather, the matter is very near to you — in your
mouth and your heart — to perform it" (30:12-14)*

In relation to this verse, the *rebbe* R' Simchah Bunim of P'shischa would often relate the following story:

In the city of Cracow lived a barkeeper R' Isaac. R' Isaac worked in a small tavern and barely managed to make ends meet. One night, he dreamt that he should travel to Prague, for there he would find a treasure chest buried under the bridge that led to the king's palace!

R' Isaac awoke from his dream and decided to travel to Prague.

When he arrived in Prague, he immediately headed in the direction of the bridge that led to the king's palace. Once there, he began digging as he had been instructed in his dream, but, much to his disappointment, he found nothing.

Bewildered and disheartened, R' Isaac sat down under the bridge, and he regretted that he had traveled so far for naught.

A non-Jew passed by and noticed the sad Jew. "Why are you so sad?" asked the non-Jew.

"I had a dream," answered R' Isaac. "In it, I was told that I would find a treasure buried beneath this bridge. I searched here, but I did not find anything."

The non-Jew laughed. "Silly Jew!" he said. "You should know better than to pay attention to a meaningless dream! I, too, had a dream that was quite similar to yours: I was told that in the city of Cracow there resides a Jew named R' Isaac, and that inside his house, beneath the oven, there is a hidden treasure. Do you think I would waste my time going there?"

When R' Isaac heard the non-Jew's dream, he became very excited. He now realized that the purpose of his trip to Prague was simply to hear the words of this non-Jew. He immediately traveled back to his home in Cracow, and, without losing any more time, he began digging under his oven. There, in his very own home, he found an enormous treasure!

So it is with all men, concluded the *rebbe*. A Jew may travel to see a *tzaddik*, and having seen him, he will return home thinking that he has done what is required of him. But such thinking is incorrect! It is specifically when he returns home that he must begin to search! Let him check the way he acts at home; let him attempt to improve his ways! If he does so, then he will merit finding a "treasure" — in his very own home!

כִּי־קָרוֹב אֵלֶיךָ הַדָּבָר מְאֹד בְּפִיךָ וּבִלְבָבְךָ לַעֲשֹׂתוֹ:

"Rather, the matter is very near to you, for you to carry out with your mouth and with your heart" (30:14)

When R' Chaim Shmulevitz was a young man, he was learning with another one of the outstanding students of the Mir Yeshivah. At one point in their learning, they had formulated seven different approaches to understanding a certain Talmudic topic. The hour, however, had gotten late, so they decided to stop for the night and return to their rooms.

The next morning, when they sat down to learn, R' Shmulevitz quickly summarized the seven different approaches they had worked on the night before.

"How are you able to remember what we learned last night?" asked the student to R' Shmulevitz. "I can't seem to remember anything!"

"What did you do after we concluded learning?" asked R' Shmulevitz.

"I went to sleep," responded the student.

"I did not," answered R' Shmulevitz. "Rather, when I returned to my room, I lay down in my bed and put my pillow over my head so I wouldn't disturb my roommates. Then, for the next few hours, I reviewed — out loud — each one of the approaches that we learned together. Is it so amazing, then, that I can remember them?"

כִּי־קָרוֹב אֵלֶיךָ הַדָּבָר מְאֹד בְּפִיךָ וּבִלְבָבְךָ לַעֲשֹׂתוֹ:

"Rather, the matter is very near to you, for you to carry out with your mouth and with your heart" (30:14)

The Tchebiner *Gaon*, R' Dov Berish Wiedenfeld, was famous for his extraordinary diligence in Torah study. Day and night he sat and toiled in Torah, not letting his thoughts drift for even one moment.

One morning, a student of R' Wiedenfeld entered his room in order to discuss a certain matter with him. Much to the student's surprise, the Tchebiner *Rav* seemed not to notice that he was there.

"I beg the *Rav*'s forgiveness," said the student, "but I have come to discuss a specific issue with him."

"What can be so pressing about your predicament that you have rushed here at midnight to discuss it with me?" asked the Tchebiner *Rav*.

"*Rebbe*," said the student, "midnight has long passed; it is already morning."

Being so engrossed in his Torah learning, the Tchebiner *Rav* had not even realized that night had passed and day had begun!

וּבָחַרְתָּ בַּחַיִּים
"You shall choose life" (30:19)

R' Chaim Chizkiyahu Medini (the *S'dei Chemed*) once related that as a youth he had not been blessed with extraordinary intelligence. He said that he had gained his mental acuity only as a result of the following story:

When he was newly married, the *S'dei Chemed* learned in a *kollel* that was funded by a wealthy philanthropist. One of the other members of the *kollel* was envious of the *S'dei Chemed*'s phenomenal diligence and success at his studies, so, motivated by his jealousy, he devised a nefarious scheme to ruin him. He went and bribed the philanthropist's Arab maid to slander the *S'dei Chemed* by telling others that he had acted immorally.

The Arab woman agreed to the scheme and began to spread the lie. The libel resulted in a terrible *chillul Hashem*, but the *S'dei Chemed* — who was mild mannered and of a gentle nature — could not muster the strength necessary to defend himself. With a ruined reputation, he left his hometown in disgrace.

A short while later, the Arab woman sought out the *S'dei Chemed* and, full of remorse, approached him to ask for his forgiveness.

In an attempt to appease him, the woman revealed to him how she had been bribed by one of his peers in an attempt to sully his name.

What shall I do? thought the *S'dei Chemed*. *On the one hand, this is a good opportunity to clear my name. On the other hand, a chillul*

Hashem has already been caused. If I now go and publicize the scheme that had been plotted against me, everyone will know how shamefully the other student acted, and I will be the cause of a second chillul Hashem! Furthermore, the student who devised this plot will be subject to untold humiliation.

The *S'dei Chemed* arrived at a decision: "Do not reveal a word of this to anyone!" he told the Arab woman.

"At that moment," the *S'dei Chemed* later recounted, "Heaven opened up the fountains of wisdom before me. I was blessed with an abundance of Divine assistance, and it is that assistance that has made me what I am today."

PARASHAS VAYEILECH

וַיִּקְרָא מֹשֶׁה לִיהוֹשֻׁעַ וַיֹּאמֶר אֵלָיו לְעֵינֵי כָל־יִשְׂרָאֵל חֲזַק וֶאֱמָץ

"Moshe summoned Yehoshua and said to him before the eyes of all Israel, 'Be strong and be firm'" (31:7)

R' MEIR SIMCHAH HAKOHEN OF DVINSK (THE *MESHECH* Chochmah) explained this verse in a unique fashion: On the one hand, the king that rules over the Jewish people is subject to the commandment, "So that his heart does not become haughty over his brethren" (*Devarim* 17:20). He is required to act lovingly toward each member of *Bnei Yisrael* and to refrain from feeling even the smallest trace of arrogance. On the other hand, when it comes to carrying out his duties as king, he must act with firm resolve. Similarly, *Chazal* state (*Kesubos* 17a), "A king that waives his honor, his honor is not waived." With this in mind, the verse can also be read as follows: "Moshe summoned Yehoshua and said to him." What was it that he said? "*Before the eyes of all Israel, be strong and firm.*" Moshe was telling Yehoshua that he must be "strong and firm" when he is standing "before the eyes of all Israel" and acting as their leader.

וְהִסְתַּרְתִּי פָנַי מֵהֶם וְהָיָה לֶאֱכֹל וּמְצָאֻהוּ רָעוֹת רַבּוֹת וְצָרוֹת
"And I will conceal My face from them, and
they will become prey; many misfortunes
and calamities will befall them" (31:17)

R' Yaakov Yosef of Polnoa explained this verse using a parable that he heard from his *rebbe*, R' Yisrael *Ba'al Shem Tov*.

A king once became angry with his son who had strayed from the upright path. To punish the son, the king commanded his servant to hit his son with painful blows.

However, as long as the king was watching, the servant was wary of striking him with a significant amount of force. What did the king do? He covered his face so as not to see his son; then the servant dealt with him appropriately.

Upon receiving his due punishment, the son began to plead for his life, begging the king to forgive him for his sins.

The same is true of the relationship between Hashem and the Jewish people, concluded R' Yaakov Yosef. The Jewish people transgress Hashem's commandments and are sentenced to be punished by the angels. However, as long as Hashem looks after the Jewish nation, the angels are unable to afflict them in any way. Therefore, Hashem states, "And I will conceal My face from them, and they will become prey; many misfortunes and calamities will befall them." In other words, only when Hashem conceals His face, as it were, are the angels capable of "hitting" the Jewish people until they fully repent.

וְעַתָּה כִּתְבוּ לָכֶם אֶת־הַשִּׁירָה הַזֹּאת
"So now, write this song" (31:19)

When R' Naftali Tzvi Yehudah Berlin (the *Netziv*) published his classic work, *HaEmek She'elah*, he arranged a large feast.

At one point during the meal, the *Netziv* rose and related the following story: "When I was a young boy, I overheard a conversation between my parents. I was shocked when my father, in the middle of a sentence, burst into tears and said, 'I have tried everything to interest our son in Torah study, yet nothing seems to work. I am afraid that I have no other choice than to teach him a trade.'"

The *Netziv* continued his story: "My father's cries touched my heart. So at that moment, I came out to my father and told him, 'Father, I promise you that from this day on, I will dedicate all my time to studying Torah!'

"Try to imagine," concluded the *Netziv*, "what would have happened had I not heard my father's weeping; I would have become a carpenter or, perhaps, a tailor. When my time to stand before the Heavenly court would have arrived, they would have shown me the *sefer HaEmek She'elah*, and they would have asked: 'Naftali Tzvi, why did you not write this *sefer*?'"

※◯❀

וְעַתָּה כִּתְבוּ לָכֶם אֶת־הַשִּׁירָה הַזֹּאת
"So now, write this song" (31:19)

Our Sages learned from this verse that each person is required to write a *sefer Torah* for himself. Why is it so important for each individual to write his own *sefer Torah*? R' Avraham Shmuel Binyamin Sofer (the *Kesav Sofer*) explained that this is so that each person can feel as though he is standing at the foot of *Har Sinai*, and he will thereby experience the elevation and excitement of receiving the Torah.

R' Eizel Charif once visited the Volozhin Yeshivah to find a suitable match for his daughter from among the students. The students of Volozhin were excited about the arrival of the *gadol hador*, and each one wholeheartedly wanted to be chosen as his son-in-law.

R' Charif turned to the young men who had gathered before him and stated: "My dear friends, I simply do not have the strength to test each one of you. I will therefore pose a question; whoever is able to provide me with an answer will be chosen as a match for my daughter."

R' Charif posed a very challenging question, and the students immediately began to search for an answer. Day and night, without break, they grappled with the question. Soon there was a long line consisting of Volozhin's best students waiting outside the room where R' Charif was staying. Each student presented him with an answer, but the *gaon* easily refuted each attempt.

Several days passed and not a single student found a satisfactory answer for R' Charif's question. Not having found the son-in-law that he was looking for, he boarded a wagon and began his trip home. After starting out, he suddenly heard yelling behind him. "Stop! Stop!" someone cried. R' Charif turned to see who was calling him, and he noticed that it was one of the students, Yosef Shlofer, running after the wagon with all his might.

The wagon driver stopped the wagon, and R' Charif questioned the young man.

"What can I do for you? Do you have an answer?"

"*Rebbe*," said Yosef as he gasped for breath, "I must admit, I do not know the answer, but I still want to know the correct answer to your question. Please tell me what the answer is!"

Immediately, R' Charif's face lit up. "Reb Yosef," he said to the young man, "you are the son-in-law that I have been searching for! If your love for Torah is so great that it brought you to chase after the wagon, then it is *you* who is deserving to be a match for my daughter."

לְמַעַן תִּהְיֶה־לִּי הַשִּׁירָה הַזֹּאת לְעֵד בִּבְנֵי יִשְׂרָאֵל:
"So that this song shall act for Me as a witness against the Children of Israel" (31:19)

From this verse we are able to gain an insight, said the *Chofetz Chaim*, into just how severe the sin of *bitul Torah*, wasting time from studying the Torah, really is.

To what can it be compared? To an expert glassmaker who taught his apprentice the fine art of glassmaking.

One day, the apprentice was working in the glassmaker's shop. The glassmaker happened to notice that the apprentice had fashioned a fine-looking glass dish. He liked it so much, in fact, that he actually requested the apprentice to let him have it.

"I will happily give it to you!" answered the apprentice. "However, you must purchase it from me."

"What nerve!" shouted the glassmaker angrily. "Was it not I who trained you and instructed you how to make this dish? Were you not sitting in *my* workshop when you made it, using *my* tools and materials? How dare you ask me to pay for it?"

Man, concluded the *Chofetz Chaim*, is the handiwork of Hashem. Hashem has granted us intellect, mouth, eyes, and the rest of our two hundred and forty-eight limbs and three hundred and sixty-five sinews.

That being the case, where do we get the nerve or the permission, for that matter, to use them in the transgression of *bitul Torah*?

כִּי לֹא תִשָּׁכַח מִפִּי זַרְעוֹ
"For it will not be forgotten by their descendants" (31:21)

At a convention of Torah leaders in Vilna, the *Chofetz Chaim* ascended the podium and addressed the assembly:

"If we want to know," said the *Chofetz Chaim*, "whether a certain tradesman, be it a shoemaker or a tailor, likes his work and finds it fulfilling, we can easily do so.

"For all we need to do is investigate whether or not this craftsman has taught his own sons the profession. If he has, we can be sure that he is happy with his work.

"The same applies to us," concluded the *Chofetz Chaim*. "If we wish to check our level of Torah and fear of Heaven, then all we have to do is check whether or not we are teaching our own children Torah! If we are, then we have a clear indicator that *we* love the Torah. But if, God forbid, we observe a father who does not do his utmost to educate his sons in the ways of Torah and *mitzvos*, then this is a clear indication that the father himself is in need of strengthening."

כִּי לֹא תִשָּׁכַח מִפִּי זַרְעוֹ
"For it will not be forgotten by their descendants" (31:21)

The *Alter* of Kelm, R' Simchah Zissel Ziv, founded an outstanding yeshivah in the city of Grobin. It is well known that the *Alter* instituted a five-minute *seder* (learning session) as part of the boys' daily schedule. Its purpose was to teach them the inestimable value of time.

In the city of Grobin resided a wealthy nobleman. One Friday night, this nobleman arranged a lavish feast to which all of the government's officers and barons were invited to attend.

As the night progressed — and the nobleman's heart became merry with wine — he began to boast about the yeshivah in his city.

"It is certainly worth your while to observe the conduct of this fine institution," said the nobleman to his guests. "The students and faculty all possess incredible self-discipline."

The officers agreed and set out toward the yeshivah riding horses and traveling in coaches. All this caused a tremendous amount of noise. When they arrived at the yeshivah, the students were in the middle of *davening Kabbalas Shabbos*. Despite all of the noise caused by the arrival of these officers, not one of the students so much as lifted his head from his *siddur*! The officers' reaction could be perfectly described by the words of the Psalmist: "They saw and were indeed astonished!" (*Tehillim* 48:6).

כִּי לֹא תִשָּׁכַח מִפִּי זַרְעוֹ
"For it will not be forgotten by their descendants" (31:21)

On the night that the son of the great *tzaddik* and kabbalist, R' Chaim Erlanger, was to become a *bar mitzvah*, his father summoned him to his study.

The young man entered the study, and his father closed the door behind him. R' Erlanger, with tears in his eyes, turned to his son and said, "My dear son, on this day that you are to become a *bar mitzvah*, I wish to give you a gift. It is a gift that will remain with you for the rest of your life!"

"What is the gift?" asked the son.

"The gift that I wish to bestow upon you," answered R' Erlanger, "is that from this day on, whenever you perform a *mitzvah*, you will receive double credit for each *mitzvah* you perform. You will receive this reward because I hereby order you to keep the *mitzvos*. Whenever you keep a *mitzvah*, you will therefore receive twice as much merit; once for the *mitzvah* itself and once for fulfilling the *mitzvah* of honoring your father. For the rest of your life, all of your *mitzvos* will be doubled."

כִּי יָדַעְתִּי אֶת־יִצְרוֹ
"For I know its inclination" (31:21)

A man's *yetzer hara* schemes against him all the days of his life and tries to make him stray from the path of Torah. It is man's duty to use every strategy at his disposal in order to defeat him.

To what can this be compared? The *Chofetz Chaim* offered the following parable: There were two countries that had been waging war for many years. One day, the king of one of the countries declared that whoever could resolve the dispute between the two countries and achieve peace would receive a very great reward — an opportunity to enter the king's vaults and take whatever he amasses in the duration of one hour.

A short while later, a certain wise man approached the king and proposed a solution to end the warfare. The king liked the plan very much and decided to use it. Eventually, peace was restored between the two countries, and, as promised, the wise man was invited to the king's vaults to collect his reward.

However, when the day of reward drew near, the king became concerned: Perhaps the wise man would take the most precious treasures in his vault. The king turned to his advisers for suggestions on how to protect his treasures.

"Your highness," said one of the advisers. "I happened to discover that this man loves music. Why doesn't the king simply place the kingdom's finest orchestra inside the vault? When the man arrives, the musicians will start playing music that will enrapture him; he will be so mesmerized by the music that he will entirely forget about the king's treasures!"

The king was very pleased with the idea.

When the wise man arrived at the palace, he was immediately taken to the king's vaults. The heavy gates to the vaults were opened, and the wise man took a step inside. But as he made his way to the riches, he was frozen in his place. For emanating from inside the vault was the sweetest-sounding music he had ever heard.

The wise man awoke from his trance and reminded himself why he had come. He took another step in the direction of the riches and tried looking through the treasures, but the beautiful music kept distracting him.

"I will only listen to these beautiful tunes for one more moment," said the wise man. But one moment quickly turned into two, then three and four....

Do not forget why you came here! he shouted at himself. But the music was simply too enchanting.

"The time is up!" announced a royal officer. The hour had passed.

"But," murmured the man, "I haven't taken anything yet!"

"Nothing you say will make a difference now," said the officer. "Your time has passed!" The man returned home sad and despondent over the once-in-a-lifetime opportunity that he had squandered. Everything had been in his hands, but he let it all slip away.

So it is in our own lives, said the *Chofetz Chaim*. Man receives a very special gift from Hashem. Over the course of his life he is given the opportunity to amass innumerable *mitzvos*.

However, the "evil adviser" — the *yetzer hara* — offers his "advice" and seduces man with trivialities that draw him away from Torah and *mitzvos*.

But then, when man reaches the end of his days and is summoned before the Heavenly court, he is painfully reminded of how he wasted his precious time, choosing to indulge in listening to worthless "music." By then, however, it will be too late.

It is incumbent upon every individual to constantly remind himself why he has come to this world. Let him not allow the *yetzer hara* to distract him from his true task: studying Torah and performing *mitzvos*!

כִּי יָדַעְתִּי אֶת־יִצְרוֹ
"For I know its inclination" (31:21)

The Ponevizher *Rav*, R' Yosef Kahaneman, related the following story: Shortly after his wedding, the *Chofetz Chaim* learned Torah under terrible conditions and dire poverty.

Each morning, the baker would give his wife a loaf of plain bread on credit and at a very inexpensive cost. She would then bring the bread home to the *Chofetz Chaim*, who would dip it in a glass of tea and eat his breakfast.

One morning, the *Chofetz Chaim*'s wife ran her usual morning errand of getting bread for her husband. But this time the baker refused to give her any, claiming that she had already accrued a large debt.

The *Chofetz Chaim*'s wife returned home empty-handed, and that day she served her husband a glass of tea without his usual bread. Upon presenting the *Chofetz Chaim* with his breakfast, she broke out in bitter sobbing.

The *Chofetz Chaim* sat quietly for some time, but then he began to pound on the table, saying, "Satan! Satan! I know exactly what you want. You would like me to put down my Gemara. I want you to know that I will not listen to you!"

"It is quite obvious," concluded the Ponevizher *Rav*, "that the *Chofetz Chaim* did not end up succumbing to his scheming *yetzer hara*. For what would the Jewish world look like had he succumbed? There would be no *Mishnah Berurah* and no *sefer Chofetz Chaim*! Nor would we have merited being led and educated by his thousands of students who went on to become the leaders of the Jewish people."

PARASHAS HAAZINU

הַצוּר תָּמִים פָּעֳלוֹ כִּי כָל־דְּרָכָיו מִשְׁפָּט
אֵ-ל אֱמוּנָה וְאֵין עָוֶל צַדִּיק וְיָשָׁר הוּא:

"The Rock! His actions are perfect, for all His ways are just. A faithful God, without injustice, He is righteous and fair" (32:4)

THERE ARE CERTAIN INDIVIDUALS, NOTED THE *CHOFETZ CHAIM*, WHO wonder why there are *tzaddikim* that live in poverty, and at times are victims of terrible misfortune and suffering. "Why do the righteous suffer?" they ask.

Their question, he said, can be answered with the following parable: There once was a wealthy individual who had an only son whom he loved dearly. One day, the son fell ill, and the father summoned one doctor after another to treat the son. But none of them had any remedy for the son's illness. But then, just when all hope for a cure had faded, an expert physician arrived from a distant country and healed the son.

"Be very careful," warned the doctor, "that your son eat no meat whatsoever! It is meat that is damaging his health. Take great care that he completely abstain from it!"

From that day on, the father kept a watchful eye on everything that his son consumed, just as the doctor had instructed.

On one occasion, however, the father's business required him to travel abroad. He therefore relayed the doctor's instructions to his servants, and placed his son under their care.

One day, the son ventured into the kitchen, and he immediately smelled the aroma of freshly cooked meat that filled the air. The young boy simply could not restrain himself; he quickly snatched a piece of meat from the pot and ran outside.

That very day, the boy took ill with the dreaded sickness.

When the father returned home, he was horrified to find his son once again bedridden. He quickly rushed to the physician who had previously healed his son and pleaded with him to once more lend his services. "This time," said the father to the doctor, "I promise you that I will not leave my house for even one moment; I will devote my full attention to my son."

The doctor agreed to return, and his treatment for the boy was once again successful. To celebrate his son's recovery, the father arranged a lavish feast and invited all of his family and friends. The tables were laden with delicacies, among them an assortment of meat dishes. The father, of course, did not allow his son to participate in the feast, as he did not want him to give in to his temptations and partake of something that would be detrimental to his health.

Look how cruel this father is, thought the guests. *Everyone is sitting and feasting on these scrumptious meat dishes, while his delightful and special son is ushered out of the dining room and not allowed to eat like everyone else.*

Now we are able to answer our initial question, concluded the *Chofetz Chaim*. There are times that Hashem causes the righteous to suffer, and we wonder, "Why?" We are like the guests at the feast who could not comprehend why the father would deprive his son of such enjoyment. Yet we must believe with unshakable faith that whatever poverty and suffering a *tzaddik* may endure is ultimately for *his* benefit!

הַצּוּר תָּמִים פָּעֳלוֹ כִּי כָל־דְּרָכָיו מִשְׁפָּט
אֵ-ל אֱמוּנָה וְאֵין עָוֶל צַדִּיק וְיָשָׁר הוּא:

"The Rock! His actions are perfect, for
all His ways are just. A faithful God, without
injustice, He is righteous and fair" (32:4)

R' Yisrael Salanter explained this verse in the following manner:
When a thief is brought before a court, he is tried and convict-
ed according to his misdeed.

It might very well be that this thief has a wife and children who rely
on his support. When he is condemned to a prison term of many years
they, too, are condemned to terrible hardship, for they have lost their
source of sustenance.

However, Hashem's judgment is altogether different! For He takes
into account the suffering of all those who will be affected by an individual's punishment.

If punishing one person will cause others to suffer unjustly, then
Hashem pardons the sinner and he will not be punished at all.

הֲלַה' תִּגְמְלוּ־זֹאת עַם נָבָל וְלֹא חָכָם
הֲלוֹא־הוּא אָבִיךָ קָּנֶךָ הוּא עָשְׂךָ וַיְכֹנְנֶךָ:

"Is this how you repay Hashem? A disgraceful and
unwise people! Is He not your Father Who acquired
you? He made you, and then established you" (32:6)

R' Moshe Berdugo (author of *Kenaf Rananim*) explained this
verse with a parable:
One day, a man was walking down a road. Suddenly, he noticed a crying baby lying on the ground alongside the road. The baby was obviously hungry and thirsty with no one to take care of it. The man, therefore,
was filled with mercy for the infant and brought it back to his house.

Once home, the man tended to the baby's needs, feeding it and giving it to drink. Since the man had no idea who the child's parents
were, he raised the baby in his home, caring for him like he would his
own son.

When the baby grew up and became an adult, the man who had adopted him expended much effort in arranging a *shidduch* for him. He succeeded in securing a *shidduch* from an esteemed family, and even promised to grant the young man a substantial dowry and a valuable gold watch. The young man, however, was far from appreciative. Instead of thanking the man who had given him so much, he complained about how offensive it was that someone of his caliber did not receive a watch of greater value!

The man attempted to pacify the *chasan*, telling him that due to the enormous expenses which the wedding was incurring, he was unable to afford a more expensive watch. He assured him that he would buy him an even fancier watch at a later date. The *chasan*, however, stubbornly refused to listen, and he began to quarrel with his adoptive father!

The father's relatives were appalled at the young man's behavior. They duly rebuked him: "What insolence! Not only are you an ingrate who does not appreciate what this man has done for you — he found you lying on the road when you were only a baby and brought you into his home; he cared for you like one of his very own children — but you are also a fool! For now that you have behaved so dreadfully who knows if your father will still be willing to give you the dowry that he had promised you!"

So it is with man, concluded R' Berdugo. Hashem bestows limitless kindness upon His creatures. In addition, he has given us the Torah and His *mitzvos* so we can have a chance to earn eternal reward in the World to Come.

When a man sins, he is "disgraceful," for instead of being grateful toward Hashem for bestowing so much good upon him, he acted with a great lack of gratitude. But a sinner is also "unwise," for on account of his transgressions, he has caused himself to lose the everlasting reward that is reserved for the righteous in the World to Come.

זְכֹר יְמוֹת עוֹלָם בִּינוּ שְׁנוֹת דֹּר־וָדֹר

"Remember days of yore; contemplate the years of one generation and another" (32:7)

In relation to this verse, the *Midrash Rabbah* comments: "Whenever Hashem brings suffering upon you in this world, remember the multitude of good things and consolations that He is going to give you in the future [in the World to Come]."

The *Chofetz Chaim* quoted the following parable in the name of R' Zev, the *maggid* of Vilna: A Jew rented an apartment from the governor of the city. On a specific day each year, the Jew appeared before the governor and paid him 300 rubles, the rental fee for the year. One year, the governor was forced to travel to another city and knew that he would not be at home on the payment day. He therefore appointed his deputy to collect the rent.

The deputy was a virulent Jew hater, and he decided to torment the Jewish renter. He notified the Jew that the governor had raised the annual fee from 300 rubles to 500 rubles per year.

On the day the rent was due, the wicked deputy arose earlier than usual and dispatched a messenger to the Jewish renter to remind him to pay on time. The poor Jew arrived before the deputy with only 480 rubles in hand; it was all that he had. He pleaded with the deputy to grant him a few more days in order to collect enough money to pay the rent. But the evil deputy adamantly refused; the Jew would have to pay the full amount by the end of the day!

The Jew did what he could to collect the 20 rubles he was missing, and he asked his acquaintances and close friends if they could lend him the money. But it was to no avail; no one had any money to lend. As the sun began to set, the hapless Jew made his way to the home of the deputy. Upon seeing that he was still missing the 20 rubles, the cruel deputy ordered that the Jew be whipped twenty times — a lash for each missing ruble.

Eventually, the governor returned to the city. The Jew turned to his wife and said, "Now that the governor has returned, I will go visit him and tell him about the ill treatment I received from the deputy."

When the governor heard the Jew's tale, he became infuriated with his deputy. He told the Jew that for each lash he had received, he would receive 100 rubles as compensation. "Since you were hit with twenty lashes, you will receive 2,000 rubles!

"Furthermore," continued the governor, "the deputy has recently built himself a new home worth 4,000 rubles. I will order him to write you a contract stating that you are now owner of half the home."

The Jew left the governor's home and was greeted by his wife who had been waiting outside. Upon seeing her husband's downcast face, however, she became concerned.

"What is the matter?" asked his wife.

Her husband told her everything the governor had said.

His wife was now confused. "So why aren't you bursting with joy?" she asked.

"I regret that the deputy did not give me *forty* lashes," answered the husband. "Had he done so, I now would have owned his entire estate and not just half!"

So it is with us, concluded the *Chofetz Chaim*. When a person is forced to endure suffering in this world, he becomes very distraught and has difficulty dealing with it. When he arrives in the World to Come, however, and he becomes aware of the enormous reward that he earned for enduring each moment of suffering, he will regret the fact that he did not suffer even more in this world.

❦

כִּי חֵלֶק ה׳ עַמּוֹ יַעֲקֹב חֶבֶל נַחֲלָתוֹ:

"For Hashem's portion is His people; Yaakov is the lineage of His inheritance" (32:9)

R' Chaim of Volozhin entered the study of his *rebbe*, the Vilna Gaon, to ask a question: "*Rebbe*, today I came across a perplexing Midrash in the second *perek* of the *Tanna D'vei Eliyahu Zuta*. The Midrash enumerates various positive qualities of Hashem; among them is that the Holy One is '*same'ach b'chelko*,' He is happy with His lot. But what does that mean? How can one say that that Hashem is 'happy with His lot' — after all, the entire world and everything in it is His?"

"A very good question, indeed," answered the Vilna *Gaon*. "But in this instance," continued the *Gaon*, "the word *chelko* refers not to His 'lot' but rather to the Jewish nation, as the verse states, 'For Hashem's portion (*chelek*) is His people; Yaakov is the lineage of His inheritance.'

"The Holy One delights in the Jewish people in all circumstances, for even when they sin, God forbid, they nonetheless remain His children! *Chazal* taught this in *Maseches Berachos* (36a), 'Even when the [Children of] Israel do not follow the will of Hashem, they are still referred to as, [Hashem's] children.'"

וַיִּשְׁמַן יְשֻׁרוּן וַיִּבְעָט
"But Yeshurun grew fat and kicked" (32:15)

T he *maggid* R' Yechiel Michel of Zlochev had a *chassid* who at one time was very poor. But then he tried his hand at business, and he quickly became a very wealthy man. However, the more his wealth and standing grew, the further he drifted from Torah and *mitzvos*.

One day, the *maggid* paid a visit to his disciple and requested that he make a charitable donation to an important cause. The *chassid*, however, evaded the request with several excuses.

The *maggid* walked over to the window and asked the *chassid* to join him. As they gazed out into the streets, the *maggid* asked him, "What do you see?"

"I see people walking through the streets," responded the wealthy *chassid*.

The *maggid* then led the *chassid* to a mirror. "Now what do you see?" asked the *maggid*.

"Now," answered the *chassid*, "I see myself."

"Do you know what the difference is between a window and a mirror?" asked the *maggid*. "A window is clear and transparent and, therefore, when you look at it, you see others. A mirror, however," concluded the *maggid*, "is coated with silver. Therefore, when you look at it, you see only yourself."

וַיִּשְׁמַן יְשֻׁרוּן וַיִּבְעָט
"But Yeshurun grew fat and kicked" (32:15)

T he *Chofetz Chaim* explained this verse by way of a parable: There were two sisters who married two brothers. One of the brothers was a wealthy businessman; the other was a destitute pauper.

One day, the poor sister went to visit the rich one. When she arrived at the magnificent palace where her sister lived, she was awestruck by its beauty and was unable to tear her eyes away from it. The palace contained large halls covered with precious rugs; splendid portraits hung on all the walls; and dozens of servants dressed in regal attire were walking about, ready to fulfil any wish of their mistress.

When they sat down to talk, the poor sister detected that her rich sister seemed unhappy. "Why are you so sad?" she asked. "You have such a magnificent home!"

"That is certainly true," her sister replied. "My husband is very wealthy and my house is extravagant, but I am treated horribly. My husband shows me no respect and he sometimes humiliates me.

"More than once I have asked myself if my lot is truly better than yours," she continued. "You may live in poverty and lack a luxurious mansion with many servants, but at least your husband respects you and values what you have to say."

There are times, concluded the *Chofetz Chaim*, when we adorn the *sefer Torah* in a beautiful silk casing and cap it with a shiny crown. We may lay the holy Torah on a golden table and then return it to an *aron kodesh* that was hand crafted and expertly designed.

Yet all of these details matter little to the Torah if we do not hearken to its words! It is as if the Torah is screaming, "I do not desire any of this glamour! Just refrain from trampling me."

Often, it is specifically the poorer congregations — congregations that may be unable to afford many of the fancy trimmings that wealthier congregations can — who accord the Torah its greatest honor by adhering to its each and every word.

Such poverty is befitting to honor the Torah and is far superior to illusory splendor. As *Chazal* state in *Maseches Chagigah* (9b), "Poverty is becoming to Israel."

וַיִּשְׁמַן יְשֻׁרוּן וַיִּבְעָט
"But Yeshurun grew fat and kicked" (32:15)

All the days of his life, R' Yisrael Salanter feared having to face spiritual challenges. The challenge of wealth, however, frightened him most of all, lest he come to personify the words of the verse, "Yeshurun grew fat and kicked."

"Hashem grants a person wealth," remarked R' Salanter, "only in order to help others! Such an individual is similar to a *gabbai tzedakah*. Who can bear such a tremendous responsibility? A rich man must always be concerned that perhaps on the outskirts of the city lives a poor man in dire straits; maybe there is a sick individual who is in desperate need of assistance; who knows if in one of these places resides an impoverished child whose parents cannot afford to hire a tutor to teach him Torah?

"This is one responsibility that I certainly do not wish to bear," said R' Salanter. "I do not want to be wealthy!"

His wife once purchased a lottery ticket. R' Salanter called two trustworthy individuals to serve as witnesses, and he told his wife in their presence: "I hereby declare that I have no share in your property, nor its produce, nor the produce of its produce until the end of time!"

צוּר יְלָדְךָ תֶּשִׁי וַתִּשְׁכַּח אֵ-ל מְחֹלְלֶךָ:

"You ignored the Rock Who gave birth to you, and forgot God Who brought you out of the womb" (32:18)

The Dubno *Maggid* explained this verse by way of a parable: There was a certain individual who was in terrible debt, owing money to all of his friends and relatives. On one occasion, he poured out his heart to a close friend of his:

"What should I do?" he asked his friend nervously. "My creditors are demanding their money, and I haven't got anything to give them!"

Though the man owed money to this friend as well, the friend did not hesitate to reply: "Let me give you a piece of advice. When the creditors come for their money, pretend that you have lost your mind. Sing and dance in front of them; they will think that your trying predicament has driven you mad and they will leave you alone."

The man was very pleased with his friend's advice, and he did exactly as he had instructed. Each time a creditor approached him for money, he would act as if he had lost his mind and the creditor would relent.

Eventually, the day on which the friend was due to be paid back arrived. When he approached the man and asked for his money, he was treated to a shocking sight — the man to whom he had given the advice now began to sing and dance *in front of him*!

"You fool!" shouted the friend to the man. "Was it not I who initially offered you this advice in order to help you escape your creditors? How dare you use it to try to deceive me?"

This is the meaning of the verse, concluded the *maggid*. "You ignored the Rock" — the Holy One did a great act of kindness for man and gave him the quality of forgetfulness. Forgetfulness is a gift for man, as it enables him to put the misfortunes that he has endured out of his mind. But man "forgot God Who brought you out of the womb" — he uses this trait to forget Hashem Himself!

כִּי דוֹר תַּהְפֻּכֹת הֵמָּה
"For they are a generation of reversals" (32:20)

The Dubno *maggid* explained this verse with a parable: The child of a rabbi and the child of a wagon driver were to be married. Since the rabbi and the wagon driver lived far away from each other, the wedding was scheduled to be held in a town that was midway between the homes of the two in-laws.

On the day of the wedding, the rabbi thought, *If I appear at the wedding dressed in my bekeshe and shtriemel — my rabbinical garb — I am likely to embarrass my mechutan.* He therefore removed his elaborate attire and, instead, donned simpler clothing. On his feet he wore boots, and on his head he placed an ordinary cap fit for a wagon driver.

A similar thought crossed the mind of the wagon driver: *It is certainly not appropriate for me to come to my child's wedding dressed like an ordinary wagon driver if my mechutan will be adorned in his rabbinical garb.* The wagon driver therefore borrowed a long silk *bekeshe* and a regal-looking *shtriemel* to wear at the wedding.

When the in-laws arrived at the wedding, everyone was under the impression that the rabbi was the wagon driver and the wagon driver was the rabbi!

Now we can gain a deeper insight into the verse mentioned above. The long and painful exile of the Jewish nation has given birth to a "generation of reversals"; our non-Jewish neighbors observed our uprightness and esteemed character and have integrated within themselves many of our lofty character traits. However, much to our dismay and shame, the Jewish people, as well, have adopted the ideals of the gentiles and have imitated their ways.

Parashas Vezos HaBerachah

אַף חֹבֵב עַמִּים כָּל־קְדֹשָׁיו בְּיָדֶךָ וְהֵם תֻּכּוּ לְרַגְלֶךָ יִשָּׂא
מִדַּבְּרֹתֶיךָ: תּוֹרָה צִוָּה־לָנוּ מֹשֶׁה מוֹרָשָׁה קְהִלַּת יַעֲקֹב:

"Indeed, You loved the tribes greatly; all their
holy ones are held in Your hands, for they
planted themselves at Your feet and took upon
themselves Your pronouncements. The Torah that
Moshe commanded us is a heritage
for the congregation of Yaakov." (33:3-4)

WHEN R' ZUSIA OF ANIPOLI READ THIS VERSE, HE EXPLAINED IT as follows: "Indeed, You loved the *amim* (the nations) greatly" — indeed, because of our many sins, Hashem has displayed some love to the nations of the world and has handed the Jewish nation into their control. "All their holy ones are held in Your hands" — but the Jews are a holy people and have refused to abandon Hashem's ways and His Torah. "For they planted (*tuku*) themselves at Your feet" — although our refusal to relinquish our holy heritage has made us subject to the beatings and derision of the gentiles — they nevertheless "took upon themselves Your pronouncements" and have never stopped declaring "the Torah that Moshe commanded us"!

תּוֹרָה צִוָּה־לָנוּ מֹשֶׁה
"The Torah that Moshe commanded us" (33:4)

Chazal assert in *Maseches Chagigah* (9b): "There is no comparison between one who recites his passage one hundred times and one who recites his passage one hundred and one times."

Chazal's statement, noted R' Yosef David Azulai (the *Chida*), is alluded to in the verse, "The Torah that Moshe commanded (*tzivah*) us," for the numerical value of "*tzivah*" is one hundred and one (90+6+5).

In a similar vein, R' Shlomo Efraim Luntshitz (the *Kli Yakar*) pointed out that the letters that make up the word, *zachar*, "remembering" — *zayin*, *chaf*, and *reish* — have the numerical value of two hundred and twenty-seven; while the letters that form the word *shachach*, "he forgot" — *shin*, *chaf*, and *ches* — have the numerical value of three hundred and twenty-eight.

If you subtract the numerical value of "*zachar*" from the numerical value of "*shachach*," you will be left with *one hundred and one*! In other words, the difference between remembering what you learn and forgetting it is reviewing the Torah passage one hundred and one times.

❧

תּוֹרָה צִוָּה־לָנוּ מֹשֶׁה מוֹרָשָׁה קְהִלַּת יַעֲקֹב:
"The Torah that Moshe commanded us is a heritage for the congregation of Yaakov" (33:4)

Rashi explains: "'The Torah that Moshe commanded us is a heritage for the congregation of Yaakov.' We held onto it and we will not let go!"

As a youth, R' Yosef Chaim Sonnenfeld studied in the Pressburg Yeshivah.

He was orderly and neat and, each week, he gave his clothing to the laundress to clean.

Although his well-to-do roommate offered to pay him for the time Chaim spent studying with him, Chaim refused to take any money. Miraculously, however, Chaim would find in the street every week the 7 *kreutzers* needed to pay the laundress.

One night, he dreamt that he saw the winning number of the government lottery.

When he awoke, he thought, *With the pittance of money in my possession, I can afford only one of two things: either my usual living expenses or the lottery ticket. What shall I do?*

On the one hand, perhaps my dream was a true one. On the other hand, with the money I have I can purchase my necessities for the next few days, and if I spend it, my learning may suffer.

If that is the consequence, then it's not worth it, thought R' Sonnenfeld. *I am not willing to risk my learning over what might be nothing but a crazy dream.*

Several days later, R' Sonnenfeld discovered that the number he had seen in his dream was in fact the number that was drawn in the lottery.

When R' Sonnenfeld would tell over the story in later years, he would continue with a broad smile, "You must think that I regretted my decision. Not at all! I gave the whole incident not a second thought and continued my Torah studies with perfect calm."

תּוֹרָה צִוָּה־לָנוּ מֹשֶׁה
"The Torah that Moshe commanded us" (33:4)

The *Chofetz Chaim* entered the *beis midrash* and saw a group of students standing around, squandering away their precious time in an idle discussion.

"I would like to tell you boys a story," said the *Chofetz Chaim*. "It is a story about a man who lost his mind and began to dismantle the railroad tracks that passed near his city."

"'What are you doing?' people screamed. 'You are going to cause a terrible catastrophe!'

"'Why is that?' laughed the man. 'This railroad track is hundreds of miles long, and I am only removing several yards of it.'

"The same applies to the Torah," concluded the *Chofetz Chaim*. "The Torah has been transmitted to us from generation to generation. One who wasted his time instead of studying is similar to the individual who removed several yards from an extremely long track.

"While he may have wasted only a short amount of time, the damage he will cause will be very great indeed."

וְעֵזֶר מִצָּרָיו תִּהְיֶה:
"May You be an aid to him from his enemies" (33:7)

Regarding this verse, the *Yalkut Meam Loez* recounted the following story: One day, a wealthy man witnessed a poor individual picking bread out of a garbage can. *If this pauper's predicament has grown so dismal*, thought the wealthy man, *then he must have given up all hope on living in this world.*

He approached the pauper and said, "I want to give some money to an individual who has lost all hope in life. After watching what you were doing, it is clear to me that you have given up all hope."

"God forbid!" declared the pauper emphatically. "My heart relies and trusts in the Holy One, Whose concern extends to all His creations! I pray each day, and I beseech Him to send me my sustenance. If you are looking to help a man who has lost hope, then I suggest that you go and bury your money — for there is no such man in the world!"

The wealthy man took the advice of the pauper, and hid the money in his yard.

That same day, the poor man found a gold coin. With joy in his heart, he went and bought a small amount of merchandise. He sold the merchandise for a profit and reinvested his earnings by buying more merchandise. He did this many times over the span of several years until he became a rich person. Eventually, he was appointed governor of the city!

In contrast, during those same years, the wealthy man lost all his wealth until he was forced to sell his home and all his belongings.

One day, the formerly wealthy man recalled the money he had buried in his yard. He decided to go to his old house at night, dig up the ground, and recover the money that he had hid there long ago.

He followed his plan, but as he was digging, the new owner of the house woke up to see an intruder digging in his yard. The owner alerted the police, and they arrived without delay. They arrested the poor man and put him in prison.

In the morning, they brought him before the governor of the city. The governor recognized the former wealthy man, but the now poor man did not realize that the governor was none other than the former pauper whom he had seen picking bread out of the trash.

The governor revealed himself to the poor man and said the following: "Look what happened! You — the one who was so proud of his wealth — were condemned by heaven to become a destitute pauper, while I — the one who had nothing yet placed my trust in Hashem — was blessed and elevated to greatness!"

כִּי שָׁמְרוּ אִמְרָתֶךָ וּבְרִיתְךָ יִנְצֹרוּ:

"For they kept Your word and preserved Your covenant" (33:9)

The *Sefas Emes* (R' Yehudah Aryeh Leib Alter) once asked one of his relatives to take his two sons, Avraham Mordechai and Moshe Betzalel, to receive a blessing from a certain Jew who lived in Warsaw.

The relative thought to himself that the man must be a great *tzaddik* if the *rebbe* himself chose this man to bless his sons. But when the relative met the man, he was surprised to discover that the man was an ordinary person.

"The *rebbe* asked that *I* should bless his sons?" asked the man. "But I am such a simple person — "

"That is what the *rebbe* instructed!" said the relative. "Please, bless them."

When the relative returned home with the children, the *Sefas Emes* told the relative more about the man: "The man is, indeed, an ordinary person. However, when a son was born to him, he decided to arrange a proper feast in honor of fulfilling the *mitzvah* of making a *bris milah*. But he did not have even one *perutah* to pay for it. Do you know what he did? He sold his pillow and blanket just so he could buy food for the *mitzvah* feast.

"This deed caused a great stir in heaven, and it was decreed that, as reward for his outstanding commitment to the *mitzvah*, any blessing he utters shall come true. Yet he does not know of his own power!"

כִּי שָׁמְרוּ אִמְרָתֶךָ וּבְרִיתְךָ יִנְצֹרוּ:

"For they kept Your word and preserved Your covenant" (33:9)

A Jew dressed in lavish attire, and clearly not religious, appeared before the rabbi of Moscow, R' Chaim Berlin.

"Rabbi," began the man, "I have a secret to confide."

"What would you like to tell me?" asked R' Berlin.

"A son was recently born to me, and I wish to circumcise him," was the man's response.

"Why is that such a secret?" asked the *rav*. "All Jews circumcise their sons."

"I am the owner of a large company," he replied, "and not one of my customers has any idea that I am a Jew. If they would know the truth, I would surely lose my livelihood, for they would not want to do business with a Jew."

R' Berlin readily agreed, and when the boy was eight days old, he went to the man's luxurious home and secretly circumcised his son.

"Please return to me in another three days," said R' Berlin to the father.

When three days had passed, the man arrived at the *rav*'s home holding a sum of money.

"I did not ask you to come because I wanted you to pay me," explained R' Berlin. "I never accept any money for the circumcisions I perform."

A look of bewilderment spread across the man's face. "But rabbi, why, then, did you ask me to come today?"

"I am interested in knowing," answered R' Berlin, "why you wanted to circumcise your son, considering the fact that you are not an observant Jew."

When the man heard these words, he broke out in bitter sobs. "I know that I have drifted far away from Judaism," he said. "I have fallen far into the depths of impurity. Yet I hope in my heart that perhaps my young son will be inspired to return to his Father in Heaven. Had I not had him circumcised, he would have had absolutely nothing to remind him of his Jewishness. This is why I wanted him to be circumcised."

זְבוּלֻן בְּצֵאתֶךָ וְיִשָּׂשכָר בְּאֹהָלֶיךָ:
"Zevulun! Rejoice when you go out [to trade], and Yissachar, in your tents [of Torah]" (33:18)

As a yeshivah student, R' Tzvi Ashkenazi (the *Chacham Tzvi*) boarded and ate his meals at the home of one of the city's laymen.

There were times when the *Chacham Tzvi*'s extraordinary diligence caused him to return from his studies later than he was expected, and this tended to upset his host's schedule.

His host decided to make him aware of this fact, so one day he spoke to the *Chacham Tzvi* about being more punctual. The host was a good person and he had no intention of offending the Torah scholar; and, indeed, he made sure to express himself as gently as possible.

The very next day, a delegation from another city arrived to see the *Chacham Tzvi*. They had come to invite him to serve as the rabbi of their city. He accepted their invitation and agreed to serve as their rabbi.

Upon taking leave of his host, the *Chacham Tzvi* blessed him: "I bless you," he said, "that you and your offspring should always merit being wealthy and prosperous. However, I want you to know," he continued, "that Heaven tested you yesterday to see whether or not you would reprimand me for my behavior. Unfortunately, you did not pass the test. Had you succeeded, I would have also blessed you with sons who would grow to be great Torah scholars."

וַיִּשְׁכֹּן יִשְׂרָאֵל בֶּטַח בָּדָד עֵין יַעֲקֹב
"Yisrael dwelt securely, alone, in the way that Yaakov [blessed them]" (33:28)

R' Yitzchak Arama (the *Akeidas Yitzchak*) told a story that relates to this verse: The king of France contracted a disease that had no known remedy. Doctors from all over the world tried their hand at finding a cure for him, but none were successful.

At one point, the king of Spain sent a Spanish physician to the French monarch. The doctor was famous as an expert in his field, and everyone hoped that he would be the one to cure the king.

But the king heard that the doctor was a Jew who had renounced his faith, and he refused to be treated by him. "Why would this Jew forsake Judaism?" he asked. "In order to find favor in the eyes of the gentiles! If he was truly well versed in the wisdom of medicine, he would have had no need to renounce his faith in order to be accepted by the gentile world! His great wisdom should have been enough to generate respect for him. This is a clear indication that he is not a great physician, and I will not allow him to examine me!"

This is also the explanation of the above verse, concluded the *Akeidas Yitzchak*. "Yisrael dwelt securely, alone, in the way that Yaakov [blessed them]." When does the Jewish people dwell securely? When they live alone without mixing with the other nations.

אַשְׁרֶיךָ יִשְׂרָאֵל מִי כָמוֹךָ עַם נוֹשַׁע בַּה׳

"Fortunate are you, Yisrael! Who is like you? A people saved by Hashem" (33:29)

R' Aharon was a simple wagon driver who earned his living by transporting clay and plaster aboard his donkey-drawn wagon. Every Shabbos, he attended the *derashah* of the *Alshich HaKadosh* (R' Moshe Alshich). One Shabbos, the *Alshich* lectured at length about the trait of *bitachon*, trust in Hashem.

"If one trusts in Hashem," said the *Alshich*, "then Hashem will provide him with all that he needs!"

R' Aharon returned home and said, "Why must I work so hard for my livelihood? After all, I trust in Hashem — He will surely provide me with all that I need!"

"But who will make sure that we have a suitable livelihood?" asked his concerned family.

"What are you worried about?" he asked them. "The *Alshich* stated explicitly that one who trusts in Hashem will not lack anything!"

That Sunday morning, R' Aharon sold his donkey and wagon to a gentile. The gentile took the wagon to a spot where he wanted to dig the soil he needed for constructing a building. As he was digging, he suddenly noticed a large chest full of gold and silver. He loaded the treasure chest onto the wagon, covered it well, and set out for his home.

In the middle of the trip, the donkey was frightened by something, and it unexpectedly jumped back. As a result, the gentile was flung off the wagon and into a ditch on the side of the road. The donkey waited for its new owner to get up, but when evening began to fall and the gentile had still not risen, it set out for R' Aharon's house, as it had been accustomed to do.

Needless to say, R' Aharon and his family wondered why their old donkey was heading toward their house carrying a covered package. When they removed the cover they were amazed to see that the package was a treasure chest filled to the brim with gold and silver! With great joy, R' Aharon and his family offered their heartfelt thanks to Hashem.

When the *Alshich*'s students heard about what had happened to the wagon driver, they asked their *rebbe*, "Why did this wagon driver merit such good fortune?"

"You should know," answered the *Alshich*, "that this simple wagon driver believed in Hashem with all his heart; he had no doubts whatsoever. That is why he merited receiving such an enormous treasure!"

This volume is part of
THE ARTSCROLL SERIES®
an ongoing project of
translations, commentaries and expositions
on Scripture, Mishnah, Talmud, Halachah,
liturgy, history, the classic Rabbinic writings,
biographies and thought.

For a brochure of current publications
visit your local Hebrew bookseller
or contact the publisher:

Mesorah Publications, ltd

4401 Second Avenue
Brooklyn, New York 11232
(718) 921-9000
www.artscroll.com